Vive les verbes français!

6,000 VERBS
to Add *Savoir-Flair*
to Your French

Vive
les verbes
français!

Dennis Long, Ph.D.

New York Chicago San Francisco Lisbon London Madrid Mexico City
Milan New Delhi San Juan Seoul Singapore Sydney Toronto

Library of Congress Cataloging-in-Publication Data

Long, Dennis.
    Vive les verbes français! : 6,000 verbs to add savoir-flair to your French / Dennis Long.
        p.   cm.
    Includes index.
    ISBN 0-07-147875-2
    1. French language—Verb.   2. French language—Textbooks for foreign speakers—
English.   I. Title.

    PC2271.L66   2006
    448.2′421—dc22   2006048246

1 2 3 4 5 6 7 8 9 10 11 12 13 14 15 16 17 18 19 20   DOC/DOC 0 9 8 7 6

ISBN-13: 978-0-07-147875-5
ISBN-10:   0-07-147875-2

Interior design by Terry Stone

This book is printed on acid-free paper.

Contents

Preface

In the quest to become more fluent in a foreign language, one must constantly build on an ever-growing foundation of new vocabulary and syntax. Achieving the goal of fluency does not come easily. Becoming facile and competent in a nonnative tongue requires, above all, mastery of the *synonym*—that is the versatility of expressing a noun, verb, or phrase in a variety of forms and nuances. This is a daunting task.

In the search for a word's synonym, one can consult a thesaurus to find a limited list of roughly interchangeable equivalents. The search for a non-synonymous, yet somewhat closely related word requires tiresome page-flipping through a dictionary. Foreign thesauruses and dictionaries abound as do compilations of colloquialisms, proverbs, and slang expressions.

The first objective of this handbook is to provide a core of one hundred twenty-five French verbs that express a range of actions, emotions, states of being, and physical activities. Around each verb is built a "verb family," not merely confined to synonyms, but that also incorporates other verbs and phrases that might logically come to mind when the core verb is expressed. For example, in researching the verb **taquiner** (*to tease*), the reader will not only find most of its synonyms (i.e., *to bother, annoy, disturb, harass*) but a number of other verbs that might be related in certain contexts of speech and literature (e.g., *to bully, intimidate, harangue, taunt, scoff,* etc.).

To stretch this formula to its extreme, under the core verb **éructer** (*to belch*), the verb family includes a large number of certainly non-synonymous verbs such as *to retch, wheeze, gripe, snooze, snore, snort, grunt, booze, disgust,* etc. Little imagination is required to visualize a slovenly, noisy couch potato planted in front of the TV set with beer in hand.

The versatility of such a format puts at the fingertips of a French learner a wider range of verbs and phrases than would otherwise be found in a standard dictionary or thesaurus. The learner is also spared the tedious task of page-flipping and cross-referencing, and can devote more time to the actual mastery of French.

The targeted reader of this handbook is the intermediate- to advanced-level student of French who is presumed to be at ease in basic conversation and reading. The reader will already be close to mastery of the skills of sentence construction, verb conjugation, and spelling. This book seeks to go beyond the simplest of foundation verbs of beginning French such as **avoir**, **être**, **faire**, **dire**, **aller**, **venir**, **savoir**, etc.

The one hundred twenty-five core verbs were not chosen because they are the most commonly used—in fact some are rather esoteric and/or antiquated. Rather, they were chosen to illustrate how mnemonics can be applied to render an initially unintelligible word into one that is familiar and recognizable.

The use of mnemonics makes memorization and learning easier. I couldn't begin to account for all the time I saved throughout medical school by recalling enzyme reactions, physiologic functions, and innumerable body parts with the help of memory aids. Even today, as a radiologist, I still find myself slipping back into the trusty, shopworn acronymic "On old Olympus's towering tops a Finn and German viewed some hops" to recall the twelve cranial nerves, rather than having to consult an anatomy text to find olfactory, optic, oculomotor, trigeminal, trochlear, abducent, facial, acoustic, glossopharyngeal, vagus, spinal-accessory, and hypoglossal nerves. If, through the use of this handbook, I can convince another language student of the utility of mnemonics, then I have achieved my second goal.

Also included in this book is a glossary containing numerous common conjunctions, adverbs, adjectives, and compound prepositions crucial for language fluency.

This work is intended as a supplement to the many excellent texts and workbooks devoted to the instruction of French, and certainly not as a substitute. While most texts are stored on the bookshelf, if a French-language student, heading off to class, crams this book in his backpack, or if a tourist jetting to Paris tosses it into her carry-on bag, then I consider the handbook a success. *Vive la langue française!*

Acknowledgments

This book is dedicated to my mother, Margaret, who instilled in me, from a young age, a love for the French language and other foreign tongues, and also to my wife, Florence, and my son, Travis, who allowed me the long hours to complete this work.

A special thank-you and acknowledgment to Marie-Gabrielle Sélarque for her time proofreading my drafts and for her thoughtful suggestions along the way. Marie has used her native French skills in the U.S. film industry, the Swiss chapter of the Red Cross, and as private instructor to the United Arab Emirates ambassador to the United Nations. She has worked translating novels from English to French and has served as director and member of the Administrative Counsel of the Alliance Française of Hawaii.

Celtic England

+

Angles
Saxons gave 100 +
most common words
Jutes

+

Norman Conquest
added
10,000 - 12,000 new words

Introduction

The Franco-English Mélange

Our modern-day English language owes a heavy debt to the Germanic tribes—the Angles, Saxons, and Jutes who invaded England across the North Sea in a series of waves beginning in the fifth century A.D. By then, Rome's protective legions had been withdrawn from its far-flung outposts, leaving Celtic England defenseless against the polyglot invaders from the East.

Just how deep-rooted the Germanic influence on contemporary English is can be seen by a computer analysis showing that "the 100 most common words in English are all of Anglo-Saxon origin." (*The Story of English*, Robert McCrum, et al., 1986.)

Over the course of several centuries of sea raids and waves of immigration by the Germanic hordes, as well as the eighth century incursions by the Danes and other Norsemen, the native Celtic tongue, admixed with vestiges of Latin, borrowed from the previous Roman occupiers, gave rise to Old English, in whose lexicon a modern reader could find many familiar words.

As nearly every student has had to memorize at some time during his or her school days, 1066 A.D. marked the year of the victory by the Norman count, William the Conqueror, over King Harold of England at the Battle of Hastings. More than just a signal conquest of title and land, the landing of William's forces on British soil that year would prove to be "an event which had a greater effect on the English language than any other in the course of its history." (*The Norman Conquest*, H. R. Lyon, 1982.)

That seminal event—the clash of two great cultures—would forever alter the sound and vocabulary of the English tongue. Over the centuries that followed, the Norman (French) influence would greatly enrich the language of the conquered—by some estimates adding some 10,000–12,000 new words to the English lexicon.

Cognates, Partial Cognates, and Help!

A quick perusal of any French textbook, newspaper, or dictionary will reveal at once a good many words that appear quite familiar to the English reader. These *cognates* (or **mots apparentés**) will have either the same or similar spelling as well as similar meaning in both tongues. Some examples are: **une distance**, **un melon**, **quadruple**, **innocence**.

Except for the infinitive verb endings peculiar to French, i.e., **-er**, **-ir**, **-re**, there exist many cognate verbs, also readily recognizable to the English speaker, such as: **causer**, **téléphoner**, **fixer**, **libérer**, **installer**, **payer**, **passer**, **admettre**, and **adresser**. (Note that **causer** also means to *chat*.)

One will also find many French words that closely resemble English words, except that their exact meanings will differ to some extent. Examples of these *partial cognates* include:

remarquer can mean *to remark* but usually means *to notice*		
agréer	*to agree*	*to recognize*
apprécier	*to appreciate*	*to pass judgment on*
chasser	*to chase*	*to hunt*
marcher	*to march*	*to walk*
monter	*to mount*	*to climb*

However, there exist an even greater number of French words that either bear some resemblance to English words but have different meanings or bear no resemblance whatsoever to English. It is to this latter category that this next section is dedicated, specifically, to verbs.

Mnemonics: The Mind Plays Tricks

It can prove frustrating to the foreign student to be confronted with an unfamiliar French verb whose spelling, pronunciation, and meaning bear no resemblance to English. The learner has the option of trying to commit the new word to memory by constant repetition or bypassing it altogether in favor of a known synonym. Many people have proposed a number of mental techniques to aid in the memorization of facts, figures, and foreign vocabularies. These methods come in a variety of forms and are known as *mnemonics* (pronounced *ne-món-ics*), which derives from the Greek *mnemonikós*, referring to the mind.

The simplest of these methods include *rhyme*, such as "Thirty days hath September, April, June, and November . . . " and *acronyms*, in which the first letter of each of the words to be memorized are combined to form a simpler word or phrase, such as SCUBA for "self-contained underwater breathing apparatus."

Some advocate the Link Method, which works by incorporating the words or items in a list or story. The success of this technique depends largely upon the strength of the visual cues provided by the recitation of the story. For instance, if required to memorize the capital cities of the United States, one might think of *Kansas* as a tin can, or *CAN-sas*, whose *TOP* is opened to allow one to *PEEK* in—hence TOPEKA, KANSAS. Or, *IDA HO* is a lovely Asian girl who likes *BOYS* a lot, thus BOISE, IDAHO.

Other memory methods, such as the Linkword Technique, formalized by Dr. Michael Gruneborg, entail the linking of a word in one language to its equivalent in another by way of an image.

Mnemonics as a Memory Aid

The mnemonic technique presented in this book can be employed by anyone with a basic knowledge of the more common Latin or Greek prefixes found in English, as well as familiarity with several simple rules of French spelling.

Used in conjunction with a knowledge of basic French verbs, prepositions, and nouns, a seemingly "foreign" French word can be rendered as a recognizable and thus easily memorized English equivalent. The first phase of the exercise requires the search for and recognition of a commonly encountered prefix and/or a spelling (or special character) equivalent peculiar to French. Become familiar with the following prefixes. They will be referred to throughout this book:

Common Prefixes (in English, of Latin or Greek origin)

a   without, not, opposite to, on, in, toward, up, out, away, of, from

com/con   together, jointly, with, mutually, collectively

con   against, opposed to, in disagreement with, to direct course or steering

de   of, from, removal, reduction, disparagement, down, away from, reversal, undoing, completely, carefully, pejorative

em/en   put on, put into, go on/into, to cover, provide for, into, within, being, becoming

entr   between

ex   out of, away from, former, opposing, without

im/in	in, into, within, inward, to cause, on, upon, toward, put in, intense
par	alongside, rear, beside, similar to, resembling, among, beyond
pre	earlier or prior, preliminary/preparatory, front or anterior, before (in time or position)
re	restoration to previous condition or position, repetition, back (to earlier state), again, repeatedly, behind, contrary, against, in response to
sub	under, beneath, inferior, secondary in rank, in place of, forming a constituent part of a whole
trans	through, across, over, beyond, above, changing, from one place to another

It is also important to recognize certain peculiarities of French spelling (special characters).

In French, the "é" (e with **accent aigu**) is often the equivalent of English "s" or "ex". For example:

French	English
étendre	extend
échanger	exchange
épice	spice
épinard	spinach
épargner	spare
écope	scoop
épine	spine
éponge	sponge

Use of the **accent circonflexe** (∧) over a vowel in French often indicates a missing "s" in English. For example:

French	English
hôpital	hospital
fôret	forest
hôte	host
pâture	pasture
fenêtre	fenestration (window)

French	English
enquête	inquest
coût	cost
côte	coast

The second phase of this technique requires a familiarity with basic French, to which are applied these rules of prefixes and spelling. With these simple aids and some degree of imagination, almost any initially unintelligible French verb can be "Anglicized" enough to allow memorization and simple recall.

However, many verbs contain no prefix or special characters. In these instances, simply finding an imaginative English sound-alike word may suffice to form a personal mnemonic link. For example:

Word: **défoncer**   meaning to smash in, bash in, bash, or batter down
Prefix: "**de-**"   can mean "down" or "undoing"
Think: "**~fonce~**"   sounds like "fence"
Picture: knocking down a fence or undoing a fence by smashing or battering it

Another example:

Word: **flemmander**   meaning to loaf about
Think: "**flem~**"   sounds like "phlegm," as in "phlegmatic." Phlegm was one of the four bodily humors thought by medieval physicians to govern man's temperament. A person having too much of the "phlegm" humor was considered sluggish.
Picture: picture a "phlegmatic" or lazy man loafing about. (phlegm = flem)

The key to making a mnemonic system of memorization successful is to use your own *imagination*. Be as personally creative as necessary in forming visual-to-verbal links to foreign words. At times your imagination may need to be stretched to form what may seem a convoluted connection between unrelated words, yet often it is the bizarre analogies that prove to be the most memorable when a mental image is conjured up in order to recall a word.

Vive les verbes français!

The following one hundred twenty-five verbs demonstrate how mnemonics as a memory aid can be used to enrich an English-speaking student's vocabulary armamentarium. Following each key infinitive is a list of other verbs and verbal expressions considered to be within its "verb family." Although not all are synonymous, there is a general applicability of these additional words to various contexts which will allow the serious nonnative French speaker and writer to become more competent.

You will find some verbs and phrases duplicated, as words often have numerous meanings and nuances related to context.

How to Use This Book

Gender

For simplicity's sake, the various gendered French particles of speech have been listed in their *masculine* singular form. These articles, nouns, adjectives, and past participles can be easily modified to their feminine form by using the standard conventions you have learned and that can be found in most French textbooks and grammar handbooks.

Abbreviations

When appropriate, the following abbreviations will be used:

m	masculine
f	feminine
pl	plural
n	noun
v	verb
adv	adverb
adj	adjective
w/	with
w/o	without
qn	**quelqu'un** (*someone*)
qch	**quelque chose** (*something*)
lit.	literal meaning
s.o.	someone
s.t.	something
m/f	male and female genders can both apply
*	a word or expression that is popular, colloquial, or slang (in French, **argot** or **langage vert**)
°	within example sentences, indicates the key verb being illustrated

Finding a Verb: French to English

To translate a verb from French to English, simply use the alphabetized index found in the back of the book. Note that some verb phrases will be preceded by one of several more common verbs such as **faire** ~, **être** ~, **avoir** ~, etc., and will be alphabetized under the heading of these verbs. Reflexive verbs will be alphabetized by the verb following the reflexive pronoun, **se** or **s'**.

Finding a Verb: English to French

The one hundred twenty-five verbs chosen to demonstrate mnemonic techniques are listed under nine categories that roughly capture the sense or feel of the verbs. Taking some time to familiarize yourself with the logic behind these headings will help make future searches for English verbs and phrases quicker and easier. Under each of the one hundred twenty-five featured verbs is a list of numerous other verbs and verb phrases within its "family." Refer to these to find the French equivalent.

Vive
les verbes
français!

1

At Work

Featured Verbs

bricoler to do odd jobs, putter about, tinker

MEMORY AID

Bricoler sounds like *brick-lay*. The verb refers to *the tinkering and odd jobs that one does around the home, in the garage, or in the yard*. Picture a do-it-yourself, jack-of-all-trades laying bricks with mortar around his home.

Other verbs in this family relate to: a host of other repairs, chores, maintenance work, and odd jobs one can do.

abonnir to mend, improve (wine)
améliorer to improve, better (health, economy)
s'arranger to make arrangements, spruce up (appearance), turn out right
attacher to attach, tie together
balayer to sweep, sweep up (dust, leaves)
bidouiller* to tinker, fiddle with
biseauter to bevel (frame, edge of table)
briqueter to pave with bricks
caillouter to lay down gravel
caler to wedge up, steady (chair leg)
chaperonner to cope (put a top on a wall)
cheviller to bolt, peg
ciseler to chisel
clouer to tack down, fix with nails
combler to fill in (hole)
corriger to correct, mend (defect)
criqueter to rasp, grate
déblayer to clear away, tidy up, do groundwork
dépanner to repair (car, machine), help out, fix (car)
dérouiller to remove rust from
désherber to weed (lawn)
entretenir to keep in repair (property, road, equipment, relationship)
épingler to pin (photo on wall, dress hem)
être réparateur to be a repairman
être rétameur to be one who tinkers

être un homme à tout faire to be one who does odd jobs
faire des petits travaux to putter about, do odd jobs
faire des travaux divers to do odd jobs
faire le dépannage to troubleshoot
fignoler* to put finishing touches to
fixer to fix, fasten, make stable, attach to
goupiller to pin, bolt, fix
guérir to heal, mend, cure
installer to fit up, install, rig up
jardiner to garden, work in the garden
lambrisser to panel (room divider, wood-paneling)
marteler to hammer
mastiquer to putty, cement
menuiser to do carpentry, saw, cut
mettre to install, put up, put in, lay, hang
moquetter to carpet
parachever to put finishing touches to
parqueter to lay a floor
passer la serpillière to mop the floor
passer la tondeuse to mow the lawn
paver to pave (street, sidewalk), lay down pavement
peaufiner to put finishing touches to
plafonner to put a ceiling to
planchéier to put down a floor, board over
polir to polish (silverware)
se porter (bien) to repair, mend (health)

raboter to plane down (wood)

raccommoder to mend, repair, fix up

raccoutrer to mend, repair, darn, patch (garment)

racler to rake, rasp, scrape (dirty pot)

rafistoler* to mend, patch up

ragréer to put finishing touches to, renovate (building)

ramoner to sweep (chimney)

rapetasser to patch, mend (clothing), cobble (shoe)

rapiécer to patch up, piece (clothing)

râteler to rake (leaves)

ratisser to rake (leaves, mowed grass), scrape

ravauder to mend, darn (clothing)

recaler to fix, fix again (stalled motor), wedge up again

reconstituer to restore (army, company)

refaire to redo, repair

regarnir to recover (furniture)

remailler to repair, mend (nets, stockings)

remanier to tinker with, revise, rework

remettre à neuf to refurbish, fix up, repair, restore condition of (home, clothing)

remodeler to remodel (organization, nose/chin in face-lift)

remonter to put together again (machine)

rénover to renovate, refurbish

réparer to repair, mend

repasser to iron (clothing), grind or sharpen a tool

repiquer to repair (road)

replâtrer to patch up, replaster

reprendre to repair, improve (machine, economy, sales numbers)

repriser to darn, mend (stocking, mitten)

ressemeler to resole (shoes)

restaurer to restore (peace, painting, monarchy)

rétablir to reestablish (health, peace, prosperity)

retaper to fix up, do up, straighten up (house, bed, car)

retoucher to touch up (makeup, text, painting)

revisser to screw back in

souder to solder, weld

tapisser to paper a wall, upholster (couch)

tripatouiller* to tinker with, fiddle with

truquer* to fix (card game, elections)

verrouiller to bolt (door, window, latch)

visser to screw (bolt)

 Le °bricolage, faire toutes sortes de petits projets manuels, est un passe-temps à la fois créatif et récréatif. Puttering, that is, doing all sorts of odd jobs, is a hobby that's both creative and recreational.

Il aime bien °bricoler chez lui. He likes doing odd jobs around his house.

Ma vieille voiture a été entièrement °retapée par le mécanicien. My old car was completely fixed up by the mechanic.

Le poste de télévision marche si l'on °bidouille* avec l'antenne. The TV set works if you fiddle with the antenna a bit.

La sculpture baroque a été °restaurée en partie grâce aux largesses d'une fondation culturelle. The baroque sculpture was restored in part thanks to the generosity of a cultural foundation.

J'ai justement °fignolé votre portrait. I just put the finishing touches on your portrait.

L'enfer est °pavé de bonnes intentions. The road to hell is paved with good intentions.

démarrer   to start (vehicle), to move off, get going

MEMORY AID
Listen to the **r's** in the word as they are pronounced gutturally in French—at the back of the throat. Picture a car with a souped-up engine roaring to life as it is started.

Other verbs in this family relate to: starting off, moving, getting going, advancing, etc.

abandonner   to leave, quit (job, place)

actionner   to bestir, rouse up, get going, drive

s'activer   to get going

agir   to act, do, take effect, influence, have an effect on

agir en solo*   to go it alone

amorcer   to begin, start, initiate

appuyer sur "lecture"   to press the "play" button (CD player, video player)

avancer   to get on, advance (idea, argument, money loan, position)

bouger   to move, budge (position, opinion)

cingler   to set sail before the wind

commencer   to start, begin (game, business, work of art)

débuter   to open, start, make a debut

défaire   to undo, unpin (hairdo, knot, lock)

déloger   to move out, dislodge (tenant, fugitive)

déplacer   to move (furniture, game piece), dislocate a joint

s'ébranler   to get underway, move out

s'émoustiller*   to bestir oneself, get going

s'en aller   to start, get off, leave

enclencher   to set in motion, engage, get underway (procedure, mechanism)

s'engager   to begin, get involved (job, training, military service)

entamer   to start up, start, institute (meal, project, negotiations)

éprouver   to test, put to the test

essayer   to try, give a try, try out (car, clothing, apparatus)

être sur pied*   to be up and about

étrenner   to use or wear for the first time

faire aller   to move, get started

faire des progrès   to make progress, advance

faire marcher   to move, get started

faire mouvoir   to set in motion

faire partir   to start, launch (rocket, firecracker)

faire ronfler son moteur   to rev up one's engine

faire table rase   to start w/ a clean slate, start from square one (w/o preconceptions)

faire voile   to set sail

faire vrombir son moteur   to rev one's engine

former   to train, educate

générer   to generate (energy), bring into existence (new chemical)

se grouiller*   to get a move on

inaugurer   to open, begin, inaugurate (monument, political term, building project)

initialiser   to initialize (computer)

initier à   to initiate s.o. into (club, fraternity, partnership)

se magner*   to get a move on

mener qn tambour battant to give s.o. a firm lead (*lit.* to lead s.o. by a drumbeat)

mettre to start, commence (activity, project)

mettre à l'allumage to switch on

mettre à l'épreuve to put to the test

mettre à voile to set sail

mettre en marche to start (machine, motor)

mettre en mouvement to move, stir, set off

mettre en œuvre to put into effect (rule, procedure)

mettre en prise to put into gear (car)

mettre en travers to heave to (boat)

mettre en vigueur to apply, start, introduce (law, program)

mettre sous tension to turn on/switch on (appliance, apparatus)

se mettre à (+ verbe) to undertake, start to do (+ verb)

se mettre à l'ouvrage to set to work

se mettre en mesure to get ready, prepare to

se mettre en route to set off (hike, trip), get going

monter sur to get on with, rouse, stir

mouvoir to move, stir, get moving

naviguer to sail off

partir to leave, depart, go away

partir scratch* to start from scratch

se prendre à (+ verbe) to set about, set about doing (+ verb)

s'y prendre to set about doing, go about

préparer to make ready, prepare

procéder to proceed, arise, originate

quitter to leave, quit (job, locale, situation, relationship)

réagir to react, respond to (stimulus, command, chemical reaction)

réamorcer la pompe* to get things going again (*lit.* to restart the pump)

recommencer to begin again, do again

se recycler to retrain, take a refresher course

redémarrer to restart, reboot (computer)

réinitialiser to reboot (computer)

rejeter to cast off, throw back (fish, object, rubbish)

rejouer to play again, replay (game, sport, theatrical scene)

se remettre to resume, start again

remonter to go up again, take up again (luggage), climb again (stairs, hill)

remuer to move, stir, rouse

se rengager to reengage, begin anew

reprendre to begin again, resume (work, study, battle, function, book, conversation)

ressortir to go out or come out again

réussir to carry out, perform (task, job, exam)

roder to break in (new motor), iron out problems

ronger son frein* to chomp at the bit

secouer la poussière* to shake off the dust, stir oneself

siéger to be in session (Congress, court, committee)

sonner le coup d'envoi* to kick-start (engine, economy)

tenter le coup* to give it a go, take a chance, chance it

tester to test (equipment, new product)

s'en tirer* to get off, get out, weasel out (tight situation, commitment)

tressaillir to start, startle s.o., cause s.o. to flinch/wince

viser à faire to aim to do

vrombir to roar, hum (engine)

Les pilotes ont fait °démarrer leurs autos. The race drivers started up their cars.
Mon projet a bien °démarré. My project got off to a good start.
Le nouvel impôt est censé °sonner le coup d'envoi* de la reprise économique. The new tax is supposed to kick-start economic recovery.
Le cortège °s'ébranla lentement vers l'église. The procession set off slowly toward the church.

démissionner to resign, give up

MOTHBALL FLEET

abandonner to give up, abandon (job, project, person)

aboutir à to end in, end at (agreement, goal)

achever to end, achieve

annuler to cancel, annul (dinner reservation, appointment, marriage, show, law)

capituler to surrender

céder to give in, submit, surrender

clore to close, end (book, speech, show, meeting)

conclure to conclude, end (treaty, business deal, contract, decision)

conclure un traité avec to make a treaty with

congédier to dismiss (employee)

se débarrasser de to get rid of (object, person, old clothing)

débaucher to lay off (employee)

déboulonner* to fire s.o., take one's job away

débouter to dismiss (legal case)

déclasser to take out of service, lower in rank, downgrade

décommander to cancel, put off

dégommer* to fire s.o.

délaisser to abandon, jilt, quit (job)

se démettre to resign

démobiliser to demobilize (military)

déposer son arme to lay down one's weapon

désactiver to deactivate, disable (bomb, chemical, computer)

destituer to dismiss (from duty), discharge (from function), depose (king/queen), impeach

donner sa démission to resign

être renvoyé to be kicked out, be booted out (bar, team, organization)

être sans travail to be out of work

faire abandon de to relinquish

faire relâche to close (theater, show)

se faire sabrer* to get fired, be flunked

faire sauter* to fire (employee)

faire une trêve to call a truce

finir to end, finish

en finir avec to make an end of

foutre qn à la porte* to fire s.o.

gicler* to get the boot, get kicked out

laisser tomber to pull the plug on, drop

libérer to let go (employees)

licencier to lay off, disband, dismiss

limoger to dismiss (employee)

livrer à to surrender, hand over (control: new leader, stolen goods: police)

mettre à pied* to lay off (workers)

mettre en disponibilité to temporarily free from work, place on reserve (police)

mettre fin à to end, put an end to

pantoufler* to leave civil service to work in the private sector

prendre congé to take leave of, take vacation

prendre la relève de qn to relieve s.o., take over from s.o.

prendre sa retraite   to retire (from job)

prendre un jour férié   to take a public holiday

proportionner   to adjust, adapt (to situation, to challenge)

quitter   to quit, leave (job, location)

quitter l'uniforme   to leave the armed forces

quitter son service   to go off duty

se recaser*   to find a new job

réformer   to discharge (soldier), declare unfit (for service)

remercier*   to dismiss s.o. from his job

remplacer   to replace (employee)

se rendre   to give oneself up, surrender

rendre son tablier   to resign, walk out, give up one's job (*lit.* to turn in one's apron)

renoncer   to resign, renounce (claim, title, throne), give up (faith, smoking, project)

renvoyer   to lay off (job), discharge (troops from service), expel (student)

résigner   to resign, give up

se résigner   to resign oneself, accept (one's fate)

résilier   to terminate, cancel, annul (subscription, lease, contract)

retirer   to retire, remove from circulation, withdraw from (competition, bank)

se retirer   to retire (from job)

retraiter   to retire (s.o., race horse), give pension (to retiree)

rétrograder   to demote (in rank, position, status)

révoquer   to remove from office (judge, civil servant)

saborder   to scuttle (ship)

sabrer*   to fire s.o., flunk (student)

sacquer qn*   to sack s.o., fire s.o.

terminer   to end (life, sentence), terminate, put an end to (suffering)

tirer à sa fin   to end (test, contract), run out (provisions, supplies)

toucher le chômage*   to be on the dole, be unemployed

En tant que maire il travaille beaucoup trop, ainsi, sa femme l'a convaincu de °démissionner de ses fonctions officielles. He works too hard as mayor, thus, his wife convinced him to resign from public office.

L'usine va ⁿlicencier les ouvriers en dépit des protestations syndicales. The factory is going to lay off the workers despite the union's protest.

Le Guide Michelin a °déclassé l'hôtel en raison d' insatisfaction des clients. The Michelin Guide downgraded the hotel's ranking because of bad service.

Le chef d'État °démissionne de ses fonctions après six années houleuses. The head of state is resigning after six stormy years in office.

Le général appela le soldat °réformé. The general declared the soldier unfit for duty.

entreprendre   to undertake, attempt, contract for, venture

MEMORY AID

"**Entre-**" means *between* and **prendre** is *to take*, so **entreprendre** is *to take on something while being between things.* (The word *enterprise* derives from **entreprendre**.) Picture a cargo ship docked between two piers taking on supplies.

Other verbs in this family relate to: venturing, establishing, incorporating, starting a business, engaging, instituting, undertaking, launching, ushering in, embarking upon, etc.

agir   to manage a business

s'agréger   to incorporate oneself into (society, organization)

s'aventurer   to venture, stake a claim, take a chance

avoir recours à   to resort to, turn to

se charger de   to undertake, attend to (responsibilities, task)

commanditer   to finance an undertaking

se comporter   to act, manage (behavior, conduct, personal bearing)

s'efforcer (de)   to endeavor (to), strive (to)

s'embarquer dans   to embark upon, launch (project, business, adventure)

s'engager à   to engage oneself, undertake, begin

englober   to incorporate, unite (companies)

ériger   to raise, set up, erect (monument, building, business)

essayer   to attempt, try (experiment, task, challenge)

établir   to establish, found (institution, business)

s'établir   to set up (business)

être à la tête d'une affaire   to head a business

expérimenter   to test, experiment, experience

faire entrer   to usher in (new era), invite in (visitor, immigrant), bring in (products)

faire une OPA sur   to take over, make a takeover bid (to control a company) (**OPA: offre publique d'achat**)

fonder   to found, set up, start up (business), lay foundation of

former en société   to incorporate

frayer   to pave the way for (new business, new venture, new method)

gérer   to manage, administer

hasarder   to venture, risk, hazard (remark, guess, bet)

implanter   to set up, establish (business)

implémenter   to implement (device, law, rule), set in motion

inaugurer   to inaugurate, open, usher in (era, political administration)

incorporer   to incorporate (business)

industrialiser   to industrialize

instaurer   to establish, institute (peace, dialog, practice, regime)

instituer   to institute, establish, introduce (rule, practice, trade relations)

introduire   to introduce, show, bring in, adopt (idea), open shop

inventer   to invent, devise

lancer   to launch, start (product, venture), introduce (product)

se lancer   to embark upon (adventure, work, project)

lier   to engage in (conversation, contract, social bond)

magouiller*   to wheel and deal, make business deals

ménager   to bring about, arrange (service, interview, meeting)

mondialiser   to become global in scope (business, communications network)

se mouiller*   to commit oneself, get one's feet wet

s'occuper à   to be engaged in (business, activity)

patenter   to license, take out a patent

pouvoir   to be able to, be allowed to, have power to

prendre la suite   to take over, take over from (business)

prendre son essor   to develop, expand rapidly (business)

préparer l'avenir   to prepare for the future

se risquer   to venture, chance, risk (business capital, investment)

soumissionner   to bid for a contract

tâcher de   to endeavor, strive, attempt to

tenir un commerce   to run a shop or business

tenter   to attempt, try, endeavor (race, legal proceeding, business venture)

Sur le commandement du roi, l'explorateur a décidé d'°entreprendre une expédition dans les arrière-pays du Nouveau-Monde. On the king's orders, the explorer decided to undertake an expedition in the hinterlands of the New World.

Cette nouvelle entreprise °prend son essor. This new business is rapidly developing.

J'ai dû °magouiller* afin d'avoir une bonne note. I had to wheel and deal in order to get a good grade.

Elle °se risque à développer le nouveau produit. She's taking a chance in developing the new product.

Qui ne °risque rien n'a rien. Nothing ventured, nothing gained.

exercer to fulfill, exercise, have (profession, job), train, practice

MEMORY AID

Exercer sounds like *exercise*. Picture a bodybuilder or someone doing aerobics as a form of exercise to train, to practice good health, and as a profession (personal trainer).

Other verbs in this family relate to: achieving, carrying out, accomplishing, working, etc. Think of verbs associated with work or careers.

accomplir to fulfill, carry out (task, assignment)

achever to achieve, complete, finish

s'acquitter de to fulfill (duty, debt, obligation), perform (duty), acquit oneself (well or ill)

aller au turbin* to go to work

assumer to take on, fulfill, take over, assume

assurer to carry out, assure that

assurer le suivi de to follow through (assignment, task)

atteindre to attain, arrive at, realize (goal, number, weight, age, prize)

avoir de la volonté to have willpower

se charger de to take interest in, attend to (task, assignment)

se complaire (de, à) to take pleasure (in)

consommer to achieve, consummate (goal, marriage), consume

se débrouiller to manage, to clear up, get out of difficulty

devenir to become (profession), change (condition, health, age, state, color)

se disposer to prepare to do s.t.

effectuer to carry out, accomplish, undergo (gesture, movement, trip, payment)

s'efforcer to strive, exert oneself

encadrer to train (a recruit)

s'entraîner to train, practice (sports, job)

être en garde to be on duty (guard, doctor)

être en mesure de (+ verbe) to be able to (+ verb)

être révolu to be completed, be accomplished

s'évertuer to strive to do s.t.

exécuter to achieve, carry out, accomplish (task, execution, murder, order, mission)

s'exercer to conduct exercises/maneuvers (military)

exploiter to make use of, exploit (land), run (business)

faire to do, act

faire au pifomètre* to do by instinct or guesswork

faire de la figuration to work as an extra (movies)

faire du volontariat to do volunteer work

faire exprès to do on purpose, do intentionally

faire l'exercice to exercise (health)

faire un stage to take a training course

fonctionner to function, operate (machine, mechanism), work (laborer)

former to train (apprentice, athlete)

gagner bien sa vie to earn a good living

gagner sa croûte* to earn one's crust (daily bread)

gagner sa vie to earn one's living

gérer to manage, handle (crisis, data, business), make do

liquider to settle, liquidate (debt, inventory, account)

se livrer à to do, carry out (exercise, analysis, experiment, study)

maîtriser to master, control (riot, language, passion, appetite, fire)

manager to manage (office, business)

marcher bien to function well (machine, car)

mener à bonne fin to carry through (assignment, task, project)

mettre à l'exécution to carry out (task, assignment)

mettre à profit to make the most of (free time), build on (idea, invention)

s'occuper de to deal with, be in charge of, look after (client, problem, task)

œuvrer to work

participer to participate (activity, adventure, game, plot)

percevoir to get paid, be compensated (money)

posséder to master (language, skill)

poursuivre to go on, continue (goal, profession)

pratiquer to practice (skill, profession, religion, method)

prendre son service to go on duty

se préoccuper to be engaged in, concern oneself with (problem, health)

se prêter à to participate in (experiment, survey, game)

professer to exercise, practice, teach

réaliser to achieve, realize (goal, desire, dream)

redevenir to return to (prior state or condition), become again

remplir to fulfill, carry out (expectations, conditions, desire, requirements)

remplir son office to serve its purpose (tool), fulfill one's duties

remplir une tâche to carry out a task

remporter to achieve, carry out (contract, prize, election, championship)

reprendre to continue, carry on with (work, studies, function, fight)

ressentir to experience, feel (burden, sensation, effects of)

satisfaire to fulfill, gratify, satisfy (need, lust, appetite, demand, assignment)

subsister to subsist, live on (income)

suffire to be enough, suffice

tenir to have under control, have hold of

traiter to process, treat (illness, sewage, minerals), handle (data), deal with

travailler to work, practice a profession

travailler au noir to moonlight or work illegally

valoir qch à qn to earn s.o. something (respect, honor, award, criticism)

vaquer (à) to attend (to), devote oneself (to) (work, hobby), be busy with (occupation)

Le vieux docteur Leclerc n'a pas encore pris sa retraite. En effet, il °exerce toujours comme chirurgien. Old Doctor Leclerc hasn't yet retired. As a matter of fact, he's still practicing as a surgeon.

Le cadre supérieur peut °gérer adroitement la crise. The senior executive can aptly handle the crisis.

Je consens à °me prêter au sondage. I agree to participate in the survey.

Elle va °se débrouiller avec les moyens du bord. She'll try to manage as best she can.

Le mécanicien s'est déjà entraîné à °effectuer des réparations d'urgence. The mechanic has already trained to perform emergency repairs.

parvenir to reach s.o. or s.t., achieve or end, attain

MEMORY AID

"**Par-**" means *alongside* and **venir** is *to come*. Picture a Coast Guard rescue boat coming alongside a stranded swimmer to help him or her reach shore.

Other verbs in this family relate to reaching a goal and achieving an endpoint and include: finalizing, gaining, succeeding, enduring, completing, pulling through, getting to the end of, resulting in, lasting, achieving, finishing off, exceeding, etc.

aborder to arrive at, enter upon (subject)

aboutir (à) to result in, end in (settlement, conclusion)

accéder to reach, arrive (destination, honor, rank, distinction)

accomplir to fulfill, realize, carry out (task, mission, military service)

accoster to berth, come alongside (nautical), go up to

achever to achieve, consummate (project, assignment, goal)

acquérir to get, gain, obtain, acquire

amarrer to moor, belay, make fast (nautical)

améliorer to improve, better (condition, health, quality of life, situation)

arriver à to reach, attain (success, goal, destination, rank, status)

arriver à bon port to arrive safely, have a happy ending

assurer la suite to follow through (assignment)

atteindre à to attain, reach (goal, target, purpose, distance)

atterrir to land (airplane)

avoir du succès to succeed at

avoir failli (+ verbe) to almost (+ verb)

bénéficier to benefit by/from, have, get

se cerner to figure out, solve, identify (problem)

clore to come to an end (show, debate)

clôturer to end, finish (debate, list, enrollment, festival)

combler to fulfill (desire, need, hope, dream)

commettre to commit, do (crime, error)

compléter to complete, finish (race, exam, project)

consommer to consummate (goal)

dépasser to pass, go beyond, exceed, overtake (vehicle, runner, limits)

doubler to overtake, pass (vehicle, person)

endurer to endure, last (difficulty, trials, pain)

évoluer to advance, evolve, change

exécuter to achieve (mission, assignment)

faire les finitions to finish off (action, final touch, project, artwork)

finaliser to finalize, achieve

finir to finish, end, end up

gagner to gain (salary, promotion, honor, prize, size, status)

se garder to last (through ordeal), keep (perishable food in refrigerator), survive

se maintenir to persist (weather), maintain (health, grades)

matérialiser to carry out, realize (project, promise, dream)

mener à bien to carry out successfully

mener à terme to bring to completion (debate, project, era, reign)

mettre au point to finalize (details)

mettre la dernière main à   to finalize (plans)

mettre un terme à   to put an end to (life, story, trip, contract)

obtenir   to get, obtain (wealth, title, possessions)

pallier   to overcome (disadvantage, difficulty)

parer à   to deal with, remedy, overcome (inconvenience, eventuality)

perdurer   to continue, endure (tradition, situation)

perfectionner   to improve (skills, condition), perfect (skills)

persister   to keep up, linger, persist

se poser   to come down, land (airplane)

poursuivre   to carry on, go on, persevere (goal, ideal), overtake

prendre la succession de   to take over, take over from

profiter de   to take advantage of (situation), make most of

progresser   to get on, progress (situation, sales, stocks, economy, disease)

rappareiller   to complete, match (clothing, articles)

se rapprocher de   to get close to (date, truth, answer)

réaliser   to realize, achieve (dream, goal, status)

réchapper   to come through, make it through (accident, illness)

recourir à   to resort to, return to (person, alternative)

remporter   to achieve (goal, victory, prize), win, succeed

réussir   to succeed at, accomplish

révolutionner   to revolutionize (method, technique, invention)

seoir   to suit, be becoming (clothing)

se solder   to end in, show (gains and losses)

solutionner   to solve (mystery, puzzle, question)

statuer sur   to give a ruling on, give a verdict (law)

succéder à   to succeed at, follow (king, time period, directorship), accomplish

suivre   to follow (example, advice, fashion, command)

survivre   to survive, outlive

tenir   to hold on, hold out, persevere (trials, tribulation)

terminer   to end, finish, terminate (job, trip, day, speech)

tirer   to get through, make it through (time period)

s'en tirer   to pull through (difficulty, trials, challenge)

tirer à sa fin   to draw to an end, draw to a close (day, test, supplies)

trancher   to solve, resolve, settle (dispute)

en venir à bout de qch   to get to the end of (goal, project, exam)

Bonnes nouvelles! Je suis °parvenu à passer mon bac! Good news! I finally managed to pass my "bac" (**lycée:** exit exam).

Enfin! Ma lettre d'amour lui est °parvenue. Finally, my love letter reached her (or him)!

Le coup d'état va °mener à terme son régime de terreur. The overthrow of the government will bring an end to his reign of terror.

Cette séance va °clôturer le festival du cinéma. This performance will bring the film festival to a close.

D'ici lundi, l'évacuation des derniers réfractaires sera °achevée. By next Monday the evacuation of the last of the stubborn resisters will be completed.

Tout est bien qui °finit bien. All's well that ends well.

peiner   to work hard, labor, struggle with a problem

MEMORY AID

Peiner sounds similar to the English word *paining—to be hurting or suffering.* Picture a weekend warrior working hard at too many chores around the house and garden and suffering the pains of overexertion.

Other verbs in this family relate to: toil, drudgery, strain, hard study, working up a sweat, being a workaholic, etc.

s'acharner   to work at furiously

s'affairer   to busy oneself (errands, housework, project)

s'affliger   to trouble oneself, self-afflict

attraper une bonne suée*   to work up a good sweat

s'autodétruire   to self-destruct

avoir de mal à joindre les deux bouts*   to struggle to make ends meet

bosser*   to work hard, slave away

boulonner*   to work hard

boulotter*   to work hard, labor

bûcher*   to work hard, study hard

chiader*   to work on, cram for (exam)

cravacher*   to work like mad

se creuser les méninges*   to rack one's brains (*lit.* méninges *(pl):* fibrous brain lining)

se crever au travail*   to work oneself to death

se décarcasser*   to work one's butt off

se défoncer*   to work like a dog

se démancher*   to work hard

se donner beaucoup de mal pour   to take great pains to

se donner de la peine   to take pains

s'efforcer   to struggle, strive

en foutre un coup*   to work hard

en baver*   to have a hard time of it

s'épuiser à faire qch   to exhaust oneself doing s.t.

s'éreinter   to break one's back, tire out

s'escrimer sur*   to struggle at (task, homework, physical labor)

être à pied d'œuvre   to be ready to get the work done, be ready to get to work

être soutien de famille   to be the family breadwinner

être travailleur (-euse)   to be a hard worker

être un bourreau de travail*   to be a workaholic (*lit.* bourreau *(m):* hangman, executioner)

s'évertuer   to struggle, do one's utmost

fabriquer en série   to mass-produce (factory item)

façonner   to work, make, fashion (item, consumer product, artwork)

faire de la peine à   to take pains to do

faire des efforts pour   to exert oneself

faire des heures sup*   to work overtime

faire des travaux tuants*   to do exhausting/killing work

faire le sale boulot*   to do the dirty work

faire les trois huit*   to work around the clock (*lit.* to work three eight-hour shifts)

faire mal à   to hurt, damage

se fatiguer   to toil, strain, tire oneself out

fournir un gros effort pour faire qch   to strain to do s.t.

se frayer (~un chemin)   to work out, carve out (niche, path, solution)

galérer*   to work hard, sweat blood

gratter*   to do a lot of paperwork

s'ingénier   to do one's utmost

labourer to toil through, plough, till, dig (soil)

marner* to work hard (*lit.* to fertilize the land)

se mettre à plat* to knock oneself out with exhaustion

y mettre du sien to pull one's own weight

se mettre en frais to go to great expense

morfler* to have a hard time of it (job, pain, illness)

mouiller sa chemise* to work up a sweat (*lit.* to wet one's shirt)

outrer to overdo (work)

ouvrager to work (handiwork, stone, metal, craft)

ouvrer to work (clay, material, metal)

pâtir to suffer, be in distress

piocher* to work hard at, grind (*lit.* to use a pickax)

se placer to find work, find a job

ramer* to work hard (*lit.* to row or paddle)

recueillir le fruit de son travail to reap the fruit of one's labor

reprendre le collier* to go back to the grindstone

se rompre la tête to rack one's brains

souffrir to endure, suffer, bear, have a hard time

subir to suffer, undergo (illness, fatigue, criticism, damage)

suer sang et eau* to work very hard (*lit.* to sweat blood and water)

se suffire à soi-même to be self-sufficient

surmener to overwork, overexert (physical limitation)

se tourmenter to self-afflict, fret, worry, anguish over

travailler au forfait to work at a fixed rate

travailler comme un forçat* to work like a slave/convict

travailler dur à to work hard at

travailler fort to toil, labor, strain

travailler pour des clopinettes* to work for peanuts

trimer* to toil, drudge, slave away

turbiner* to work hard, toil

vivoter to struggle, live a hand-to-mouth existence

vivre à la dure* to live a rough life

L'assassin a été condamné aux travaux forcés à perpétuité. **Tous les jours il °peine dans la mine de sel.** The murderer was given a life sentence of hard labor. Every day he toils in the salt mine.

L'examen est demain? Purée!* Il me faut °chiader* toute la nuit. The test is tomorrow? Darn it!* I'll have to cram* for it all night long.

À l'aise Blaise! C'est facile ce boulot. Je ne °me suis pas décarcassé.* No sweat . . . piece of cake!* That job was easy. I hardly worked up a sweat.*

J'ai °pioché* sur mes devoirs—c'est un travail tuant.* I slaved away* on my homework—it's a tough job.

primer   1. to prevail, dominate
2. to award a prize to

accorder à   to award (favor, permission, allowance, value)

accrocher une victoire   to post a win, mark a win, register a victory (sports)

adjuger   to award (prize, title, item at auction)

aduler   to adulate, admire, flatter, praise

allouer   to allocate, grant (salary, allowance, time off)

avoir du succès   to succeed, be successful

avoir la main   to lead (race, contest)

avoir la vedette   to have star billing (star of stage or cinema)

se bonifier   to improve (condition, situation, health)

caracoler en tête*   to be ahead of the pack, be in the lead

célébrer   to celebrate (birthday, success), observe (holiday)

chanter victoire   to crow, boast, exult

commémorer   to commemorate, honor memory (s.t., s.o.), serve as a memorial

couronner   to crown, award prize to

débuter   to lead, play first, open, debut

décerner   to award (prize, money), confer honor

décrocher   to get, obtain (prize, contract)

décrocher la timbale*   to hit the jackpot*

se démarquer de   to distinguish oneself from

dépasser   to exceed (vehicle, race, speed limit, spending limit)

dépouiller le scrutin   to count the votes

devancer   to get ahead of, arrive before, outstrip, get in front of

se distinguer à   to excel at (skill, academics)

dominer   to dominate, prevail over, rule, overcome (weakness), overpower (foe)

doubler   to overtake, pass ahead of (lead race car, front runner)

élire   to elect (leader, politician)

s'emporter sur   to excel at, gain the upper hand (solution, contest, competition)

être à la tête de   to head, lead (race, list, ranking)

être au top*   to be the best in one's field

être en progrès   to be improving, be making progress

être en tête   to be in the lead (race)

être premier ex æquo   to tie for first place

être primé   to be award-winning

être survolté*   to be worked up, be boosted up, be jacked up*, be psyched up*

étrenner   to try for the first time

excéder   to exceed (distance, time period, strength, in profession)

exceller to excel (athletics, profession, academics)

faire des prouesses to work miracles

faire figure de favori to be looked on as the favorite (for promotion, horse race)

faire le trou to open up a lead (sports)

faire prime to be at a premium (exchange rate, value)

faire recette to be a big success

faire son come-back* to make a come-back (retired boxer)

faire un tabac* to be a big hit

faire une bonne prestation to put up a good performance

gagner d'une tête to win by a head (horse race)

guider to lead, guide, be at the head (hike, profession)

hiérarchiser to prioritize (tasks)

honorer to honor (with award/title, commitment, one's word)

jouer atout to play a trump (cards)

jouer le premier to lead (sports, races)

mener to lead (race, election, political party, conversation, business, hike)

monter dans les sondages to climb in the polls (elections)

monter en grade to be promoted

monter en puissance to gain ground, increase in importance

pallier to overcome (difficulty)

parfaire to perfect (knowledge, skill, talent)

précéder to be in front, lead, precede (race, parade, in career)

prendre du galon* to get promoted (*lit.* **galon** *(m)*: stripe indicating military rank)

prendre la tête to take the lead (race, election, poll)

prendre qn de vitesse to beat s.o. (race)

prévaloir to prevail (fight, politics, legal judgment)

priser to prize, value, hold in high esteem (award, recognition, object, person)

se profiter contre to stand out against

se rabattre devant to cut in front of (another car, s.o. in line)

rallier to rally, win

recevoir (être reçu à) to pass (exam)

récompenser to award, reward (prize, recognition)

recueillir to win (election, net profit, money)

réélire to reelect

se réformer to reform, mend one's ways

se réhabiliter to rehabilitate oneself, recover one's good name

renchérir sur to improve upon, go one better

être renommé to be famous, be praised

renommer to reappoint

reprendre haleine to catch one's breath

reprendre le dessus to regain the upper hand

reprendre ses forces to regain one's strength

réussir à to succeed at

succéder à to succeed (in time, throne, administration)

surclasser to outclass (rank, talent)

surmonter to top, overcome (fear, difficulty, obstacle)

surpasser to exceed, surpass, excel (agility, talent, speed)

survivre to survive, outlive

truster to monopolize (market, product)

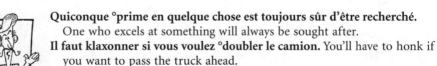

Quiconque °prime en quelque chose est toujours sûr d'être recherché. One who excels at something will always be sought after.

Il faut klaxonner si vous voulez °doubler le camion. You'll have to honk if you want to pass the truck ahead.

Cette étude scientifique est °menée par un médecin belge. This scientific study is headed by a Belgian physician.

Vos gros efforts ont °pallié votre manque d'expérience. Your strong efforts made up for your lack of experience.

2

At Leisure

Featured Verbs

allaiter to breast-feed, suckle, nurse

MEMORY AID

"A-" can mean *toward*, and **lait** means *milk*, so "**a-lait**" can mean *to come toward with milk*. Picture a mother nursing her baby with breast milk.

Other verbs in this family relate to the loving and nurturing activities that a mother would share with her newborn and include: pampering, fondling, cooing, comforting, pacifying, cuddling, bathing, pleasing, rocking, loving, etc.

adorer to love, adore

affecter to move s.o. emotionally

aimer to love, be in love (with)

alimenter to feed (person, animal, steam boiler), supply (money), fuel (engine, inflation)

attendrir to soften, touch, move (emotionally)

avoir un béguin pour* to be sweet on*

baigner to bathe, give a bath to

baiser to kiss (Caution! Now the verb is more commonly used to mean "to screw*")

batifoler* to fondle, play

bercer to cradle, rock (baby)

boire au goulot to drink from the bottle

chanter une berceuse to sing a lullaby

chatouiller to tickle, please

chérir to cherish, love dearly

chouchouter* to pamper

choyer to pamper, pet

consoler to comfort, console

débrailler to uncover one's breast

détacher to wean, remove from (nursing baby)

donner le sein à un bébé to breast-feed

donner naissance to give birth

donner un baiser à qn to kiss s.o.

dorloter to fondle, pamper, pet, coddle

élever to nurse, bring up, raise (child, cattle)

embrasser to kiss, embrace

emmailloter to swaddle, swath

emmitoufler to wrap up warmly

endormir to rock to sleep

engendrer to beget, produce (children), breed (discontent, quarrel)

engloutir to suck down

entretenir to nourish, support (infant, family, relationship, garden)

s'éprendre de to fall in love with, become enamored with (s.o., s.t.)

étreindre to cuddle, embrace

faire des mamours* to fondle, pet, caress

faire faire son rot à un bébé* to burp a baby

faire un câlin à qn* to cuddle s.o.

frayer to lay eggs, spawn (fish)

garder to nurse (the infirm)

gazouiller to gurgle (baby)

glouglouter* to gurgle

langer to change (baby's diaper)

mignarder to fondle, pet, indulge

nourrir to suckle

nourrir au biberon to bottle-feed

pacifier to pacify

se pelotonner to snuggle up

raffoler to dote; ~ **de** to be fond of

réconforter to comfort (with words, with presence)

recoucher to put back to bed (baby)

repaître to feed, nourish (baby, sheep)

roucouler to coo, gurgle (baby)

rouler une pelle* to kiss; ~ **à qn** to give (someone) a French kiss

serrer dans les bras to cuddle

servir de mère à   to mother
sevrer   to wean (infant, young animal)
soigner   to care for, nurse, look after
se soucier   to care, mind, be concerned (welfare, health, condition)
sucer   to suck

tempérer   to soothe, ease (pain, suffering)
tenir à   to care about, be fond of
téter   to suck (baby), breast-feed
tomber amoureux de   to fall in love with (s.o.)
traire   to milk (cow)

La future maman a décidé d'°allaiter son bébé au lieu de le nourrir au biberon. C'est plus naturel. The mother-to-be has decided to breast-feed her baby instead of bottle-feeding him. It's more natural.

Se brisant, les gigantesques plates-formes glacières °donnent naissance à des icebergs de la taille de pays. When giant glacial platforms break they give rise to icebergs the size of countries.

L'intérieur de la chambre est °baigné d'une douce lumière. The room's interior is bathed in a soft light.

On lit dans les Écritures, Luc 2, que les bergers ont trouvé le nouveau-né Jésus °emmailloté et couché dans une crèche. One reads in the Scriptures, Luke 2, that the shepherds found the newborn Jesus wrapped in swaddling cloth and lying in a manger.

arborer   to wear, sport, display, show

accommoder   to dress, trim (food dish, window display)

afficher   to display, make a show of, parade

affubler   to deck out, dress up in (clothing)

agrémenter (de)   to embellish, adorn (with)

s'ajuster   to dress, deck oneself out

apprêter   to dress, get ready

assaisonner   to dress (salad)

avoir du chien*   to be stylish, be sexy

bien s'habiller   to dress smartly

se botter   to put one's boots on

se boutonner   to button one's coat

se coiffer   to put one's hat on, do one's hair

couvrir   to cover (with hat or shawl)

se couvrir   to cover oneself

couvrir d'un manteau   to cloak

se cravater   to put on one's tie

décorer   to decorate, set off (with ornaments/trim/color)

se déguiser   to put on fancy attire, disguise

draper   to drape, cover (shawl, scarf)

se draper   to wrap oneself up, show off

embellir   to adorn, embellish (person, garden, town, food platter)

endimancher   to put on one's best Sunday clothes

endosser   to put on, don (clothing, uniform)

enfiler   to put on, slip on (dress, pants)

enjoliver   to embellish (with ornaments/trim/color)

enrichir   to embellish, add to, enrich (spirit, work of art, language, collection)

ensevelir   to enshroud, wrap in a shroud (for burial, e.g., corpse, mummy)

être habillé de   to be wearing

être mal/bien fringué*   to be poorly/well-dressed

être peinturé*   to wear gobs* of makeup

être vêtu de   to be dressed in, wear

exhiber   to display, show, exhibit (body, animal, document, art, wealth)

exposer   to put on display, show off, show (merchandise, painting, ideas, facts)

faire l'ornement de   to adorn

faire parade de   to sport, show off (wealth, clothing)

faire sa toilette   to dress, wash, prepare oneself

fringuer*   to dress, get dressed

garnir   to garnish, adorn (clothing, food)

se glisser dans   to slip into (dress, bed)

s'habiller   to dress, dress up, dress oneself

s'habiller en habit noir   to dress in formal evening wear

insinuer   to slip into, insinuate oneself into (dress)

lisérer   to trim a dress with piping

mettre   to put on (clothes)

mettre dans un linceul   to enshroud (corpse for burial)

mettre en valeur   to enhance (estate, wealth, property, inheritance)

mettre sur les trente et un*   to be dressed to the nines,* be dressed in fancy attire

modeler   to model (clothing)

montrer   to show, display (idea, object, example)

se nipper*   to get dolled up,* get dressed up

orner   to adorn, embellish, deck out

s'orner   to adorn/decorate oneself

panser   to dress (a wound), groom (horse)

parer   to adorn, attire (dress, jewelry)

parer de bijoux   to bejewel, adorn with jewelry

passer   to put on (apparel)

pavoiser   to dress (a ship)

porter   to wear (clothing, jewelry, eyeglasses, beard)

porter la tenue de soirée   to wear evening attire

présenter des vêtements   to model (clothing)

se reboutonner   to rebutton one's coat

revêtir   to dress, put on, cover (naked body), take on (appearance, shape)

se rhabiller   to put one's clothes back on

se saper*   to get dolled up,* get dressed up

tendre   to drape (curtain, wallpaper, tapestry)

théâtraliser   to dramatize (story), adapt (book to stage)

travestir   to dress up (in drag), disguise (truth, words)

se travestir   to put on fancy dress, dress in drag

vêtir   to clothe, put on, dress

voiler   to veil, cloak, disguise

"Comme il est beau!" pensaient toutes les jeunes filles lorsqu'il °arborait son smoking. "How handsome he is!" thought all the young girls as he sported his tuxedo.

Le mannequin est °vêtu d'un ensemble bleu clair et d'un chapeau assorti. The model is wearing a light blue ensemble with a matching hat.

La hôtesse °agrémenta son repas d'une divine mousse au chocolat. The hostess embellished her meal with a heavenly chocolate mousse.

Le nouveau pape était °paré d'une soutane de soie blanche, d'une pèlerine rouge et d'une calotte. The new pope was attired in a white silk cassock, a red cape, and a skullcap.

décontracter   to relax (muscles, tension)

MEMORY AID

"De-" means *undoing* or *reversal*, and the **"~contracter"** fragment sounds like *contracted*, meaning *pulled* or *drawn together*. Picture an uptight, stressed businessman who, in anticipation of having to go to work in the morning, is tightly wound up or contracted into a frazzled state of tension. Then picture him later in the evening, returning home after first stopping at the bar for a few cocktails with his friends, being "de-contracted" or unwound, unraveled, and relaxed.

Other verbs in this family relate to: unwinding, lazing about, loafing, napping, lounging, idling, kicking back, loitering, refreshing, reviving, reinvigorating, resting, etc.

s'accorder une trêve   to allow oneself a rest, call a truce (warring parties)

s'amuser en chemin   to loiter

s'assoupir   to grow drowsy/sleepy, doze

avoir la cosse*   to be lazy

avoir un poil dans la main*   to be extremely lazy (*lit.* to have hair growing on one's hand)

badauder*   to lounge, loiter, rubberneck

battre le pavé*   to loaf about town

se bronzer   to get a tan

brunir   to get a tan

chômer   to be idle, unemployed

débander   to slacken, relax (blindfold, bandage, spring), become limp (penis)

débrouiller   to unscramble (problem, puzzle, confusion)

décompresser   to relax, decompress (person, pressure, built-up tension)

décramponner   to relax one's hold

se défouler*   to let off steam*

se délasser   to relax, rest

se délecter   to enjoy oneself, delight in (doing s.t.)

dépelotonner   to unwind (curled-up cat, watch spring)

dérouler   to unwind, uncoil (cassette tape, cable, yarn ball)

desceller   to loosen (rock, stuck object), unseal (package)

se désempeser   to become limp (unstarched shirt)

détendre   to slacken, loosen (watch spring, cord, grip, tension)

se détendre   to relax, loosen (body, facial muscles, cord, tension)

dévider   to unwind (tape reel, spool, yarn ball)

dormir   to sleep, be asleep, lie dormant

enfiler des perles*   to laze around, do nothing (*lit.* to string pearls)

s'étaler   to loll, stretch oneself out

être appuyé paresseusement   to lounge, loaf

être assoupi   to doze, be dozing

être bien portant   to be in good health, (**être mal portant:** to be in poor health)

être couché   to lounge, be lying down

être de repos   to be off of work, be at rest

être désœuvré   to be idle, unoccupied

être en congé sabbatique   to be on sabbatical leave, take a year off

être en étude   to have a study period

être en villégiature   to be on vacation

être pantouflard*   to be a stay-at-home type

fainéanter   to loaf, be idle

faire de la rééducation   to have physical therapy/physical rehabilitation

faire la grasse matinée to sleep deeply/soundly, sleep in
faire la sieste to take a nap (siesta)
faire la teuf* to party*
faire le paresseux to be idle
faire un roupillon* to take a nap, doze
flâner to loaf, lounge
gésir to lie, recline
se gîter* to sleep
se guérir to get better, heal
hâler to tan
hiberner to hibernate
se lever de to recover from
lézarder* to sunbathe, soak up rays* (like a lizard)
se ménager to take it easy
passer le temps to idle time, kill time
patienter to be patient
se pieuter* to hit the sack, take a nap, go to bed
pioncer* to get some shut-eye
piquer un roupillon* to have a nap
se prélasser to lounge, bask in the sun
prendre du repos to take a rest
radoucir to pacify, appease, soften
se rafraîchir to rest, be refreshed, be cool
ragaillardir to perk up, cheer up (attitude, physically, outlook)
se rajeunir to make oneself look younger
se ralentir to slacken (pace, step)
rasseoir to calm, compose, settle (tempers, mixed liquids)
rasséréner to restore serenity, pacify
se rassurer to put one's mind at ease
ravigoter* to refresh, revive, perk up
se ravigoter* to perk up, recover one's drive
raviver to revive, freshen up (colors)
se recharger ses accus* to recharge one's batteries*
recréer to take recreation, amuse oneself
se refaire to recoup one's strength, recover
refroidir to relax, slacken (tension, enthusiasm)

se régaler to enjoy oneself, entertain each other
se réjouir to take delight in, be delighted; ~ **de faire:** to be delighted to do
relâcher to slacken, loosen (grip, embrace, muscle, spring, bond)
se relâcher to grow slack, grow loose, relax (muscle, morals, attention, grooming)
relaxer to relax (muscle, bond)
se remonter to recover one's strength or spirits
se renouveler to be renewed, be revived (contract, governing body, incident)
se reposer to relax, rest, settle down, lie down
reprendre haleine to take a breather,* catch one's breath, relax
respirer to catch one's breath
se ressouder to mend (fracture), heal
se ressourcer* to recharge one's batteries,* renew one's energy
se restaurer to rebuild one's strength, get well
rester zen* to remain serene, remain unfazed
se rétablir to reestablish, restore oneself; ~ **de:** to recover from (injury, illness)
se retremper* to be invigorated
revigorer to revive, cheer, invigorate (breeze, fresh air, meal, beverage)
revivifier to revive, regenerate (strength, mind, spirit, plant)
se rôtir au soleil* to bask in the sun
roupiller* to doze, snooze
sommeiller to doze, lie dormant
soupirer to sigh, gasp, breathe forth, heave a sigh
se tanner to tan oneself
traîner to loiter, kick back
vaquer to be on vacation, take a break
végéter to vegetate

Aujourd'hui, avant l'examen, elle est extrêmement tendue. Demain, elle sera plus °décontractée. Today, before the test, she's very tense. Tomorrow she'll be more relaxed.

J'ai beaucoup de choses à faire. Je n'ai pas le temps de °flâner. I have lots of things to do. I don't have time to lounge around.

Le gourmet est connu pour °se délecter de plats exotiques et de vins millésimés. The gourmet is known for enjoying exotic dishes and vintage wines.

Les deux adversaires politiques °s'accorderont une trêve pour la fête nationale. The two political opponents will call a truce for the national holiday.

Cœur qui °soupire n'a pas ce qu'il désire. A sighing heart is not satisfied.

MEMORY AID

"De-" means *to undo* and *frizz* means *to form hair into small, tight curls or tufts.* **Défriser** sounds like *"de-frizz"*—to undo frizzy hair. Picture a girl using a hair iron to straighten or uncurl her frizzy hair.

Other verbs in this family relate to: smoothing, untying, untangling, adjusting, taming, unraveling, resolving, unpleating, unwrinkling, combing, and hair care, etc.

ajuster   to adjust (belt, tie, drain pipe)

apprivoiser   to tame (animal, difficult person)

avoir la boule à zéro*   to have a bald head

avoir le melon déplumé*   to have one's head shaved bald, have a bald head

débrouiller   to straighten out (problem), untangle

décorder   to untwist, unwind (string, bond, cable)

défaire   to undo (hairdo, clothing, bedspread, knot), unpack (suitcase)

défausser   to straighten (kink, bend, twist)

défroisser   to smooth out (wrinkled paper, bed sheet)

dégager les cheveux   to cut back/shorten (hair)

se dégarnir   to go bald, lose one's hair

délier   to untie, release, undo (bond, knot, obligation, promise)

démailler   to undo the mesh of a net

démêler   to untangle, unravel, comb out

dénatter   to unbraid, unplait (hair)

dénouer   to untie, unknot

dépêtrer   to disentangle, extricate (tight spot/situation, mud hole)

déplier   to unfold, lay out (newspaper, handkerchief, sofa bed)

déplisser   to unpleat (skirt)

déployer   to unfold (wings), unroll (map, fabric), unfurl (flag)

se déplumer*   to lose one's hair

déraidir   to unbend, unstiffen

dérider   to unwrinkle (forehead)

désentortiller   to untwist, unravel (ribbon, rope)

détordre   to untwist, unravel (rope, cable)

détresser   to unravel, unplait (hair braid, plait)

détrousser   to let down, untruss, undo (gear, travel kit)

dompter   to tame, subdue (animal, river, nature, passions, emotions)

dresser   to straighten (bed, ladder)

effiler   to unravel, unweave

égaliser   to smooth over (hair, rough terrain)

érailler   to fray, unravel (rope, ribbon, tie)

étriller   to comb (horse), fleece (sheep)

se faire coiffer   to have one's hair done

se faire déboiser la colline*   to get one's head shaved (*lit.* to deforest the hill)

se faire faire un brushing   to have one's hair blow-dried

se faire faire un shampooing   to get a shampoo

se faire faire une coupe-brushing   to get a haircut and blow-dry

se faire faire une coupe de cheveux   to get a haircut

se faire faire une mise en plis   to get one's hair set

se faire faire une permanente to get a permanent (hair perm)

lisser to smooth, smooth out (paper, mustache, crease)

maîtriser to tame, control (passion, appetite, wild animal)

mettre de l'ordre dans to put in order (objects, personal affairs)

se peigner to comb one's hair

rebrousser to turn one's hair up

rectifier to straighten, adjust, reform, rectify, set straight (course, trajectory)

redresser to straighten (wire, nail)

rendre droit to straighten, make straight

rendre raide to make straight (posture, hair, limb, cloth)

résoudre to resolve (conflict, puzzle, difficulty)

toiletter to groom (animal)

Michelle est allée chez le coiffeur pour se faire °défriser. Michelle went to the hairdresser to get her curly hair straightened.

Le cow-boy s'efforce de °dompter le cheval sauvage. The cowboy struggles to tame the wild horse.

Pour éviter une catastrophe en plein vol, le pilote était en mesure de °rectifier le trajet de l'avion furtif. To avoid an in-flight accident, the pilot was able to straighten out the trajectory of the stealth bomber.

Le voleur a été °maîtrisé par la police et placé en garde à vue. The robber was subdued by the police and taken into custody.

MEMORY AID

"**É**" can be the French equivalent of "*ex*," so "**épan~**" is similar to *expand*. Picture a pregnant mother-to-be with a large, bulging, greatly expanded tummy, who is happy, radiant, and in full bloom.

Other verbs in this family relate to: flowering, flourishing, thriving, being fertile, being fruitful, bearing, producing, giving birth to, fertilizing, etc.

accoucher   to be in labor, have a baby, give birth

accroître   to enlarge, augment (size, power, privilege, funds)

adopter   to adopt (child, traits), accept (s.o.), pass (law)

affruiter   to bear fruit (fruit tree, investment, efforts)

avoir de la prestance   to have style

avoir la main verte*   to have a green thumb*

avoir le ballon*   to be pregnant (*lit.* to have a ball . . . under one's dress)

bourgeonner   to bud, grow, flourish (flower, shrub)

concevoir   to conceive, become pregnant

couver   to incubate, hatch, sit on an egg

croître   to swell, sprout, grow (number, size, volume)

donner le jour à   to give birth to

éclore   to hatch, to flower, blossom, bloom, nurture (talent), kindle (emotion)

enfanter   to give birth to, beget

engraisser   to fatten (cattle, person, state coffers), enrich

engraisser de fumier   to fertilize with manure

engrosser qn*   to get or make s.o. pregnant

s'enrichir   to thrive (financial account, culture, civilization)

être en cloque*   to be pregnant (*lit.* **cloque** (*f*): blister)

être en travail   to be in labor (pregnant mother)

être enceinte   to be pregnant

faire naître   to produce, cause to spring forth in life

faire souche   to found a family

féconder   to make fertile/fruitful, impregnate, fertilize

se fendre   to be ready to burst (ripe fruit, fissured rock, dam)

fertiliser   to fertilize

fleurir   to flower, blossom, flourish

frayer   to lay eggs, spawn (fish)

fructifier   to bear fruit (tree, idea, investment)

germer   to sprout, germinate (seed, grain, idea)

gondoler   to bulge, crinkle (paper, wood)

grossir   to swell, become larger (waistline, sea, animal, tumor, crowd)

imprégner   to impregnate

mettre au monde   to give birth (*lit.* to bring into the world)

se multiplier   to multiply (people, plants, insects, prices, problems), be fruitful

mûrir   to mature (fruit, idea, project, abscess, pimple), ripen

pondre   to lay (egg), produce

pousser bien   to thrive (crops, herbs, investment)

procréer   to procreate, beget

produire   to produce (results, energy, factory output), bear (fruit, interest)

prospérer   to thrive, prosper (person, business, animal, plant, investment)

provenir   to issue from, spring from

rabonnir   to improve (wine)

rajeunir   to rejuvenate (medical care, potion, beauty product, rest, business), renew

refleurir   to blossom again

régénérer   to blossom again, regenerate

renaître   to be born again, revive, regrow

se reproduire   to reproduce (animals, plants, organism, phenomenon, error), breed

reverdir   to revive, make green again

revivre   to live again, come to life (comatose patient, usage, outdated fashion)

tuméfier   to swell (tumor, bruise, black eye)

venir au monde   to be born (*lit.* to come into the world)

Comme elle est contente! La grossesse l'°épanouit. How happy she is! Pregnancy makes her bloom.

Pierre °adopta la langue autochtone de sa nouvelle patrie. Peter adopted the native tongue of his new homeland.

Dans le poulailler, la volaille s'agite. La grosse poule a °pondu. In the henhouse the birds are astir. The fat hen has laid an egg.

Le vol 142 °provient de Moscou à destination de Berlin avec deux cents passagers à bord. Flight 142 originates in Moscow and flies to Berlin with two hundred passengers on board.

La reine s'oppose à toute initiative qui puisse faire °accroître les tensions entre les deux pays. The queen opposes any legislation that might increase tension between the two countries.

MEMORY AID

"**Éruct~**" sounds similar to *erupt*. Picture a massive burp erupting from the gaping mouth of a beer-guzzler like a plume of ash and lava belching forth from a volcano.

For this verb family, picture the wide range of noises, activities, and bodily functions one might expect from a lazy couch potato who plans to spend the weekend in front of the TV with beer and snacks. A few verbs in this family relate to: grunting, sweating, boozing, breaking wind, snoring, vomiting, etc.

aller à la selle* to have a bowel movement

aller au renard* to vomit (*lit.* to give food to the foxes)

avoir des démangeaisons to itch

avoir du mal à respirer to wheeze

avoir la colique* to gripe, complain, bellyache

avoir la gueule de bois* to have a hangover (*lit.* to have a wooden face)

avoir un haut-le-cœur to gag, retch

avoir un renvoi to belch

baver to slobber, dribble

se beurrer* to get plastered,* get sloshed* (drunk)

boire sec to drink heavily

bougonner* to grumble

bouquiner* to spend time reading

brouter to graze (cattle, sheep)

chier* to defecate

chiquer to chew tobacco

cracher to spit

se cuiter* to get plastered* (drunk)

se curer le nez to pick one's nose

se curer les dents to pick one's teeth

déféquer to defecate

dégobiller* to vomit, puke

dégoûter to disgust, gross out, be repugnant

dégueuler* to vomit

se désaltérer to quench one's thirst

donner la colique à* to gripe, complain

s'ébrouer to snort (horse)

écœurer to disgust or sicken s.o., nauseate

s'enivrer to get drunk/intoxicated

s'esclaffer to guffaw, laugh loudly

éternuer to sneeze

être en nage to be dripping with sweat

être rond comme une bille* to be blind drunk*

être rond comme une queue de billard* to be roaring drunk*

évacuer le couloir* to vomit (*lit.* to clear the hall)

faire dodo* to snooze

faire la tournée des bars to pub-crawl

faire un sort à* to polish off* (bottle, plate)

flairer to sniff, sniff out (clues), inhale (fragrance)

fumer to smoke (tobacco)

gargouiller to rumble, gurgle (stomach)

gémir to groan, wail, whimper

gerber* to throw up, vomit, puke*

gicler* to spray (vomit)

se gratter to scratch oneself

grimacer to grimace

grincer to grouse, gnash (teeth)

grogner to grouse, grunt, growl, groan

grommeler to mutter to s.o.

gronder to rumble (stomach)

lâcher un pet* to break wind, fart

lâcher un vent* to break wind

laisser dégoutter* to dribble (urine, drink)

manger malproprement   to be a messy eater

maugréer (contre)   to grumble (about)

se moucher   to blow one's nose

pétarader*   to break wind, pass gas, fart

péter*   to break wind

picoler*   to booze*

se pinter*   to booze*

piquer du nez*   to snooze*

pitonner*   to channel surf, zap* (between TV channels)

prendre un pot*   to have a drink (wine, beer, coffee, tea)

puer   to stink

râler*   to moan, grumble

recracher   to spit out

regorger   to regurgitate

régurgiter   to regurgitate

renâcler*   to snort, grumble, moan

rendre   to vomit (polite: to give back), bring up (vomit), be sick

renifler   to sniff, snivel

répugner (à)   to disgust, repel

respirer bruyamment   to wheeze

révulser   to disgust, revolt s.o.

ronchonner*   to grumble

ronfler   to snore

roter*   to burp

roupiller*   to snooze*

rouspéter*   to gripe, grouse*

schlinguer*   to stink

sentir le pourri   to smell bad

siffler*   to guzzle down* (food, drink)

sommeiller   to snooze*

souffler   to pant, puff

se soûler*   to get drunk

soulever l'estomac   to have one's stomach turn

suer   to sweat

tousser   to cough

transpirer   to perspire

uriner   to urinate

vomir   to vomit

zapper*   to channel-surf (TV)

Pendant que son mari regarde les temps forts du match à la télé et lit les nouvelles, il s'enfile* encore une bière, puis, il °éructe sans s'excuser. While her husband watches the game highlights on TV and reads the news, he gulps down another beer, then belches without apologizing.

Eh monsieur! Quand vous aurez fini de vous °gratter le cul* je voudrais du pain! Hey waiter! When you've finished scratching your behind* I'd like some bread!

Qui a °lâché un pet*? Il n'y a tout simplement pas d'excuse pour ce genre de grossièreté dans un café. Who broke wind? There's simply no excuse for such crude behavior in a café.

Une nuit, °faisant la tournée des bars, l'ivrogne s'est fait prendre dans une bagarre de ruelle. One night while making a pub crawl, the drunkard got mixed up in a brawl in the alley.

MEMORY AID

"Frisson~" sounds a bit like *freezin'*. Picture an arctic explorer caught in a freezing snow drift shaking and shivering. This group includes conditions that can make one shiver, shudder, or shake.

Other verbs in this family relate to: quivering, vibrating, fluttering, freezing, being frightened, wriggling, reverberating, resonating, chilling, shaking, etc.

agiter   to shake (person, flag, cocktail), agitate, jiggle

avoir des chocottes*   to have the jitters

avoir la frousse*   to be scared stiff (*lit.* **froussard*** *(m)*: chicken,* coward)

avoir la trouille*   to be scared stiff, (~ **bleue***) to be scared shitless*

avoir le trac*   to be scared, have stage fright

(les) avoir à zéro*   to be scared out of one's wits

avoir peur   to be scared

branler   to shake, quake, waver, be rickety (ladder, table leg, loose tooth)

cailler*   to be cold (e.g., Ça caille! It's freezing!)

congeler   to freeze, congeal, gel

se dégonfler   to lose courage

être bleu de froid   to be very cold (*lit.* blue with cold)

être effrayé   to be afraid, be frightened, be startled, be alarmed

être frigorifié*   to be frozen stiff

être gelé d'effroi   to be frozen with fright

être glacé d'effroi   to be frozen with fright

être muet de terreur   to be scared speechless

être pétoche*   to be scared stiff

être transi de froid   to be numbed by the cold

faire grise mine* à qn   to give s.o. a cold shoulder* (*lit.* to give a gray look)

faire vibrer   to vibrate (tuning fork), twang (guitar string)

ficher la trouille* à qn   to scare the pants off* of s.o.

ficher une de ses frousses* (à qn)   to scare the hell out of* (s.o.)

figer   to freeze, congeal

flageoler*   to quake (i.e., knees with fright)

fredonner   to hum (tune, bee, machinery, motor)

frémir   to shiver, vibrate, tremble (in horror, in fright, in anger)

frétiller   to wriggle (fish), wag (dog's tail)

se geler   to be frozen, to freeze

gigoter*   to wriggle, squirm

glacer   to chill, ice, freeze

grelotter   to shiver, tremble (with fear, with excitement)

morfondre   to be chilled, shiver (with cold)

ondoyer   to undulate, ripple (lake surface)

onduler   to ripple, undulate (laser beam, sound wave, belly dancer)

osciller   to vibrate (tuning fork), waver between (temperature, prices)

palpiter   to quiver, flutter (heart)

se pétrifier   to freeze, be petrified (with fright)

prendre   to freeze, congeal, curdle (milk)

redouter   to fear, dread, be afraid of

refroidir   to chill (food, enthusiasm, atmosphere)

répercuter   to reverberate (sound, echo), have repercussions (consequence)

résonner   to resonate (footstep), resound (echo)

retentir (de)   to resound (with), resonate (acoustics, physics)

réverbérer   to reverberate (sound), reflect (light)

se rider   to ripple, become wrinkled (skin, face, fruit)

secouer   to shake (person, thing)

trembler   to tremble (earthquake), shiver (with fright, with cold)

trembloter   to quiver, flicker, shudder

tressaillir   to shudder (in pain), shiver, quiver (with excitement, with pleasure)

vibrer   to quiver, waiver (voice)

voltiger   to flutter about, hover (bird, helicopter, butterfly)

Le brouillard au cimetière cette nuit-là m'a fait °frissonner. The graveyard fog that night gave me the shivers.

Le pilote °redoute que les égratignures à la surface de la carrosserie puissent modifier son aérodynamisme. The race driver fears the scratches on the car body may alter its aerodynamics.

Il ne se souvient pas des paroles du tube, donc il le °fredonne. He can't remember the words of the hit song, so he hums it.

Quel cloporte*! Il me °fiche* une de ses frousses*! What a creep! He scares the hell out of me!

MEMORY AID

Gober is spelled similar to *goober*, a Southern slang for *peanut*. Picture a fat, voracious baseball fan wolfing down or gulping down handfuls of peanuts (goobers).

Other verbs in this family relate to: devouring, stuffing oneself, imbibing, chewing, digesting, snacking, pigging out, nibbling, eating, drinking, engulfing, etc.

abîmer   to engulf, swallow up (in emotion, in grief)

absorber   to eat, drink, imbibe

aimer la bonne chère   to love one's food

assouvir   to glut, satiate, gratify, surfeit (taste, thirst, lust)

avaler   to swallow, gulp, inhale (food, drink, bad news)

avaler de travers   to swallow s.t. down the wrong pipe

avaler d'un trait   to swallow in one gulp

bâfrer*   to guzzle,* booze,* pig out*

boire   to drink

boire d'un trait   to drink down in one gulp

boire/manger jusqu'à satiété   to drink/eat one's fill of

bouffer*   to gobble up* (fast food, precious time)

bouffer à la pelle*   to stuff one's face*

boulotter*   to eat, put away* (meal)

buvoter*   to sip, tipple (wine)

casser la croûte*   to have a bite/snack (*lit.* to break bread/crust)

collationner*   to have a snack

croustiller*   to bite, eat, munch

déglutir*   to swallow

déguster   to taste (wine), sample (cheese), enjoy (meal, coffee)

dévorer   to devour (food, good book)

digérer   to digest (food, knowledge)

s'empiffrer*   to stuff oneself*

s'enfiler*   to wolf down* (food, drink), knock down (beer)

enfourner*   to wolf down*

engloutir*   to swallow, wolf down*

engouffrer*   to swallow down

enliser   to engulf (in mud or sand)

ensevelir   to swallow up, absorb (work, responsibility, grief)

s'envoyer*   to knock down (beer, etc.)

être repu   to be full, be sated

faire festin   to feast

faire gras   to eat meat

faire ripaille*   to feast

farcir   to stuff with meat, cram

festoyer   to feast

se forcer à manger   to force-feed oneself

se gaver de*   to stuff with,* devour (food, good novel)

se goinfrer*   to stuff oneself,* pig out*

gorger   to gorge, glut, soak up (food)

goûter   to taste, snack, take tea

s'hydrater   to drink lots of fluids

ingérer   to ingest

ingurgiter   to gulp down, swallow down

intérioriser   to internalize (nutrition, advice, teachings)

jeûner   to fast, abstain from food and drink

lamper*   to guzzle* (drinks)

mâcher   to chew, munch

mâchonner*   to chew

mâchouiller*   to chew

manger à sa faim   to eat until full, eat one's fill

manger avec une lance-pierre*   to grab a quick bite to eat

35

manger comme quatre*   to eat like a horse*

manger gras   to eat fatty food

manger hors foyer   to eat out (e.g., at restaurant or fast-food shop)

manger un morceau   to have a bite to eat

mastiquer   to chew

s'en mettre plein la lampe*   to stuff one's face*

se mettre plein la panse*   to stuff oneself*

mordiller   to nibble at

mordre sur   to eat into, bite into

paître   to graze, feed (animals)

phagocyter   to engulf (biology) (*lit.* cellular digestion)

picorer*   to peck, nibble (snack foods, hors d'œuvres)

se pourlécher   to lick one's lips

prendre du rab*   to eat more food, take a second helping

puiser   to imbibe, draw/fetch up (water)

rassasier   to satisfy, satiate, fill (hunger, curiosity, lust)

ravaler   to swallow again (anger, dignity, pride), choke back (tears)

se remplir   to fill oneself, become full

se repaître   to feast on, indulge in, feed on

se resservir   to serve oneself again, take seconds

se restaurer   to have s.t. to eat

ronger   to gnaw at (rat, acid, hunger, rust, rot)

satisfaire sa faim   to satisfy one's hunger

satisfaire sa soif   to satisfy one's thirst

siffler*   to guzzle down* (beer)

siroter*   to sip

souper   to have supper

se taper*   to put away* (meal)

se taper la cloche*   to stuff one's face* (*lit.* to hit the dish cover/stew pan)

Quelle poire*! Il °gobait le baratin* du démarcheur à domicile. What a sucker! He swallowed the door-to-door salesman's pitch, hook, line, and sinker.

L'athlète est contraint d'°ingurgiter chaque jour 5.000 calories afin de maintenir sa force. The athlete has to gulp down 5,000 calories daily in order to maintain his strength.

À partir de lundi, les clients pourront °déguster les nouveaux mets du chef. Beginning Monday, the customers will be able to sample the chef's new specialties.

Le gros gourmand °engloutit* plus de cinquante canapés et un gâteau aux fruits d'une seule traite. The fat glutton wolfed down* over fifty canapés and a fruitcake in one sitting.

MEMORY AID

"**Héberge**" sounds like *auberge*, meaning *an inn or public-house that lodges travelers or guests*. Picture a youth hostel or **une auberge de jeunesse**, which houses or shelters backpackers or cross-country bikers overnight.

Other verbs in this family relate to: harboring, protecting, welcoming, quartering, accommodating, keeping safe, shading, etc.

abriter   to shelter, shade, protect

accommoder   to accommodate, adapt, reconcile (differences), to fit, to suit

accueillir   to welcome, accommodate (guests, requests)

ajuster   to fit, adapt, adjust to (lifestyle, preferences)

s'ajuster   to accommodate s.o. (needs, preferences, values)

cacher   to hide, conceal

cantonner   to billet, put up in quarters

caserner   to quarter in barracks (soldiers)

chambrer   to lodge (together), keep confined (people)

couvrir   to cover (tarpaulin, lid, blanket), roof

donner asile à   to harbor (criminal)

entretenir   to entertain (company, relationship, questions), foster, support (idea)

être en couveuse   to incubate, be in an incubator (hen egg, premature newborn)

être en villégiature   to stay in the country

fournir   to provide, furnish (lodging, provisions)

garder   to watch over, take care of, guard

garer   to shelter, cover, protect from (rain), provide refuge

gîter   to provide lodging, provide shelter (tourists, guest)

hiverner   to winter, lodge for the winter

loger   to lodge, put up, quarter (guest, friend)

loger chez l'habitant   to billet, quarter

ménager une place pour   to make room for (overnight guest, dinner guest)

mettre en quarantaine   to quarantine (animal, prisoner of war)

occuper   to inhabit, occupy (country, town, apartment, seat)

ombrager   to shade, protect (tree, parasol), overshadow s.o.

ombrer   to shade (tree), shadow (police suspect)

parer   to shelter, guard (against attack, blow), parry (sword thrust)

percher   to perch, roost (vulture, chicken)

se prémunir contre   to protect oneself from (unforeseen expense, danger)

préserver   to preserve, keep safe (valuables, rights, loved ones)

protéger   to protect

receler   to harbor, conceal from justice (criminal)

recevoir   to receive, host, accommodate, take in, entertain (visitors)

recevoir qn sous son toit   to receive s.o. as a guest

recueillir   to gather, shelter (refugee, homeless, orphan, animal)

se réfugier   to take refuge (displaced refugee, fugitive)

réoccuper   to reoccupy (surrendered town, vacated seat, prior position)

reposer sur   to be built on (foundation, results, assumption, theory)

rester   to remain, stay (at home, in bed, in same position)

soustraire à   to shield from (harm, injustice, UV radiation)

se terrer   to hole up, lie low (fugitive, social recluse)

Le gouvernement a construit un grand ensemble afin d'°héberger les sans-abri qui vivent dans des conditions épouvantables. The government built a housing project to shelter the homeless who live under appalling conditions.

Une cellule psychologique d'urgence a été installée pour °accueillir les proches des victimes. An emergency psychiatric unit was set up to accommodate the victims' families.

L'hôte a °accueilli chaleureusement la délégation française. The host warmly welcomed the French delegation.

Cet immeuble °abrite le siège du gouvernement intérimaire. This building houses the seat of the interim government.

MEMORY AID

"**Install~**" in French is essentially the same as the English *to install*; as a reflexive verb, **s'installer** means *to install oneself*. Picture a family having themselves installed or settled into a new neighborhood much like a mechanic would install a new machine part.

Other verbs in this family relate to: taking root, residing, dwelling, living, being stationed, nesting, inhabiting, being established, sojourning, locating, resettling, being parked, being headquartered, etc.

accoutumer to accustom, habituate (lifestyle, environment, habit)

s'ancrer to establish oneself, take root, get footing in (idea, belief, superstition)

s'assagir to settle down, quiet down (noise, commotion)

asseoir to establish (reputation, authority, theory)

se camper to plant oneself (in s.o.'s path, on s.o.'s doorstep)

coloniser to settle, colonize

crécher* to live, inhabit, dwell

demeurer to live, lodge, reside

se déposer to settle (legal testimony), put down (object), drop off (package)

domicilier (à) to live (in)

emménager to move in, settle in (house)

s'enraciner to put down roots, settle down, become established, take up residency

s'établir to set up, be established (newlyweds, business, cannon emplacement)

être en garnison à to be stationed at (soldier)

être garé to be parked, be stationed (vehicle, airplane)

être occupant sans titre to be a squatter/illegal occupant

faire étape à to stop off at, make a stopover at (trip, boat cruise)

faire souche to found a line (family)

se fixer to settle down, become established (neighborhood, profession)

garder la maison de qn to house-sit

se garer to take cover, get out of the way, park

habiter to inhabit, dwell (house, town, planet)

habiter intra-muros to live in town

instaurer to institute, establish (government, regime, peace, institution)

localiser to locate (place, address), pinpoint (location)

se loger to lodge, take up one's abode

mettre en place to install (new law, leader, appliance)

se nantir de to take possession of, provide oneself (provisions, weapons)

se nicher to nest, nestle (bird, newly-weds)

occuper to occupy (residence), live at

pendre la crémaillère* to have a house-warming party (*lit.* to hang a pothook)

poireauter* to take root, tarry, wait, hang out (bar, pool hall, friend's house)

se poser to set up, alight, land on (airplane, insect)

positionner to locate, position (object, star, map coordinates)

prendre racine to take root, become established (business), outstay one's welcome

raccoutumer to get used to, re-accustom oneself (locale, climate, habit)

se ranger   to settle down, go straight (criminal)

se réimplanter   to relocate, reestablish oneself (profession, business)

rentrer au gîte   to return home

se repérer   to find one's bearings

résider   to reside, dwell (home, city)

rester   to dwell, stay, remain (location, domicile, physical state)

en rester à   to go no farther than (boundary, limitation)

retrancher   to entrench oneself (in solitude, soldier)

sédentariser   to settle, populate (frontier)

séjourner   to sojourn, stay temporarily

siéger à   to have headquarters at (United Nations, business)

se situer   to place oneself, be situated

squatter*   to occupy a home (illegally)

squattériser*   to squat,* settle unoccupied land

se stabiliser   to settle down, stabilize (prices, inflation, balance)

stationner   to be parked, park (car), be stationed (troops)

subsister   to subsist, live on (bread and water, income), remain

transplanter   to resettle elsewhere

se trouver   to find oneself (in situation/location), to be (at or in)

vivoter   to live poorly, scrape by (poor, unemployed)

vivre   to live, be alive, exist, live on (land, salary)

Les colons °se sont installés sur un terrain reculé où ils ont fondé une pittoresque ville frontalière. The colonists settled in a remote area where they founded a quaint border town.

Raoul est en retard. Si on °poireautait* ici au bistrot jusqu'à ce qu'il arrive? Ralph is late. Let's hang out* here at the bistro until he arrives.

L'enflure °s'installa en réaction de l'entorse. The swelling set in as a result of the sprain.

Le bombardement a visé la ville ancienne où °se trouve un immeuble abritant une cellule terroriste. The bombing targeted the old town where a building is located that harbors the terrorist cell.

MEMORY AID

"**Ôte~**" sounds like **haute**, meaning *high* or *elevated*. Picture a boy's mother removing his wet, dirty T-shirt high above his head. This category includes verbs relating to removing, lifting off, or taking away from a body or fixed point, or removing a covering or clothing.

Other verbs in this family include: to unclothe, slip off, strip, uncover, undress, divest, peel off, make naked, etc.

décaper to clean off, scour (pot), strip off (paint), sandblast

décoiffer to take off a hat, undress hair

découvrir to uncover, expose (casserole dish, body part, pirate treasure, ruins)

se découvrir to expose or uncover oneself

déculotter to take off pants

défeuiller to take the leaves off

défiler to slip off (skirt, pants)

déflorer to deflower (plant, virgin)

défroquer to unfrock (priest)

dégainer to unsheath (sword)

se dégarnir to strip oneself (clothing), go bald, be cleared (store shelves)

déplumer to deplume (bird, bald man)

dépouiller to strip (clothing), unclothe, go through (document), skin (rabbit)

se dépouiller de to strip oneself of (clothing, possessions)

déshabiller to unclothe

se déshabiller to undress

détacher to take off, release, remove (stains, clothing, etc.)

dévêtir to divest, undress

se dévêtir to take one's clothes off

dévoiler to unveil (painting, defects, weakness), uncloak, divulge (truth)

écorcher to skin (knee), peel (fruit, tree bark), fleece (sheep)

enlever to remove (feet from table, stain, dust cover), take off, peel off (wet shirt)

épiler to remove hair from

éplucher to peel, clean (shrimp, fruit, vegetables)

hausser to lift up, raise (shoulders, prices, salary)

hisser to lift, hoist, raise, run up (flag)

larguer to let out (sails), cast off, release, jettison

mettre à nu to make naked, make exposed

muer to molt (bird)

ôter to slip off (T-shirt)

peler to peel off (fruit skin, sunburn)

perdre to shed (leaves, fur)

perdre ses poils to molt (dog, cat)

plumer to pluck (chicken), fleece* s.o. (of money)

relever to raise up, lift up again

retirer to take away, withdraw, take off (coat, gloves)

verser to shed (tears, blood)

Tu sors de la boue trempé et grelottant! °Ôte vite ta chemise! You're soaked in mud and shivering! Quickly, take off your shirt!

Sa vésicule biliaire enflammée a été °enlevée par une opération chirurgicale. His inflamed gallbladder has been removed surgically.

Des dommages à la couche d'ozone peuvent °hausser la température terrestre et ainsi provoquer le réchauffement climatique. Damage to the ozone layer can raise earth's temperature, thus causing global warming.

°Épluche les crevettes avant de les couper en tranches. Peel the shrimp before slicing them up.

°Déshabiller Saint Pierre pour habiller Saint Paul. To rob (*lit.* to undress) Peter to pay (*lit.* to dress) Paul.

MEMORY AID

Sombrer sounds somewhat like *sombrero, the high-crowned, wide-brimmed Mexican hat.* Picture someone sinking or being engulfed in a heavy, oversized sombrero. See also **soupeser** (to feel the weight of, weigh in one's hand), page 284.

Other verbs in this family include: to plunge, dip, dive, immerse, flounder, drown, sag, yield to, give in to, faint away, get bogged down, fail, falter, flood, submerge, run aground, etc.

s'absorber   to be absorbed (in task, in study), be engrossed, be completely taken in

s'affaisser   to sag, collapse, cave in (road, soil)

s'affaler   to slump, collapse (into armchair), flop down

s'en aller en fumée   to founder (plans, attempt), struggle

aspirer   to suck in, draw in (air, liquid)

bredouiller   to sputter, stammer (words), falter (step)

broncher   to falter, reel, stumble, trip

capoter   to founder, capsize (boat)

céder à   to yield to, give in to (conqueror)

couler   to sink, slip, run down (business venture, leaky boat, poll ranking)

couler à pic   to sink straight to the bottom (anchor, torpedoed ship)

couler bas   to founder (person, boat)

couler dans   to slip into (bad habit)

se débattre   to flounder, struggle (business, swimmer)

déchoir   to sink, decline (prestige, fortune, influence, faith), fall off

décliner   to wane (health, sunlight, popularity), fall off

défaillir   to swoon, faint away, fail (memory, strength, willpower, courage)

déférer   to yield, give in to (police authorities)

descendre en piqué   to dive, swoop down (eagle, dive-bomber)

descendre en vrille   to spiral downward (airplane)

désenfler   to go down, become less swollen (bruise, insect bite)

ébouler   to sink, fall in (cave, wall, cliff)

échouer   to run aground, fail, miscarry (person, plan, attempt, project)

s'effondrer   to founder, sink (hopes, dreams, ship)

s'embourber*   to get bogged down* (in mud, in work)

enfoncer   to sink, fail, plunge (dagger, stake), sink into (chair, vice, fog)

s'engluer*   to get bogged down* (problem, situation)

s'enliser   to get bogged down, get stuck (in mud, sand)

être abîmé   to be engulfed, be swallowed up (despair, ruin, emotion)

être avalé   to be swallowed up (food, by flames)

être dans la panade*   to be in a mess*

être dans ses petits souliers*   to be ill at ease

être englouti   to be engulfed (waves, mudslide)

faire naufrage   to be wrecked, be shipwrecked

faire trempette*   to have a quick dip* (pool)

faire un plongeon   to make a dive (swimmer, goalkeeper)

fléchir   to sag (economy), flag (attention, interest), droop (pants, diaper)

foirer* to fall through (plans)

immerger to immerse (in water, in sludge, in study)

s'immerger to immerse oneself (foreign language, project)

inonder to submerge, flood (tidal wave, phone requests, fan mail)

louper* to botch,* fail (opportunity), miss (train, date)

noyer to flood, drown (s.o. else, car engine)

se noyer to drown (accident)

patauger to flounder, struggle, splash, bog down (in details, in work)

péricliter to be in jeopardy (economy, business)

périr noyé to drown, die by drowning

se plier à to bend, yield to (pressure, requests)

plonger to dip, plunge, immerse, swoop (bird, airplane), dive (submarine)

ployer to sag, bend, give way (plank, tree branch, back)

redescendre to walk down, drive down (hill), lower again, come back down (to earth)

se rendre à to give in to, surrender to (authorities, reason, passion)

renfoncer to drive deeper (stake), pull on further (hat)

se rétamer* to take a dive (grade point average), flunk (exam, job)

saper to undermine (morale, castle wall, efforts)

sauter le pas to take the plunge

se soumettre to give in to, comply with (authority, regulations)

stagner to stagnate (pond water, economy, relationship)

submerger to submerge (flooded land, submarine)

tomber dans to fall into (well, trap)

tremper (dans) to dip (into) (crackers: soup)

se vautrer to slouch/sink into (comfortable armchair)

 Après avoir heurté l'iceberg le navire s'est mis à °sombrer. After hitting the iceberg the ship began to sink.

Lors de son traitement pour la toxicomanie, le patient est °tombé dans un état végétatif. While being treated for drug addiction, the patient lapsed into a vegetative state.

Quant aux élections, le taux de participation s'était °effondré à 50 pour cent, soit son niveau le plus faible. As for the elections, the rate of participation had fallen to 50 percent, its lowest level.

°Trempez les ciseaux et le coupe-ongles dans cette solution pour les désinfecter. Dip the scissors and the nail clippers in this solution to disinfect them.

MEMORY AID

"**Traîn~**" sounds like the English word *train*, which refers to something that *follows* or *is drawn behind*, as part of a gown that *trails* behind the wearer. Picture a king wearing a robe with a long, resplendent train that drags or trails behind him, drawn by servants. The sheer weight of the robe train slows him down. See also **épuiser** (to exhaust, drain, use up, tire, wear out), page 277.

Other verbs in this family include: to pull, tug, languish, waver, dawdle, loiter, falter, limp, shirk, pause, procrastinate, waffle, stagger, delay, stall, stall for time, be a slowpoke, etc.

ânonner   to mumble one's way through

s'arrêter   to pause, loiter, lag

atermoyer   to procrastinate

s'attarder   to loiter, linger

attirer   to draw, attract (attention, crowd), lure (into a trap)

s'avachir   to flag, lose energy, get out of shape, grow flabby

avancer à l'aveuglette   to grope one's way along

avoir les doigts de pied en éventail   to be idle, be lazy, do nothing (*lit.* to fan out one's toes)

béquiller   to walk on crutches

boiter   to limp, be lame

broncher   to stumble, trip, falter

buller*   to laze around,* loaf*

chanceler   to stagger, wobble (person, top), falter (government)

circuler à vitesse réduite   to drive at a slower speed

clochardiser*   to be a bum (*lit.* **clochard** (*m*): bum, hobo, vagabond)

se dandiner   to waddle (duck, fat man)

déboîter   to pull out of joint, dislocate (shoulder, object)

défaillir   to falter (strength, willpower, conviction)

draguer   to drag, dredge (canal, swamp)

entraîner   to drag along, carry along (cart, loose debris)

entraîner à contrecœur   to drag along reluctantly (husband to a shopping mall)

époustoufler*   to stagger, boggle* (mind, senses)

s'éterniser   to drag on, stay too long (visitor)

être à la remorque   to trail behind (laggard, little child)

être la lanterne rouge*   to lag behind (*lit.* to be the train's caboose)

être lessivé*   to be beat,* be all-in,* be worn-out

être limace*   to be a slug,* be a slow-poke*

être sur les rotules*   to be beat,* be all-in*

faiblir   to flag, weaken (courage, strength, pulse, voice)

faire du délayage   to waffle, be hesitant, be indecisive

faire du nombrilisme*   to contemplate one's navel,* zone out*

faire du surplace*   to move at a snail's pace,* get nowhere fast*

faire grève   to go on strike (labor union)

faire languir qn*   to keep s.o. waiting

faire une pause   to take a break

glander*   to screw around,* mess around,* hang around,* loaf about*

hésiter   to hesitate, pause, waver

lambiner*   to dawdle,* dilly-dally*

languir   to languish, droop, flag (plant, business, economy)

louvoyer   to beat around the bush,* prevaricate

luxer   to pull out of joint, dislocate (shoulder)

manquer de zèle   to lack enthusiasm

mariner*   to hang about,* stew about* (decision, commitment)

se morfondre   to languish, mope around

mouliner   to reel in (fish)

musarder   to dawdle

muser   to loiter, dawdle

pêcher au chalut   to trawl, drag net (fisherman)

pédaler*   to get nowhere fast* (wasted effort)

prendre son temps   to take one's time

prolonger   to prolong, drag on (time, conversation, suffering)

ralentir   to slow down (pace, car speed)

ralentir le pas   to slow down (pace, step)

ralentir le train   to slow down

se rechigner (à)   to balk (at), hesitate

remorquer   to tow, haul, pull (train)

renâcler à faire   to be reluctant to do

rester sur la touche*   to be sidelined,* stay on the bench (sports)

rouiller   to rust (iron), grow rusty (muscle, athlete), be impaired (memory)

somnoler   to be sluggish, be sleepy

stagner   to stagnate (person, economy, relationship)

stationner   to stop, stand, park (vehicle)

stopper   to stop (vehicle, action, person)

tarder   to tarry, loiter, delay

tarder à   to delay (action, arrival, decision)

se tasser   to slow down, subside (aging process, agility)

tâter   to hesitate, balk (indecision)

temporiser   to play for time, stall, delay

tergiverser   to hem and haw, dither, procrastinate

tirer   to drag, tug, pull (furniture, trailer, handle, rope, curtain, drawer)

tirer au flanc*   to shirk, avoid work

tirer fort   to tug (rope, barge)

tituber   to stagger (drunk, dizzy person)

touer   to tow, tug (tugboat)

tourner au ralenti   to idle, go at a slower speed (vehicle)

traînailler*   to dawdle, loaf about*

traînasser*   to dawdle, loaf about*

trébucher (sur ou contre)   to stumble (over)

trimballer*   to trail along, lug around* (luggage, person, flu)

user de faux fuyants   to evade the issue

vaciller   to vacillate, waver, sway to and fro, be unsteady

zoner*   to bum around*

Ce badaud***! Comme il °traîne! Il n'a rien foutu*** **de la journée.** That idler! How he dawdles! He's done nothing all day long.

Je n'ai pas °tardé à lui envoyer ma réponse. I didn't delay in sending him my reply.

Le remorqueur °remorqua le pétrolier qui s'était brisé en deux sur le récif de corail. The tugboat towed the oil tanker that had broken in two on the reef.

Cette cérémonie grandiose a °attiré le gratin* **politique et aussi le gotha*** **d'Hollywood.** That spectacular ceremony attracted the political elite and also Hollywood's "high society."

MEMORY AID

"Voûte" sounds similar to *vault*, meaning *an arched structure forming a roof or ceiling*. The verb is reflexive, meaning *to arch oneself*. Picture an old bishop stooping over to pick up something. In doing so, his kyphotic back is angled and bent like a gothic arch or vault.

Other verbs in this family include: to bow, incline, lean, list, curve, hunch, nod, droop, slope, be crooked, kneel, lower, etc.

s'abaisser   to stoop, humble oneself, be servile, be submissive

s'accroupir   to squat (on haunches), crouch, hunker down

s'agenouiller   to kneel

s'appuyer   to lean (against a wall)

arrondir   to give curved shape to, round off (object, contour, gemstone)

arrondir le dos   to hunch one's back

avoir le dos voûté   to have a hunchback

baisser d'un cran   to lower a notch (alert level, TV volume, thermostat)

se baisser   to bend down, lower oneself, duck

bomber   to cause to curve or arch (chest, back)

cambrer   to bend, curve, warp (wood, metal, back)

cintrer   to arch, curve (wire, door archway)

courbaturer   to make s.o. feel stiff all over

courber l'échine*   to kowtow,* bow down to s.o. (*lit.* **échine** (*f*): spine, backbone)

se courber   to bow, bend down, be curved

crocher   to bend like a hook

se déculotter*   to lie down and take it* (punishment)

se déroger   to lower oneself, demean oneself

se détendre   to become slack, become less tense (person, face), sit back

dévaler   to descend, slope (hill, roof), go or rush down (river)

se diminuer   to lower oneself, humble oneself

être bossu   to be hunchbacked

être en pente raide   to slope steeply (cliff, roof)

être maussade*   to be sullen, depressed

être traviole*   to be crooked (painting, line, finished product)

fléchir   to bend, bow (knees, metal rod)

gîter   to lean, list, run aground (ship)

hocher la tête   to nod one's head

s'humilier   to humble oneself, lower oneself

s'incliner   to bow, incline oneself, recline (in chair), bow down, kowtow (to s.o.)

s'incurver   to curve (road, line)

se mettre en portefeuille   to jackknife oneself (diving)

se pencher   to bend (over ship railing), stoop, be inclined (tree)

se pencher au dehors   to lean out (window)

plier   to bend over, sag (floor, tree, resistance)

se ramasser   to crouch

se ravaler   to lower oneself, debase oneself

ravilir   to degrade, lower (esteem, opinion, self-worth)

rebaisser   to lower again (price, rate)

se repentir   to repent (of sin), regret (actions, words), humble oneself

saluer   to bow, salute, greet
saluer bas   to bow deeply
saluer qn d'un signe de tête   to nod
  one's head (to acknowledge or greet
  s.o.)

tomber   to droop (popularity), sag
  (spirits, curtains)
se tapir   to crouch, squat
se tordre de   to be doubled up with
  (laughter, pain)

Elle remarquait que le vieil évêque avait le dos très °voûté. She was
  noticing that the old bishop's back was very stooped.
Le chevalier °salua le défi de son adversaire d'un signe de tête. The knight
  acknowledged his opponent's challenge with a nod of the head.
**Dans la basilique Saint-Pierre presque deux millions de fidèles °saluèrent
bas devant le catafalque du pape.** In Saint Peter's Basilica nearly two million faithful
bowed deeply before the pope's catafalque.
Le chalutier sortit de la trombe marine °gîtant à tribord. The trawler came out of the
waterspout listing to the starboard side.

3

Neighbors

Featured Verbs

comploter to plot

ambitionner to aspire to (career, honor)

apprécier to estimate (price, distance), perceive, discern, appreciate (help)

apprendre to learn (facts, skill), acquire knowledge, learn of, find out

apprêter to prepare (food), get ready to do s.t.

arriver à comprendre to figure out

aspirer à to aspire, aim for (career, honor, title)

assimiler to equate, make similar (ideas, comparative data)

s'assurer to ascertain, verify, make certain

s'aviser to think of, be minded (of), realize

avoir besoin (de) to want, have need (of)

avoir des visées sur qch/qn to have designs on s.t./s.o.

avoir du goût pour to fancy, desire

avoir l'intention de to intend to

calculer to calculate, compute

cerner to figure out, solve, close in on (solution)

choisir to choose, select, elect, pick out

cogiter to cogitate, think about, dream up

comprendre to realize, understand, comprehend, conceive

compter to calculate, reckon, count, tally, enumerate, weigh (facts)

concerter to devise, plan, conceive of (plan)

concevoir to conceive, plan, design

concocter to concoct

confédérer to combine, enter into a confederation

conférer to confer, consult together

conjecturer to conjecture, speculate

conjoindre to unite together

connaître to know

considérer to consider, think, ponder

conspirer to conspire, plot

constater to ascertain, prove, verify (death), certify, note (details)

contempler to contemplate, meditate, reflect upon, consider thoughtfully, ponder

convoiter to covet, crave, desire that which is another's

coordonner to coordinate (efforts)

couver to prepare in secret

croire to believe, have faith in, think, deem

décider to decide, determine

déduire to infer, deduce, reason

délibérer to deliberate over (jury, judge), ponder, weigh (evidence)

désirer to want, desire, wish

destiner to destine, to purpose

déterminer to determine, ascertain, decide

digérer to ponder, discuss (idea, proposal)

élucubrer to dream up, envision, fancy

envisager to envision, plan
estimer to estimate, assess
être au parfum* to be in the know*
être en séance to be in session
(Congress, court)
étudier to study, examine
étudier à fond to study in depth
évaluer to estimate, value, assess, evaluate
évoquer to call to mind, recall
examiner to examine, discuss, inspect, investigate
faire des projets to make plans, scheme
faire un vœu to make a wish
se figurer to fancy, imagine, believe
se forger to imagine, fancy, conjure up
formuler to formulate (idea), detail, express (sentiment, thought), make known
fricoter* to cook up,* plot, scheme
gamberger* to brood, think hard about
garder secret to keep s.t. secret
idéaliser to idealize, glorify, conceive an idea or ideals
imaginer to imagine, conceive
s'imaginer to dream, suppose
s'informer de to ascertain, be apprised of
intégrer to integrate (ideas, math)
intriguer to scheme, puzzle
juger to consider, think, judge, deliberate
machiner to contrive, plot, conspire, devise
manigancer* to contrive, plot, conspire, wheel and deal*
manquer de to want, be in need of
méditer to plan, meditate, muse
méditer sur to ponder, meditate over
mijoter* to cook up* (mischief)
opter to choose, decide, opt
ourdir to plot, concoct (secret plans)
pactiser avec l'ennemi to collude with the enemy
penser to think, reflect, consider
peser to ponder, weigh (options, consequences)
piger* to get it,* understand it
planifier to plan, organize (expenses, blueprints)

pontifier to pontificate, act pompously
préméditer to premeditate
prendre en compte to consider, weigh (options, idea)
préparer to hatch (plot), prepare, arrange, make ready
programmer to plan, arrange, schedule (calendar), program (computer)
projeter to plan, design, scheme
proposer to propose, intend, suggest, advise, offer (suggestion), nominate
se proposer de to intend to, plan to
raisonner to reason, argue, study, talk over
rappeler to recall to mind, remember, recollect
rationaliser to rationalize, think rationally (reason, logic, empiricism)
se raviser to change one's mind, decide against
réaliser to realize, be aware of, understand
réexaminer to reconsider, reexamine (evidence), reassess
réfléchir to reflect, ponder, think upon
regarder to think about, notice
remâcher* to brood over, ruminate, meditate at length, muse
se remémorer to remember, recall
remettre to remember, recall
repenser to rethink, reconsider
se représenter to imagine, visualize (face, person)
résoudre to solve, decide on, resolve (conflict, puzzle)
ressouvenir to recollect, remember
retenir to remember, recall
se retracer to recall to mind, retrace in one's mind
retravailler to give more thought to
retrouver to remember, recall (person, idea, detail)
rêvasser to daydream, muse
rêver to dream, dream of, muse
rêver tout éveillé to daydream
revoir to review, revise (homework, list)
ruminer to ruminate, muse, ponder, mull over
ruser to use cunning, use trickery

savoir to know, be aware of, realize, comprehend

songer to think of, dream of

souhaiter to wish, desire

se souvenir to remember, recall, be mindful of

spéculer to speculate

supposer to suppose, assume, presume, speculate

supputer to calculate, compute (data), work out (computations)

tenir de grands conciliabules to hold secret talks/great consultations

tenir pour vrai to believe in, believe to be true

tirer to draw up (plan), print (newspaper, magazine)

tracer to plot (graph, boundary line, route)

tramer to plot, hatch s.t., brew (plans)

vérifier to ascertain, verify

visualiser to visualize (idea), picture (in mind), imagine

vouloir to intend, want, desire, wish

Les deux agents secrets °complotaient un attentat à la bombe et d'autres actes de terrorisme outre-mer. The two secret agents were plotting a bomb attack and other acts of terrorism overseas.

Au moins 70 pour cent des images réalisées ont été °jugées ayant une bonne valeur diagnostique. At least 70 percent of the images taken were considered to be of diagnostic quality.

Le journal hebdomadaire est °tiré à 50.000 exemplaires avec un point mort à 20.000 exemplaires. Fifty thousand copies of the weekly newspaper are printed with a break-even point of 20,000 copies.

Davantage de recherche est nécessaire pour mieux °comprendre le changement cellulaire aboutissant à une tumeur. More research is needed to better understand the cellular changes that result in a tumor.

Les chefs sont encouragés à °concevoir des plats équilibrés pour satisfaire les exigences des clients au régime. The chefs are encouraged to create balanced, healthy dishes to satisfy the demands of the dieting customers.

concourir

1. to compete with
2. to contribute, work together, cooperate

With

accentuer to accentuate (taste), emphasize (similarities, word)

accommoder to reconcile, conciliate (differences, misunderstanding)

agir de concert avec to act in concert with s.o.

appareiller to match up (socks), pair with (shirt and pants)

apparenter to ally, connect by marriage (noble families)

appuyer to support, uphold (political candidate, social cause)

s'appuyer sur to depend on (person, welfare check)

s'associer à to partner with (business, project, law firm)

avoir trait à to be connected with, be concerned with (details, ideas)

se caser* to find a partner (single person)

coïncider to coincide, happen at the same time, correspond exactly, be identical

collaborer to collaborate (book, song, research)

commercer to trade (business, countries)

concurrencer to compete with (product, business)

contribuer to contribute (donation, effort, to results)

coopérer to cooperate (project), collaborate (song, book)

égaliser to equalize, level out, make equal (chances, salaries, social status)

encadrer to train, manage, take in hand (recruit, intern, trainee)

s'entendre to act in concert, agree with (friend, family member)

s'entraider to assist one another

étayer to shore up, support (wall, hypothesis)

être à l'aide de to give aid/assistance to

être au service to be of service

être en phase* to be on the same wavelength* (friends)

être en pourparlers avec to start talks/negotiations with (diplomat)

être le partenaire de to be partners with

être utile to be useful (person, tool)

faire bloc to join forces (allies, nations)

faire des remerciements to thank, give thanks

faire du bien à to benefit (good night's sleep, medicine, kind words)

faire équipe to team up with

fréquenter to consort with, date, go steady

inviter to invite (guest, criticism)

jouer franc-jeu to play fair

jouxter to be next to (garage, house), border on (empty lot)

juxtaposer to juxtapose, place side-by-side (color samples, before-and-after photos)

négocier to negotiate, trade

nouer to strike up a friendship, start a relationship

obtempérer to obey (king/queen)

opposer to bring together (ideas, people, colors) (See also the following list "Against")

passer le témoin to pass the baton (sprinters)

se raccommoder to reconcile (quarreling lovers), set right

se raccorder to fit together (electric plugs/devices), blend

rallier to rejoin, rally around, regroup, rally

se ranger de côté to side with

se rapporter to relate to, bear relation to (subject, idea)

réconcilier to make up with (rivals, lovers)

régler to deal with, settle (account), pay for

remercier to thank, give thanks

se rencontrer to meet, meet with

renfoncer to reinforce, strengthen, drive deeper (stake, pole)

réunir to get together, join, unite (family, rope ends)

revaloir to repay, be even with (See also the following list "Against")

servir to serve, assist (person, cause)

supporter to support (person, object, idea, cause)

tolérer to allow, tolerate (difference of opinion), bear (pain)

traiter de to deal with (problems, requests), negotiate

Against

s'accorder (ne pas ~) to disagree

se brouiller avec qn to have a falling out with s.o.

confondre to baffle, confound

contester to contest, dispute

contraindre to constrain, suppress (free speech), quell (dissent)

contrarier to thwart, baffle (plans), irritate

contrecarrer to thwart, oppose (plans)

contredire to contradict

courir contre to run against (rival candidate)

défier to challenge, defy, dare

déjouer to baffle, foil (plans, plot)

déranger to inconvenience, disturb (person, routine, tranquility)

se désolidariser de to dissociate oneself from (person, organization)

différer to differ (opinions), disagree (fashions, customs)

discriminer to discriminate against

discuter to argue about (prices), debate (issues, ideas)

disputer to dispute, contend for (trophy, football match, race)

se dissocier to break up (group)

empêcher to hinder, get in the way (object, person, law)

entrer en lice to come into contention (ideas, viewpoints)

être aux prises avec to struggle with (difficulty, illness)

être coude à coude* to be neck and neck* (race, election) (*lit.* elbow to elbow)

faire concurrence to compete with

faire échouer to foil, cause to fail (plans, negotiations, test)

frustrer to frustrate, foil (plans, hopes)

gêner to hinder, impede (person, progress)

s'immiscer to interfere in, meddle in (plans, affair)

incommoder to inconvenience (situation, heat, rain, traffic, delay)

se liguer contre   to league against, team up against, oppose (enemy)

omettre   to leave out, omit

opposer   to oppose, go against (rival, government) (See also the previous list "With")

prendre sa revanche sur   to take one's revenge on

se quitter   to split up (relationship)

se rebeller   to rebel, revolt

retarder   to hinder, impede (progress, search, sale, person), set back (clock)

retenir   to detain, hold back (crowd, mudslide, stampede)

revaloir   to get even with s.o., return in kind (See also the previous list "With")

rivaliser (avec)   to rival (competitor), vie with (rival)

traverser   to thwart, frustrate, challenge (opposition)

Tous vos efforts °concourent à la réussite de la compagnie. All your efforts contribute to the company's success.

Les deux candidats °courent coude à coude dans les sondages. The two candidates are running neck and neck in the polls.

Nos grévistes °se liguèrent et °se rebellèrent contre les forces de l'ordre. Our strikers united and rebelled against the police force.

Le premier ministre refuse de °négocier directement avec les ravisseurs. The prime minister refuses to negotiate directly with the kidnappers.

Les soldats se postent le long de la rue barricadée afin d'°empêcher les éventuels pillages dans les banlieues désertées. The soldiers are posted along the barricaded road in order to prevent possible looting of the deserted suburbs.

confondre 1. to confound, confuse, mix, mingle
2. to amaze, astound

MEMORY AID

"**Confond~**" sounds like *confound*, meaning *to bewilder*, *confuse*, or *mix up elements or ideas*; someone who is *confounded* is *confused* or *befuddled*. The verb's second meaning is *to amaze* or *astound*. Picture the clown act in a three-ring circus. Their hectic, confused antics cause them to collide and commingle, forming a mass of jumbled torsos and twisted limbs. Their physical agility and their juggling and balancing skills amaze and astound the audience. See also **enchevêtrer** (to tangle up, entangle, tie in knots), page 160.

Other verbs in this family include: two subgroups based on their similarity to the meanings of "to mix" or "to amaze."

To Mix

accourir (à, vers) to flock (to) (ticket office, movie premiere, holy shrine)

achopper (sur) to stumble (over) (rock, obstacle, words)

aller de guingois* to go haywire,* become jumbled/confused

amalgamer to amalgamate, mix, combine (metals), confuse (ideas)

bader* to bungle,* mess up,* screw up*

bousculer to jostle, bump into (crowd)

brasser to stir, mix (food ingredients, deck of cards)

brouiller to scramble, mix up, confuse (ideas, words, TV transmission), blur (view)

cafouiller* to be in a mess,* be struggling (candidate in polls, new business)

se coaliser to combine, unite, coalesce (chemicals), league (nations)

combiner to combine, blend, fuse (ingredients, styles, ideas)

complexifier to make more complex (solution, situation, equation)

compliquer to complicate (situation, idea)

confluer to unite (rivers, bloodlines)

conjoindre to join together, unite (families, electrical connections)

côtoyer to mix with (styles, flavors), meet (people at a club)

désordonner to throw into confusion, disturb (tranquility, equilibrium, order)

désorganiser to disorganize, disrupt (meeting, bedroom, schedule)

emberlificoter* to mix up (ideas, words)

emmêler to entangle (yarn, hair, relationship)

s'empresser (de) to press, crowd around (celebrity, victim), hasten to

encombrer to jam (telephone lines), encumber (hallway), clutter (room)

entrelacer to interlace, intertwine (vines, ribbons)

entremêler to intermingle, intermix (ideas, items, ingredients)

faire des balourdises* to klutz about,* go about clumsily

faire des singeries* to clown around*

faire le pitre* to clown around*

se faire mitrailler par* to be mobbed by (adoring fans, swarm of bees)

fondre to combine, blend (colors, liquids, sounds), smelt (minerals), melt

fusionner to blend, merge (ore, colors, liquids, populations, towns, companies)

homogénéiser to homogenize, make homogeneous (milk, ethnic populations)

impliquer to involve (in project, in plot, in activity)

incorporer to integrate, mix (ingredients, elements, mechanical parts)

malaxer to mix, knead (clay, dough) massage (muscle)

mélanger to mix, mingle (people, ingredients, ideas)

mêler to mix, mingle (liquids, chemicals, colors, people)

métisser to mix blood, crossbreed

se mouiller dans* to get mixed up in (affair, relationship)

panacher to mix (salad), variegate (flower colors)

se presser to crowd, press together (people)

regrouper to group together, consolidate (companies, objects, pieces, parcels, people)

rencontrer to meet with, encounter

se serrer to crowd together, huddle (around campfire, lovers)

touiller* to stir (coffee), mix (salad)

tremper dans to be mixed up in (crime)

To Amaze

abasourdir to bewilder, stun, stupefy

ahurir to astound, confuse, stupefy, daze

charmer to charm, enchant, bewitch, captivate

déconcerter to baffle, disconcert

désorienter to bewilder, disorient, confuse

divertir to entertain, amuse, be entertaining

ébahir to astound

s'ébahir to wonder at, be amazed

éblouir to fascinate, amaze, dazzle

ébouriffer* to startle, amaze

émerveiller to amaze, astonish

enchanter to charm, enchant

épater to amaze, astound

étonner to amaze, astound, stun

étourdir to stun, daze, bewilder, make giddy

intriguer to puzzle, bewilder

méduser to transfix, dumbfound

mystifier to mystify, hoax

passionner to fascinate

séduire to fascinate, charm, seduce

sidérer to dumbfound, stagger

stupéfier to amaze, astound, stupefy

surprendre to surprise

 Au centre-ville °se confondent une variété de magasins—le magasin de fleurs, la charcuterie, la boucherie, la confiserie, la crémerie et la boulangerie. Downtown there's quite a variety of shops: the florist, the pork butcher, the butcher, the confectioner, the dairyman, and the baker.

Nous voulions que le public soit °impliqué dans toutes les décisions. We wanted the public to be involved in all the decisions.

Les deux familles, partageant le même deuil, vont °se côtoyer devant les obsèques du roi défunt. The two families, united in mourning, will meet at the funeral services of the late king.

Hier soir les visiteurs du musée furent °ahuris par le "tableau vivant"—une exposition de vingt femmes et hommes nus. Museum visitors last night were stunned at the "living painting"—a display of twenty nude women and men.

convenir à   to suit, fit, match
convenir de   to admit, agree on, acknowledge

[Note: **convenir à** conjugated with **avoir**, but **convenir de** conjugated with **être**]

MEMORY AID

"**Con-**" means *together* or *with* and **venir** means *to come*, so **convenir** can mean *to come together*. Picture two foreign ambassadors, who harbor different views on politics and diplomacy, agreeing to meet to discuss terms of peace, mutual respect, and coexistence. They each agree to formulate foreign policies to match the other's.

Other verbs in this family include: to avow, harmonize, compromise, forgive, associate with, convene, reconcile, concur, concede, appease, settle, get along with, pledge, pardon, etc.

accéder   to accede, consent to (request, prayer), grant (wish)

accepter   to accept (offer, present, invitation)

accommoder   to suit, accommodate (differing opinion)

accorder   to concede, bring into harmony (people, colors), admit (truth)

s'accorder sur   to agree upon, concur (treaty, decision)

acquiescer   to acquiesce, give in to, consent to

adapter   to make suitable, to fit (mechanical pieces, decor, personalities)

admettre   to admit (truth), accept (excuse, theory), pass (exam)

affirmer   to affirm, confirm, assert, vouch

ajuster   to suit, accommodate (temperature setting, different beliefs), fine-tune

aller à   to suit, match (colors, style)

apaiser   to appease (crowd, person, animal), slake (thirst, hunger)

approuver   to approve, ratify (nomination, contract, idea, treaty)

avaliser   to endorse (idea, cause), guarantee, support (candidate)

avoir des atomes crochus (avec qn)   to get along, hit it off, have s.t. in common (with s.o.) (*lit.* to have linked atoms)

avoir une liaison   to have an affair (romantic)

avouer   to admit (guilt), avow (truth, love), acknowledge (weakness, fault)

battre sa coulpe   to admit one's guilt, confess to (crime, sin)

coexister   to coexist, live together (people, nations)

commettre   to commit, entrust, appoint, empower (with responsibility)

concéder   to grant, concede (privilege, rights)

confesser   to acknowledge, admit, confess (guilt, sin)

confier   to confide (in friend, in lawyer), entrust (secret, possessions)

se confier   to trust in, confide in (friend)

confirmer   to confirm (reservation, appointment)

conformer   to conform (to norm, expectations, shape)

consentir   to consent, agree

se contenter de   to settle for, be content with

convoquer to convene (session of Congress, court)

coordonner to coordinate

cracher le morceau* to spill the beans,* come clean,* admit

se décider pour to settle on

dialoguer to talk, engage in dialog

donner suite à to accede, agree, consent

engager to pledge (word, honor), engage (dialog)

s'engager to covenant (negotiations, business deal, politics)

engager sa parole to pledge one's word

s'entendre avec qn to get along with s.o., agree with s.o.

entériner to confirm, ratify (contract, judicial ruling)

être conforme to be in agreement, certify, conform (to original, to specification)

être d'accord to be in agreement, agree, concur, be in accord

être disposé to be willing (to do s.t.)

être peu disposé to be unwilling

exaucer to grant (wish), fulfill (desire), answer (prayer, request)

excuser to excuse, pardon, forgive

faire chorus to be in agreement with

faire la paix fo make peace

faire un vœu to vow, pledge

frayer avec to associate with (friend, business partner)

fumer le calumet de la paix* to bury the hatchet* (*lit.* to smoke the peace pipe), make peace (with s.o.)

garantir to pledge (support), assure, guarantee

harmoniser to harmonize (music, colors, relationship)

honorer to keep one's word, honor (pledge, commitment)

imiter to imitate (person, voice), impersonate (celebrity), mimic (sound, symptom)

jurer to vow, pledge (oath, promise)

se livrer à to entrust oneself to (assignment, study, exercise, project)

mettre d'accord to reconcile (differences)

obtempérer à to comply with (rules, law, authority)

pactiser avec to make a pact or covenant with

parlementer to reach a truce, come to terms, negotiate, parley

se parler to talk to each other, discuss

parvenir à un accord to reach a settlement

passer la poigne* to extend the hand of friendship

plaire à to suit, please

prêter to favor, impart (aid, support), lend (object, assistance)

prêter serment to pledge an oath, promise

promettre to promise

se rabibocher* to make up, patch up differences*

se raccommoder to make it up (to s.o.) (because of hurt feelings or misunderstanding)

se raccorder to blend, fit together (plumbing, electrical plugs)

racheter to atone for, make amends for

rajuster to settle, reconcile (differences), tidy up (house)

se ranger à to go along with (decision), side with

rapatrier to reconcile, repatriate (exile)

rapprocher to reconcile, bring together (objects, people, nations)

ratifier to ratify (pact, treaty)

rationaliser to rationalize, conform to reason, make rational (idea, theory)

réadmettre to readmit, admit again (club member, ticket holder)

réconcilier to reconcile, make up (warring nations, lovers)

reconnaître to admit, acknowledge, recognize (credentials, authority, sovereignty)

régler to settle (account, bill)

régler les différends to settle differences

se rencontrer to agree (people), coincide, to be found (disease, condition)

renouer avec to resume relations with

réunir   to convene, meet, reconcile

revendiquer   to be responsible for, claim (rights, paternity), admit to (crime, deed)

sacrifier à   to conform to (fashion, tradition, law), support, endure (loss)

stipuler par contrat   to covenant, make a pact, draw up a contract

tenir parole   to keep one's word

toper*   to agree, agree to (deal)

traiter   to negotiate, deal with (complaint, concern, business, legal case)

transiger   to compromise (standards, in terms of an agreement)

vérifier   to verify (account, data, truth, suspicions)

vivre en osmose avec*   to live in harmony with

voir du même œil   to see eye-to-eye, be in agreement, be in accord

Je suis plus intelligent que toi! °Conviens-en! I'm smarter than you! Admit it!

Les profits de vos investissements durant cet exercice financier ne °garantissaient pas une telle rentabilité à l'avenir. Your investment gains this fiscal year didn't guarantee similar future profitability.

Un éclaireur °tient parole toujours. A scout always keeps his word.

Le célibataire solitaire °avoua n'avoir que cinq rancards* par an. The lonely bachelor admitted to having only five dates per year.

Jeanne est fiable. Elle °honore tous ses engagements. Jean is reliable. She keeps all her commitments.

Les beaux esprits °se rencontrent. Great minds think alike.

to bother, annoy, rile, pester **embêter***

MEMORY AID

"**Em-**" means *being* or *becoming*, and **une bête** is a *beast* or *dumb animal*, so **embêter** can mean to *become like* or *act like a dumb animal*. Picture someone as stubborn as a mule, refusing to be budged. The poor person trying to get the reluctant beast to move would be quite annoyed and bothered.

Note: This verb family contains words that convey a stronger sense of irritation and imply more malicious intent than those found under **taquiner** (to tease), page 88.

Other verbs in this family include: to menace, enrage, bully, torment, terrorize, dismay, distress, upset, anger, offend, exasperate, horrify, disrupt, badger, hamper, tick off, etc.

---

s'acharner contre   to pester, to hound (bad luck, injury)

agacer   to annoy, pester, irritate, vex, rile

altérer   to trouble, upset (person, object), adulterate (medicine)

angoisser   to distress, agonize, cause anguish

se becqueter   to peck one another (birds)

bisquer*   to be vexed or riled

bourreler   to torment, rack (pain, guilt, anguish)

brimer   to bully, aggravate

brutaliser   to bully, ill-treat

casser les pieds à qn*   to be a pain,* be a pain in the ass*

chagriner   to bother, annoy, cause chagrin

chahuter   to make a racket,* create an uproar, be rowdy

consterner   to dismay, cause consternation

contrarier   to annoy, bother, irritate

contrister   to vex, grieve, sadden

courir qn*   to bug s.o.,* annoy s.o.

courir sur les haricots*   to get on s.o.'s nerves (*lit.* to step on s.o.'s beans)

déconcerter   to disturb, confuse, thwart, discomfit

défriser*   to bug s.o.*

dépiter   to vex, spite (s.o.)

déplaire   to offend, displease (person, odor, situation)

déranger   to bother, disturb, annoy, vex, perturb

emmerder*   to be a pain in the ass* (vulgar)

empoisonner*   to irritate, bother (*lit.* to poison or administer poison to)

ennuyer   to pester, bother

enquiquiner*   to irritate, annoy, bother

exaspérer   to exasperate, irritate

fâcher   to anger, offend, grieve, make angry

faire enrager   to rile, enrage

faire injure à qn   to offend/hurt/insult s.o.

faire suer qn*   to drive s.o. mad (*lit.* to make s.o. sweat)

gêner   to bother, hamper, impede, be in the way, interfere with

harasser   to harass

harceler   to harass, pester

horrifier   to horrify

horripiler*   to exasperate

impatienter   to bother, irritate

importuner   to bother, disturb

incommoder   to disturb, bother (noise, odor)

indigner qn   to make s.o. indignant

indisposer   to upset, annoy (person, remark), ail (disease, heat)

insulter   to insult, offend, cuss out, treat rudely

interférer   to interfere (in affairs, in conversation), come between (people)

interloquer   to disconcert, nonplus, baffle, perplex, dumbfound

intimider   to intimidate, bully

irriter   to irritate, anger, gall, bother, bedevil, peeve, frustrate

jouer les trouble-fête*   to be a spoilsport*

léser   to wrong s.o.

martyriser   to torture, bully

menacer (de)   to menace, threaten

mettre au supplice   to cause s.o. agony, torment

molester   to trouble, molest (sexually), manhandle (police), harass

navrer   to dismay, disconcert, perturb, ruffle

outrager   to outrage, insult, offend

parasiter   to get in the way of, interfere with (person, obstacle)

passer un savon*   to tick s.o. off* (*lit.* to pass s.o. a bar of soap)

perturber   to perturb, disrupt, disturb (person, peace, situation, order)

pleurnicher*   to whimper, whine, snivel*

pourchasser   to badger, pursue, hound (fox, escaped criminal)

pousser une gueulante*   to kick up a stink*

prendre qn à rebrousse poil*   to rub s.o. the wrong way*

relancer   to pester, hassle, badger, pester (weakling), harass (taxpayer)

tanner*   to drive s.o. up the wall,* annoy, pester, peeve

taper qn sur les nerfs*   to get on s.o.'s nerves

tarabuster*   to pester, badger, bother, niggle*

terroriser   to terrorize

tirailler   to plague, gnaw at (guilt, pain, doubt, remorse)

torturer   to agonize, torture

tourmenter   to torment, agonize

tracasser   to pester, trouble, disquiet, cause to fret

troubler   to trouble, disturb (person, peace), blur (judgment), muddy (water)

turlupiner*   to bother, bug s.o., be domineering

tyranniser   to bully

vexer   to vex, plague, annoy

Tu es un âne*! Comme tu m'°embêtes* avec ton opiniâtreté! You're such a jackass*! Your stubbornness bugs me*!

Le discours incendiaire du sénateur fit °bisquer* les défenseurs de la constitution. The senator's inflammatory speech riled the defenders of the constitution.

Une telle manifestation de grossièreté me °consterne beaucoup. Such a display of raunchiness causes me much consternation.

L'aumônier est °agacé par ceux qui prennent de telles hypothèses pour paroles d'Évangile. The chaplain is annoyed at those who consider such theories as Gospel truth.

Elle est °incommodée par la poussière et le bruit du chantier à côté de chez elle. She's bothered by the dust and noise from the construction site next door.

to inquire into, hold an inquiry, **enquêter (sur)**
investigate, conduct a survey

s'adresser à/chez   to inquire, address (a question to)

affirmer sous serment   to swear under oath

arpenter   to survey (land)

briguer   to solicit (support), canvass for (votes), court (voters)

cadastrer   to survey (for zoning ordinance, property boundaries)

chaîner   to measure with a chain (land)

chercher   to look for (s.o., s.t.), look into (evidence, files), seek, search for

citer   to cite, summon, arraign (legal)

compulser   to inspect (documents)

demander   to ask, inquire

demander du secours   to ask for help (police, teacher)

se demander   to question, interrogate, wonder, ponder (mystery)

embrasser du regard   to survey (the horizon, the entire vista)

s'enquérir de   to inquire about (information, whereabouts, s.o.'s health)

enquêter sur   to conduct an inquiry, inquire about (time, weather, s.o.'s health)

estimer   to appraise (art, property, damages), value, estimate (price, worth)

étêter   to poll, do a head count (voters, constituents)

évaluer   to appraise, determine value of

examiner   to investigate, look for

examiner à fond   to probe in depth

exiger   to demand, entreat, beseech

expertiser   to survey, appraise, assess, determine value of (gem, land, damages)

explorer   to explore (land, options), inquire into, scout (terrain)

faire du racolage*   to solicit (votes, contributions)

faire la quête   to pass the hat around* (for handouts)

faire le beau*   to sit up and beg (dog)

faire le levé de   to survey (land)

faire le recensement   to take inventory (merchandise)

faire plancher*   to grill, interrogate (prisoner)

faire une étude de   to study, investigate, perform a study (scientific, medical)

faire un inventaire   to take an inventory/survey

faire un sondage   to carry out a survey, conduct a poll

fouiner*   to nose around, snoop* (detective, spy)

fureter to snoop, rummage about, ferret (detective)

s'informer de to inquire, ask about

s'inquiéter de to worry about (s.o.'s health, luck)

intercéder to intercede, plead s.t. on behalf of s.o., mediate in a dispute

interjeter appel to lodge an appeal (law)

interpeller to question, call out to (police)

interpoler to question, call for questioning (police)

interroger to question, interrogate (suspect, prisoner)

s'interroger (sur) to wonder (about), question

interviewer to interview (TV guest, job applicant)

invoquer to plead (innocence, ignorance), call upon (legal rights, God)

jauger to size up (opponent, competition)

juger to judge, try, pass sentence (court of law)

jurer to swear, take oath, vow (court)

lever le plan de to survey (property, terrain)

se mêler de to pry into (affairs, s.o.'s business)

mendier to beg (pauper)

mettre en cause to call into question, suspect, blame

passer en revue to survey, look over, peruse (book), read attentively

passer le chapeau* to pass the hat* (for handouts)

perquisitionner to make a search (police investigator)

pétitionner to petition (court), make a request

plaider to plead (innocent/guilty, cause), litigate (law)

poser to question, request (vacation, time off)

postuler to solicit, apply for (job, position)

prier to beseech, request, invite, pray, beg (favor, God)

priser to appraise, value (worth, price)

quémander to beg for (handouts, food), fish for* (compliments)

questionner to question, quiz, interrogate

quêter to seek, look for (truth, approval), beg (pity)

recenser to take the census of, record, verify, inventory

rechercher to look for, search for, pry into, seek

réclamer to entreat, beseech, demand, ask for

recourir to appeal (law)

(en) redemander to ask again, ask for more (second helpings of dinner)

remettre en cause to question, suspect, call into question

se renseigner sur to seek information, make an inquiry, inquire into

requérir to request, require, requisition

réquisitionner to requisition (supplies), commandeer (military service)

revendiquer to demand, ask for, claim, make demands (rights, legal recognition)

scruter to investigate, scrutinize (personal data), peer into (darkness)

solliciter (de) to seek (from), appeal to

sommer to summon, call up (legal witness)

sonder to probe, search, investigate, sound out (person), poll (opinions)

soutirer à to extract (information), squeeze out (confession, money)

spéculer to speculate, reflect, consider

supplier to implore, beg, beseech

tendre le chapeau* to pass the hat* (for handouts)

La police conduisait une °enquête sur la disparition du forçat. The police were conducting an investigation into the convict's disappearance.

Cet appareil mécanique permettra aux °enquêteurs de °scruter le cœur du volcan. This mechanical apparatus will enable the researchers to peer into the volcano's core.

Le procureur avait °requis vingt ans de prison ferme et dix ans avec sursis. The prosecutor had asked for twenty years of mandatory incarceration with ten years of probation.

Certains citoyens °s'interrogent sur la pertinence de cette décision politique. Some citizens question the relevance of this political decision.

L'avocat °intercéda pour son client et °plaida la cause de celui-ci auprès du juge. The attorney interceded on his client's behalf, pleading his case before the judge.

s'entraider to help one another

aboucher to bring together (things, people)

accommoder to adapt (lifestyle), accommodate, fit, adjust (to handicap)

administrer (à) to minister, administer (to) (sick, church congregation)

agréger to admit into a society or club

aider to help, succor, aid, go to s.o.'s aid

aller au secours de qn to go to s.o.'s aid

aller de pair avec to go hand in hand with

améliorer to make better, improve (conditions, health, quality of life)

apporter son soutien à to support, bring aid (emotional, physical, financial)

s'appuyer sur (qn) to lean on (s.o.)

assister to help, assist, give aid

avoir du piston* to have friends in the right places

avoir trait à to be related to, have to do with (characteristics, features)

calmer to calm, soothe (nerves, person, spirits)

compatir to sympathize, be compatible (with)

confluer to meet, unite (rivers, roads)

conjoindre to conjoin, unite (families, forces)

coopérer to cooperate, work together

délivrer to rescue, set free (hostage), free from (debt, obligation)

devoir (à) to owe (to), be obliged (to)

donner un coup de main to lend a helping hand

égaliser to level out, equalize (opportunities, chances, welfare benefits)

embrancher to recruit, hire, join up (pipes, railroads, roadways)

s'enfuir to elope (lovers)

entretenir to maintain (relationship, goodwill, conversation)

épauler to assist (s.o.), give a hand (to s.o.), shoulder (a burden)

épouser to marry

être solidaire de to stand by s.o., show solidarity

être tributaire de to be dependent upon (vassal to king/queen), be a tributary (stream)

faciliter to make easier (task, usage), help along (journey)

faire du troc to barter, swap

faire venir le médecin to send for the doctor

fêter to celebrate, fête (anniversary, victory)

se fiancer to get engaged (to marry)

fraterniser to fraternize (person, country)

garantir to guarantee, insure (fire/health/life insurance), pledge (support)

gracier   to pardon s.o., grant a pardon (king, judge)

harmoniser   to harmonize (music, colors, relationship)

indemniser   to compensate for, reimburse (loss, damage)

s'interposer   to intervene, be intermediary (between rivals, to settle dispute)

intervenir   to intervene, step in, arbitrate (debate, argument)

inviter (à)   to invite (to)

se marier   to get married

médicamenter   to medicate, treat s.o. (ill)

mettre à l'aise   to ease, put at ease

mettre qn en selle*   to give s.o. a boost* (*lit.* to help s.o. into the saddle)

niveler   to level, level out (social conditions)

s'occuper de   to attend to, care for (needs, client, invalid, infant)

officier   to officiate (ceremony, marriage)

offrir   to offer, tender (drink, advice, services)

pallier   to overcome (handicap, obstacle, hurdle)

passer devant monsieur le maire*   to get married (*lit.* to go before the mayor)

payer   to pay, reward, hire

pistonner*   to pull the strings for s.o., use influence to help out a friend

plaire (à)   to please, appeal to, give pleasure to

pousser   to help along (job applicant, trainee, novice)

prendre qn en main   to take s.o. in hand, help

se prêter   to lend oneself to, favor, countenance (assistance, cause)

prêter secours à qn   to go to s.o.'s rescue

privilégier qn   to favor s.o. (privilege, rights, promotion)

proposer   to offer, suggest (help, idea)

protéger (de)   to defend, protect (from)

régaler qn   to treat s.o. to (meal, drink)

relayer   to take over from, relieve (shift worker)

se relayer   to relieve one another, work in shifts

relever la garde   to change the guard, relieve s.o.

remplacer   to take the place of, replace s.o., stand in for s.o.

rendre service à qn   to be of service to s.o.

ressusciter   to revive, resuscitate (economy, drowning victim)

réveillonner   to celebrate Christmas or New Year's Eve (with a party)

satisfaire   to satisfy (needs, requirements, appetite, lust)

sauver   to save, rescue (victim, hostage)

seconder   to assist, support, back up (person)

secourir   to rescue

sécuriser   to give a feeling of security to (s.o.), reassure (s.o.)

servir   to attend to (needs, business, dinner guest)

servir à   to be of use to/in (tool, equipment, device)

servir d'aide à   to look after, support

servir d'appui   to look after, support

servir de   to serve as, act as, act in capacity as (role, job, responsibility)

soigner   to take care of, look after, treat (ill, baby, elderly)

soulager   to relieve, ease (pain, suffering, thirst)

se soulager   to help one another

soutenir   to support, prop up (legs, scaffold), uphold (law, rights, tradition)

se substituer   to substitute for s.o.

succéder   to succeed, follow, take over from (vice-president, first runner-up)

supplanter   to replace (old parts), supersede (new technology, new knowledge)

suppléer à   to substitute for, make up for (person, loss, defeat)

supporter   to bear, endure (pain), support (person, object)

se supporter   to bear with each other, tolerate one another (faults, weaknesses)

syndicaliser   to unionize, form a union

syndiquer   to unionize

tabler sur qn   to count on s.o., rely on s.o.

traiter   to treat (wounds, infection, the ill)

tranquilliser   to ease, soothe (pain, nerves), reassure (s.o.)

travailler en tandem   to work in tandem

troquer   to swap, trade, barter (goods, services)

venir à la rescousse   to come to the rescue

venir en aide à qn   to come to s.o.'s rescue

Maman et Claire °s'entraident avec le ménage. Mother and Claire help one another with the housework.

Jeanne d'Arc fut victorieuse dans sa quête. Elle °délivra Orléans assiégé. Joan of Arc was victorious in her quest. She set free besieged Orleans.

En plus de ses œuvres caritatives en Asie, elle °apporte son soutien aux réfugiés africains. Besides her charity work in Asia, she lends her support to the African refugees.

Le mandat autorise les troupes onusiennes à °intervenir pour porter secours à la population civile. The mandate authorizes the U.N. troops to intervene in support of the civilian population.

Notre but est d'°améliorer les conditions sanitaires de ce quartier pauvre. Our goal is to improve the health conditions of this slum.

MEMORY AID

"**Gronde~**" sounds like the verb *to ground*, which can mean *to confine someone to home as punishment for a misdeed*. Picture a teenager who has returned home late after his curfew being grounded by his irate father who proceeds to scold and reprimand his son.

Other verbs in this family include: to tell off, blame, demean, rant, rave, censure, criticize, upbraid, admonish, exhort, rebuke, forbid, fly off the handle, scoff, humiliate, reprove, etc.

abaisser qn   to humiliate s.o.

admonester   to admonish, berate, reprimand

affliger   to afflict, trouble, distress, chasten

apostropher   to reprimand, call s.o. into question brusquely

avilir   to demean, shame (person), debase (person, currency)

avoir à redire à   to find fault with

en avoir gros sur la patate*   to be upset

en avoir marre*   to be fed up with,* be sick of* (s.o., s.t.)

blâmer   to chide, blame, reprove

brocarder   to criticize, taunt

censurer   to criticize, censure, find fault with, blame

chapitrer   to reprimand, rebuke

cingler   to chastise (person), lash, sting (rain, whip, wind)

commenter   to criticize adversely

contrister   to grieve, sadden, vex

corriger   to correct (misbehavior, fault, defect), chide, reprove

critiquer   to censure, criticize (person, painting), blame

débiner*   to denigrate, vilify, disparage

décourager   to dishearten, discourage

décrier   to decry, criticize, run down s.o.

discriminer   to discriminate against

donner un coup de semonce*   to reprimand, rebuke

engueuler qn*   to bawl s.o. out*

enguirlander qn*   to tell s.o. off*

épiloguer   to criticize, find fault, censure

épingler*   to lay into* (s.o.), criticize harshly

être dans la moise*   to be up the creek,* be in trouble

être victime de sévices   to be an abuse victim

exhorter   to admonish, exhort (s.o. to do s.t.)

faire des reproches à   to criticize, find fault, reproach

faire la critique de   to criticize (person, painting, job performance)

se faire du mauvais sang*   to get upset

se faire rabrouer   to get shouted at

gourmander   to chide, reprimand

haranguer   to harangue, rant, rave

hausser le ton   to raise one's voice

houspiller   to scold

humilier   to humiliate, mortify (person)

imputer à   to attribute to (quote, blame, accident), charge to (account, s.o.)

s'indigner de   to get indignant about

injurier   to abuse, insult

mécontenter   to displease, dissatisfy, disgruntle

mésallier   to disparage, belittle, slight, disgrace

mettre en garde contre   to warn against

morigéner   to scold, reprimand, rebuke

outrager   to insult, offend, outrage

passer un savon*   to lay into* (s.o.), give (s.o.) a dressing-down, chide, reprimand

pénaliser   to penalize (person, sports team), punish

pester   to rant, rave, storm, rail, fulminate, curse

piquer une crise*   to fly off the handle*

pontifier   to lay down the law

s'en prendre à   to take it out on, put blame on

priver de sortie   to ground (a teenager), forbid from going out (on a date)

prohiber   to forbid, prohibit (illegal drugs, entry)

rabrouer   to rebuke sharply

rager   to be in a rage, be angry

railler   to scoff at (person, idea), sneer, deprecate

ravauder*   to scold, chide

rectifier   to correct (error, calculation, trajectory, course), rectify, reform

regretter   to be sorry for, regret, repent

rejeter la faute sur   to blame, put blame on

rembarrer*   to tell s.o. off*

reprendre   to reprove, scold

réprimander   to reprimand, censure

reprocher   to blame, upbraid, rebuke, find fault

reprocher qch à qn   to rebuke, upbraid s.o. for s.t., blame for

réprouver   to condemn, disapprove of

ressasser   to harp on, repeat tediously

rompre avec qn   to break up with s.o. (relationship, friendship)

rugir de colère   to roar with anger

scandaliser   to outrage, scandalize, shock, dishonor, disgrace (moral sense)

semoncer   to rebuke, reprimand, lecture

seriner qch à qn   to drum s.t. into s.o.

sermonner   to harangue, harp on, sermonize

serrer la vis à qn*   to crack down on s.o.* (*lit.* to tighten the vise on s.o.)

sonner les cloches à qn*   to tell s.o. off* (*lit.* to ring s.o.'s bells)

sortir de ses gonds*   to fly off the handle*

subir la carence affective   to suffer emotional deprivation

tenir rigueur à qn   to hold it against s.o.

trépigner de colère   to be hopping mad

trouver à redire à   to find fault with

vitupérer contre   to rant and rave about, berate, rail against

vociférer   to shout angrily

vocaliser   to vocalize, use the voice, give vocal expression to (idea, concern)

en vouloir à qn   to hold a grudge against s.o.

Le père a °grondé son fils car celui-ci avait menti à ses parents. Il a privé de sortie son adolescent mécontent. The father scolded his son for lying to his parents. He grounded his disgruntled teenager.

Des électeurs ont °épinglé le ratage budgétaire de son administration. Voters severely criticized the budgetary failure of his administration.

Nos canons °grondants étaient assourdissants. Our booming cannons were deafening.

Le tonnerre °grondait si fort que l'enfant ne pouvait pas dormir. The thunder roared so loudly that the child was unable to sleep.

Depuis le haut du minaret, la voix °exhortait les fidèles musulmans à prier. From the top of the minaret, the voice called the faithful Muslims to prayer.

MEMORY AID

"**Jacasse**" sounds a lot like *jackass*. Think of *loud gossiping* and *jabbering* similar to the *braying* and *hee-hawing* a noisy jackass would make.

Other verbs in this family include: to gossip, gab, banter, yap, blab, chat, noise about, make a racket, ramble on, murmur, jest, stammer, stutter, prattle, jeer, grumble, carp, niggle, etc.

aboyer   to bark (dog)
avoir bon bec*   to have the gift of gab*
avoir de la tchatche*   to have the gift of gab*
avoir du bagou*   to have the gift of gab*
avoir la langue bien pendue*   to be a chatterbox,* have the gift of gab* (*lit.* to have a well-hung tongue)
babiller   to babble, prattle, chat, gossip, blab*
badiner   to jest, banter
bafouiller*   to stammer, talk nonsense
balbutier   to stammer, stutter
baragouiner*   to jabber,* talk gibberish
baratinerˣ   to chatter, chat up
bavarder   to chatter, gossip
bégayer   to stutter, stammer, lisp
braire   to bray (donkey)
bredouiller   to babble, stammer, stutter
calomnier   to slander, libel (the press)
cancaner*   to gossip, tattle,* invent stories, spin tales
clabauder*   to clamor, make a loud outcry, create a hubbub/din/blare
converser   to converse, hold conversation
cousiner*   to hobnob, be cronies (*lit.* to call s.o. cousin)
déclamer   to spout, mouth off, rant, rave
déconner*   to talk nonsense, bullshit*
dégoiser*   to talk a lot, spout off at the mouth*
déjanter*   to talk nonsense, go crazy

déplorer   to bemoan (one's fate), lament (loss), express deep sorrow
dire des niaiseries   to talk rubbish*
dire des plaisanteries   to tell, crack jokes
divaguer   to talk nonsense, ramble on, digress (from topic), talk insanely (psychiatry)
draguer*   to chat up,* pick up (street-walker)
ébruiter   to make known, noise about, spread (news, gossip)
s'entretenir   to converse, have a discussion, have a conversation
être le bon bec   to be a chatterbox,* gossip
être prolixe   to be talkative, be verbose
être un moulin de paroles*   to be a chatterbox* (*lit.* to be a windmill of words)
être une pipelette*   to be a chatterbox*
faire des commérages*   to gossip about
faire du boucan*   to make a racket*
faire du plat*   to chat
faire du potin*   to gossip, make a racket*
fanfaronner   to talk big,* be a blowhard,* act swanky,* talk cocky*
gazouiller   to babble, prattle, twitter
glapir   to snap out, yelp, bark (dog)
goguenarder   to banter, jeer
haranguer   to harangue
héler   to hail, call (taxi)
hurler   to howl, roar, scream
jaboter*   to chatter, prattle
jacter*   to chatter, blab,* yap*

japper to yelp, yap, yip (dog)

jaser to chatter, gossip

lier conversation to engage in conversation

se moquer de to scoff at

murmurer to murmur, mutter about

palabrer* to chat away, talk incessantly

papoter* to chatter, chat, shoot the breeze*

parler avec abandon to speak freely, talk without constraint

parler dans le vide* to waste one's breath,* talk vacuously/aimlessly

piailler* to rant, squawk (bird), speak rapidly and incessantly

se plaindre de to complain about

plaisanter to jest, banter, joke

radoter to ramble on, talk idly

railler to banter, jest, scoff at, gibe

répliquer to reply, retort (verbally), retaliate (verbally, militarily)

répondre to answer, reply, respond

ronchonner* to grumble, bellyache*

talonner* to niggle,* carp*

tchatcher* to chat

trinquer* to schmooze, chat, gossip

Je n'arrivais pas à dormir! Les voisines d'à côté ont °jacassé toute la nuit. I couldn't sleep at all! The next-door neighbors chattered all night long. **Es-tu sourd? Ta radio ne °hurle pas assez?** Are you deaf? Isn't your radio loud enough?

Elle demeure hospitalisée dans le service gastro-intestinal après °s'être plainte de vomissements et de douleurs à l'estomac. She remains hospitalized in the gastrointestinal ward after having complained of vomiting and stomach pains.

Le premier ministre est censé °s'entretenir avec les dirigeants religieux koweïtiens. The prime minister is supposed to meet with the Kuwaiti religious leaders.

MEMORY AID

In French, a **marchand** is a *merchant* or *shopkeeper*. The English word *merchandise* is derived from **marchand**. Picture a customer haggling over the price and trying to get a bargain price for an item of merchandise from a merchant.

Other verbs in this family include: to quibble, wheel and deal, split hairs, talk business, purchase, overcharge, discount, fuss over, charge for, sell off, rip off, sell at cut-rate, etc.

achalander* to attract customers, draw in business

acheter à bon compte to buy at a good price

acheter à prix d'or* to buy at outrageous price

acheter cher to buy at a high price

arnaquer* to rip off,* cheat

baratiner* to sweet-talk,* chat up

brader to sell off, sell at cut-rate, have a clearance sale

se brouiller to have a falling out with s.o.

se chamailler* to bicker, squabble

chercher la petite bête* to split hairs,* niggle*

(se) chicaner (sur)* to quibble (over)

chinoiser* to split hairs, trifle, quibble

chipoter* to haggle, trifle

colporter to hawk merchandise, peddle wares (street peddler)

conclure un marché to strike a bargain

couper les cheveux en quatre* to split hairs*

débattre sur to discuss, debate, argue

dédommager to make amends for, compensate for, make up for (loss)

dégrever to reduce the tax on (product), give tax relief to (taxpayer)

déposer une plainte to lodge a formal complaint

écorcher le client* to fleece the customer* (*lit.* to skin)

ergoter (sur) to quibble (over)

ergoter sur des vétilles to quibble over trifles

escompter to discount (banknote, bill, exchange rate)

être mesquin* to split hairs,* be stingy

être radin* to be stingy, be a tightwad*

être une aubaine to be a bargain, be a windfall, be a godsend

s'expliquer to quarrel, have a fight

facturer à qn to charge s.o. for, bill s.o., give s.o. a bill

faire des commissions to go shopping

faire du scandale to make a scene, create a fuss

faire du troc to barter, swap (goods, services)

faire la chochotte* to make a fuss, fuss over

faire le colportage to peddle (wares), hawk (merchandise)

faire le créancier importun to dun, demand payment

faire marché to bargain, strike a bargain

faire une bonne affaire to get a good deal/bargain

faire une ristourne to give a discount

lécher les vitrines* to window-shop (*lit.* to lick the windowpanes)

magouiller* to wheel and deal,* scheme

mévendre to sell at a loss

négocier to bargain, negotiate

s'opiniâtrer to be obstinate, insist, be stubborn

parler affaires   to talk shop, talk business

payer plein pot*   to pay full price/full fare

perdre son sang-froid   to lose one's cool

porter plainte   to make a formal complaint

racheter   to buy back, repurchase, buy another, buy more, buy out

saler*   to overcharge for, inflate (sales price)

supplier   to beg, beseech, entreat

surfacturer   to overcharge (product, client, interest on, loan)

surfaire   to ask for too much, overrate (person, worth), inflate (reputation, value)

tarifer   to set a price, fix the price, set a rate

troquer   to swap,* barter, trade (goods and services)

vétiller   to trifle, split hairs*

Elle n'a pas de moyens financiers. Forcée à être judicieuse dans l'achat de vêtements, elle °marchande avec les vendeurs. She doesn't have the financial resources. Having to be prudent in her clothing purchases, she haggles with the salespeople.

Si on faisait du °lèche-vitrines au centre commercial cet après-midi? How about going window-shopping at the mall this afternoon?

Le poissonnier °faisait du colportage dans la ruelle exiguë. The fishmonger hawked his wares in the cramped alleyway.

Aucune récompense pour sauver ton chien? Ne °sois pas mesquin*! No reward for rescuing your dog? Don't be stingy!

MEMORY AID

Nier sounds like the Russian word *nyet*, meaning *no*—a word one will often use *to deny something*. Picture a Soviet general slamming his fist down to deny a request made of him, shouting out the word Nyet!

Other verbs in this family can apply in a wide range of situations where the word "no" might be used, including: to cancel, disallow, prohibit, forbid, expel, disavow, disown, protest, repeal, quash, put off, veto, disapprove, refute, break a promise, object, prevent, nullify, etc.

annuler   to cancel, annul, void, rescind, abolish (pact, contract, treaty, agreement)

apostasier   to apostatize, deny the faith, abandon one's faith/religion

avoir tort   to be wrong

bannir   to prohibit, banish (usage, disease), exile, reject (person, offer)

boycotter   to boycott

censurer   to censor, rebuke formally, censure

congédier   to dismiss, discharge (employee), disband (army, organization)

critiquer   to censure, blame, disapprove

débouter   to dismiss a case (legal)

décevoir   to disappoint, cause disappointment

décliner   to decline, refuse, turn down (offer, invitation)

décommander   to cancel, annul (meeting, dinner engagement, order)

défendre   to disallow, prohibit (activity, entry, usage)

démentir   to deny (rumor, news), refute (testimony), disappoint (hopes)

dénier   to deny (claims, guilt), refuse (s.o., s.t.)

désapprouver   to disallow, disapprove (action, conduct)

désavouer   to disavow (involvement, paternity), disown (child, responsibility)

dessaisir   to dismiss or remove a legal case from court, take off the record

disconvenir   to deny, disown

disqualifier   to disqualify (athlete)

écarter d'un geste   to wave away, wave aside, turn away (hand gesture)

empêcher de   to forbid, prevent from

être blackboulé*   to be blackballed,* voted against, denied admission to (club)

éviter   to avoid, evade, shun, stay clear of, dodge

excommunier   to excommunicate, disfellowship (church), bar from religion

exempter (de)   to exempt (from), free from obligation (payment, military service)

exiler   to banish, exile

exonérer (de)   to exempt (from) (blame, taxes, import duty)

finir   to end, finish, terminate

hocher la tête   to shake one's head (to say no)

infirmer   to invalidate, quash (judgment)

s'ingérer   to obtrude, interfere, meddle with, force upon s.o. (opinion, oneself)

interdire   to prohibit, forbid, ban, proscribe

invalider   to nullify, invalidate, void, disable

manquer à sa promesse   to renege, break a promise

manquer sa parole   to break one's word, renege

mettre à l'index   to blacklist, boycott, put on list of disapproved/disavowed (person, business)

mettre des coupures   to censor (news article, book)

mettre le holà à*   to put on hold, veto (*lit.* holà: hold on a minute!)

négliger   to neglect (appearance, s.o.), omit, be careless about (advice)

obvier   to prevent, obviate, render unnecessary, eliminate need for

opposer son veto à qch   to veto s.t. (amendment, law)

parjurer   to perjure oneself, lie (under oath)

se priver   to go without, deprive oneself of (food, medical attention), deny oneself

prohiber   to prohibit (alcohol, illegal entry)

proscrire   to outlaw, banish, proscribe, ban (drugs, activity, ideology)

protester   to protest (one's guilt), express opposition (politics), resist (authority)

quitter   to discharge, give up, lay aside (responsibility, task)

récuser   to deny (accusation), object, challenge (judge, witness)

se récuser   to decline (participation), excuse oneself (testimony), resist (authority)

refouler   to expel (aliens), turn back (crowd)

refroidir   to put off s.o., quash (enthusiasm), "turn off" (s.o.)

refuser   to disallow, deny, refuse, decline

refuser l'entrée à   to turn away (client), deny s.o. entry

réfuter   to refute (claim), disprove, prove erroneous (person, information)

rejeter   to reject, deny (request, claim, illegal alien, ballot proposal)

renier   to renounce, disown, break promise

renoncer   to renounce, disclaim, disown, give up (faith, throne, opinion)

renverser   to overthrow (government, chair, person), knock over (bottle, pedestrian)

renvoyer   to dismiss (employee, club member), expel (student), send back (letter)

répudier   to renounce (faith), repudiate, deny, disown (son)

résilier   to cancel, terminate (contract, lease, subscription)

révoquer   to revoke (license), recall, repeal, cancel, remove from office (civil servant)

snober*   to snub (person), turn up one's nose at* (offer, party)

terminer   to terminate (employment, contract, agreement)

Lors du procès, l'accusé a °nié toutes les inculpations prononcées par le juge. Juge: Au bagne avec ce récidiviste! During the trial, the accused denied all the indictments charged to him by the judge. Judge: Lock up this repeat offender!

Le patronat °interdit explicitement l'embauche de postulants non vaccinés. The employers expressly forbid the hiring of any unvaccinated applicants.

Elle s'est convertie au culte même si les anciens lui °refusaient le droit de lire les écritures. She joined the sect even though the elders forbade her from reading the scriptures.

En raison de la grippe, j'ai été contraint d'°annuler mon déplacement à Marseille. Because of the flu, I was forced to cancel my trip to Marseille.

La compagnie aérienne °dément toute culpabilité et ingérence dans les affaires syndicales. The airline company denies all guilt and interference in the union's business.

to specify, make clear, state precisely **préciser**

MEMORY AID

"**Précise~**" is spelled exactly the same as the English word *precise*, which means *clearly defined* or *delineated*, *exact*, *distinct*, or *correct*. Picture a mathematics professor using precise terminology to clearly define the equation he has written on the board so that there is no ambiguity.

Verbs in this family include those that enumerate, set boundaries, qualify, and quantify. Included are: to detail, declare, enunciate, articulate, clarify, designate, classify, denote, express, decree, point out, measure, calibrate, calculate, proclaim, stipulate, explain, etc.

accentuer   to emphasize (differences), accentuate, stress (syllable)

affirmer   to assert, vouch, declare, affirm, claim, maintain that

approfondir   to delve into, examine closely, go into detail (research, study, evidence)

appuyer sur   to emphasize (word, syllable)

arrêter   to decree, resolve, decide (place, date)

articuler   to articulate (words), enunciate (phrase, ideas)

attester   to attest, certify, avouch, witness, testify

bien articuler   to enunciate clearly (words), articulate clearly (ideas)

calibrer   to calibrate (machine, rifle), gauge, grade (eggs, fruit)

caractériser   to characterize, describe

cartographier   to map, map out, draw a map

chiffrer   to calculate (math, expenses), cipher, code, assess (damage, losses)

chronométrer   to time (stopwatch)

clarifier   to clarify (situation, instructions), remove impurities (butter)

classifier   to classify, catalog, categorize

codifier   to codify (law), reduce to a code, arrange, systematize

comptabiliser   to count (computer calculations)

constater   to state, decree, certify (authenticity), observe (detail), notice, take note of

déclarer   to state (opinion, fact), declare (love, war, innocence, income)

décrire   to describe, depict (in words)

délimiter   to set boundaries of (precinct, subject), delimit (responsibility), determine

démontrer   to demonstrate (theory), prove (experiment), show (necessity, urgency)

dénombrer   to number, enumerate, count (computer)

dénommer   to designate (alternate), appoint (to office)

dénoter   to denote, indicate, reveal, indicate, mark

désigner   to designate, denote, detail, assign (duty), refer to, appoint (to office)

détailler   to explain in detail, itemize, give details

déterminer   to determine, ascertain, settle

dévider*   to recount, explain

dresser   to draw up, make up (list)

élucider   to clear up, elucidate, clarify (problem)

énoncer   to state, express, enunciate, pronounce clearly

énumérer   to enumerate, number, itemize, list, count up

épeler   to spell a word (aloud) (See
orthographier in this section)

étalonner   to standardize, calibrate
(mechanic, physicist), set standards for
(test)

être en filigrane   to be implicit (*lit.* to be
as integral as a watermark)

expliciter   to make explicit, explain

exposer   to state, explain (thesis,
hypothesis, plan, idea)

exposer en détail   to detail, state in
detail

exposer sa thèse   to explain one's
theory/hypothesis

exprimer   to express (opinion, talent),
formulate (idea), convey (idea), say

exprimer clairement   to articulate, state
clearly

exprimer de façon cohérente   to express
coherently

extérioriser   to express openly,
externalize (emotions), act out (frustra-
tion)

faire du prosélytisme   to preach
(gospel), try to convert

faire état de   to report (facts), state
(intention, fear)

faire part de   to inform, announce,
break the news

faire prendre conscience   to bring into
focus (issues, details)

faire remarquer   to point out, make
one's point

faire (un) reportage sur   to write a
report on, report on (TV, radio)

faire sonner un mot*   to emphasize a
word

fixer   to set a date (appointment,
rendezvous)

formuler   to express (criticism, sentiment), make known (complaint,
opinion)

indiquer   to indicate, show, point out

indiquer du doigt   to point (with
finger), point out (s.o., s.t.)

individualiser   to individualize, tailor to
(fit needs, individual requirements)

informer   to inform, make known

mesurer   to measure, calculate, proportion, size up (problem, item), moderate
(voice)

métrer   to measure (by the yard)

mettre les points sur les "i"*   to dot all
the "i's,"* get all the details right

minuter   to time (activity, race), record,
keep minutes (meeting)

montrer   to indicate, demonstrate, teach
(lesson by a gesture, by an example)

narrer   to narrate, tell (story), recount
(tale)

nombrer   to number, reckon (days,
years), count

normaliser   to standardize (product),
normalize (diplomatic relations)

nuancer   to explain every nuance or
shade of meaning, to detail (description)

numériser   to digitize (camera,
computer)

numéroter   to number, assign numbers
to, count off (items, soldiers)

opiner   to give an opinion, opine

orthographier   to spell a word (in
writing) (See **épeler** in this section)

ponctuer   to punctuate (spelling),
emphasize, place emphasis (remarks)

prétendre   to claim (rights, title), aspire
to (honor)

proclamer   to proclaim, announce,
disclose

proférer   to utter, pronounce, offer
(help, advice)

professer   to profess (love), claim, state
that

promulguer   to make known (law,
decree), declare publicly, announce
officially

publier   to publish, proclaim, make
public, issue

qualifier   to describe (goals, standards),
qualify (remark)

quantifier   to quantify

raconter   to tell, recount (story)

raconter en détail   to detail, tell in detail

raffiner   to split hairs, argue over
details, make fine distinctions

regarder à la loupe   to examine in detail
(*lit.* **loupe** *(f)*: magnifying glass)

réitérer   to reiterate, repeat, emphasize (a point), make clear (opinion)

relater   to state, tell (account, story)

remontrer   to point out, show again, re-teach

renseigner   to give information, direct, give directions (to stranger), inform (details)

repartir   to answer, retort (Note: *répartir* is a different word, see page 239.)

répertorier   to list, record (information)

rétorquer   to answer back, retort

scander   to stress a phrase, chant (slogan)

sélectionner   to highlight (computer)

signaler   to point out, give description of

singulariser   to make conspicuous, make noticeable, single out (an individual)

souligner   to emphasize, underline, highlight

spécialiser   to specialize (product, talent, medical/legal practice)

spécifier   to specify, state specifically

stipuler   to stipulate, specify

surligner   to highlight (with marker pen), emphasize (key points)

synchroniser   to synchronize (clocks, schedules)

témoigner que   to testify that, confirm

tracer   to outline (plan of action/attack), trace out (plans, details)

traduire   to translate (foreign language), convey (thought), make manifest (idea)

À la gare, la voix du haut-parleur °précisait les départs et les arrivées des trains. The voice over the train station loudspeaker gave details concerning the train departures and arrivals.

Citant la nouvelle amitié franco-américaine, le maire °exprima l'immense gratitude normande. Citing the new Franco-American friendship, the mayor expressed Normandy's immense gratitude.

Elle demanda un divorce en °faisant état de différends insurmontables. She asked for a divorce, citing irreconcilable differences.

On ne peut pas °décrire la douleur d'une telle blessure! One cannot describe the pain of such an injury!

Tous ses récits sont °ponctués par une blague. All of his stories are highlighted by a joke.

préconiser   to recommend, advocate

MEMORY AID

"Pre-" means *before* or *beforehand*, and the **"~réconise~"** fragment sounds somewhat similar to *recognize*. So, with a stretch of the imagination, **"pre-conise"** can be thought of as *recognizing beforehand*, and if someone *recognizes* something *beforehand* as being a good bargain or useful, he can *recommend* it to others and *advocate* its use or purchase. Picture an ingenious Neanderthal recognizing the potential in a circular rock in its natural state before anyone else. So he recommends or advocates the new granite wheel to his fellow cavemen as an item they cannot afford to be without. History's first salesman!

Other verbs in this family include: to approve, ratify, commend, laud, justify, propose, prescribe, popularize, endorse, urge, choose, exhort, coax, sanction, testify, suggest, etc.

accentuer   to stress, accentuate (details), highlight (features, advantage)

acclamer   to cheer, acclaim, praise

accommoder   to support, adapt (to change, to situation)

agréer   to officially sanction, authorize, accredit (business, college credits)

alléguer   to urge, allege, plead, advance, put forward (idea), quote (text, author)

amadouer   to coax, flatter, wheedle (s.o. into doing s.t.)

applaudir   to applaud, commend, praise, approve

approuver   to approve (of), sanction, ratify, consent, authorize (treaty, nomination)

appuyer   to support, uphold, insist, stand by (person), endorse (idea)

appuyer sur   to emphasize, stress (syllable)

autoriser   to authorize, sanction, allow

avaliser   to endorse (candidate), guarantee, support (cause, idea)

breveter   to obtain or grant a patent

certifier   to certify, vouch for, testify

choisir   to choose, pick out, elect, select

concerner   to be of importance to, to matter to

confier (à)   to commend, entrust (for safekeeping)

conseiller   to advise, offer advice, advocate, recommend, counsel

convaincre   to convince, persuade

convier   to invite (to party, on a date), ask, suggest

défendre   to advocate, defend, support (rights, cause)

départager   to decide between, settle votes

détromper   to convince, disabuse, persuade

disséquer   to analyze (data), dissect (sentence, biology frog)

dogmatiser   to state dogmatically, state with authoritative assertion

donner son avis   to advise

éclairer   to enlighten (mind), illuminate (path), throw light on (subject), clarify

élaborer   to elaborate (details), refine (plan), outline (project)

élire   to choose, elect, select, pick

entériner   to ratify (contract, judicial ruling), confirm

être partisan de   to advocate, recommend, champion (cause)

évangéliser   to preach the Gospel, evangelize

exalter   to extol (virtues), exalt, praise, glorify

exemplifier   to exemplify (ideals, traits), illustrate with examples

faire de la publicité pour qch   to advertise s.t.

faire l'éloge   to praise (s.o. or s.t.), give eulogy (funeral)

faire preuve de sagesse   to be sensible

faire respecter   to uphold (law)

faire un avenant à   to endorse (candidate, contract), amend

faire valoir   to put forward (argument, theory), assert (rights)

glorifier   to glorify, honor, praise

homologuer   to approve, ratify (treaty), officially recognize (sports record), sanction

illustrer   to illustrate, give an example of (plans, ideas)

implorer   to implore, supplicate, beg

impressionner   to impress (s.o.), make an impression on, have an impact (on s.o.)

inculquer   to impress (upon s.o.), instill (knowledge), teach, implant (idea)

inspirer   to suggest, incite (reaction, riot), inspire (confidence, trust)

intercéder   to intercede, plead s.t. on behalf of s.o.

justifier   to justify (action, decision), attest, explain (stance)

légaliser   to legalize

légitimer   to legitimize, make lawful, make authentic/genuine, authenticate (brand)

louer   to praise (king, God), commend, extol (virtues)

magnifier   to idealize, glorify, praise

miser sur   to bank on, bet on (idea, horse)

motiver   to justify (conduct, behavior)

mythifier   to glamorize (person, past)

opter   to choose, decide, opt

parier   to bet, wager, gamble on

passer un vote   to take a vote

persuader   to persuade, win approval

pistonner*   to pull strings for,* use one's influence for

plaider   to defend (s.o., ideal, cause), plead (for defendant, for mercy, ignorance)

prêcher   to exhort, extol, praise

préférer   to prefer, favor

prescrire   to recommend (method, book), prescribe (medicine), lay down (law)

priser   to esteem, estimate, appraise (worth, value)

prôner   to advocate, commend, laud, extol

prononcer   to declare one's sentiments, declare, say

proposer   to propose, offer (idea, solution)

ratifier   to ratify, approve of, commend, authorize

recommander   to advocate, recommend

remémorer   to bring s.t./s.o. to mind

en remontrer (à)   to give advice, admonish

respecter   to respect, honor, esteem (person), prize, observe (law), keep (promise)

revendiquer   to claim responsibility for (deed, crime), claim (rights, recognition)

sanctionner   to sanction, approve, authorize

sensibiliser qn à qch   to raise s.o's awareness of s.t.

sous-entendre   to imply (hidden meaning), insinuate (sexual innuendo)

soutenir   to support, sustain (s.o.'s claim, tradition, rights)

suggérer   to suggest, advise, counsel

supplier   to supplicate, implore, beg s.o., plead with

supporter   to support (person, idea), uphold (law), endure (pain, trials)

témoigner en faveur de   to testify in favor of

trier   to sort out, select, handpick

trier sur le volet   to handpick (employee, partner, fruit)

trouver bon que   to approve

tuyauter*   to give s.o. advice or a tip

vanter   to praise, commend, extol, boast, show off, brag

voter   to vote, vote for

vulgariser   to popularize (for general public, e.g., song, style, method)

Le diplomate °préconise au roi de signer le traité. The diplomat strongly recommends that the king sign the treaty.

Des vagabonds sans terre °revendiquent ce territoire vierge pour une future mère patrie. Homeless drifters lay claim to the virgin territory for a future homeland.

Le président °prôna "l'esprit de liberté" lors des cérémonies fêtant les anciens combattants. The president commended the "spirit of freedom" during the ceremonies honoring the war veterans.

La directrice exige que la gestion mette en vigueur les changements °préconisés par le rapport. The director insists that management implement the changes as recommended by the report.

La fin °justifie les moyens. The end justifies the means.

MEMORY AID

This verb is easy to recall. **Résumer** sounds exactly like **résumé**—a *summary, summing up, or abbreviated list of one's training or job experiences, submitted when applying for a position.* The word is recognized by French and English speakers alike. Picture a job applicant's *curriculum vitae* or *résumé* summarizing his or her accomplishments.

Other verbs in this family include: to abridge, recapitulate, recap, add up, overview, highlight, outline, emphasize, condense, simplify, generalize, skim through, review, revise, update, etc.

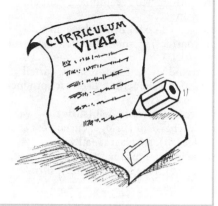

abréger to abbreviate (words), abridge (text), shorten (visit, lifespan), clip, cut short

additionner to sum up, total up (numbers), add up

alambiquer to refine, distill (chemical, liquor, complex idea)

borner to bound, set limits, mark out (terrain, boundary)

briefer to brief, summarize, give concise advice or instruction

condenser to condense, sum up, abridge (text), make denser (liquid)

conter to recount (tales, adventure), tell (story), relate (details, history)

donner un aperçu to give a brief overview (project, situation), give a general survey

dresser to draw up (report)

effleurer to touch upon (subject), skim the surface of (detailed report/study)

estimer to estimate (price, distance), assess (value, damage)

être contenu to sum up (terms of letter), be contained (in box, in file)

faire de la paraphrase to paraphrase (sentence)

faire de la synthèse (de) to summarize (points of lecture)

faire l'addition de to sum up, add up, total

faire le point sur to sum up, point out key ideas (lecture)

faire le récit de to give an account of (tax record, tale, narration)

faire mention de to mention, make brief note of, make mention of

faire savoir to inform, make known

faire un topo sur qch* to give a summary, give a rundown of

faire un tour d'horizon to make an overview of

feuilleter to leaf through, skim through (book, file)

frôler to touch on lightly (topic, subject)

généraliser to generalize, make generalizations

globaliser to generalize, make global or worldwide in application or scope

limiter to limit, bound, confine, fix limits

mentionner to mention, note briefly

mettre à jour to bring up to date, update (file, calendar, news)

mettre au courant to brief, bring up to date (news, project)

mettre au point to summarize, review

offrir une mise au point to give an outline (project, plan)

prononcer to declare, pronounce (legal sentence), articulate, say, give a talk

qualifier to qualify (goal, standards, remark), describe (project, conduct)

raconter to tell, relate, narrate

réactualiser to update, bring up to date (news, data)

récapituler   to recapitulate, sum up, recap

rédiger   to edit, draft, draw up (contract), compile (dictionary), write (article)

restreindre   to limit, restrict, curtail (expense, appetite), decrease (production)

retracer   to relate, tell (story)

retrancher   to abridge, curtail, cut short (speech), subtract (math)

rétrécir   to limit, narrow (scope, road, orifice), take in (dress size), shrink (cloth)

réviser   to revise, review, make revision (rough draft), reorganize, reevaluate, edit

schématiser   to schematize, oversimplify (issue), simplify (blueprint), diagram

sensibiliser qn à qch   to make s.o. aware of or sensitive to s.t.

simplifier   to simplify (subject, details)

sommer   to sum up (investigation, findings)

souligner   to underline, emphasize

surligner   to highlight (key points, with marking pen)

symboliser   to symbolize, represent

L'avocat peut °résumer son procès en quelques mots. The attorney can summarize his case in just a few words.

Pour des renseignements, consultez la liste °mise à jour chaque semaine. For information, consult the list which is updated weekly.

La commission a °qualifié de "satisfaisant" son dossier comportemental. The panel judged his behavioral file to be "satisfactory."

Des problèmes de santé mentale sont une conséquence d'une telle activité, °souligne le rapport psychiatrique. The psychiatric report emphasizes that mental health problems result from such activity.

MEMORY AID

Sus, as part of **en sus**, means *in addition to*, and the "**~cite**" fragment is spelled like the second part of the English *incite*, meaning *to provoke to action* or *stir up*. Thus "**sus-cite**" can be thought of as an element that is added to something, *provoking or stirring up action*. Picture an instigator placing a firecracker in a crowd of protestors, thus adding an unexpected element of surprise to the activity that is sure to provoke hostile action and likely a riot.

Other words in this family include: to excite, aggravate, incense, stimulate, rouse, bestir, cause, enliven, bring about, rekindle, inflict, foment, waken, urge, revive, cajole, inflame, charm, captivate, influence, stir up, motivate, invoke, etc.

acharner to madden, embitter (foe, wasp)

actionner to bestir, arouse, activate ("on" switch), operate (machine)

agacer to provoke, set on edge, rile, annoy, bedevil

s'aggraver to worsen, aggravate (health, unemployment)

agiter to stir up (trouble), disturb (peace, tranquility), agitate (crowd)

allécher to allure, lure, attract, entice, tempt, make one's mouth water (scent)

amadouer to coax, cajole (s.o. into action)

ameuter to stir up, rouse, excite, draw a crowd

animer to enliven, animate, rouse, excite

appâter to bait (person, fish, wild game), lure, entice (sexually)

attirer to entice, lure (into trap), win over

attiser to stir up (tension, anger, revolt), incense, fan (flames)

avoir pour l'origine to be caused by, be incited by

avoir recours à to resort to (action), have recourse to

avoir une incidence sur to affect, have an impact on

axer (sur) to center (on) (key point, issue), focus (on)

captiver to captivate, charm

charmer to charm, enchant, bewitch

courroucer to provoke, anger, irritate

déplaire to displease, offend (situation, person, comments)

donner prise à to give rise to, elicit (effect, outcome, result)

draguer*** to try to pick up girls or guys

drainer*** to attract, bring in (clients, public)

égayer to enliven, cheer up, brighten up (person, atmosphere, room)

émouvoir to excite, arouse (emotion), disturb, perturb

encourager to incite, encourage (activity, person), urge, urge on

engager to invite (conversation, participation), induce, urge, enlist

enjôler to seduce, cajole

entraîner to bring about, influence (event, action, emotion, outcome), involve, entail

envenimer to inflame, stir up (quarrel)

s'établir to set up, establish (position, ground rules, tradition)

être à l'origine de to be behind, be the cause of

être le boute-en-train*** to be the life of the party**

éveiller to awaken, arouse (passion), be aroused, wake from sleep, stimulate (debate) évoquer   to call to mind, bring up (subject), recall

exalter   to fire (imagination), excite (mind)

exciter   to arouse, excite, stir up, inflame (passion), stimulate (sexually)

s'extasier   to be enraptured, go into raptures

fâcher   to anger, offend

faire du remue-ménage   to create commotion, stir up activity, create hustle and bustle

faire du scandale   to make a scene, create a scandal

faire faire un soubresaut à qn   to give s.o. a start, startle s.o.

faire naître   to cause, give rise to (suspicions)

fomenter   to stir up, foment, incite (riot, anger), brew (trouble), agitate

fricoter*   to cook up s.t.* (plan, trouble)

générer   to generate (energy, excitement, emotions)

inciter   to incite (riot), instigate, brew (trouble)

induire   to induce, lead to (action, outcome, results)

infléchir   to affect (decision), modify (strategy), change the emphasis of (politics)

infliger à   to inflict upon (defeat, wounds), impose on (tax)

influencer   to influence, have an effect on

influer sur   to influence

insinuer   to insinuate, imply, seep into (odor, liquid)

inspirer   to prompt, inspire (confidence), incite (action), arouse (suspicion)

instiller   to instill (values, moral sense), implant (ideas in mind)

insuffler   to inspire, motivate

intéresser   to interest, captivate, concern

inviter   to invite (criticism, critique, ill will, misunderstanding)

invoquer   to invoke (Fifth Amendment rights, wrath of God, prayer)

irriter   to irritate, incense, inflame (emotions, gallbladder, appendix)

manier la carotte et le bâton*   to entice with carrot and stick approach

mériter   to deserve, call for, merit (honor, blame), be worthy of (praise)

mettre en exergue   to give rise to, bring out (evidence)

motiver   to bring about, cause, motivate (action)

se mouvoir   to move, bestir oneself, start moving

occasionner   to bring about, cause (accident, effect)

offusquer   to offend (s.o.), dazzle

opérer   to bring about (action, illness), operate (tool, surgeon), carry out (reform)

perpétrer   to perpetrate (crime, abuse)

perpétuer   to perpetuate (usage, tradition)

persuader   to persuade, convince of, talk s.o. into

piquer   to goad (into action), spur, arouse (interest), sting (needle, insect)

pousser à   to instigate, provoke (action, reaction), motivate (person)

pousser à agir   to motivate, cause to act

prendre son pied   to have an orgasm, get off* (sexually), have one's way with (sexually)

presser   to urge, push (to action), impel, compel

provoquer   to excite, provoke, incite, arouse, induce

puiser (dans)   to draw (from) (inspiration, example)

ragaillardir   to enliven, cheer up

ragoûter   to restore appetite of, stimulate, stir up

rallumer   to rekindle (love, flame), revive (relationship, interest)

ranimer   to restore to life, revive, enliven, pep up

réagir   to react (person, chemical), respond to (threat, stimulus)

réchauffer   to reanimate, stir up, reheat (food, relationship)

relancer   to revive (debates), boost (economy), reopen (negotiations)

remettre dans l'esprit   to remind, bring to mind again

reprendre ses sens   to regain consciousness

ressortir de   to be a result of

résulter de   to result from

retentir sur   to have an effect on

réveiller   to arouse, awaken, rouse

révolter   to stir up, rouse

séduire   to charm, seduce, appeal to, allure, lure (into trap)

solliciter   to incite, call into action, entreat

sortir de   to come of, result from (as consequence of an action)

soulever   to raise (issue, question, suspicion), stir up (debate), arouse (anger)

stimuler   to incite, stimulate, excite

subjuguer   to captivate (audience), charm, enthrall, enrapture

tonifier   to stimulate, tone up (muscle), add new life to (economy, spirit, hair)

trancher dans le vif   to take drastic action, take drastic measures

Le nouveau roman incendiaire de l'auteur avait °suscité des controverses. The author's new inflammatory novel had raised some controversy.

Le paysage est °égayé par le chant des oiseaux. The countryside is enlivened by the singing of the birds.

Son corps brûle les calories beaucoup plus vite que la moyenne, °entraînant une perte de poids. His body burns calories much faster than normal, resulting in weight loss.

L'inculpé a refusé de °réagir aux informations de la presse faisant état du vol. The accused refused to respond to press information regarding the theft.

Proverbe français: N'°éveillez pas le chat qui dort. French proverb: Let sleeping cats [English: dogs] lie.

taquiner   to tease, plague

MEMORY AID

The "**taqui~**" fragment sounds like *tacky*, meaning *shabby* or *lacking style*. One who makes a *tacky* comment to someone else is often saying something *classless, critical,* or *offensive*. Picture two spiteful little kids teasing one another by making taunting jests and tacky comments.

Note: This verb family contains words that convey a *less threatening sense of irritation* and imply more *benign intent* than those found under **embêter** (to bother, annoy . . .), page 61.

Other verbs in this family include: to scoff at, scorn, mimic, ape, needle, boo, deride, ridicule, taunt, lampoon, bother, harass, make fun of, snigger, pester, satirize, etc.

---

affrioler   to tempt, entice

allumer   to tease (sexually)

asticoter*   to tease, needle, pester

badiner (avec)   to toy with, dally, trifle with, jest, take lightly

bafouer   to ridicule, jeer at, scoff at, flout (law, authority)

berner   to ridicule, deride, make a fool of, fool, hoax

brocarder   to ridicule, taunt, criticize

chahuter   to heckle

chambrer*   to tease, make fun of

chansonner   to lampoon, satirize

charrier*   to tease, pull s.o.'s leg,* kid s.o.

chiffonner*   to tease, vex, perturb, bother

conspuer   to boo, shout s.o. down

contrarier   to annoy, bother, vex

crisper (qn)   to cause (s.o.) to fidget, get on (s.o.'s) nerves

s'égayer aux dépens de   to laugh at s.o.'s expense, make fun of

embrasser de questions   to heckle

énerver   to bedevil, rile (s.o.), unnerve (s.o.)

ennuyer   to bother, hassle, annoy, pester, badger

faire des astuces   to make wisecracks/jokes

faire des sottises   to be naughty (child), do a silly thing (adult)

faire la satire de   to satirize

faire le zouave*   to play the fool

faire marcher qn   to pull s.o.'s leg,* fool s.o.

flirter   to flirt, be trifling, be coy

hanter   to haunt (ghost, memories), stalk s.o.

harceler   to harass, badger

huer   to boo, deride, mock, ridicule

importuner   to bother, trouble, inconvenience

incommoder   to disturb, inconvenience, trouble

irriter   to irritate, annoy, peeve, rag on,* gall

jouer un mauvais tour   to play a dirty trick on

se jouer de qn   to make fun of s.o.

lutiner   to tease, pester, plague, be mischievous, be impish (*lit.* **lutin** *(m)*: imp, elf)

mettre en boîte*   to make fun of, pull s.o.'s leg*

mimer   to mimic, ridicule, pantomime, mime

minauder   to smirk, simper, smile in a silly way (derogatory)

se moquer de   to make fun of, tease, ridicule

narguer   to scoff at, scorn, disdain

oser   to dare (to do s.t.), venture, take the challenge

parodier to parody, burlesque, ridicule by mockery and satire

pointiller to tease, bicker, be fussy, be a fuddy-duddy*

pourchasser to badger, hound, chase (fox, escapee)

rabaisser to demean, disparage (person, effort), put s.o. down, insult

railler to taunt, scoff at, mock, sneer at

reprocher to taunt, upbraid, blame (for error, fault), rebuke, criticize

ricaner to sneer, sniggle,* giggle (foolishly), snigger*

ridiculiser to ridicule, make fun of, poke fun at

rigoler to laugh, joke, kid,* poke fun

rire au nez to laugh in s.o.'s face

se rire to mock, make sport of

riser to laugh in s.o.'s face

sangloter to sob

singer to ape, mimic, imitate (mockingly) (*lit.* **singe** (*m*): ape, monkey)

stimuler to goad, rouse, prod (s.o. to irritate or incite)

tarabuster* to pester (person), bother (thought, deed)

tirailler to tease, pester, gnaw at (doubts, worry)

tirer la langue à to stick one's tongue out at

titiller to titillate, excite, tease

tourner qn/qch en ridicule to ridicule s.o./s.t.

tracasser to worry, niggle (doubt), disquiet (uncertainty), trouble

Pierre, arrête-toi! Tu °taquines ta pauvre sœur sans trêve! Peter, stop it! You tease your sister incessantly!

Saute! °Ose, si tu peux! Ah la vache*, il saute! Il a °osé! Jump! I dare you! Wow, he's jumping! He did it!

La vaurienne °s'égaye aux dépens des plus petits mômes.* That good-for-nothing laughs at the expense of the littlest kids.

Le benjamin °mime constamment les actions de son frère aîné, un ado*. The youngest child constantly mimics the scheming of his older brother, a teen.

°Rira bien qui °rira le dernier. He who laughs last laughs best.

trôner   to lord over, sit imposingly

MEMORY AID

Un trône is a *throne* or *the seat of royalty*. A sovereign, who is *enthroned*, can wield limitless power over his subjects and *lord* his supreme authority over them. Picture a despotic king sitting imposingly atop his throne with all the imperial powers he wields as monarch.

Other verbs in this family relate to: a ruler holding supreme power over his domain and subjects and all the attitudes, airs, authority, and pretensions associated with his office as well as his abuses of power.

amnistier   to pardon by amnesty

s'annexer   to commandeer, seize, confiscate (property, person)

anoblir   to raise to the rank of nobility

asservir   to enslave, subjugate

assujettir   to subjugate, subdue

avilir   to debase (person, currency), degrade, disparage

avoir la haute main   to have supreme control, have the upper hand

chapeauter   to be the head of, supervise

cirer les bottes de qn   to lick s.o.'s boots, brownnose

se consacrer à   to devote oneself to (religion, job, cause, hobby)

contrôler   to control, master, be in control, dominate

couper   to trump (cards)

couronner   to crown (with honor, king/queen), award prize to (author, artwork)

crâner*   to show off, be proud, be boastful

daigner   to deign, condescend, stoop to a lower level (socially)

damer   to crown s.o. (checkers)

déborder   to go beyond (limit), overflow (river), exceed (rights)

décaver   to win the whole stakes from, to clean out s.o., ruin s.o.

déclarer   to proclaim, make known (decree), declare (war, martial law)

déclasser   to take from one social class to another, degrade in rank/status

décorer   to confer upon (titles, medals)

décréter   to decree, declare, order, enact (law, legislation)

se dédier à   to devote oneself to, dedicate oneself to (religion, s.o., cause)

défrayer la chronique   to be in the news, be the talk of the town

dégrader   to degrade, debase (money, person), cheapen, damage, vilify

déifier   to deify, elevate to the level of a god

demander   to order, command, assert, call for

démoraliser   to demoralize, discourage, dishearten

démunir   to strip of, deprive, leave unprovided (land, money)

dénigrer   to disparage, vilify

dépasser   to exceed, surpass (limit, measurable quantity, value, expectation)

déposer   to depose (king, etc.)

dépourvoir   to leave unprovided for, deprive (rights, nourishment, possessions)

se dépraver   to become corrupt, lack all morals

déprécier   to belittle, disparage, denigrate (s.o.), depreciate (currency, value)

déprimer   to depress (morally, physically), discourage, deject

dérouter   to lead astray (evil ruler), reroute (airplane)

désaffectionner   to cause s.o. to lose affection

désappointer   to disappoint, frustrate (hopes, desire, expectations, plans)

désavantager   to handicap, put at a disadvantage

déserter   to forsake, abandon (post, family, cause)

désespérer   to drive to despair

déshonorer   to disgrace, dishonor

désillusionner   to disillusion, disappoint

désobliger   to displease, be unkind, be inhospitable, be uncooperative

désorienter   to lead astray, disorient, bewilder

détenir le pouvoir   to be in power (king/queen, political party), hold power

détrôner   to dethrone (king/queen), oust (champion), supplant (style, product)

se dévergonder   to become dissolute (leader, society), debauch, become corrupt

dévoyer   to lead astray, corrupt (youth, society), become delinquent (student)

dîmer   to levy a tithe, require payment of a tenth of revenue

se disculper (de)   to exonerate (from), vindicate (of crime/wrongdoing)

diviniser   to deify (s.o. or s.t.), praise to the heavens, sing praises of

dominer   to lord it over, preside over, rule, outclass, overcome (defeat), overpower

dominer sur   to dominate, surpass, overpower (rival)

dompter   to subjugate, subdue (peasants, animal, passions, nature)

édicter   to decree, issue an edict

égarer   to lead astray (morally), mislead (person)

s'enhardir   to become bolder

s'enorgueillir de   to pride oneself on, boast

entrer dans la légende   to become a legend

étatiser   to bring under state control

être assujetti   to be subjugated (peasant, serf)

être aux manettes*   to be in charge, be in control

être doué de   to be endowed with (talent, good looks)

être mat   to be in checkmate (chess)

exalter   to exalt, glorify (God), laud (virtues), praise, intensify (odor, pride)

excéder   to exceed (rights, power, boundary), overtax, overburden

exploiter   to exploit (land, natural resources, peasant labor), make use of

exulter   to exult, rejoice, be jubilant

faire de la lèche*   to be a bootlicker, be a brownnoser,* be a butt-kisser*

faire de l'élitisme   to be elitist, be snobbish, act socially superior

faire de l'épate*   to show off, be a braggart, be boastful

faire de l'esbroufe*   to show off, bluff

faire de l'étalage*   to flaunt (acquaintance, wealth), show off, be showy

faire des châteaux en Espagne*   to build castles in the air, have grandiose dreams

faire des chichis*   to put on airs, be a showoff,* make a fuss

faire des manières   to put on airs, be showy, be ostentatious

faire échec au roi   to checkmate (chess)

faire la java*   to live it up,* enjoy life

faire le faraud   to strut, pose, swagger

faire le maître   to lord over, rule over, preside over, dominate

faire le renchéri*   to put on airs, be ostentatious

se faire mousser*   to blow one's own horn*

se faire plébisciter   to be elected by an overwhelming majority

fidéliser   to build loyalty, build a faithful following

se flatter   to pride oneself, flatter oneself

frimer*   to show off, boast

gémir sur son sort   to bemoan one's fate

glorifier   to glorify, honor

se glorifier   to glory in (honors, accomplishment), revel in glory

gouverner   to govern, control, rule

gracier   to grant a pardon to, pardon (transgression, debtor)

idolâtrer   to idolize (movie star), worship (pagan god)

immortaliser   to immortalize, make immortal, memorialize (war dead)

s'intituler   to be titled (lord, earl, duke)

introniser   to enthrone (king/queen, Pope)

jouer atout   to trump (cards), play a trump card

jouer les vedettes*   to act like a star

légiférer   to legislate (senate), create laws

lever une dîme sur   to levy a tithe

maîtriser   to lord it over, master, control (peasants, subjects, passions, fire)

mater   to checkmate (chess)

mépriser   to look down on (person), scorn (advice, danger)

mésuser (de)   to abuse, misuse

mettre échec et mat   to checkmate (chess)

se mirer   to admire oneself

monopoliser   to monopolize (business, conversation)

octroyer   to grant (land, financial grant), concede, allocate (funds)

oindre   to anoint, appoint to office

oppresser   to oppress (heat, anguish, environment)

opprimer   to oppress (lower class), subjugate (peasants)

ordonner   to command, direct, govern, dictate

outrepasser   to exceed, go beyond (limit), overstep (authority), override (veto)

parapher   to put one's flourish or initials to (document), sign (law)

pardonner   to pardon, forgive, grant pardon

passer à la postérité   to go down in history

se pavaner   to strut, walk proudly

persécuter   to persecute, oppress (lower class), harass

pervertir   to pervert, corrupt (morals), adulterate (food, chemicals)

planer   to look down (on) (from high perch), be menacing, menace

plastronner   to strut, swagger

se plier à   to abide by, submit to, give in to, yield to

policer   to establish law and order, civilize

polir   to civilize, refine (barbarian)

pontifier   to act or speak pompously, lay down the law

posséder   to possess, be master of (wealth, land, power, possessions, talent)

pourrir   to go bad (situation), become rotten (fruit, tooth, spoiled child)

préjudicier   to be prejudicial, be detrimental (legal decision), to harm (health, morals)

prescrire   to stipulate (law), prescribe (medicine, method), lay down the law

présider   to preside over (meeting, senate)

prétexter   to pretend, feign

se prévaloir   to boast, take advantage, pride oneself on (accomplishment)

prévariquer   to betray s.o.'s trust

priser   to take snuff (inhaled tobacco)

priver   to deprive (rights, possessions), bereave, keep from having (sleep)

profiter de   to take advantage of, profit, gain

prospérer   to prosper, thrive (riches, business, power, authority)

réduire en esclavage   to enslave

se régaler   to regale oneself, feast

régenter   to domineer, lord it over, rule over, dictate to

régir   to rule, govern, administer

réglementer   to regulate, make rules

régler   to rule, regulate, order

régner   to reign (king/queen), rule (political party), prevail (opinion, belief)

rendre hommage à qn   to pay homage to s.o.

se rengorger   to carry one's head high, give oneself airs

se reposer sur ses lauriers   to rest on one's laurels

réprimer   to repress (insurrection, emotions), restrain, crack down on (crime)

respecter to respect (authority), revere (king/queen, law), observe (rules)

révérer to revere, treat with reverence

rouler sur l'or* to be rolling in money*

rugir to roar (lion, storm), bellow (person), snarl (beast)

sacrer to crown, anoint, consecrate

se signaler to distinguish oneself

se singulariser to make oneself conspicuous, make oneself stand out (from crowd)

snober* to snub, turn one's nose up at* (person, offer, food)

sommer qn to command s.o.

soumettre to subject (people), put down (rebellion)

statuer to decree, ordain (law), determine (judge)

superviser to supervise (person), oversee (project)

surclasser to outclass (talent, rank, prestige)

surpasser to exceed, excel, outdo (talent, intelligence, performance, speed)

se targuer de to boast about, pride oneself on

taxer to tax, impose a duty on

tenir le haut du pavé* to lord (it) over*

tirer orgueil de qch to take pride in s.t.

titrer to confer a title on (aristocrat), run as a headline (press), label (alcohol proof)

tonitruer to boom, blare, blast, thunder (loud person, loudspeaker)

tonner to boom, thunder (artillery, loud voice)

trompeter to trumpet abroad, proclaim (joyous news, royal decree)

truster to monopolize, have a monopoly of (market share, product), corner (market)

usurper to usurp, seize, hold (power, position, possessions)

vanter la marchandise* to show oneself off

se vanter to boast, brag, gloat

vénérer to venerate (idol, memory of s.o.), worship, honor

vivre dans l'opulence to live the opulent life

Le portrait du patron °trône sur le bureau afin d'intimider les employés. The boss's picture sits imposingly on the desk in order to intimidate the employees.

Selon le porte-parole, de nombreux foyers ont été °privés de courant et d'eau. Numerous homes lost electrical power and water supply, according to the spokesman.

Le temps est venu pour moi de me retirer en tant que dirigeant et de me °consacrer à ma vie privée. The time has come for me to retire as director and to devote myself to my private life.

Elle °profite de ses vacances à la station thermale alpine. She takes advantage of her vacation at the Alpine thermal spa.

Le PDG peut °s'enorgueillir d'un bilan économique robuste. The CEO can be proud of a strong economic balance sheet.

4

At War

Featured Verbs

acheminer to send forward, dispatch

s'acheminer to make one's way toward

activer to get going (plan), speed up (work)

aller (à, de) l'avant to go forth, go forward, (**de**) to forge ahead

avancer to go forward (troops, theory, clock, date), advance (idea, army), push on

s'avancer vers to head for, progress toward, move forward toward

se balader* to stroll, gallivant,* go for a walk

convoyer to send out on convoy (ships), to escort (vehicles), ferry (cargo)

dépayser to send away from home, give a change of scenery, disorient (s.o.)

dépêcher to dispatch, send quickly, do quickly

déployer to deploy (troops, forces, flag)

déroger to deviate (from standard), go astray, depart from (rules, guidelines)

se destiner à to be destined for, have for a destination

se diriger vers to head toward, home in on (target), zero in on, make toward (ship)

donner le feu vert* to give the "go-ahead," give the green light

s'ébranler to get underway, move on, move off (train, vehicle, procession)

s'écarter de la ligne droite to veer away from the straight and narrow

émettre to send out, broadcast, emit (TV signal, odor), issue (ticket), give off (heat)

envoyer to send off, dispatch (letter, package), remit (money), send out (troops)

envoyer chercher to send for s.o.

éperonner to spur, urge forward, hasten (*lit.* **éperon** (*m*): spur)

escorter to guide, usher, escort (armed guard, on a date)

expédier to dispatch, send off, forward (letter, package), ship (raw material)

expédier à l'avance to send in, advance (loan), send ahead (scout)

faire avancer le schmilblik* to help things along

faire entrer to send in (troops)

faire ressortir to bring out again (old joke, winter coat), go to relieve (troops)

faire sortir to send out (dry cleaning), take out (trash, car from garage)

faire suivre to send after, forward (mail)

faire venir to send for (help, doctor)

garer to pull over, move aside, park (car), station (train), dock (canoe)

hâter to bring forward, hasten, forward, rush, speed

lancer to send forth (plea), cast (dice), launch (rocket), hurl (rock, dart)

se lancer to embark on (adventure, quest, crusade), go into battle

mal conseiller to misguide, misadvise

mener to lead (business, cause), control (army, enterprise), guide (tour)

mener la bande to lead the pack

mettre le cap sur to head for, make toward (nautical)

se mettre en route to set out (for destination), get going, move off

mobiliser to mobilize (for war), rally (troops), marshal (resources)

obliquer to turn off (path), bear to (the right), skew (boat)

ordonner qn à to order s.o. to

partir en éclaireur to go on ahead, scout ahead

poster to station (guards), post (fort sentry)

promouvoir to advance (idea), promote (product), pitch (idea), boost (sales)

propulser to propel (rocket, astronaut), send forward, hurl (projectile), drive (car)

reconduire to lead back, send home, show out

redéployer to redeploy (troops)

réexpédier to send on (to new destination), send back, re-forward (mail)

reformer to reform (troops), discharge from service (soldier)

se régler sur to be guided (by example, principles)

réintégrer to reinstate (position), restore (rights), return to (prior status)

renvoyer to send (an object left behind)

roder to get the show on the road

router to route (mail), dispatch, sort and mail (letters)

Silencieusement, l'espion s'est °acheminé vers le laboratoire souterrain. Silently, the spy made his way toward the underground laboratory. **Un convoi de blindés et de chars °s'ébranla vers le conflit.** A convoy of armored combat vehicles and tanks got underway toward the battle. **En tant que routier j'°achemine des poutres et des poutrelles vers le chantier.** As a truck driver I dispatch girders and beams to the construction site. **Notre maison d'édition propose de °lancer un nouveau mensuel axé sur les spectacles, les tendances et les restos à la mode.** Our publishing house plans to put out a new monthly magazine focused on shows, trends, and fashionable restaurants. **Tout chemin °mène à Rome.** All roads lead to Rome.

affronter to confront, face

MEMORY AID

The **"affront~"** fragment is spelled the same as the English word *affront*, meaning *to meet face-to-face defiantly* or *to confront*. When someone rises to a challenge he puts up *"a front"* to confront or *meet his opposition head-on*. Picture two menacing wrestlers challenging one another. They both show off their muscular chests (fronts) and stand fearlessly chest-to-chest to confront one another.

Other verbs in this family include: to challenge, brave, contest, stand up to, pick a fight with, quarrel, flout, defy, contend, argue, resist, withstand, dispute, vie, offend, take a stand, etc.

s'aborder to accost each other, address (threat)

accuser qn de to accuse s.o. of

s'affirmer to assert oneself (opinion, talent)

s'affronter to face one another, come up against (competition), brave (danger)

arguer de to protest that, claim, argue for (belief), give reasons for

arguer que to argue that, contest that

s'arracher les yeux* to have a violent quarrel

avoir une prise de bec* to quarrel

se braquer* to dig one's heels in,* challenge s.o.

braver to brave (danger), be courageous, defy (challenge, odds), stand up to

se buter to dig one's heels in, be stubborn, be persistent

chercher des ennuis to look for trouble

chercher noise à qn to try to pick a fight with s.o.

chercher querelle avec qn to pick a fight with s.o.

se colleter* to come to grips with s.o.

confronter to confront (accuser, fears), disagree with, compare (points of doctrine)

contester to contest, dispute, debate, object to, question (credentials, validity)

défendre to stand up for (person, belief), advocate (cause)

se défendre to defend oneself (opinion, position)

défier to challenge (s.o., results), dare (s.o.), defy, withstand (insults)

en démordre (ne pas)* (to refuse) to budge an inch

déroger à to go against (rules, authority)

discuter avec to argue with

disputer to argue, contend, wrangle, quarrel, contest, dispute

donner la réplique à to play opposite (in movie, on stage), give s.o. a cue (on stage)

donner un camouflet (à qn)* to affront, offend, insult (s.o.) (*lit.* **camouflet** *(m)*: puff of smoke blown in s.o.'s face)

se dresser face à to stand up against (challenge, opponent)

s'élever contre to rise up against

être en litige to be in dispute/conflict, be in litigation (law)

être en réaction contre to be in reaction against, be in response to (decision, critique)

être impertinent to be impertinent/rude/impudent

se fâcher avec/contre to be upset with/at

se fâcher tout rouge to become furious

faire face à to face up to (challenge, faults), oppose, cope with, be met with (danger)

faire offense à to offend, insult

se faire du mauvais sang*   to get oneself upset

fusiller qn du regard*   to look daggers at s.o.*

s'imposer   to assert oneself, show one's superiority, stand out (talent, quality)

insulter   to insult, affront, speak disparagingly, treat rudely, curse, cuss

jeter pavé dans la mare*   to make waves,* cause trouble, stir up trouble

jouer dans la cour des grands*   to play ball with the big boys*

lancer un défi   to challenge (to a duel), defy (challenge)

lutter corps à corps   to fight hand-to-hand

marcher sur les brisées de qn*   to trespass on s.o.'s turf*

se mesurer   to vie, contend, be in contention (sports)

se mesurer à   to pit oneself against, confront (trials)

se monter à la hauteur   to rise to the challenge

narguer   to defy, flout, disdain, scoff at (threat)

offusquer   to offend (person, odor, remark)

s'opposer   to resist, set oneself against

planer sur   to hang over (threat), threaten, menace

polémiquer (sur)   to argue (about), argue in controversy (politics, news editorial)

se positionner   to take a stand (opinion)

se poster   to take a position (soldier, in an argument)

se pousser   to shove one another

précariser   to make insecure, jeopardize (job, status), make unstable (position)

prendre position   to take a stand

provoquer qn en duel   to challenge s.o. to a duel

quereller   to quarrel with, have words

récuser   to challenge (jury, witness, testimony), object to (law)

regarder en face   to face up to (responsibility, weaknesses)

regarder qn droit dans les yeux   to look s.o. straight in the eye

relever le gant   to accept a challenge (from opponent) (*lit.* to pick up a tossed gauntlet)

répondre   to talk back, answer back, react

résister à   to resist, withstand, stand up to (s.o.), fend off (threat, attack, enemy)

rétorquer   to retort, return in kind, pay back (insult), counterargue

rompre avec qn   to break up with s.o. (relationship)

tenir bon   to hold one's position

tenir en respect   to keep s.o. at bay

tenir tête à   to stand up to (enemy, challenge)

voir rouge*   to become livid with rage

Le vieux baleinier, battu par la tempête, °affrontait l'orage de plein fouet. The old, weather-beaten whaling ship faced the thunderstorm head on.

Le juge l'°accuse d'avoir du sang sur les mains. The judge accuses him of having "blood on his hands."

Des soucis d'une réduction de salaire éventuelle °planent sur les pourparlers budgétaires. Concerns of a possible salary reduction are threatening the budgetary discussions.

La veuve de la victime °s'oppose vivement à la libération proposée du criminel endurci. The victim's widow strongly opposes the hardened criminal's proposed release.

astreindre   to compel, subject, force upon

alléguer   to urge, advance (proposal, program), put forth (opinion, idea)

asservir   to enslave, subjugate (people), force into slavery/servitude

assujettir   to compel, subjugate, subdue (country, people)

charger   to burden, load (camera with film, ship containers)

contraindre (à, de)   to compel, coerce, constrain

contrevenir   to violate, infringe upon (law, regulation)

demander   to demand (respect, action), require (obedience), call for (new measures)

effectuer   to assign, appoint (for assignment)

être d'astreinte   to be on call (doctor), be on duty

être obligatoire   to be necessary

exciter   to urge, make excited, agitate, stimulate (caffeine), arouse, energize

exiger   to demand (answers, action), require (toy: assembly, plant: water)

faire plaisir à   to oblige

falloir   to be necessary/obligatory, be needful (should, must)

forcer   to force (s.o., lock), compel, oblige, coerce, strain (voice)

forcer qn à faire qch   to pressure s.o. to do s.t.

imposer   to tax, impose (law, tax), force (obedience)

insister (sur, à)   to insist (upon)

mettre à l'amende   to fine, charge a levy/fine, give a ticket (parking, speeding)

nécessiter   to compel, oblige, be needful, need, demand, require

obliger (à, de)   to obligate (rule, law), bind, compel, require, force (oppressor)

obtempérer   to obey (authority), bend to (higher power)

percevoir   to collect (taxes)

persuader   to induce, persuade, prevail upon (for favor)

porter à (qn à faire qch)   to urge (s.o. to do s.t.), incite

pousser   to impel, push (heavy object), drive (cattle, slaves)

pousser en avant   to urge on, motivate (employee), drive s.o. (to action)

prélever   to impose/levy tax

presser qn   to hurry s.o., urge s.o.

recourir à la force   to resort to force

réduire (en)   to compel, oblige, reduce to (slavery, rubble, ashes)

rendre sujet à   to subject to (scrutiny, experimentation, suffering)

requérir   to require, call for (cooking ingredients, attention, caution)

soumettre qn à   to subject s.o. to (condition, punishment, humiliation)

subjuguer   to subjugate, enslave, make captive

taxer   to tax, impose taxes

violenter   to constrain, force, violate, do violence to

vouloir absolument   to insist, insist upon

Papa °astreignait Étienne à tondre la pelouse avant de sortir avec ses copains. Papa used to force Stephen to mow the lawn before going out with his friends.

Il roulait en sens inverse et heurta le réverbère. Pour cela le gendarme lui °imposa une amende. He was driving the wrong way and hit a streetlight. For that the constable gave him a ticket.

Sa conduite malveillante a °soumis son épouse à une souffrance monumentale. His malicious conduct subjected his spouse to tremendous suffering.

Il avait ignoré l'ordre du policier de cesser ses agissements, avant d'°obtempérer finalement. He had ignored police orders to cease his activities, before finally complying.

bouleverser to overthrow, upset, agitate, overturn

abolir to abolish (slavery, law), outlaw (rule, usage)

affoler to throw into a panic (crowd, stock market)

agiter to perturb, agitate (liquid), trouble (peace, quiet), bustle about (waiter)

basculer to topple over, knock off balance, tip up

cabrer to revolt, rebel (rioters), rear up (horse), buck (bronco)

se cabrer to revolt, fly into a passion

causer des ravages to wreak havoc

chambarder* to turn upside down, create a ruckus*/an uproar/an upheaval

chambouler* to turn things upside down (household), ruin (project), shatter (s.o)

chavirer to capsize (boat), overturn (apple cart)

couver to brew or stir up (trouble)

culbuter to upset violently, overthrow (monarchy), topple (vase), tip over (chair)

déborder to overrun, flow over, flood (river), exceed (limits), boil over (soup)

déclamer to rant, rave, rail against (s.o., institution)

défaire to defeat, undo, unmake (government, social hierarchy, relationship)

démolir to demolish (car), pull down (building, theory), ruin (reputation)

déranger to disturb (peace), upset (tranquility, status quo), unsettle, derange, trouble

dérégler to unsettle (emotionally), upset, perturb (mechanism), lose (radio signal)

désarticuler to upset, dislocate (shoulder, clock gear, mechanism)

détrôner to dethrone (king/queen), oust (political party, administration)

détruire to destroy, demolish

ébranler to disturb, unsettle (bad news), shake (train, car), make shaky (foundation)

envahir to invade (country), overrun (weeds), flood, (market)

être le tapeur* to be rackety,* boisterous

exaspérer to enrage, exasperate

exterminer to exterminate (termites), destroy (population), commit genocide

extirper to exterminate, destroy, uproot (weed), eradicate (cancer)

faire des vagues to make waves, create a ruckus

faire du raffut* to kick up a fuss*

faire du vacarme* to make a racket/ruckus*/hubbub

faire enrager to enrage, infuriate

faire grève   to strike, go on strike (labor union)

faire irruption dans   to invade (ants, army), overrun, burst in (room), barge into

faire le poirier*   to do a headstand, turn oneself upside down

faire un tapage*   to create an uproar/row

faire une émeute   to riot

faucher   to mow down (wheat, enemy), reap (crops), flatten (car)

fulminer contre   to rant/rail against

inciter qn à agir   to rouse, incite

inciter une révolte   to incite a riot

infester   to overrun, infest (rats, roaches), invade

infliger des dégâts   to inflict damage on

s'insurger   to rebel, rise up (in revolt)

manifester   to demonstrate (in the streets)

mettre à l'envers   to turn upside down (barrel, picture), put on backwards (shirt)

mettre dessus dessous   to turn upside down

se mettre en grève   to go on strike

se mutiner   to mutiny

protester   to protest, express dissent (ideology), resist (authority), strike against

se rebeller   to rebel

réclamer   to object, complain, protest (**contre**), demand (ransom), claim (right)

récrier contre   to protest, cry out against

remuer   to upset, turn over (compost, dirt), stir up (sand), toss (salad)

renverser   to overthrow (government, authority), remove from office (coup d'état)

retourner   to turn upside down (sand pail), shake, turn over (omelette, mattress)

révolter   to revolt, rebel

révolutionner   to revolutionize, radically transform (social hierarchy, idea, method)

se soulever   to revolt, rise up (rebellion), arise (opposition)

supprimer   to abolish, suppress (rights, freedom), phase out (product, subsidy)

tempêter   to rant and rave

troubler   to perturb, trouble, disturb (sleep, peace, digestion), disrupt (order)

troubler la tranquillité publique   to disturb the peace

verser   to upset, overturn (fuel drum, vehicle)

La nouvelle de son décès les a °bouleversés profondément. The news of his death deeply upset them.

Raoul, dont l'univers est déjà °basculé, est harcelé par des conditions psychiatriques. Ralph, whose world is already in turmoil, is further tormented by psychiatric troubles.

Les pêcheurs bretons °fulminent contre le blocus de tous les ports de la façade atlantique. The fishermen of Brittany are railing against the blockade of all the Atlantic ports.

Bon nombre de consommateurs °réclament une compensation financière pour faire face à la flambée du prix du mazout domestique cet hiver. A good many consumers are demanding monetary compensation to offset the skyrocketing price of heating oil this winter.

carboniser to burn to cinders, reduce to ashes

MEMORY AID

The "**carbon~**" fragment is the same as the English word *carbon*. To *carbonize* something is *to reduce it to elemental carbon: ashes, cinders, charcoal*. Picture a large fire reducing a subdivision of wooden homes, or a forest, to ashes.

Other verbs in this family include: to char, inflame, incinerate, cremate, raze, commit arson, scorch, grill, blaze, flame, explode, heat, smolder, catch fire, flare, smoke, detonate, etc.

allumer to kindle, light a fire

attiser to make or stir up a fire

attraper un coup de soleil to suffer a sunburn

brûler to burn, scald (hot water), burn down (village), sear, scorch

brûler sans fumée ni flamme to smolder

calciner to burn to cinders

chambrer to warm to room temperature (wine)

charbonner to char, to blacken with coal

commettre incendie volontaire to commit arson

couver to smolder (fire, passion, jealousy), be brewing (plot)

cramer* to burn, go up in flames, be on fire (house, forest), scorch (clothes)

détoner to detonate (dynamite, bomb)

s'échauder to burn or scald oneself, wash in hot water

embraser to set on fire, inflame, set ablaze, fire, kindle

enfiévrer to inflame (passion), fire, rouse (sentiment), make feverish

enflammer to inflame, set fire to

enfumer to smoke out (room, bugs)

être en flammes to blaze, be afire

être victime d'une insolation to suffer sunstroke

exploser to explode (bomb, population), blow up (bridge), detonate, flare up

faire éclater to explode s.t., pop s.t. (firecracker)

faire sauter to explode (a mine)

flamber to blaze, flame, flare (tree, campfire)

flamboyer to flame, flare, blaze, be flamboyant

fumiger to fumigate (home against termites)

griller to scorch, grill, burn

hâler to tan (suntan, leather)

s'immoler par le feu to set oneself on fire, self-immolate

imploser to implode (vacuum tube)

incendier to burn down, set fire to

incinérer to incinerate (rubbish), cremate (cadaver)

marquer au feu chaud to brand (cattle)

mettre le feu à to set on fire, set fire to

porter qch à incandescence to heat s.t. white-hot

prendre to begin to burn, catch fire (by accident), light (matchstick)

prendre feu to catch fire (forest, house)

raser to raze, tear to the ground (village)

se réchauffer to grow warmer, warm oneself up

réduire en cendres to reduce to ashes

renflammer to rekindle (fire, romance)

rougeoyer to glow red

rougir to become red-hot

roussir to scorch (sun), singe (with iron), sear (steak), turn brown (leaves)

tiédir to grow lukewarm, take the chill off (champagne, water)

tourner en surrégime to be overheating (engine, economy)

Après le grand incendie, la forêt était totalement °carbonisée. After the huge conflagration, the forest was reduced to ashes.

Des émeutiers ont °incendié au moins vingt véhicules le long du boulevard. Rioters burned up at least twenty vehicles along the boulevard.

Une seule roquette a °explosé dans la zone tampon hier. Aucune victime n'a été signalée. A lone rocket exploded in the buffer zone yesterday. No casualties were reported.

Les tensions politiques sont °attisées par des conflits fonciers. The political tension is stirred up by conflicts over land.

se chamailler to squabble, wrangle, bicker

ETCECI DE

HIC FRANCI PUGNANT

MEMORY AID

With a bit of imagination, the "**chamaill~**" fragment resembles *chain mail*, the flexible armor covering comprised of joined metal links that *wrangling* knights would want to wear to protect themselves against enemy sword thrusts. Picture a scene from the famous Bayeux Tapestry (**la Tapisserie de Bayeux**), in which the warriors are well-covered from neck to toe in protective chain mail warring, wrangling, and bickering with one another. See also **mater** (to subdue), page 121, and **terrasser** (to bring down, overcome), page 132.

Other verbs in this family include: to assail, fight, wrestle, attack, kill, vanquish, strike, stab, wage war, battle, skirmish, injure, brawl, scuffle, grapple, quarrel, duel, beat up, clash, etc.

accrocher avec qn to fight s.o.

s'acharner sur to go at relentlessly (foe, homework, novel)

affronter to confront, face (enemy, danger), come up against (opposition)

agresser to attack, assail, start a fight

assaillir to assail (fortress), attack (enemy), bombard (with questions)

assassiner to assassinate, murder

attaquer to attack, assail, assault

se bagarrer to brawl, scuffle, fight

batailler to battle, fight, give battle, be at war

bâtonner to cudgel, cane, club (riot police)

battre en brèche to batter, breach (enemy defense)

se battre avec/contre to fight, do battle with, combat

se battre bec et ongles* to fight tooth and nail

se battre en duel to duel, fight a duel (with pistols or swords)

se bigorner* to fight

blesser to wound, injure

se bouffer le nez* to fight, wrangle

se brouiller to quarrel, have a falling out, scuffle

canarder* to take pot shots at* (*lit.* to shoot at ducks)

canonner to attack with artillery/cannons

chicaner* to fight, quibble about

se colleter* to scuffle, grapple

se coltiner* to have to put up with (person, work)

combattre to fight against, wage war, combat, struggle, oppose (enemy, idea)

contre-attaquer to counterattack

donner l'assaut à to assault, assail

donner une pêche à qn* to smack s.o. across the face

empiéter to invade, encroach upon (territory), infringe (on s.o.'s property), impinge

escarmoucher to skirmish, squabble

escrimer to fence (sport with swords)

être en conflit to clash, conflict with

être rancunier to bear grudges

se fâcher avec/contre to quarrel with

faire la guerre à to wage war with

faire la tête au carré à qn* to smash s.o. in the face*

faire rage to be fierce, rage

faire tort à to injure, wrong (s.o.), damage (s.o. or s.t.)

faire un attentat   to attack, assault, commit an attack/crime/outrage

faire une échauffourée   to skirmish with, clash with

faire une embuscade   to ambush

faucher   to mow down, cut down (enemy), strike down (illness)

ferrer   to strike (at bait, e.g., fish)

fondre sur qn   to swoop down on s.o., attack

frapper   to strike, stab, hit, chop, deliver a blow, smash, smack, knock, shoot (gun)

fulminer contre   to verbally attack, denounce

fustiger   to flay, whip

garder rancune à qn   to bear s.o. a grudge

guerroyer (contre)   to wage war (on)

jouer des coudes   to push, shove, elbow

lancer un brûlot contre*   to launch a scathing attack on

léser   to injure, hurt, harm, damage

livrer bataille à   to do battle with

lutter   to fight, wrestle

mener une attaque (contre)   to lead an attack (against)

militer (pour/contre)   to fight (for/against)

mitrailler   to machine gun, gun down

nuire à   to injure (person, health), harm

offenser   to injure, hurt, offend

parer   to fend off, guard against

passer qn à tabac*   to beat s.o. up

porter atteinte à   to damage, attack, harm

prendre à partie   to assault, assail, attack, start a fight

s'en prendre à   to go at (physically), take on (s.o.), set upon, take a swing at (s.o., s.t.)

se rebiffer (contre)*   to hit back at

répliquer   to reply, retort, answer back, retaliate (verbally, militarily)

repousser   to fight off, repel (invasion), reject (offer), snub, rebuff, beat back (foe)

se riffer*   to fight, quarrel

riposter   to retaliate, fight back, fire back, counterattack

rudoyer   to bully, treat roughly

sangler   to deal a slashing blow

souffleter   to slap in the face, box the ears of (boxer)

se torcher*   to fight, beat s.o. up

triompher   to triumph, win, prevail (army, reason), rejoice, gloat (over victory)

tuer   to kill, murder, slay, gun down

vaincre   to vanquish, overpower, defeat, finish first, beat (opponent)

venger   to avenge, take one's revenge

en venir aux mains   to come to blows

Flûte*! Quelle histoire! Les gosses* de mon jardin d'enfants °se chamaillaient toute la journée. Drat!* What a hassle! My kindergarten brats* bickered all day long.

Dans son for intérieur elle espère que la vérité °triomphera et que la paix régnera à jamais. In her heart of hearts she wishes for truth to triumph and for peace to rule forever.

Le maire °milite pour une interdiction totale de l'ingérence municipale dans ses affaires personnelles. The mayor is fighting for a total ban on municipal interference in his personal business.

Lors d'un stress, les niveaux élevés sanguins d'adrénaline et d'autres hormones peuvent °porter atteinte au muscle cardiaque. During stress, the elevated blood levels of adrenaline and other hormones may damage the heart muscle.

châtier   to punish, chastise

brêler (breller)   to lash, whip (as punishment, gale force winds)

brutaliser   to ill-treat, abuse, bully

cingler   to lash, sting (rain, wind, branch, whip)

condamner à mort   to sentence to death

condamner qn à (#) ans de prison   to sentence s.o. to (#) years in prison

condamner qn aux travaux forcés   to sentence s.o. to hard labor

corriger   to correct (error, criminal behavior), punish, thrash

cravacher   to horsewhip

crucifier   to crucify

décapiter   to behead, decapitate

déchirer   to torture, rend, tear apart

défavoriser   to penalize (court decision, law), put at a disadvantage (economically)

déférer   to refer to court, hand over (to judge, authorities)

discipliner   to discipline, punish (child), control (impulse), keep tidy (hair)

donner une contravention   to fine, ticket (police)

donner une fessée*   to spank, give a spanking, paddle

échapper à la punition   to escape punishment

écoper d'une punition*   to be punished (law), get a jail term, take the rap* (for crime)

écorcher   to flay (animal), skin (with whip), grate on (nerves)

écrouer   to imprison, lock up, incarcerate

électrocuter   to electrocute

employer la manière forte   to use strong-arm methods

emprisonner   to imprison, confine, put in prison

être atteint (de)   to be ill, be suffering (from), be affected (by) (cancer, illness)

être au supplice   to be in agony

être fusillé   to be shot by firing squad

être guillotiné   to be beheaded by guillotine

exercer des sévices sur   to abuse, ill-treat

faire des sanctions contre   to impose sanctions against, punish, discipline

faire (du) mal à   to harm, hurt

faire le procès de qn   to put s.o. on trial

faire souffrir (qn)   to torture, pain s.o., cause s.o. pain/suffering

faire un exemple de qn   to make an example of s.o.

flageller   to whip, flog, lash

fouetter   to whip (cream, prisoner), beat (eggs)

fourguer*   to flog

froisser   to wound (body), offend (feelings), dent (car), bruise (skin, pride)

fustiger   to flog, whip, flay

griffer   to scratch, claw

guillotiner   to behead/decapitate by guillotine

incarcérer   to incarcerate, imprison

inculper   to charge, indict (law)
infliger des sévices   to inflict punishment/suffering
infliger une peine à   to penalize (judge, jury), inflict pain
lapider   to abuse, pelt, stone to death
lyncher   to lynch, hang (by the neck)
malmener   to manhandle, ill-treat, mistreat, mishandle, stun (s.o.)
maltraiter   to abuse, ill-treat, mistreat
martyriser   to torture, torment, make a martyr of
mettre au martyre   to torture (*lit.* to make a martyr of someone)
mettre en prison (geôle, bagne*)   to put in prison, imprison, jail, put in jail
meurtrir   to bruise (flesh, ego, fruit)
mutiler   to mutilate, disfigure, maim, injure severely
nuire à   to harm (s.o., health, reputation), prejudice (law trial)
passer en cour martiale   to court-martial
pâtir (de)   to suffer (because of)
pénaliser   to penalize (sports), punish (person)
persécuter   to persecute, harass
poursuivre qn en justice   to prosecute s.o. by law
punir   to punish, chastise (child, criminal), correct (bad behavior), discipline
purger une peine   to serve a sentence (prison)
réformer   to reform (delinquent), improve, make changes, declare unfit (for service)

se réformer   to improve, mend one's ways
se reprendre   to correct oneself, pull oneself together
sanctionner   to sanction, penalize (error), punish, discipline (team, student)
scorifier   to scarify, lash, scar
servir de marchepied à qn*   to be a stepping stone for s.o.*
sévir contre   to deal with severely
souffrir   to suffer, bear, endure (pain, hardship, heat)
souffrir de privations   to endure hardship
soutirer qch à qn   to squeeze s.t. out of s.o.
stresser   to put under stress, stress out
subir   to suffer, submit to (damage, attacks, pain, criticism)
tanner le cuir à qn*   to tan s.o.'s hide,* whip s.o.
terrifier   to terrify
torturer   to torture, torment, treat cruelly
tourner le couteau dans la plaie*   to rub salt in the wound*
traduire qn en justice   to bring s.o. to justice
traiter mal qn   to treat s.o. badly
traumatiser   to traumatize
tuer par injection mortelle   to kill by lethal injection
vexer   to hurt, vex, irk, miff, irritate
violenter   to assault (sexually), do violence to (s.o.)

Le tribunal a °châtié le prévenu sous l'inculpation de meurtre prémédité et l'a condamné à perpétuité. The court punished the accused with the charge of premeditated murder and sentenced him to life imprisonment.

Désormais, les détenus devront °subir un examen physique obligatoire tous les trois mois pour vérifier leur santé. Henceforth, the prisoners will have to undergo a quarterly health check-up.

Il hésite à °purger sa peine jusqu'à ce que son avocat fasse un appel. He's hesitant to serve his sentence until his lawyer files an appeal.

Selon les prises de sang elle °est atteinte de leucémie. She suffers from leukemia, according to the blood tests.

emplafonner* to smash into

abattre to abolish, batter down (house, wall), strike down, cut down (tree)

abîmer to ruin, damage (building), spoil (clothing), injure (s.o.), gum up (machine)

s'aborder to run afoul of each other (two ships)

accidenter to damage (vehicle), injure (person)

amocher* to bash up* (car), mess up* (person, object)

asséner to strike a blow, deal a blow (to s.o.)

assommer to knock down, knock out (boxer), crush (ego), stun (s.o.)

bombarder to bomb, shell (artillery)

bousculer to jostle, throw into disorder, shake up (old notions, habits, tradition)

bousiller* to smash up,* wreck, botch,* screw up,* muck up,* bungle*

briser to break (bone), shatter, smash, crack (glass), ruin (life), end (career), bust*

buter contre to hit, strike

cabosser* to dent (car), bump, indent, belt (s.o.)

casser to break (neck, bone), crack, smash (window), chip (tooth)

choquer to shock, clash, stun, traumatize, offend

cogner to knock, beat up, thump, knock in, hit, slug,* poke (with fist), whomp,* sock*

craquer to break up (iceberg), crunch (ice), crack (wood), fall apart (plans, business)

crasher to crash (car, computer), crash land (airplane)

défoncer to smash in (door, wall), bash in, stave in (barrel), tear up (road)

dégrader to damage, cause to fail, deteriorate (building, health, weather, relations)

délabrer to shatter, ruin (house, wall, equipment)

démolir to demolish (house, car, reputation), wreck (plans), dilapidate (home)

détériorer to damage, impair, deteriorate (health, furniture)

détruire to destroy, ruin, demolish, violate, blast (hope, reputation)

dévaster to devastate, lay waste, ravage (crops, countryside, culture)

écraser to run over (car), crush, ruin, squash, mash (potato), grind (seed), swat (fly)

s'effriter to crumble, disintegrate (rock), be eroded (power, authority)

endommager to damage, injure, smash, destroy, hurt, harm, corrupt (computer data)

entraîner une dégradation de to damage, weaken, degrade

entrer (dans) to run into (wall, trouble), come in, go in, fit in, penetrate

entrer à la resquille* to gate-crash* (party, rock concert), sneak in

entrer en bombe* to come bursting in, burst in

entrer en collision avec to collide with, crash into each other

entrer en coup de vent* to burst in (party crasher), breeze in* (late for class)

érafler to scratch (car paint), graze, scuff (shoe), key (vandalize car), scrape (skin)

esquinter* to smash up,* bash* (car), ruin (vision), pan (film critic), beat up (s.o.)

être en panne to be broken down (car engine)

être pris en sandwich entre* to be sandwiched between*

exploser to explode (dynamite), go off (bomb), burst (fireworks), blast

faire tort à to harm (s.o., s.t.), damage, wrong (s.o.)

fracasser to shatter, break into pieces, crash

fracturer to fracture, break (bone, safe, lock, door)

frapper to strike, hit, knock, bump, smite, run into (with car), smash, slam into, belt*

frapper du poing to thump (with fist), punch

freiner à mort* to slam on the breaks

gâter to damage, spoil (environment, child, fun), blemish, harm (mind, judgment)

gêner to jostle, interfere with

gifler to slap in the face, box the ears of

gourmer* to box, thump, pummel (boxer), curb (horse)

happer* to hit (by vehicle)

heurter to hit, collide, bump into, strike against, dash into (wave)

imploser to implode, collapse inward (vacuum tube)

léser to damage, injure, harm

nuire à to harm, hurt, jeopardize

percuter to crash, strike, percuss, ram in, impact (missile)

péricliter to be in a state of collapse (economy, relationship)

pilonner to ram, shell (artillery, air strike)

planter to crash, drive in with force, jab (s.o.), hammer (nail)

plastiquer to blow up (with **plastique** explosive)

provoquer le naufrage de to wreck (ship), shipwreck

pulvériser to pulverize (rock, opponent), smash (world record)

ratatiner* to wreck (house), smash to pieces, total (car)

ravager to devastate, ravage (village, countryside), scourge, desolate

se rentrer dedans to crash into one another

rompre to break (silence, spell, dish), shatter, burst, break off (communication)

ruiner to shatter, ruin (reputation), destroy (crops, economy)

smasher to smash (tennis ball)

souffler to destroy (bomb, explosion)

souffleter to box, slap, swipe a blow (boxer)

se tamponner to run into, collide (vehicles)

taper* to hit, slap, smack (face), beat (rug)

tomber en panne to break down (car), fail (machine, motor)

tomber en rade* to break down, run out of gas (car)

voler en éclats to shatter (glass, cup)

Quelle malchance! Le chauffeur ivre a brûlé le feu rouge et a °emplafonné* le fourgon de police. Il est dans le pétrin*! What bad luck! The drunk driver ran the red light and smashed into the police wagon. He's really in a stew*!

Un sans-abri est mort; °happé par un train dans des circonstances encore indéterminées. A homeless man is dead; hit by a train under as yet undetermined circumstances.

La chute d'une tuile isolante peut °endommager le bouclier thermique de la navette spatiale. An insulation tile coming loose could damage the space shuttle's heat shield.

L'explosion d'une bombe artisanale a °soufflé les vitres de la caserne de pompiers d'après la porte-parole. The explosion of a homemade bomb blew out the windows of the fire station according to the spokeswoman.

On ne fait pas d'omelette sans °casser des œufs. You can't make an omelette without breaking some eggs.

MEMORY AID

"En-" can mean *to put into*, and the "~tour~" fragment is the same as **tour** *(f)*, or *tower*. Thus, "en-tour~" can mean *to put into a tower*. Picture a fairy-tale king putting the princess into his towered fortress to encircle her in safety and to surround her with impregnable walls.

Other verbs in this family include: to guard, keep, watch over, lock up, insert, encompass, fence in, confine, pen in, safeguard, shut in, cage, imprison, detain, wall in, cordon off, etc.

aller en taule*   to go to jail

assiéger   to besiege, lay siege to (castle), mob (department store), surround (actor)

balustrer   to rail in, surround with railing (balcony, mezzanine)

barricader   to barricade, lock in

border   to border, edge, line (path with flowers, street with trees), tuck in (blanket)

cacher   to hide, conceal, keep secret

cachotter   to conceal, make a mystery of, be secretive (*lit.* **cachot** *(m)*: dungeon)

ceindre   to encircle (perimeter), encompass (area), gird (loins), enclose (garden)

ceinturer   to girdle, surround (village), grab by the waist (person)

cercler   to ring (barrel), encircle (the globe), rim

cerner   to ring, surround, encompass, hem in (enemy), zero in on* (problem)

claquemurer   to coop up,* imprison, shut s.o. away (inmate)

cloîtrer   to immure, shut up in (recluse), enter a convent/monastery (nun, monk)

clore   to close (shutters, door, gate), end (show, debate), enclose (park)

clôturer   to fence in (garden, field)

coffrer*   to throw in jail

confiner   to confine, imprison, incarcerate

conserver   to keep, preserve (fruit), pickle, store (item), conserve, guard with caution

consigner   to confine to barracks (troops), put a deposit on (soda bottle)

défendre (de)   to defend (innocent, rights, helpless), protect, shield from (danger)

désinvestir   to raise the siege of (castle, town)

détenir   to hold (prisoner, suspect), detain (power, authority), confine

écrouer   to imprison, lock up, lock away, incarcerate

encadrer   to surround, frame, bracket (picture, diploma)

encercler   to encircle (garden), circle (word on page), surround (enemy)

enclaver   to enclose, hem in (crowd), isolate (landlocked country)

encoffrer   to shut in, cage, lock in (chest, box) (*lit.* **coffre** *(m)*: chest, safe)

enfermer (dans)   to lock in, shut in, enclose

englober   to encompass (the globe), encircle, include (parts of whole), blanket (area)

enserrer   to enclose, lock up, hem in

entourer de murailles   to wall in (village)

envelopper   to envelop, wrap up, enclose, surround, encircle, shroud, veil, cover

environner   to encompass, surround, enclose

escorter to escort (on a date, with bodyguard), accompany, usher, guide

être bien installé to be ensconced, be securely placed, be settled in (home, position)

être emmené sous escorte to be taken under guard

être sous les verrous to be behind bars (jailed prisoner)

faire surveiller to guard (prisoner), stake out (area), monitor (exam), keep watch

fermer à clef to lock up, lock (door, safe, room)

garder qch/qn sous surveillance to keep s.t./s.o. under guard

grillager to enclose with wire fencing/wire screen/wire mesh

griller to enclose with iron railings

incarcérer to incarcerate, imprison

inclure to enclose (in letter), insert (in mailing), include, leave in, keep in

investir to surround (army), place in control (police)

isoler to isolate, insulate (wire, cold), separate from, seclude, sequester (witness)

isoler par cordon to cordon off (police barrier)

mettre au bloc* to slap in jail*

mettre au trou* to put in the slammer,* throw in jail

mettre en cage to cage, put in a cage (animal)

mettre en garde à vue to place in police custody

mettre en prison to put in prison

mettre sous séquestre to sequester (witness), isolate, impound, confiscate (evidence)

monter la garde auprès de to stand guard over

ourler to hem in, crowd (*lit.* **ourlet** *(m):* hem or hemline of a skirt)

palissader to stockade, fence in, put a fence around, surround with fortifications

se parquer to be placed in an enclosure, be penned in (cattle), be packed in (fish), park (a car)

prémunir to secure beforehand, protect against (hurricane, financial loss)

se prémunir contre to guard against (danger, illness)

préserver to keep safe (loved ones), defend (home, country, liberty)

protéger (contre) to protect (from)

receler to harbor, conceal (secret, treasure, fugitive)

reléguer to shut s.o. up, relegate (to lower status), consign, exile

renfermer to close up, contain (box, carton), enclose, hold, incorporate (parts)

resserrer to pen in, close up (gap), restrain, squeeze (vise), retighten (knot, bolt)

sauvegarder to safeguard (peace), protect (home, money), save (computer data)

serrer to lock up, tighten (knot, belt), keep close together (lines, words), clench (fist)

tenir to hold (water, pose, contents), retain (liquid), contain (box)

veiller sur to watch over, look after (flock, children)

Le célèbre chef-d'œuvre de De Vinci est arrivé au Louvre, °entouré de gardes armés et de chiens bergers allemands. Da Vinci's famous masterpiece arrived at the Louvre, surrounded by armed guards and German shepherds.

Un grillage rouillé °clôture le chantier désaffecté. A rusty wire fence surrounds the empty work site.

Des renforcements nous ont délivrés de l'ennemi qui nous °enserrait. Reinforcements rescued us from the enemy who had us surrounded.

Des ténèbres épaisses l'°environnaient à minuit. Thick darkness enveloped her at midnight.

MEMORY AID

Recall that "**é**" may indicate a missing "*s*," therefore "**é-touffe**" becomes "**s-touffe**," which resembles *stuff*. One can *choke* or *suffocate* if something is *stuffed* into one's mouth. Picture a loud fool being asked to keep quiet and to "Stuff it!" The verbs in this group relate mostly to choking or stifling a person. See also **coincer** (to jam, wedge), page 144.

   Other verbs in this family include: to cram, block, muffle, smother, obstruct, strangle, seal, fill, be quiet, suppress, stifle, hush, silence, gag, stop up, thwart, have a stranglehold on, etc.

MMMMFF!

apaiser   to quiet (crowd), allay (pain), calm (animal)

assourdir   to muffle, silence (noise), make deaf, deafen (by loud noise)

avoir la mainmise sur   to have a stranglehold on (power), have a grip on

bâillonner   to gag, muzzle (enemy, opponent, dog)

barrer   to obstruct, thwart (effort), bar (passage), cordon off/close (crime scene)

bloquer   to block (road, progress), barricade, halt, arrest (motion), hinder, impede

boucher   to stop up, choke, plug, obstruct, fill (crack, hole), cork (bottle), stuff (hole)

bourrer*   to stuff, fill, cram,* pack, wad, tamp (gunpowder charge)

brider   to bridle, restrain, curb, keep in check (wild horse, spending, passions)

bûcher*   to cram* (for school exam)

contrarier   to thwart (efforts, plans), baffle

encombrer   to obstruct (drain, filter), jam (roadway, telephone lines)

encrasser   to clog (machinery), clog up (drain, filter)

endiguer   to hold back (tears, emotion), curb (violence), dam (river)

engorger   to block, obstruct (hose, road), clog (drain), be engorged (liver, vein)

s'engouer   to choke oneself

étrangler   to strangle, choke s.o.

faire barrage à   to block (road), dam (river), bar (traffic)

faire de l'obstruction   to obstruct, block, hinder

faire silence   to hush, keep quiet, keep silent

faire taire   to hush/quiet s.o.

fermer   to close off, shut, close (mouth, door), bar, seal (envelope), turn off (light)

feutrer   to muffle, deaden (sound), mat (wool)

garrotter   to strangle (by executioner), tie down (arms), cut or bind (wings), pinion

juguler   to suppress, stop (illness, desire, inflation, revolt)

obstruer   to obstruct, block (path, artery)

obturer   to block, close (gap), fill (tooth), seal (crack)

plomber   to seal, fill (tooth)

réduire au silence   to silence (s.o.)

refouler   to choke back (tears), turn back (crowd, attack)

suffoquer   to suffocate, stifle, choke (victim, smoke, tears)

supprimer   to suppress (freedom, evidence, emotion)

se taire   to keep quiet, maintain silence, be silent, hush up, shut up

tamponner   to plug, stop up (leak, blood flow), dab (wound, tears)

tranquilliser   to quiet (storm), tranquilize (animal, person)

traverser   to thwart (progress), oppose, challenge (opposition)

Quelle chaleur accablante! On °étouffe cet été! What oppressive heat!
We're suffocating this summer!

Ils se sentaient °étouffés dans leur petit bouge.* They felt their tiny hovel
to be stifling.

Elle pouvait à peine parler, sa voix °étranglée par l'émotion. She could
barely speak, her voice choked with emotion.

**Le patron de la braderie va embaucher davantage de vendeurs afin d'°apaiser la
grogne* de ses clients.** The discount store owner plans to hire more sales personnel
in order to alleviate his customers' discontent.

MEMORY AID

Subtracting the letters "**l**" and "**u**" from **flinguer** leaves *finger*. Picture the finger of a hit man on the trigger of a pistol as he guns down a rival gangster.

Other verbs in this family relate to: killing, being killed, and dying. Included in this verb family are: to perish, bump off, commit suicide, kick the bucket, croak, die, wound, hunt, kill off, drop dead, shoot down, execute, assassinate, mortally wound, etc.

abattre   to shoot, shoot down (enemy), slaughter (animal)

abréger les souffrances   to put an end to suffering (e.g., euthanasia)

agoniser   to be at the point of death, be dying, be in death throes

aller à la chasse   to go on a hunt (for wild game)

appuyer sur la gâchette   to pull the trigger of a gun

assassiner   to assassinate, kill

blesser à mort   to mortally wound

blesser par balle   to wound with a bullet

butter*   to kill

canarder*   to take potshots at*

chasser   to hunt, go hunting (game), go shooting

clamser*   to croak,* die

claquer*   to kick the bucket*

se crever*   to kill oneself

décéder   to die, pass away

décharger   to discharge a firearm, empty a gun (into the crowd)

décocher   to shoot (arrow), fire, let fly (arrow), deliver (blow)

démolir   to shoot down (theory, idea, argument)

disparaître   to become extinct (dinosaurs, endangered species), disappear, vanish

écraser   to murder, kill off

éliminer   to kill off, liquidate (debt, enemy)

être atteindre d'une balle   to be hit with a bullet

être cuit*   to be done for,* have had it* (e.g., "he's had it for tonight!")

être dans l'état de mort cérébrale   to be brain-dead

être dans un coma dépassé   to be brain-dead

être fusillé   to be shot by firing squad

être mort par surdose   to be killed by an overdose (drugs)

exécuter   to execute (mob rival, condemned criminal)

faire feu sur   to fire on, shoot at

faire périr   to kill

se faire rectifier*   to be (get oneself) bumped off*

fusiller   to shoot, gun down, execute by firing squad

garrotter   to strangle s.o. to death

immoler   to kill as a sacrifice (lamb), slay, sacrifice

lâcher la rampe*   to kick the bucket*

lancer à   to shoot (rocket, missile)

lapider   to stone to death

liquider*   to kill, kill off (mob rival)

massacrer   to massacre, butcher

mettre à mort   to put to death

monter en flèche   to shoot up (rocket)

mourir   to die, pass away, expire, succumb

mourir de vieillesse   to die of old age

mourir un héros   to die a hero's death

occire   to slay, kill (used only as infinitive, **occire**, or past participle, **occis**)

ôter la vie de qn   to take s.o.'s life

se passer   to die, pass away (person, custom), elapse (time limit)

périr   to die, perish, decay, decease, pass away

prédécéder   to predecease, die before s.o.

se putréfier   to decompose, rot

ratiboiser*   to bump off* (s.o.), do in* (s.o.), kill

y rester*   to die

se shooter*   to shoot up* (drugs)

sonner l'hallali*   to go in for the kill*

succomber   to die, succumb (to terminal illness)

supplicier   to execute, put to death

se supprimer   to take one's own life, commit suicide

tirer au jugé   to fire blindly

tirer sur qn   to shoot at s.o., fire a gun at s.o.

tirer un coup de balle   to shoot (bullets)

tomber raide mort   to drop dead

trucider*   to bump off,* kill

tuer   to kill, slay, gun down, murder, do in (s.o.)

zigouiller*   to kill s.o., do s.o. in*

Au cours d'un règlement de comptes, le tueur à gages a °flingué le chef du gang rival. During a "settlement of accounts," the hit man gunned down the rival mob boss.

Le survivant n'est pas °décédé, mais son état de santé nécessite un traitement dans l'unité de soins intensifs. The survivor didn't die, but his condition requires treatment in the intensive care unit.

Des insurgés ont °tiré plusieurs obus de mortier sur l'ambassade étrangère. Insurgents fired several mortar shells at the foreign embassy.

Tristement, dans sa ville, au moins trente enfants par an °meurent aux mains de leurs parents ou tuteurs. Sadly, in her city, at least thirty children die annually at the hands of their parents or guardians.

Quiconque se sert de l'épée °périra par l'épée. He who lives by the sword dies by the sword.

Note: The use of **haïr** is mostly confined to literature. In everyday speech, **détester** is more commonly used to express *hatred* or *a strong dislike*.

MEMORY AID

Haïr is spelled similarly to the English word *hair*. Picture a woman in a beauty salon who has just had her hair done by a novice stylist. She is appalled at the results and so detests or hates her hair.

Other verbs in this family include: to dislike, scorn, disdain, dread, disavow, avoid, reject, deplore, spurn, rebuff, revile, snub, hold a grudge against, disapprove, embitter, distrust, etc.

---

abhorrer   to abhor, hate, loathe
abominer   to detest, abominate, hate
aigrir   to embitter (person), make bitter, make sour (personality, relationship)
aimer (ne pas)   to dislike
avoir de la rancœur contre qn   to feel resentment toward s.o.
avoir de l'animosité contre   to feel animosity toward
avoir du dégoût pour   to dislike, be disgusted by
cracher son venin*   to spit out one's venom*
craindre   to dislike, dread (person, situation)
dédaigner   to despise, disdain, look down on (person), treat with contempt
déplorer   to hate, deplore, bemoan (fate), lament (loss)
désapprouver   to disapprove (action, conduct)
désavouer   to disown (child), disavow (involvement, knowledge of)
détester   to hate, loathe, detest
être en pétard*   to be raging mad
être hostile à   to be hostile toward
éviter   to avoid, shun, stay clear of, dodge, circumvent (area)
exécrer   to loathe, abhor (person, thought)
faire à contrecœur   to be loath to do

fuir   to shun, avoid, flee from (temptation, place), shrink from (danger)
garder rancune à qn   to hold a grudge against s.o.
haïr qn comme la peste*   to hate s.o. like the plague*
s'indigner (de)   to get indignant (about)
mécontenter   to displease, disgruntle, dissatisfy
se méfier de   to distrust, mistrust
mépriser   to despise (person), scorn (advice, danger)
narguer   to scorn (danger, threat), disdain, scoff at (person)
nier   to disown, deny (guilt, request), negate
rabrouer*   to snub, treat with scorn or contempt, dismiss, rebuke
rebuter   to rebuff, repulse, snub, rebuke (offer, the devil)
rejeter   to reject (person, object, results)
rembarrer*   to snub, tell s.o. off
repousser   to spurn (amorous advances), reject, rebuff, decline (invitation)
tempêter   to rage (storm, temper), storm (in temper tantrum), rant and rave
vilipender   to revile, vilify, malign, lambaste, defame, denigrate
en vouloir à qn   to bear a grudge against s.o.

Il °haïssait tellement son concurrent qu'il a lancé une campagne de dénigrement. He hated his opponent so much that he launched a hate campaign.

L'ambassadrice °déplore que des étrangers aient une opinion très négative de son pays. The lady ambassador hates the fact that foreigners have a negative opinion of her country.

Marie s'excuse auprès de toi. Ne lui °garde pas rancune. Pardonne-lui. Mary apologizes to you. Don't hold a grudge against her. Forgive her.

Le ponte* °rabroua* le petit galopin* en lui refusant l'aumône. The bigwig* treated the little street urchin with contempt, refusing him a handout.

MEMORY AID

The "**mat~**" fragment is spelled the same as the English word *mat*, meaning *a floor pad used to protect athletes or wrestlers from injury*. Picture a bully wrestler subduing and suppressing his puny opponent by smashing him into the mat. Whereas the verbs included in the **affronter** family (page 98) relate to the initial confrontation with an enemy/opponent, the verbs in the **mater** family carry on from there to include the various nuances of physical violence resulting from a quarrel. See also **terrasser** (to bring down, overcome, beat), page 132.

Other verbs in this family include: to ransack, violate, pillage, break, lay waste to, plunder, ravage, ravish, beat up, crush, knock out, maul, create havoc, squash, flatten, defeat, bash, etc.

abolir to abolish (institution, usage, slavery)

accabler to crush, overwhelm (heat, fatigue, grief), overburden (work)

amocher* to bash up* (s.o., object), mess up*

anéantir to annihilate, destroy, crush (opposition, grief)

aplanir to flatten, make flat (surface, terrain), iron out (differences), smooth over

asséner une sacrée raclée* to beat the crap* out of s.o.

assommer to knock s.o. out, stun, crush

assujettir to subdue, subjugate, subordinate (people, country, clause)

bousculer to jostle, shake up, push, knock over (vase, object)

broyer to crush (limb), grind (seeds, grain, food)

concasser to crush (rock), concuss (skull), pound

dauber* to mock, make fun of, wreck, mess up*, beat (with stick) (*lit.* **dáraba:** to beat [Arabic])

déboîter to dislocate (joint)

décimer to decimate, kill ¹⁄₁₀ᵗʰ of (army), kill many

déferler to break (waves), sweep through (enemy horde, riots)

déjouer (un complot) to foil (a plot)

démantibuler* to break (into pieces), dislocate (joint), break up, break apart

démembrer to dismember (limbs), break up (into pieces), carve up (turkey, empire)

démettre to dislocate, put out of joint (shoulder, knee)

déplumer to despoil (crops, forest)

désoler to devastate, lay waste to (army, fire, plague), afflict, distress

desservir to harm (person, cause), do disservice to (interests)

détruire to destroy, ruin, blast, demolish

dévaster to devastate, lay waste to (crops, village)

disloquer to dislocate (joint), dismantle (organization, empire)

écrabouiller* to crush, smash, squash (bug, soda can)

écraser to crush, squash, flatten, stomp on (cigarette), grind down (foe), thrash (foe)

éliminer to eliminate, liquidate (stock, debt), decimate (enemy)

enfreindre to break (law, promise), violate (law, probation, contract, curfew)

enlever to remove (nuisance, stain, hope), kidnap

enlever de force to rape, commit rape, violate

estourbir* to stun, render senseless, knock out, crush

éteindre to extinguish (fire), put out (cigarette, light), shut down (computer), douse

s'étriper* to make mincemeat of one another, tear each other to pieces

faire du grabuge* to create havoc, create a ruckus, stir up trouble, wreak havoc

faire du tort à to cause s.o. harm

faire échouer to defeat (plans, efforts)

faire souffrir (qn) to cause to suffer, hurt (s.o.), cause pain, inflict suffering

faire subir des pertes à l'ennemi to inflict losses on the enemy

faire un maul* to maul, handle roughly, beat, tear (bear attack)

flanquer une taloche à qn* to slap s.o., cuff s.o., box (s.o.'s ears)

flanquer une torgnole à qn* to wallop s.o.

fouler to tread, trample down (crops), stampede, press (grapes), crush (underfoot)

fracasser to shatter, break into pieces, wreck

fracturer to fracture, break (bone, safe, lock, door)

frapper to hit, bash, strike, belt, knock, buffet, smite, bring down (opponent)

froisser to hurt, crush (ego), crumple (paper), damage, dent

juguler to repress (desire, appetite), curb (disease), halt (inflation)

limer to file down (metal, wood), file (nails)

matraquer to club, beat s.o. up with clubs

mettre à feu et à sang to sack, pillage, loot (village)

mettre à sac to sack, ransack, pillage

nuire à to harm, injure, hurt (person, reputation, health)

percuter to strike (vehicle), percuss, impact (missile, rocket)

piétiner to tread or trample underfoot

piler to pound, crush (ice, grain), shell, bombard (artillery), pulverize

piller to pillage, plunder, ransack (village), pilfer, loot

pilonner to ram, pound (rocket, mortar), shell (artillery)

pulper to make into pulp (fruit, wood shavings)

pulvériser to pulverize, annihilate (opponent), smash to powder (rock)

râper to grind, grate (cheese, carrot), file down (tool), rasp (wood)

rapiner to pillage, plunder, forcibly seize (property)

ravager to ravage, devastate (land, opponent)

ravir to carry off (victims), ravish (captives), rape

réduire en bouillie* to beat to a pulp*

réduire qn à l'impuissance to render s.o. powerless

réduire qn en marmelade* to reduce s.o. to pulp*

refréner to bridle (passions), restrain, control, curb (desire, appetite)

reprendre le dessus to regain the upper hand

réprimer to subdue, repress (emotion, uprising), suppress (tears, anger)

restreindre to restrict, restrain, curtail, keep under control, hold back (horse, anger)

rétamer* to knock out, wipe out,* demolish, make drunk

retrancher to curtail (visit, payment, access to), cut short (trip)

rompre to break (silence, promise), break off (contact), sever (alliance)

rosser* to thrash, beat up, hammer (s.o.), lambaste (with a cane)

rouer de coups to beat unmercifully

saccager to wreck, destroy (countryside), devastate, pillage (village)

se serrer   to squash, scrimp (belt), squeeze in (tight seat), clench (handshake)

soumettre   to put down (revolt), subdue (enemy), subject to (law, master)

spolier   to despoil, plunder, ravage, deprive of (possessions)

supprimer   to suppress, delete (word), abolish (law), eliminate (poverty)

tabasser*   to beat up, clobber,* hit

talocher*   to cuff,* drub,* box (s.o.'s ears)

vaincre   to defeat, vanquish, come out on top

se viander*   to smash oneself up*

violer   to transgress, violate, rape, infringe

Les gendarmes ont °maté l'émeute qui avait éclaté au stade. The police put down the riot that had broken out at the stadium.

Hou!* Cet enfoiré* a °assommé notre attaquant de soutien. Coup franc! Boo! That bastard hit our forward over the head. Free kick!

Le soldat avoue que sa principale préoccupation est de rester en vie plutôt que de °vaincre l'ennemi. The soldier confesses that his main concern is to stay alive rather than to defeat the enemy.

Dû au syndrome de stress post-traumatique, le patient était °anéanti, choqué et paralysé émotionnellement. Owing to post-traumatic stress syndrome, the patient was crushed, shocked, and emotionally paralyzed.

maudire to curse

MEMORY AID

"**Mau~**" is similar to **maux**, the plural form of **mal**, meaning *evil, ill, misfortune*; **dire** is *to say* or *speak*. Thus, **maudire** is *to speak evil* or *curse*. Picture a village shaman performing an incantation and pronouncing or saying a curse intended for a rival tribe. Some of the verbs in this category deal with the world of spirits, the occult, and the attempt to rid oneself of evil influences.

Other verbs in this family include: to vilify, bewitch, jinx, profane, cast a spell, bedevil, damn, libel, slander, swear, hex, defame, sin, transgress, conjure up, exorcize, haunt, etc.

affliger   to vex, trouble, ail, afflict (illness), pain, distress

agonir   to insult grossly, hurl insults (at s.o.)

anathématiser   to anathematize, pronounce a curse

avoir la guigne*   to be jinxed*

baptiser   to baptize (immerse in water), christen, anoint

blasphémer   to blaspheme, speak in vain

calomnier   to libel, slander (s.o.'s reputation)

charger de malédictions   to curse, put a curse on

commettre un péché   to sin, commit a sin

communier   to receive communion (church), receive the sacrament (bread and wine)

conjurer   to conjure up, to exorcize, ward off (demons, spirits)

croire aux esprits   to believe in ghosts

damner   to damn, condemn to everlasting punishment, curse, swear at, ruin, doom

déblatérer   to rail against, utter violent abuse

dégrader   to degrade (morals), vilify (person), damage (reputation)

déguignonner   to lift a curse from, exorcize, cast out spirits

désenvoûter   to undo a curse or spell, exorcize (demon), cast out spirits

diaboliser   to demonize, turn into a demon, possess by a demon

diffamer   to vilify, defame

dire des jurons   to swear, curse

dire des méchancetés   to say nasty things

dire des saletés   to use filthy language

ensorceler   to bewitch, hex, jinx

entrer en transe   to go into a trance/hypnotic state

envoûter   to bewitch, curse, hex

être possédé   to be possessed (spirits)

exorciser   to exorcize, cast out spirits

faire tourner les tables   to hold spiritual séances, contact the dead

faire une imprécation   to curse (s.o.), place a curse on (s.o.)

fulminer   to send forth maledictions or religious decrees, inveigh against

hanter   to haunt (ghost, memories)

huer   to boo (s.o.), hoot (owl)

jeter l'anathème sur   to curse s.o., put a curse/hex on s.o.

jeter un sort (sur, à)   to cast a spell on, curse, jinx

lanciner   to haunt (memories, song), nag (doubt, pain)

mal faire   to do evil

maugréer   to curse, swear, fume, grouse

médire   to speak ill of, slander, badmouth (s.o. or s.t.)

mettre à l'index   to blacklist, boycott

obséder   to haunt, bedevil, obsess about (thought, lust)

se parer de   to ward off (evil)

pâtir de   to be bedeviled by, suffer (because of, on account of)

pécher   to sin, transgress, offend

pester contre qn   to curse s.o., rail at s.o., swear at s.o.

porter la guigne à qn*   to jinx s.o.* (*lit.* guigne *(f)*: bad luck)

prier   to pray to (God, idols)

profaner   to defile (religion), profane (the sacred), debase, desecrate (idols, church)

psalmodier   to chant (i.e., musical chant, Gregorian chant)

se répandre en injures   to pour out insults

sacrer   to curse, swear

sacrifier (à)   to sacrifice (to) (pagan deity)

scander   to chant (slogan, curse)

supplier   to pray, supplicate (God), beg for (mercy, forgiveness, favor)

taxer   to call s.o. something (a name), accuse s.o.

 °**Maudit soit le jour où je me suis décidé de m'associer avec vous!** Cursed be the day that I decided to go into partnership with you!

L'éventualité d'un groupe terroriste en possession d'une arme nucléaire °**hante les dirigeants mondiaux.** The possibility of a terrorist group possessing a nuclear weapon haunts the world leaders.

Le forban va °**baptiser son nouveau navire "La Sorcière de la Mer".** The pirate plans to christen his new ship "The Sea Witch."

C'est cette église que sa famille fréquente pour °**communier tous les dimanches.** This is the church her family attends to partake of the sacrament each Sunday.

rattraper to catch, recapture, make up for

MEMORY AID

The "**rattrap~**" fragment looks and sounds just like *rattrap* in English. Picture a baited rattrap set to catch a pesky rodent.

Other verbs in this family include: to track down, hunt down, regain, ensnare, trap, booby-trap, arrest, seize, grab, harness, yoke, apprehend, win back, grip, catch, redress, recoup, etc.

accoster to accost, capture, hook, capture (person), berth (ship)

alpaguer* to collar s.o.,* catch s.o., snag* (thief)

appréhender to apprehend, catch, arrest

arrêter to capture, arrest, detain, bring to a halt, stop

atteler to harness (mule), yoke (ox), hitch up (horse), tether

attraper to catch (ball), capture (animal, thief), seize, grab (arm)

capter to catch, gain, capture (attention), harness (energy), get (TV reception)

capturer to catch, capture (thief, animal)

choper* to catch, nab (crook), catch (flu)

colleter* to seize by the neck, to collar s.o.

s'emparer de to seize, grab, snatch, get ahold of, secure, take possession of

empoigner to grab (person, object), seize, grasp, collar (s.o.)

épingler to pin (butterfly in a collection, dress hem, brooch pin, blame on s.o.)

faire une belle pêche to make a good catch (fish)

se faire pincer to get caught (in the act), be nabbed

intercepter to intercept (ball, radio signal), seize (drug shipment)

mettre en cage to cage, put in a cage (animal)

se mettre au courant to catch up with (news, gossip)

piéger to trap, set a booby trap, set a trap

pincer to grip, seize, hold, catch (thief), pinch (nose), bite (cold wind)

poursuivre to pursue, hunt (wild game, escaped convict)

prendre to capture, catch, seize, take hold of, clutch, claim, pick up

prendre au piège to ensnare, trap, catch (in a trap), seize

se prendre to be taken (seriously), be caught (in a trap, by police)

préserver to preserve, safeguard (rights, job)

ratteindre to retake (lead in race), catch again (front runner), take over (first place)

se réconcilier to make up with, reconcile (loose ends), get back together (lovers)

reconquérir to regain, win back (lead), regain (dignity), recover (territory)

recouvrer to regain, recover (losses), recuperate (health), recoup (expenses)

récupérer to recover (health), recoup (lost time, wages), salvage, reclaim (title)

se redresser to redress (wrongs), turn around, put right, right itself (boat)

regagner to win back, regain (ground, upper hand, lead)

rejoindre to get back to, catch up with, return to, rejoin (parts), link up (chain, s.o.)

se remettre to recoup, recover, be on the mend (illness, injury), get over (flu)

remonter to come back, return (to surface, to origin), climb back, perk up, rise again

repiquer* to catch again, catch up with (police), rerecord (song), record (song copy)

reprendre to recapture, catch again

ressaisir to seize again, take again, regain (lead, self-control, momentum)

se rétablir to recover, restore (economy, calm, peace), regain (balance)

retenir to get hold of again, restrain (person)

retrouver to regain (status), find again (employment), rediscover (love), meet (date)

revenir sur to catch up with, go back over (problem, decision)

saisir to catch, seize (s.o. or s.t., opportunity), grasp (concept), latch on to (idea)

saisir l'occasion to seize the opportunity

sauver to save (from danger), salvage (working parts)

séduire to ensnare, allure, lure (into trap), seduce, captivate (with charm)

surprendre to be caught (in rain, high tide)

tendre un piège à qn to set a trap for s.o.

tomber dans un traquenard to fall into a trap (*lit.* **traquenard** *(m)*: trap)

traquer to track down (news lead), hunt down (animal, crook), hound (paparazzi)

Avec un nouveau moteur, le pilote du Grand Prix a °rattrapé son retard et a regagné la tête de la course. With a new engine, the Grand Prix driver made up his lost time to regain his lead in the race.

Des autorités proposent d'°arrêter le parrain sous le prétexte de proxénétisme. Authorities intend to arrest the godfather for soliciting prostitution.

L'ouragan menace de frapper la ville à moins qu'il ne °remonte en direction de la mer. The hurricane threatens to strike the town unless it turns back toward the sea.

Notre armée °s'est emparée du siège de l'ennemi situé à la lisière de la forêt. Our army gained possession of the enemy headquarters located at the forest's edge.

remporter to win, get, carry off (prize, victory)

MEMORY AID

"Re-" means *again* or *repeatedly*, and **emporter** means *to carry away* or *take away*. Thus, "**re-emporter**" can be thought of as *carrying away* something or *winning again*. Picture a victorious soccer team rejoicing as they carry away the championship trophy that they've won again. Also, they carry off their team captain on their shoulders after this repeat victory. The verbs in this category relate to both nuances of **remporter**. See also **primer** (to prevail, dominate), page 16.

Other verbs in this family include: to win back, win over, rally, score a goal, triumph, prevail over, glory in, drub, take away, convey, lead away, remove, overcome, etc.

battre   to beat, vanquish, defeat, win (game), demolish, pound, strike

conquérir   to conquer, win over (opponent, audience), win

défaire   to defeat (competition, rival power, hypothesis)

déménager   to move (house), physically move (furniture, household items)

éloigner   to remove, take away, put off (meeting), go away (fear), pass (danger)

emmener   to convey, lead away, invite along, drop off (s.o.), give s.o. a lift, carry

empocher   to win, carry off (prize)

emporter   to carry away (furniture, wounded), remove, storm (castle), take by force

l'emporter sur   to overcome, prevail over (technique, idea), get the upper hand

enlever   to take off, carry off (object, money, victory), kidnap

entraîner   to drag or carry away, win over (with enthusiasm, with logic)

s'estomper   to fade away (colors, memories)

être victorieux   to be victorious

étriller*   to drub,* beat, pound, beat emphatically (*lit.* **étrille** *(f)*: horse currycomb)

faire moche*   to score a bull's-eye*

foutre une taule*   to thrash, punish, beat up (in sports competition)

gagner   to win (game, sports event, title, prize, recognition)

gagner au loto   to win the lottery

gagner du terrain   to gain ground (in race), make progress

se glorifier   to boast, glory in, revel in (glory, victory)

marquer un but   to score a goal (soccer)

mener   to take, conduct (meeting), guide (tour), lead (cause), head (organization)

s'octroyer   to win, claim (medal, award)

ôter   to remove (item), take away (s.o.'s life), take off (shirt), to subtract (math equation)

porter   to carry (title, badge of honor), bring to completion

prédominer   to prevail over, predominate, prevail (opinion, impression, argument)

prévaloir   to prevail, win (game, contest)

rallier   to rally, win over, win (support, voting rights)

reconquérir   to regain (crown, dignity), reconquer (country), win back (title)

regagner   to win back, regain (lead, upper hand), return to (prior status)

régner   to prevail (peace, belief), reign (king/queen), exercise dominion over (country)

rosser*   to trounce, thrash, beat (with cane), hammer out (victory)

supplanter   to supersede (new method, new technology), override (old method)

surmonter   to overcome, surpass (hurdle, crisis), weather (storm), master, prevail

survivre à   to outlast, live through (trials, hard times), survive, outlive (person, idea)

toucher   to win (card game, lottery)

transporter   to convey (idea), move (cargo), uplift (emotion), transport (cargo)

triompher   to triumph, prevail (reason, peace), rejoice, gloat (over victory), exult

se vanter   to boast, pride oneself, brag, exult

Aujourd'hui, en football, l'équipe française a °remporté la victoire, 2 à 0, contre l'équipe hollandaise aux quarts de finale de la Coupe Mondiale. Today, in soccer, the French team gained a victory, 2 to 0, against the Dutch team in the quarterfinals of the World Cup.

Le mouvement contre la hausse du taux de chômage °gagne du terrain parmi des syndicalistes. The movement opposing the increasing unemployment rate is gaining ground among union members.

Notre candidat est le premier à °remporter trois élections législatives d'affilée. Our candidate is the first to win three consecutive elections.

Le conquérant °ôta le joug d'oppression des épaules des paysans. The conqueror lifted the yoke of oppression from the shoulders of the peasants.

Il faut °battre le fer pendant qu'il est chaud. Strike while the iron is hot.

repousser to push back, repulse

acculer to bring to a stop, drive into a corner, bring to bay, drive to brink (of ruin)

ajourner to put off, adjourn (meeting, process), postpone, defer

aliéner to alienate (newcomer), estrange (spouse), dissociate from (s.o.)

aller à rebours to go backwards, go against the grain

bannir to banish (s.o., word, subject), expel (diplomat), dismiss, prohibit (usage)

barrer to thwart, obstruct (passage), barricade (road), close off (to public access)

blâmer to reprove, reproach, reprimand

bouder to snub, turn one's nose up at, sulk, refuse to talk

censurer to censure, criticize, rebuke formally, censor

cesser to stop, break off (contact, relations), discontinue, trail off (remarks), cease

chasser to drive away (evil spirit), dispel (rumor), chase away, dismiss (idea), evict

combattre to repel (enemy, odor), fight against, contend for (legal stand), oppose

contrarier to thwart (amorous advances), counteract (chemical reaction), check

contrecarrer to thwart (plans, efforts)

débusquer to drive out (person, animal)

décaler to put back (furniture to prior location), set back (clock, time of departure)

dédaigner to disdain, spurn (s.o.'s advances), turn down (reward), ignore (injury)

désamorcer to defuse (bomb, situation), forestall (event, inevitable), postpone

différer to procrastinate, postpone, put off (engagement, deadline)

écarter qn du coude to elbow s.o. aside

éconduire to dismiss (visitor), show s.o. out, reject (suitor), turn away (solicitation)

faire reculer to push back (horse), force back (foe), drive back (wilderness)

faire renvoyer to expel (student), dismiss (employee), exile, send back (letter)

faire sortir qn to drive s.o. out, show s.o. out the door

frustrer to foil, frustrate (plans, enemy attack)

inverser to reverse (direction), invert (object)

limoger to dismiss (employee)

louper* to flunk, fail (opportunity, exam)

mépriser to spurn (advice, help), disdain, scorn

mettre en retard to delay, set back (timetable), make late, make overdue, put behind

mettre la holà à qch* to put a stop to s.t. (inappropriate behavior)

mettre qn à la porte to kick s.o. out

ostraciser to ostracize (newcomer), shun, give cold shoulder to, exclude (newcomer)

parasiter to get in the way of (person, obstacle)

passer à la trappe* to be given a push* (e.g., overboard)

pousser to push (to deliver baby), heave, shove (object, stalled car)

rebrousser chemin to turn back (direction), retrace one's steps

rebuter to repulse, rebuff, snub, rebuke, send away, reject (person, offer)

récalcitrer to be refractory, resist, reject, be recalcitrant, be unyielding

réfléchir to throw back, reflect (sound, light), repel

refouler to hold back, force back (crowd), drive back, repress, expel, flow back

rejeter to push back, reject, throw back (fish into pond, object)

relancer to throw back (ball)

rembarrer* to snub, repulse, give cold shoulder to* (s.o.), send s.o. packing

remettre to postpone (date, meeting), put off (engagement, decision)

reporter to postpone, put off (deadline, engagement), adjourn (meeting)

reprendre to reprove, correct (error, student), use again (idea, tool)

réprimander to rebuke, reprimand

retarder to set back (clock), delay, retard, be slow

retenir to hold back (crowd, mudslide), hold (breath)

surseoir à to postpone, stay (judgment, execution), defer (deliberation) (*lit.* **sursis** *(m)*: legal reprieve or suspended sentence)

suspendre to suspend (action), postpone, break off (talks), adjourn (meeting)

 À la plage, son pied a heurté quelque chose dans le sable—un petit rocher. Elle l'a °repoussé du pied. At the beach, her foot struck something in the sand—a small rock. She kicked it out of the way.

Après s'être approvisionné, le navire °reprit la mer. After stocking up with provisions, the ship headed back to sea.

Soupçonné d'avoir soutenu des groupes liés au terrorisme, il a été °refoulé à la frontière. Suspected of having supported groups linked to terrorism, he was turned away at the border.

La police va °bannir toute circulation au centre-ville à partir de 0800 h en prévision du grand défilé syndical. The police are going to ban all downtown traffic beginning at 8:00 A.M. in light of the expected large union parade.

terrasser to bring down, overcome, strike down

abaisser to abase, to bring low, lower (volume), pull down (lever), put down (siege)

abandonner to surrender (army, weapon, rights, power)

abattre to strike down (enemy), kill, shoot down (plane), put down (sick animal)

abolir to abolish (segregation, slavery)

aborder to land, reach land (ship)

atterrir to land (airplane), touch down (space shuttle orbiter)

battre to beat, pound, pummel, buffet, flail, strike, smash, batter

céder to give up, yield, surrender, cede (control, right of way, battlefield)

couper to cut down (enemy, tree), hew (wood), crop (hair), slash (prices)

crouler to collapse (building), make collapse (in ruin), fall down (rock pile)

se déchirer to tear one another to pieces (enemies), be torn (shirt), burst (sack)

dégommer* to knock down (bowling pin), zap,* hit, down (plane), unseat (rival)

délabrer to shatter (house, equipment), ruin, tear to pieces (clothing)

se déliter to disintegrate, crumble (values), fall apart (government, structure)

démobiliser to demobilize (military)

démonter to dismantle (machine), take apart (gun, clock), remove (tire, shutter)

démunir to disarm, strip of ammunition, leave unarmed

dénuder to strip (leaves, clothes, power, title), leave destitute, lay bare

désactiver to deactivate, disable (bomb, apparatus, computer)

désarmer to disarm (enemy, bomb, s.o. with smile/charm), uncock (gun trigger)

désassembler to dismantle, disassemble, take to pieces

désemparer to cripple or disable (ship)

dévorer to destroy (plague, epidemic), devour (locusts: crops)

écloper to disable, lame, make lame, handicap, cripple

s'écrouler to collapse, fall down, cave in, demolish, devastate, be overcome (heat)

envoyer qn au tapis* to floor s.o.,* knock s.o. to the floor

estropier to cripple, maim, handicap, make lame

être débordé to be overcome, overwhelmed, be overrun (borders), overflow (river, pot)

être en réanimation to be in intensive care (hospital)

être en rééducation to undergo physical rehabilitation

être la proie de to fall prey/victim to

être sinistré to be stricken (ill), be the victim of (disaster), be blighted by (pollution)

faire chuter qn to bring s.o. down, knock down s.o., cut down s.o.

faire naufrage to collapse, founder, shipwreck (boat, business), be shipwrecked

faire subir une défaite à l'ennemi to inflict defeat on the enemy

faire tomber to knock down, strike down, knock over, bring down (price, regime)

faire un tacle to tackle s.o., make a tackle (soccer, football)

faire une culbute to do a somersault

faucher to flatten, knock down, cut down (enemy, grass)

flanquer qn/qch par terre* to throw s.o./s.t. to the ground

foudroyer to strike down (illness, gunshot), blast (lightning)

gauler to beat trees, knock down with a pole (fruit)

humilier to humiliate, humble, abase

se livrer (à) to surrender, give up (to) (police, authorities)

mordre la poussière* to bite the dust,* be defeated, be taken down (by opponent)

paralyser to paralyze, lame, palsy, cripple, hamstring, render immobile

planter to crash (computer), dump (work), drive in (stake), hammer (nail)

prendre un gadin* to fall flat on one's face*

rabattre to beat down, cut down, bring down, knock down again, shut (lid, cover)

ramasser* to fall over, take a beating

ravaler to abase, lower (dignity, moral standards)

rebaisser to humiliate, humble, fall again (temperature, stock prices)

recaler to fail/flunk s.o. (exam)

se réceptionner to land (from a fall), bring down (inflation, interest rate)

réduire to cut down, reduce (price, weight), pare down, scale down, cut back (usage)

rendre boiteux to lame, cripple, render s.o. lame

se rendre à to surrender to (enemy, police, passions)

résorber to bring down, reduce (inflation, stock price)

ruiner to ruin (economy, reputation), destroy (crops), cause ruin

saper to undermine (enemy castle wall, morale)

sonner* to knock out, stagger, ring s.o.'s bell*

tackler to tackle (football, soccer)

tomber to fall (snow, rain, scaffolding, wall, stock prices)

tomber à la renverse to fall flat on one's back

Le captif était °terrassé à cause des sévices corporels et de la douleur accablante. The captive was overwhelmed by the physical abuse and crippling pain.

Le cascadeur °s'est réceptionné sur un grand matelas pneumatique. The stuntman landed on a big air mattress.

Utilisant son manche à balai, l'amateur des jeux en lignes °dégomma* des cibles ennemies sur l'écran. Using his joystick, the online gaming enthusiast zapped enemy targets on the screen.

L'éléphant déchaîné fut °abattu de vingt tirs de fusil. The rampaging elephant was brought down by twenty rifle shots.

transpercer to pierce through, run through

affûter to sharpen, grind (knife, ax)

crever to split, burst, rend, tear, puncture (tire), poke out (eye), pierce (eardrum)

cribler (**de**) to riddle (with wounds), pierce all over, bombard

darder to spear, dart, hurl, beam (sun's rays)

déchirer to rip open (sack), tear apart, rend (fabric), split open, rip (to pieces)

défoncer to stave in, tap (cask, barrel), plough deeply (farm)

donner un coup de lancette to lance, spear with a lance

driller to drill, bore a hole through

éborgner to poke out s.o.'s eye (*lit.* **borgne**: blind in one eye)

embrocher to skewer (shish kebob), put on a spit (pig)

empaler to impale, pierce with a sharp stake, put on a spit

encastrer dans to embed into (slot), build in (appliance), fit (parts), recess (switch)

encorner to gore, toss (mad bull)

enfiler to pierce, pass through, thread (needle), string (beads), screw* (sexual)

enfoncer to drive in, jab (dagger, stake), stick in (pin, thumbtack)

enfouir to bury (treasure), insert, plough, plant (pole, stake)

enfourcher to pierce with a pitchfork

engager to insert (key)

être le feu de lance de to spearhead (attack, plan)

faire une piqûre à qn to give s.o. a shot or injection

ferrer to nail (shoe)

forer to drill (wood, hole, for oil), bore (tunnel, well)

harponner to spear (fish), harpoon

injecter to inject (with syringe), shoot up/mainline* (heroin), perfuse

inoculer to inoculate, give an injection to

introduire to put in, bring in, insert (key)

jouter to joust (knight), tilt (with lance)

larder to run through, pierce, insert bacon or fat into lean meat

mettre une sonde à qn to put a catheter in s.o. (bladder)

pénétrer to penetrate (bullet, needle), pierce (skin), enter (locale, group), trespass

percer to bore or drill a hole, make an opening, pierce, puncture

percer d'un coup de lance to spear, lance

percer un tunnel dans to tunnel through (mountain, wall)

perforer to perforate, bore, drill, make hole(s) in, pierce

piquer to puncture, stick, prick (needle, insect), poke

plonger to dip, immerse, dive in (pool), plunge (into darkness, into deep sleep)

poignarder   to stab, knife

pointer   to pierce, stab, prick

pousser   to poke, grow (sprout), thrust, heave (sigh)

précipiter   to plunge, fall (rain, snow), precipitate (chemistry)

prélever   to remove (organs), take samples (tissue, blood)

riposter   to parry, thrust (sword)

sabrer   to cut or strike with a saber, slash to pieces (text), cut out (phrase)

saigner   to stick, bleed (animal)

sasser   to pass through a lock (boat)

sonder   to catheterize (bladder)

traverser   to penetrate, run through, pierce, go through (projectile, tunnel, road)

trouer   to pierce, make a hole in, rip (trousers), burn hole in (cigarette: rug)

vriller   to pierce, bore into (wood, metal)

Attention! Un coup de fusil! La balle a °transpercé son casque et a pénétré jusqu'au crâne. Watch out! A gunshot! The bullet pierced his helmet and lodged in his skull.

Ses paroles nous °transpercèrent jusqu'au fond de nos âmes. His words pierced us to the very depth of our souls.

D'après les données, le scientifique précise que le nouveau virus peut °traverser des préservatifs. According to the data, the scientist confirms that the new virus can pass through condoms.

Des rayons cosmiques ont suffisamment d'énergie pour °pénétrer d'épaisses couches de métal lourd. Cosmic rays have sufficient energy to penetrate thick layers of heavy metal.

5

Machines and Tools

Featured Verbs

abréger   to shorten, abridge, abbreviate, end

araser   to erode (embossed logo), level (wall), plane down, make level

banaliser   to trivialize, treat s.t. as being unimportant or insignificant

condenser   to condense (book), reduce volume, compress (time), make compact

couper   to cut (hair, wire), clip, pare, shave, chop (tree), break up (day, trip)

découper   to carve (turkey), cut out (scissors), cut up (paper), dissect (film, text)

décroître   to diminish, decrease (intensity), lessen (wind, sound) subside (fever)

défalquer   to deduct (taxes, from total), take off (extra charges)

dégager   to cut back, shorten (hair)

dégraisser   to cut back (staff, budget), slim down, cut off (fat), trim edges (table)

diminuer   to diminish (size, volume), fall (temperature), wane, tail off (sound)

ébrancher   to trim, prune (tree, shrub), lop off (treetop)

écourter   to shorten (pole, trip, text), crop, cut down (number of words), cut short (visit)

élaguer   to lop, prune (shrub, tree)

émonder   to prune, lop (tree, hedge)

s'espacer   to become less frequent (symptoms, visits)

expurger   to expurgate (book), remove passages from text, purge (text)

faucher   to mow (lawn)

froncer   to contract, wrinkle (forehead), frown, gather (fabric)

grignoter   to erode gradually (beach), nibble (food), gnaw, pick at (dinner)

maigrir   to grow thin (person, army, troop ranks), lose weight, slim down

mettre en minuscule   to put in small (lowercase) letters (e.g., "a" not "A")

miniaturiser   to miniaturize (toy soldiers, scale model), make miniature (camera)

minimiser   to minimize, play down (bad news), understate, trivialize (importance)

minorer de (x)%   to reduce by (x)% (e.g., taxes, salary)

modérer   to reduce (impact, speed), restrain (spending), curb (appetite, desire)

rabaisser   to reduce (prices)

rabougrir   to stunt (growth), dwarf (plant, person), shrivel (leaf)

raccourcir   to shorten, curtail, abridge, shave, trim, clip (hair), lessen (size, extent)

racornir   to shrivel up, dry up (skin, leather, parchment)

rapetisser   to shorten (day, length), shrink, make smaller, diminish (shadow, image)

se ratatiner   to shrink, shrivel up (old person), become wizened (elderly)

recéper   to cut back or clear (woods)

recoquiller   to curl up, shrivel, turn up (dog-eared book page)

se recroqueviller   to curl up, shrivel (leaf, paper), huddle up (s.o.), cower (in fear)

réduire   to reduce, diminish, cut down, lessen, push down (inflation), scale down

se réduire à   to be reduced to (basics), boil down to (simple terms), amount to (sum)

resserrer   to abridge, tighten up (credit, circle, net), narrow (bridge, path)

restreindre   to curtail (spending), cut down, limit, decrease (output), narrow (scope)

retrancher   to abridge, cut short (speech, story, quantity)

rétrécir   to contract, narrow (road, orifice), limit (scope), shrink (circle of friends)

se rider   to shrivel up (face, fruit)

rogner sur   to cut back on (prices), cut (corners, expenses)

sous-estimer   to underestimate (value, capability, opponent)

sous-évaluer   to undervalue (price, business, worth), underestimate (risk)

suivre un régime   to be on a diet

tailler   to cut, hew (stone), carve, prune (tree), trim, whittle (wood, prices)

terminer   to end, top off, cut off (negotiations, speech, telecast, contact)

tondre   to shear (sheep), clip (hair, hedges), mow (grass)

tronquer   to truncate, abbreviate (text, remarks), cut short (sentence)

Arrête ton verbiage! °Abrège! Stop your verbose lecturing! Get to the point!

Laissez-moi °abréger une longue histoire. Let me make a long story short.

Le président allemand °écourta ses vacances pour affronter les problèmes du terrorisme et de la sécurité de l'état. The German president cut short his vacation to address the issues of terrorism and state security.

Nos ennemis ont °sous-estimé la résistance de notre peuple. Our enemies have underestimated the resilience of our people.

allonger to lengthen, elongate, extend

MEMORY AID

Allonger is spelled similarly to *a longer* in English. Picture the wooden marionette Pinocchio. Whenever he tells a lie he grows a longer nose. His nose lengthens and extends farther from his face.

Other verbs in this family include: to prolong, persist, grow, increase, expand, broaden, stretch out, maximize, exceed, proliferate, multiply, abound, exaggerate, go beyond, etc.

s'agrandir to become greater or larger (person, animal), expand, increase in size

s'allonger to grow taller, lie down (person), recline (on bed), stretch (limbs)

arrondir to extend, enlarge, fill out (stomach, face)

augmenter to grow, augment, increase, enlarge, raise (taxes), climb (profits), boost

croître to grow (plant), increase, sprout (seed), lengthen, swell (river), wax (moon)

cultiver to grow (crops), cultivate, cause to grow (crops, flowers)

décoiffer to let down (hair)

décroiser to unfold (arms), uncross (legs), untwine (string), unravel (rope)

défaire to let down (hemline), lengthen (skirt)

dégourdir to stretch (legs)

déployer to stretch out, spread (wings)

détirer to stretch (clay, dough, rubber band), draw out (vowels)

se développer to spread (custom, influence), develop (idea), build up (muscle)

s'élargir to stretch (legs), widen (horizon), expand (group), broaden (shoulders)

en rajouter* to exaggerate (truth, proportions), add to, tack on (extra features)

étendre to extend, broaden (scope, horizon), stretch out (s.o.), spread out (paper)

étirer to stretch, lengthen, elongate, stretch out

être en expansion to expand, spread, be expanding (economy, influence, suburbs)

être gisant to be lying (dead, ill), be outstretched

s'exacerber to increase, become more intense (pain), heighten (sensation)

exagérer to exaggerate (truth), amplify, accentuate, play up, make too much of

excéder to exceed (time limit), go beyond (capability), surpass, overtax (strength)

filer to draw out, prolong (musical note), pay out (fishing net/line, cable)

foisonner to abound (ideas, enthusiasm), increase, multiply, be abundant (fruit)

grandir to grow, increase, enlarge, grow bigger, grow larger

grossir to grow, grow bigger (waistline, tumor), put on weight

laisser pousser to grow (plants)

majorer de to increase by (numbers, size, weight)

maximiser to maximize, make bigger, make larger, enlarge to maximum size

mettre en majuscule to put in capital (uppercase) letters (e.g., "A" not "a")

pérenniser   to perpetuate, make perpetual, make long-lasting

pousser   to grow (hair)

proliférer   to proliferate, reproduce, produce new growth or parts, grow rapidly

prolonger   to extend (trip, railroad), prolong (time, life), persist (effect)

proroger   to prolong the time of, extend (time period), defer (deadline)

rallonger   to lengthen, extend (day, garment)

renforcer   to grow in strength, reinforce (troops, wall), strengthen (currency)

surestimer   to overestimate (importance, worth), overvalue (price, art), overprice

surévaluer   to overvalue (currency, cost), overestimate (influence, difficulty)

surexploiter   to overexploit (land, resources)

se tapir to lurk, hide away

tendre   to stretch (archer's bow, spring, muscle)

En défaisant l'ourlet, la couturière a °allongé la jupe de six centimètres. By letting down the hem, the seamstress lengthened the skirt by six centimeters.

Selon des chiffres boursiers, la livre britannique est °surévaluée par rapport à l'euro. According to stock market figures, the British pound is overvalued compared to the euro.

Bien qu'elle continue à se guérir, il semble que les médecins ont °surestimé ses capacités de récupération. Although she continues to get better, it seems the doctors have overestimated her ability to recover.

Au clair de la lune, les éclaireurs °s'allongèrent à même le sol dans des sacs de couchage. By moonlight, the scouts stretched out on the bare ground in sleeping bags.

brancher to plug in, connect, branch off

accéder à to tap into (power source), gain access, get into (locale)

accoupler to couple with, mate, match up (people, plugs), link (word and sound)

appareiller to install equipment, fit with (hearing aid, artificial limb)

assurer la correspondance to connect (train, plane)

bifurquer to bifurcate (angle [geometry]), branch off (side street), fork (road)

communiquer avec qn to connect with s.o., communicate with s.o.

connecter à to connect to/with (electrical parts, internet server)

se connecter sur to plug into (computer)

dériver to shunt, divert (electric current), branch off (plugs, wires)

détourner de to divert from, turn aside, turn away from (water flow)

dévier to deviate (compass needle), divert (traffic), deflect (bullet), realign (road)

se diversifier to branch out, be diversified (business), vary (method, exercise)

divertir to divert (attention, investment money), misappropriate (funds), move to

se diviser to divide (cell), split up (groups), divide into (chapters), fork (road)

emboîter to fit together, interlock (puzzle pieces, machine parts)

s'embrancher to branch off, fork (road, tubing)

enter to graft (tree branch), engraft, join

s'entrecroiser to crisscross, intersect (lines, wires, roads)

être branché to be forked, bifurcated (road, tubing, tree branch), "plugged in"

faire la ponction à to tap into (surgery), insert biopsy probe into (organ)

greffer to graft (skin, bone, plant), transplant (tree, liver, kidney, bone marrow)

intercaler to switch in, plug in (electric appliance)

joindre to combine, join, put together, blend, link, unite, bring together, conjoin

mettre en perce to put on tap (beer)

raccorder à to connect to, join, crossconnect (phone lines, electric wires)

ragrafer   to hook again, reclasp

se ramifier   to branch out (business), ramify (nerves), divide (rail line, network)

relier   to connect with, link with, connect up, link up, bridge, bind (hardbound book)

segmenter   to segment, divide, split into parts/segments

subdiviser (en)   to subdivide (number, plot of land), divide into smaller parts

tirer   to tap (liquor)

tracer   to spread roots (tree), burrow (gopher holes), mark out (gridlines)

Où se °branche cette prise de courant? Where does this plug plug in?

D'ici on peut °accéder au salon par ce long couloir. From here you can access the living room by this long hallway.

Le fort champ magnétique peut °dévier le trajet d'une aiguille ou déloger un marqueur tissulaire. The strong magnetic field is capable of deflecting a needle pass or dislodging a tissue clip.

Notre ville est bien desservie. Il y a un train et un autobus °assurant la correspondance avec Paris. Our town is well served by public transportation. There are a train and a bus linking us with Paris.

MEMORY AID

The "**coin~**" fragment is spelled the same as the English word *coin*. Picture a caller in a phone booth frustrated as the coin he tries to deposit for a call gets wedged in the coin slot. See also **étouffer** (to choke, suffocate), page 115.

Other verbs in this family include: to close, fasten, secure, lock, block, obstruct, trap, snare, pinch, bar, squeeze, tie up, muzzle, bolt, goof up, make firm, be glued to, be packed, etc.

accaparer   to corner (the market), monopolize (conversation, business)

accrocher   to stick, jam (zipper), hit a snag/hitch (negotiations)

accrocher à   to hang on, hook on, snag on (sweater: nail)

affermir   to make firm, make secure, reinforce (wall), strengthen, tone up (muscle)

arriver à saturation   to reach the saturation point, become jammed/congested (traffic, phone lines)

attacher   to stick, tie up, attach, affix, bind, fasten, hitch, fix, secure, anchor

attraper   to catch, nab, grab (arm, s.o.), catch hold of (animal)

bâcler   to bar, stop, secure (door, window), obstruct (traffic, port)

barrer   to block, seal off (access road), bar (entry, access), close (road)

bloquer   to block, jam (mechanism), lock, obstruct (traffic), freeze (funds)

boucher   to fill in (hole, crack), stuff (hole), plug (leak), clog (sink)

brouiller   to jam, cause interference (TV/radio signal), blur (outline, view)

cadenasser   to padlock, lock up with a padlock

caler   to wedge, wedge open (with a prop, with a door jam)

cochonner*   to botch* (job), mess up,* goof up* (project)

coller   to stick (glue), adhere to

colmater   to plug a leak, caulk, stop up clog (drain)

embourber   to get (a vehicle) stuck in the mud

encombrer   to obstruct, jam (phone lines), clutter (room)

encrasser   to clog up (drain, filter), clog (machinery)

endiguer   to dam (river), embank, form a dike, form a levee or seawall

enfoncer   to wedge, stick in, drive in (pole, stake), push in, hammer in, imbed

engorger   to block, obstruct (road, tear duct), clog (drain), congest (sinus, organ)

enrayer   to jam, slow up (traffic, progress), jam up (road, pipe), check (progress)

être bondé   to be packed, be crowded, be crammed full (bus, arena)

être rivé à   to be tied to (seat), be glued to (TV), be riveted to (show)

faire le blocus de   to blockade (port), embargo, block (shipment)

fermer   to close (door), secure, fasten (collar, shirt), shut up (mouth), obstruct (path)

fermer à clef   to lock (door), lock up (room)

se gourer*   to goof up,* screw up,* botch*

gripper   to jam, block up, seize up (mechanism)

immobiliser   to immobilize, stop, halt, catch, trap

s'ingérer   to obtrude, interfere, be an interference, be an obstruction

lock-outer   to lock out (during a labor strike)

mettre en sûreté   to secure (safety device, lock), put s.t. in a safe place

mettre une muselière à   to muzzle (animal)

museler   to muzzle, gag, put on a gag

obstruer   to obstruct, block (artery, passageway)

pincer   to pinch (finger: door), grip (tongs, tweezers)

se planter*   to mess up (calculation), crash (computer), jam up

prendre au piège   to trap, snare (animal), entrap

presser   to squeeze, crowd, compress, squash

serrer   to squeeze, tighten (grip), clamp (jaw, vise), be too tight for (shoe, pants)

verrouiller   to lock, bolt (door, latch)

 Quelle histoire!* Le jeton est °coincé dans la fente. Comment puis-je téléphoner? What a hassle!* The token is stuck in the slot. How can I make a phone call?

L'astronaute doit °colmater les espaces entre les tuiles isolantes de la navette Discovery. The astronaut must plug the spaces between the insulation tiles on the shuttle Discovery.

J'ai une grande bannière que je veux °accrocher sur mon balcon pour accueillir la reine. I have a big banner that I want to hang on my balcony to welcome the queen.

Certaines lois sociales risquent de °s'ingérer dans la vie familiale. Some social laws threaten interference in family life.

composter to date, stamp (ticket)

affranchir to put a stamp on, apply postage to

agrafer to staple (papers)

annuler to cancel (ticket, bank check, application)

contrôler to stamp, register, check (validity), verify, monitor (surveillance)

coudre à to tag, sew on, sew to, fasten to (button, tag)

dater to date, put a date on, assign a date, determine a date (age, fossil, document)

décommander to cancel (order, invitation, appointment)

décomposer to break up, decompose (cadaver, vegetable matter, mulch)

dégrafer to remove a staple (paper)

effacer to erase, obliterate, rub off, rub out, white out, eradicate (mark)

émarger to sign, initial (document, check), make marginal notes

empreindre to imprint, stamp, impress (seal, medal), mark

estamper to stamp (ticket, envelope), punch (ticket), print (image)

estampiller to stamp, punch, mark, press (sealing wax)

étiqueter to label, make a label, tag, ticket

homologuer to ratify (treaty), approve, officially sanction

imprimer to imprint, impress, stamp

invalider to invalidate (ticket), void (credit card charge, data entry)

marquer to mark (grade, score, tag), stamp, post (score, tally), tag (price), signal

mettre un tampon sur to put a stamp on

oblitérer to obliterate, cancel (stamp)

offusquer to obfuscate, hide (truth, clues), dim, keep from view

poinçonner to punch, stamp (ticket, design in metal)

rendre valable to validate (ticket)

repérer to make a guiding mark on (map), localize biopsy site (medicine)

révoquer to repeal (law, ordinance), cancel (contract)

scanner to scan (computer)

sélectionner to highlight (computer), select icon (computer)

surligner to highlight (with marker pen)

tamponner to stamp (envelope), put a stamp on

timbrer to stamp (letter), put a stamp on

valider to validate, make valid, authenticate (lottery number), ratify (contract)

vérifier to verify (date, number), audit (tax return, account)

viser to stamp (document)

S'il oublie de °composter son billet le contrôleur va lui donner une amende. If he forgets to punch-date his ticket the conductor will give him a fine.

L'aiguille et le fil servent à °repérer la tumeur pour la chirurgie effractive à suivre. The needle and wire serve to localize the tumor for the open biopsy to follow.

Il vous faut °composter votre billet pour le °rendre valable. You'll have to punch your ticket to validate it.

Il est probable que votre médaille ait été °poinçonnée par le bijoutier. It's likely your medal was stamped by the jeweler.

déboucher to uncork, unplug, unblock

MEMORY AID

"**De-**" means *removal* or *from*, and the
"**~bouche~**" fragment is the French word meaning
mouth. Thus, **déboucher** can be thought of as
removing the cork from the mouth of a bottle.
Picture a wine connoisseur uncorking a bottle of
wine. See also **déchaîner** (to unleash, let loose),
page 186.

　　Other verbs in this family include: to disgorge,
unstop, clear, extract, take out, unscrew, force
open, pull free, pull out, unpack, unstick, uncoil,
undo, take off, unsheath, uproot, core, etc.

arracher to extract (tooth), uproot, pull
or tear away, pull out (hair, nail)

arroser* qch to pop a cork (celebration)

béer to be wide open, yawn, gape
(wound, mouth)

commencer to open (bottle, package)

crever to pop (cork), tear open (artery)

déballer to unpack, unbox, unpackage

déblayer to remove, clear away (leaves,
debris), clear up, clear ground (for
planting)

débloquer to unjam, release, unblock,
free (account), unfreeze (salary), clear
(traffic)

débrancher to unplug (appliance), tune
out (radio), disconnect (plug, life
support)

décapsuler to take the top off (soda
bottle, pill bottle)

décoller to unstick, take off (jet),
detach (sticker, label), unstick, steam
off (stamp)

défaire to undo, unpack (luggage)

dégainer to unsheath (sword), draw
(sword, pistol)

dégorger to disgorge, unstop, clear

déloger to dislodge, remove (obstruction, tenant)

déplacer to dislodge, remove (furniture)

déplomber to take the seal off, take out
a filling (dental)

dérouler to uncoil (thread, bobbin,
wire, red carpet)

desceller to pull free, pull out (thorn,
stuck object)

se desceller to come loose (stuck object,
plug), come undone, come unsealed

désenclaver to open up (region, neighborhood)

désencombrer to clear (airway, path),
remove obstacles/impediment

désengorger to relieve the burden on
(service backlog, waiting line, facilities)

désopiler to clear of obstruction
(esophagus, trachea, bowel [medicine])

dévisser to unscrew (woodscrew, bolt)

entamer to open (bottle)

entrouvrir to open a little, open
partway

évider to hollow out (log), core (apple),
scoop out

extirper to pull out, weed out, root out
(weeds), eradicate (crime)

extraire to extract (tooth), take out,
remove (bullet), dig out, wring out,
quarry (ore)

lever les scellés to remove the seals
(medicine bottle, package)

ouvrir to open (door, bottle), unstop,
undo (wrapper), unlatch, pry open,
break open

ouvrir de force to force open (door,
safe)

retirer de to remove from, take out
(cork)

rouvrir to reopen, open again, open
anew (package, door, discussion,
tunnel, store)

sauter to pop out (cork)

tirer to extract, pull out, tap (liquor),
wrench (s.t. stuck), draw out, tug out
(cork)

Le sommelier °débouche la bouteille de vin avec le tire-bouchon. The wine-steward uncorks the wine bottle with the corkscrew.

Des forces de l'ordre ont °délogé les extrémistes de leur bastion de l'opposition. Law officers ousted the extremists from their strongholds of resistance.

Le patient devrait subir une angioplastie: intervention pour °déboucher ses artères coronariennes. The patient would need to undergo an angioplasty; a procedure to unblock his coronary arteries.

Ce fabricant cosmétique a récemment °entamé la production d'un nouveau parfum à son usine. That cosmetics manufacturer recently started production of a new perfume in his factory.

La trachéotomie aide les infirmières à mieux °désencombrer ses bronches. The tracheotomy helps the nurses to keep his bronchi clear.

déclencher to trigger, set off, release

MEMORY AID

"**De-**" means *undoing* or *reversal* and "**~clench~**" is the same as the English word *clench*, meaning to *grasp or grip tightly*. Thus, "**de-clench~**" can mean to *undo a tight grasp or grip*. Picture first a hand tightly grasping a grenade and its safety lever. Then picture it releasing its grip, thereby triggering or setting off an explosion.

Other verbs in this family include: to launch, detach, unbind, unhook, unclasp, work loose, unlatch, provoke, slacken, relax, switch off, cast off, jettison, activate, ring the alarm, etc.

amorcer to set off (bomb), trigger, prime (pump, gunpowder), initiate, start (war)

crocheter to pick the lock of, jimmy* (safe lock, car ignition)

débloquer to release, unlock, release (mechanism), unfreeze (device), loosen (bolt)

décharger de to release, discharge, unload (baggage), bleed (fuel line), vent (anger)

décoincer to unstick, work s.t. loose, unloosen, unjam

décrocher to unhook (latch), uncouple (trailer, wagon), take phone off the hook

défaire to undo (clasp, button, hairdo)

dégoupiller to pull the pin out (grenade)

dégrafer to unclasp, unhook, remove staple (paper)

délier to unbind, untie (knot), undo, release

dénouer to unknot, disentangle, unravel, undo, untie, let down (hair)

désenrayer to unlock, unstick (tires)

desserrer to unclench (vise), loosen (nut, screw), make less tight (cord), unfasten

détacher to detach (string, lacing, paper from pad, fruit from tree)

se dévêtir to undress

élargir to release (captive), free (prisoner), let out (skirt/pants waistline)

exploser to explode (bomb, TNT), detonate, skyrocket (oil prices)

faire basculer to toggle (switch), topple (vase), tip over (chair)

faire exploser to explode, set off (bomb), release (grip)

faire jouer un ressort to activate a spring

imploser to implode (vacuum tube)

interrompre to break off (conversation, negotiation), switch off (electricity, power)

lâcher to let go of, drop (bombs)

lancer to launch (missile), throw (javelin, discus), launch (catapult)

larguer to cast off, drop (military airlift), jettison (bomb)

lever le loquet de to unlatch (door, chest)

partir to go off (gun), fire off (missile)

provoquer to provoke, set off (reaction)

relâcher to release, slacken, relax (grip, spring tension, muscle)

roder to break in (car engine), work out kinks (mechanism, show, muscle)

sauter to set off (landmine), blow up, explode

sonner l'alarme to sound/set off the alarm

sonner le tocsin to ring the alarm

susciter to arouse, instigate, provoke, incite, alarm, cause alarm

tirer la sonnette d'alarme to set off the alarm

toucher to have an effect on (outcome, condition), affect (action, illness)

Cette cellule photoélectrique °déclenche l'alarme de l'usine. This electric eye sets off the factory alarm.

Ce problème de santé, relativement bénin, °touche plus de 25 pour cent des hommes. This relatively benign health condition affects more than 25 percent of men.

Le réservoir à combustible °largué depuis l'avion de bombardement frappa de plein fouet le petit aéronef. The fuel tank jettisoned by the bomber hit the small aircraft head-on.

L'État est en train d'°amorcer une guerre totale pour supprimer le mouvement des activistes. The State is about to launch an all-out war to suppress the activists' movement.

diriger to steer, pilot, guide

administrer   to direct, govern, manage, administer (business, organization)

aiguiller   to direct, orient, shunt to, send (in the direction of)

aligner   to lay out in a line, align, line up (ticket line), dress (troop ranks)

aller à la dérive   to drift toward, drift, be adrift (boat), be rudderless

amorcer un virage   to take a turn (vehicle), go into a turn (road)

apprendre à conduire   to learn to drive (car)

aspirer à   to aim at, aim for (glory, title, achievement)

s'avancer vers   to head toward, move toward

avoir pour but   to aim toward, have as a goal, have as a destination

axer sur   to center on (target, goal)

barrer   to steer (ship), scuttle (ship)

battre pavillon de   to sail under the flag/ensign of (country)

changer de direction   to veer toward, steer toward, change direction

cibler   to target (archery, riflery, business goal), aim toward, set goal for

coucher en joue   to aim rifle at (*lit.* to seat the gun butt against the cheek)

décoller   to take off (planc), lift off (rocket), become airborne

empiéter   to encroach upon (property), impinge upon, obtrude

établir sa position   to get one's bearings, get oriented

être au volant   to be at the wheel (vehicle)

faire route vers   to steer toward, be bound for, head for

faire un virage sur l'aile   to bank (plane)

faire un zoom sur   to zoom in on (camera)

faire voler   to fly, pilot (aircraft, space vehicle)

se focaliser (sur)   to focus (on) (person), be focused on (attention)

se fonder   to go by (decision, theory), be based on (data, findings)

gérer   to guide, manage, lead, administer (business, computer data, crisis)

gouverner   to steer (boat), direct (business), govern (country)

guider   to guide, direct, lead (hike, tour, spiritually)

indiquer le chemin   to give directions, point out the way

louvoyer   to tack (sailboat)

manœuvrer   to maneuver (vehicle), operate (machine), manipulate (person)

marcher au radar   to be on autopilot (plane)

mettre en joue   to take aim at (target)

mettre le cap sur   to be headed toward (ship), set a course for

mettre qn sur la voie   to put s.o. on the right track

naviguer   to navigate, sail, fly, pilot

naviguer à vue   to navigate visually (airplane, ship)

orienter   to guide, get one's bearings, point toward, direct (tourist, research)

piloter   to pilot (ship, plane), guide, run (business, project), show around (tourist)

pointer vers/sur   to point at (finger, gun), aim at, aim toward

porter juste   to hit home (insult, comment, missile), be on target (missile launch)

porter sur   to focus on, center on (issue), be about (text content), concern (details)

se porter   to be directed, go toward, move toward, direct oneself toward

prendre pour cible   to target, aim at, shoot at

prendre son essor   to fly up, fly off, take flight (bird, plane, dream, ambition)

prétendre à   to aspire to, aim for (goal, work, honor)

recadrer   to refocus (action, goals)

recentrer   to refocus, redefine (goals)

rectifier   to change or straighten one's direction

rectifier le tir   to correct the range (shooting), adjust one's tack (ship)

référer à   to refer to (matter, issue, complaint), have reference to

relâcher   to put into port (ship)

remettre à flot   to refloat, bring back on an even keel (ship)

repérer   to locate, spot, pinpoint (landmark), get one's bearings (map, compass)

se repérer   to find one's way around, get one's bearings

stabiliser   to stabilize (price, economy, situation)

survoler   to fly over (in airplane), skim through (book), skim over (question)

tâtonner   to feel one's way along, grope along, fumble one's way along

tenir en laisse   to keep on a leash (animal)

se tourner vers   to turn toward, head toward, aim toward, look to (leader), turn to

trouver ses repères   to get one's bearings, find landmarks

s'y trouver   to find one's way (around town)

varier   to change, vary, depart (from norm, from usual), diversify (interests)

virer   to veer toward, tack (nautical), bring about (boat), swerve

virer sur l'aile   to bank (plane)

viser à   to aim at, point at, zero in on (target), have a goal (business), aim (gun)

viser juste   to hit the mark, aim accurately (target, goal)

voler   to fly (plane, bird)

Le gourmand rebondi s'est °dirigé en hâte vers le buffet. The plump glutton hastily steered toward the buffet table.

Notre décision °se fonde sur des données scientifiques. Our decision is based on scientific data.

Les trois aéronefs ont °décollé pratiquement au même instant. The three aircraft took off almost simultaneously.

C'est un cancérologue qui °dirige la recherche dont les résultats paraissent dans le journal. A cancer specialist, whose results are published in the journal, is directing the research.

Sa recherche est °axée sur la régénération des cellules souches. Her research is centered on the regeneration of stem cells.

ébaucher to sketch out, draw an outline

MEMORY AID

The "**ébauch~**" fragment is spelled similar to the English word *debauch*, meaning *to corrupt* or *pervert* (morally). Also, the "**~bauch~**" sub-fragment sounds somewhat like *botch*, an English slang term meaning *to mess up* or *foul up*. Picture an artist distracted by the beauty of his portrait model. As he sketches her form on canvas the distraction causes him to botch his work. The resultant canvas is corrupted or debauched.

For this category, think of the verbs that might be overheard in the studio of an artist, graphic designer, or architect—verbs in this family relate to putting pen, pencil, or paint to paper: to portray, depict, mark out, engrave, daub, scrawl, scribble, paint, shade, touch up, doodle, do graffiti, make a rough sketch, outline, etc.

aménager to lay out (plan), develop (land), plan (project), convert (garage to room)

baliser to mark out (area), prepare terrain, blaze (trail)

barbouiller to scrawl, scribble, daub paint

bomber to spray paint (car, graffiti)

borner to mark out, line, set limits for, delimit (extent)

brosser to paint, sketch out in paint, brush on (paint)

buriner to engrave, etch/cut/carve a design (glass, wood, metal)

caricaturer to draw a caricature of

crayer to mark up with chalk

crayonner to draw with a pencil

décalquer to transfer a decal, trace (design)

délimiter to mark out, set boundaries (field, precinct)

dépeindre to portray, depict, describe (in artwork, in words)

dessiner to sketch, draw, design (engineer, architect), outline, compose (artwork)

dessiner qch à grands traits to make a rough sketch of s.t.

dessiner très vite to do a quick sketch

donner un aperçu to outline, give an overview of (situation)

élaborer to map out (plan, vision), elaborate (details), refine (technique, process)

envisager to envision (final product), contemplate, envisage, picture in one's mind

esquisser to sketch, draft (speech, project), outline (project), sketch out (plans)

estomper to shade or blur (drawing)

exposer les grandes lignes de to outline (details, plans)

faire le brouillon to do a rough draft (report), do a rough sketch (art)

faire un croquis to make a preliminary sketch, do a rough sketch, silhouette

faire un tracé to draw an outline, lay out, block out (rough design elements)

faire une croquade to make a rough sketch

faire une pochade to do a rough sketch, dash off (a quick note or sentence)

figurer to represent, appear (in list), depict, show, symbolize

gribouiller to scribble, doodle, scrawl

griffonner to scribble, jot (notes)

hachurer to make hatch marks (relief map or to shade a design)

illustrer   to illustrate (book, idea), exemplify, give examples, demonstrate (idea)

incarner   to incarnate, represent (work, person), play (actor)

marquer   to mark (with ink), label (merchandise), brand (cattle, criminal)

paperasser*   to scribble, rummage through old papers

peindre   to paint (portrait, house), apply paint, color

peinturer   to daub, apply paint with hasty or crude strokes, paint (Canadian French)

prendre au pochoir   to stencil (*lit.* **pochoir** *(m)*: stencil)

recopier   to make a copy of, transcribe, copy out again

reprendre   to touch up (painting), alter, redo (artwork, project)

représenter   to depict, show (painting), stand for (idea), symbolize, represent (icon)

retoucher   to touch up (painting, photo), alter (text, clothing, art)

revoir sa copie   to go back to the drawing board

signer   to sign (document, check, work of art), make one's mark

strier   to streak (colors)

taguer*   to do graffiti

tracer   to draw, mark out (grid lines), outline (route, blueprint), rule (lines: ruler)

tracer le contour de   to outline, draw an outline

tracer un trait   to draw a line

zébrer   to stripe, make streaks on

Dans la salle de réunion, l'architecte °ébauchait les projets d'un nouveau gratte-ciel. In the conference room, the architect was outlining the blueprints for a new skyscraper.

Le livre °dépeint l'accusé comme le cerveau d'une opération clandestine. The book portrays the accused as being the brains of a clandestine operation.

Je ne peux pas concevoir votre proposition pour le nouvel immeuble. °Faites-moi un brouillon. I can't envision your proposal for the new building. Draw me a sketch of it.

Les dessins humoristiques servent à °illustrer, de manière ludique, l'importance d'un dispositif de sécurité aérien. The cartoons serve to illustrate, in an entertaining way, the importance of an aerial security plan.

effacer   to erase, rub out, delete

anéantir   to wipe out, destroy, eliminate (enemy, competition)

aseptiser   to disinfect, sterilize, make germ-free, make aseptic

assainir   to clean up, purify, disinfect

biffer   to cross out, erase, blot out, cancel (error)

blondir   to bleach, lighten (color, room)

déblayer   to clear away, tidy up, clean up (trash)

déboiser   to clear of trees, remove trees

décrasser   to clean, scrub, scour (pots), clear (lungs with fresh air)

décrotter   to get the mud off (tires, boots), remove rough edges (from s.o. uncouth)

démazouter   to remove the oil from

déminer   to remove the mines from (minefield)

dépolluer   to clean up, rid of pollution (air, water, land)

déraciner   to eradicate (weeds)

désembuer   to de-mist, defog (mirror, glass) (*lit.* **buée** *(f)*: condensation, steam)

desservir   to clear (table), clear away (dinner serving)

déteindre   to remove the color, fade, lose color (fabric, photo)

donner un coup de chiffon   to wipe with a rag

donner un coup de torchon   to wipe with a rag

écarter   to remove (person, object), discard (card, idea), reject (offer, s.o.)

éditer   to edit, publish (book, newspaper), supervise publication

s'effacer   to withdraw, move aside, step aside, take a backseat

élider   to cut out, delete, leave out, eliminate (vowel), omit or slur (syllable, vowel)

enlever   to remove (stain), take away (thought from mind)

épousseter   to dust (house)

épurer   to purge, refine (molten ore), purify (water), clarify

éradiquer   to eradicate (disease, weeds), erase, eliminate (germs), remove all traces of

érafler   to scratch out, scratch (paint), scuff (shoe)

essuyer   to wipe (table), dry, wipe up (spill), sop up (soup: bread), dust off

exclure   to exclude, dismiss (theory), omit (word)

extirper   to pull out (splinter), eradicate (crime), root out (evil, vice)

faire la lessive   to do the laundry

faire la plonge   to do the washing up, wash (the) dishes

faire le nettoyage par le vide* to throw everything out, clean up

faire le ravalement de to clean, give a facelift to (building), renovate

faire une rature to make a deletion, make an erasure, erase

frictionner to rub (with eraser, sponge, rag, towel), rub down

frotter to rub (to clean), scrub, brush, polish

gommer to erase (mistake, memory), rub out (with eraser)

innocenter de to clear of, acquit (law)

laver to clean, launder, hose down, wash down, wash

laver au jet to hose down (sidewalk, dirty car)

nettoyer to cleanse, clean, sanitize, launder, clean out, disinfect, unclutter, mop up

passer un coup de chiffon to wipe with a rag, wipe down

purger to purge, cleanse, purify, scour, bleed (fuel line)

purifier to purify (metal, air, water), make pure

radier to erase, strike out (name on list), disbar, cross off (name)

raturer to delete, alter, erase, make a deletion

ravoir qch to get s.t. clean (fabric, metal), recover (health), regain (sanity)

rayer to cross out (name on list), erase (error)

reblanchir to whitewash, bleach again

récurer to scour (sink, pot), clean, scrape out

refondre to revise (project, system), overhaul (text, dictionary)

rincer to rinse (mouth, sink), wash, wash out

savonner to wash, lather, wash with soap

supprimer to remove (obstacle), delete (error, word), eliminate (unemployment)

tamponner to dab (wound), mop, swab, wipe (sweat, fluid)

torcher* to wipe up, mop up, wipe (table, baby's bottom)

 La mauvaise note, "F", sur son bulletin scolaire a rapidement °effacé la possibilité de passer son concours. Évidemment, il va rater les maths et devra redoubler. The bad grade of "F" on his report card quickly eliminated the possibility of his passing his exam. Obviously, he's going to fail in math and will have to repeat a grade.

À huit heures pile, la bombe atomique °raya la ville de la carte. At precisely 8:00 A.M., the atomic bomb wiped the town off the map.

Quant à votre tumeur, selon les résultats des prélèvements tissulaires, on peut °exclure un carcinome. As for your lump, according to the results of the tissue samples, we can rule out a carcinoma.

Le chef exige que tous les fruits de mer soient bien °nettoyés avant la consommation. The chef insists that all seafood be well cleaned before consumption.

empâter to thicken, make sticky

MEMORY AID

"**Em-**" means *becoming* or *being*, and "**~pâte~**" is equivalent to the English word *paste*. (Recall the rule that the French **accent circonflexe** "**^**" can indicate a missing "*s*" in English, thus "**â**" means "**as**".) So, "**em-pâte**" or "**em-paste**," in English, is *to be* or *become like paste—thick and sticky*. Picture a grade-school artist trying to create a construction paper work of art but only succeeding in becoming stuck in thick, sticky library paste. See also **empailler** (to stuff, pack with straw), page 224.

Other verbs in this family include: to make firm, harden, intensify, strengthen, fortify, pad, reinforce, make a paste, congeal, clot, fatten, enrich, insulate, grow stronger, plump up, etc.

---

affermir to make firm (commitment, scaffolding), strengthen (relations), reinforce

s'affermir to grow strong, become strong (s.o., muscle), be established (business)

bétonner to lay/pour concrete, play tough defense (football, soccer)

cailler to curdle (milk), clot (blood)

calorifuger to insulate (against heat loss)

capitonner to pad, stuff (pillow, upholstery)

cimenter to cement (sidewalk, friendship), solidify, reinforce, consolidate

coaguler to coagulate (blood, gelatin), clot, curdle (milk)

coller to paste, glue, bond, epoxy

se coller to cling to (s.o.), stick to like glue, cuddle* (lovers), get cozy*

congeler to congeal, freeze, solidify, gel

corser to intensify (difficulty), stiffen, thicken (plot, soup), complicate (situation)

croître to increase (size, volume)

cuirasser to harden, fortify, steel, armor (vehicle), plate with armor

décrasser to tone up (physique)

emballer to pack, wrap, box up, wrap up

empaqueter to pack, wrap, bundle, bundle up

empeser to starch (shirt collar), stiffen

enduire de colle to coat with paste

endurcir to harden, toughen (mental attitude, physique, resolve), make hard

enforcir to strengthen, grow stronger, gather strength (hurricane, invalid)

engraisser to fatten (cattle, waistline, wallet)

enrichir to enrich, embellish (with ornamentation, with decoration)

épaissir to thicken (sauce, paint), make heavy, fill out (face), get thicker (hair)

faire bouffer to fluff up (pillow), puff up (sleeves)

faire une pâte to make a paste

faire ventouse to adhere, stick to (suction cup, decal, self-adhering soap dish)

farcir avec to stuff with (turkey dressing, foam), fill with (ideas: head)

figer to congeal, clot, coagulate (blood, sauce, gelatin), freeze

fortifier to steel, fortify (castle), strengthen (muscle), gird (loins)

garnir to pad (upholstery), garnish (food), cover with (garnish)

grossir to make bigger or greater (cattle, hogs, fruit, waistline)

lier to thicken (sauce, soup, gravy)

se lier to thicken (sauce), become thick, become close (friends)

muscler   to strengthen (economy, business)

se muscler   to develop one's muscles

poisser   to make sticky (hands), pitch (cover with tar for roofing/waterproofing)

raffermir   to make firm, strengthen (economy), steady (prices), firm up (muscle)

raidir   to stiffen, harden, make inflexible, tense (muscle), make taut (rope)

reboiser   to reforest, retimber, thicken vegetation

réconforter   to fortify (with food, alcohol, encouragement)

rembourrer   to pad (bed, clothing), stuff (cushion, sofa)

rembrunir   to stiffen (person), cloud over (sky)

renforcer   to reinforce, strengthen, solidify (position), cement, fortify, bolster

resserrer   to grow stronger, tighten up (grip), tighten (belt), strengthen (relations)

tapisser   to upholster, pad, stuff (sofa, mattress)

tapoter   to plump up, fluff up (pillow, comforter)

Le goudron frais sur l'autoroute a °empâté les pneus de sa nouvelle voiture de sport. The fresh tar on the highway made the tires of his new sports car sticky.

Viens °te coller* à moi! J'ai une bouteille de bon vin et des fraises. Let's get cozy!* I have a bottle of good wine and some strawberries.

Les mineurs doivent °reboiser la galerie de la mine au fur et à mesure qu'ils gagnent du terrain. The miners must shore up the mine shaft little by little as they make headway.

Lorsqu'il vit le visage du fantôme, son sang °se figea dans ses veines. Seeing the face of the ghost made the blood in his veins freeze.

enchevêtrer to tangle up, entangle, tie in knots

avoir trait à to be connected with (idea, feature, concept), be related to

baratter to churn (butter), stir (sauce)

câbler to twist into a cord or cable

cafouiller* to be in a mess,* be struggling (in polls, business), bumble*

clocher to hobble, go amiss (engine, mechanism), be awry, be defective

clopiner to hobble, lame, be lame, be halt, hobble along

compliquer to entangle, complicate (situation, relationship)

contourner to distort, contort, skirt around, go around (roadblock), hedge (guess)

corder to twist into cord

cramponner to cramp, fasten with cramp-iron (to hold stone and timber together)

déchirer to mangle, rip up, tear up (paper), tear (clothing)

défigurer to distort (face), deform (shape), disfigure (statue), deface (painting)

déformer to deform, distort, wring (rag), contort (face), warp (judgment), skew

disloquer to dislocate (joint)

embrouiller to mix up, scramble, confuse, perplex, tangle, entangle, fog up, muddle

emmêler to tangle (hair, yarn, relationship)

empêcher to impede, fetter, hinder (progress)

empêtrer to entangle, enmesh (wire, yarn, fish net, lies)

enchaîner to shackle, link (words), connect, string together (beads), chain (to post)

s'entortiller to entangle oneself, twist oneself around

essorer to wring out (rag), twist, compress, wring (hands), spin-dry (clothes)

estropier to cripple, distort (word), mutilate (pronunciation), twist (meaning)

être tapissé de to be covered/carpeted with (wall: photos, hill: snow, skin: warts)

faire des nœuds to knot up (rope, hair), snarl, tangle

se faire un chignon to tie up one's hair in a bun

feutrer to become entangled or interwoven into a thick mass, be matted (hair)

ficeler to bind, do up (dress)

fouler to twist, sprain (joint)

se lover to coil up (cat: fireplace, snake), curl up (with book), wind up

luxer to dislocate (joint)

menotter to handcuff, put handcuffs on (s.o.), shackle, manacle, cuff (s.o.)

se mouiller dans to get mixed up in (relationship, trouble)

moutonner to curl, frizzle, make woolly or fleecy (hair, sweater)

mutiler to maim, mutilate, mangle

natter to twist, tangle, plait, braid (cord, hair), make a pigtail (hair)

se pelotonner to roll oneself up, curl up

plisser to pleat (skirt), pucker up, screw up (face), wrinkle (brow)

se ramasser to curl up, crouch, crouch down (to spring like a tiger)

se rattacher to be linked up, be connected with, reattach to

se recroqueviller to huddle oneself up, curl up (in blanket), cower (in fear)

se replier to twist oneself, writhe, fold up again, withdraw (troops)

resserrer to cramp (vise), tighten (hug, grip, discipline)

se resserrer to be contracted, confine oneself, close (pores), narrow, draw in (close)

retarder to impede (progress), hinder (bad weather)

sangler to strap tightly, lash tightly, cinch (strap, belt)

serrer un nœud to tighten a knot

se télescoper to have a multivehicle pileup

tendre to tighten, tense (muscle, spring tension)

tordre to distort, contort, twist (ankle), bend (pipe, branch), wring (hands, rag)

torsader to twist (cord, hair, cable), torque (physics)

tortiller to twist, wiggle, squirm, roll (twine)

touiller* to stir (soup, coffee), toss (salad)

tourbillonner to swirl, whirl around (dust cloud, snow), form eddies (sea)

tourner to stir, toss, turn, rotate, revolve, gyrate, bend (direction), deviate (course)

tournoyer to spin, whirl around, whirl (dancer), swirl (smoke, water), flutter (leaf)

tresser to plait (wire, straw), braid (hair), twist, enlace (ribbon)

tricoter to knit (sweater, scarf)

virevolter to twirl around, spin around (dancer, acrobat)

Le menteur chronique s'est °enchevêtré dans ses excuses et ses explications. The chronic liar became entangled in his excuses and explanations.

Le forcené restait °menotté avant d'être guillotiné par le bourreau. The madman remained handcuffed before the executioner killed him by guillotine.

Les cadres surchargés ont dû °enchaîner réunion sur réunion. The overworked executives had to attend meeting after meeting.

Mon patron °empêcha l'embauche du postulant en raison de fausses informations sur le formulaire. My boss prevented the applicant from being hired because of falsified information on the application form.

entrechoquer   to knock/dash together, click together

ballotter   to shake, rattle, toss about (boat), roll around (object), bounce (belly)

bousculer   to jostle each other (crowd)

briser   to shatter, burst, crack (ice, glass), break apart, smash to smithereens

se briser contre   to dash against

cahoter   to jolt, jostle, jerk about (bumpy wagon), lurch

choquer   to shock, dash against, clink glasses, jar on (ears, nerves), shake up

se choquer   to collide with one another (cars, meteorites)

clapper   to clack, smack (tongue)

claquer   to chatter (teeth)

cliqueter   to clink (glasses), clank, clatter (plates), jangle (keys), click (lock)

cogner   to hit, bump, knock, thump, strike against, stub (toe), slap

se cogner   to knock against, hit against, bump up against

cramer*   to short out/burn out (electrical plug or circuit)

craqueler   to crackle, crepitate, crack (paint, plaster, sidewalk)

craquer   to crack, crackle, snap, creak, crunch

crépiter   to crackle, sputter, patter, rattle

débâcler   to break up (ice), collapse (government)

ébranler   to shake (foundation, confidence), disturb, unsettle (investors)

ébrécher   to crack, chip (nail polish, dish, paint, tooth), notch, dent

effaroucher   to shock, startle, alarm, scare, scare away, frighten away

électrifier   to electrify, provide with electrical current (house, city)

électriser   to electrify, inflame (passion), enthrall, thrill

électrocuter   to electrocute (accident, capital punishment)

entrer en collision avec   to collide with, bump into, crash into

étoiler   to crack (glass), stud with stars

être criard   to clash (colors), be loud (clothing), discordant

être en désaccord   to be discordant (sound, personalities, clothes)

se fendiller   to crack (porcelain, earth, plaster), chap (skin, lips)

se fendre   to crack, split, burst asunder (dam, tree struck by lightning)

se fissurer   to crack, become fissured (rock, sidewalk, plaster)

gourmer*   to thump, box (prizefighters)

grésiller   to crackle (radio signal), sizzle (steak, French fries)

se heurter à   to crash into, collide with, run up against (wall), run afoul of (law)

jouxter   to be next to, abut (people, objects, property lines), border on (empty lot)

jurer   to clash (colors), jar/jolt (words)

porter un toast à qn   to toast s.o. (cocktails)

prendre un coup de jus*   to get a shock (electrical), get a jolt*

se rentrer dedans   to crash into, bump into (one another)

retentir   to reverberate (echo), ring out (bell, noise, alarm)

secouer   to jolt, bump, shake (hand, rug), jerk, shake off (dust, crumbs), nod (head)

se tamponner   to crash into each other (trains, cars)

tinter   to clink (glasses)

trinquer   to toast, clink glasses (to toast s.o.)

 Elle avait si froid que ses dents °s'entrechoquaient sans pouvoir s'arrêter. She was so cold that she couldn't keep her teeth from chattering.

Une tragédie ou même un stress profond peuvent °choquer le cœur et produire des symptômes imitant une crise cardiaque. A tragedy or even a strong stress can shock the heart to produce symptoms mimicking a heart attack.

La roquette s'est °brisée en éclats en plein ciel à la suite d'une défaillance technique. The rocket broke into pieces while in flight due to a technical failure.

Des cloches d'église ont °retenti pour marquer le moment précis où le peuple avait proclamé son indépendance. Church bells rang out to mark the exact moment the people proclaimed their independence.

épointer   to blunt, dull, break the point off of

MEMORY AID

Recall "**é**" can be equivalent to "*ex*" in English and "*ex*" means *without*. The "**~point~**" fragment is spelled like the English word *point*, as in *the tip* of a spear or a sword. Thus, "**ex-point~**" can mean *without the tip or point*. Picture a medieval guard's spear being rendered useless or blunted by having its tip removed, therefore leaving it without a point.

Other verbs in this family include: to deaden, tarnish, fade, tone down, soften, smooth, level, make even, decline, diminish, flatten, grind, polish, file down, file off, sand, crop, etc.

abêtir   to dull (senses), blunt (mental capacity), addle (brain), make stupid

affadir   to make dull or flat (taste)

s'affaiblir   to fade, weaken, abate, grow dim, become weak (s.o., sound, light)

amortir   to deaden, weaken, break (a fall)

amputer   to amputate (arm, leg, tree branch)

aplanir   to smooth (surface), level (terrain), make even (rough spots)

baisser   to decline, reduce the height of, flag, droop, lower, turn down (radio, heat)

décapiter   to behead, lop (tree)

décapsuler   to take top off (bottle)

décliner   to wane, be on the decline (influence, prestige, profits, stock prices)

se décolorer   to fade, discolor

décroître   to diminish (sound), wane (moon phase), decrease, subside (flood)

dégraisser   to trim the edge (wood), skim off (fat), cut off fat (meat)

se délaver   to lose color, fade (ink, blue jeans, inscription)

délustrer   to take the gloss or luster off of (silverware, polish, glassware)

dépolir   to make a surface dull, frost (glass)

désamorcer   to defuse (bomb, crisis), nip in the bud (idea)

diminuer   to decrease (size, volume), reduce (weight), die down (noise), let up (rain)

ébouter   to cut the end off of (pole, vegetable, wire)

ébrancher   to trim (shrub), prune (tree)

écailler   to chip (varnish), flake, peel off (paint, nail polish), scale (fish)

écimer   to top (plant, tree), cut top off (vegetation)

écorner   to dehorn (cattle)

écourter   to crop (hedge), cut short (sentence, visit)

écrêter   to lop off, prune (tree)

édulcorer   to tone down (criticism, harsh rhetoric), soften, water down (text)

égriser   to grind, polish

émonder   to prune, crop (tree), lop (tree top)

émousser   to dull, blunt (intellect, sword), lose sharp edge (wit), wane (appetite)

étêter   to cut the head off (tree)

s'évanouir   to fade, vanish, disappear, fade away

s'éventer   to become flat (wine), evaporate

exciser   to excise, cut off, remove surgically (wart, cancer, mole)

faire décroître   to decrease (productivity, noise, power), diminish, wane, lessen

hébéter   to dull (intellect), make stupid, besot, stupefy

incliner   to decline (slope, angle), slant, tilt

limer   to file down (rough edge), file off (wood, metal), file (fingernail)

lisser   to smooth, polish (shoes, wood, metal)

mater   to make dull, make matte or dull (gloss finish, paint), dull (sound)

meuler   to grind down (metal, wood), grind

perdre son lustre   to lose luster

poncer   to sand, sand down, sandpaper, rub with an abrasive

raccourcir   to cut/clip (hair), trim/shorten (skirt, beard)

râper   to grate (cheese), grind, rasp

raser   to shave off (beard, hair), scrape (car against wall)

rendre moins aigu   to dull, make less sharp (razor, sword), lower pitch (voice)

rendre terne   to make dull (color), make lackluster, make matte (paint)

roder   to grind, polish (rough surface), break in (engine)

rogner   to cut, pare, crop, clip, prune, trim

ronger   to corrode (rust, acid), gnaw (rat), nibble, rot

sabler   to sand down, sandblast

sablonner   to scour with sand

scier   to saw off, saw, cut with a saw, hew (lumber)

tailler   to prune, trim (tree, mustache), whittle down (wood, resistance), clip off

ternir   to dull, deaden, tarnish, fade (luster, shine, color, sheen)

tronquer   to cut short (speech), truncate (apex [geometry]), cut off end (log)

Le fer de la flèche s'est °épointé sur le bouclier du guerrier. The tip of the arrow broke off against the warrior's shield.

°Rognez-vous un peu la monnaie de tous vos clients dans cette bâtisse*? Do you shortchange all of your clients in this dump*?

La canicule estivale °baissa le niveau de la nappe phréatique. The summer heat wave lowered the level of the water table.

En raison d'une tempête violente, le paquebot fut contraint d'°écourter son périple océanique. Because of a violent storm, the passenger ship had to cut short its ocean voyage.

fossoyer   to dig (ditch or trench)

MEMORY AID

The "**foss~**" fragment is found in the English word *fossil* (*the remnants of an organism from a past geological age*). Fossils are usually found by archeologists digging in the ground or unearthing debris. In French, a **fossoyeur** is a *gravedigger*. Note that the verb **fossoyer** is an antiquated word. Nowadays, **creuser** is more commonly used for *to dig*. Picture an archeologist digging a deep trench while excavating fossils. See also **ébouer** (to scavenge, clean out), page 252.

Other verbs in this family include: to unearth, rummage, excavate, pry, ferret, find, ransack, raid, explore caves, bury, hoe, weed, disinter, remove turf, exhume, dredge, delve into, etc.

arracher   to dig up, uproot (weed), weed out (evil), snap up (item), tear off (label)

bêcher   to dig, dig into

biner   to hoe, dig again

braquer*   to raid (bank, hoarded treasure)

butter   to unearth, dig up, earth up

canaliser   to install pipes, dig a canal

chambouler*   to rummage, turn everything upside down (household)

creuser   to dig, excavate, scoop out, burrow (mine, tunnel), hollow, sink (well), bore

creuser des galeries   to tunnel, dig tunnels

déblayer le terrain   to level the ground, clear the way (for talks), prepare the way

décacheter   to unseal, remove seal, tear open (package)

défoncer   to dig deeply, dig a trench, deep plough (farm)

dégazonner   to remove turf from

dégotter*   to dig up, find

déraciner   to pull/uproot (weeds, shrub), weed (lawn)

désensabler   to dig out of sand (car), dredge (canal)

désensevelir   to exhume (cadaver, mummy)

déterrer   to unearth, dig up (secrets), dig out (pipe), disinter (coffin)

dévaliser   to raid (refrigerator, pantry), burgle (house), rob (bank)

dévaser   to dredge (canal, trench) (*lit.* **vase** (*f*): mud, ooze, silt, sludge)

échopper   to gouge, gouge out, dig out (with tool)

s'enraciner   to become entrenched, take root (habit, idea), put down roots, implant

ensevelir   to bury, to enshroud for burial

s'établir fermement   to become entrenched (habit, idea, person)

être une croqueuse*   to be a gold digger* (**de diamants**), be a fortune hunter*

excaver   to excavate, dig out, hollow out (tunnel, mine)

exhumer   to exhume, excavate, dig up (coffin/cadaver)

extirper   to weed out, root out, pull out (plant)

extraire   to mine (gold, minerals), extract, quarry (ore), dig out

faire de la spéléologie   to go cave exploring (spelunking)

faire des fouilles   to dig, excavate (archeological dig), search (police), frisk (cops)

faire des travaux de terrassement   to do excavation work, do earthwork (landscaping)

farfouiller*   to rummage about, search among (items)

foncer   to sink (well), deepen, bore (well, cesspool), dig a hole

fouiller   to excavate, search, rummage, delve into, ransack

fouiller de fond en comble   to ransack, search from top to bottom

fouiner*   to nose about,* pry into (affairs, secrets)

fureter   to ferret, rummage about (detective, forensic investigator)

gouger   to gouge, dig out (with tool)

houer   to hoe (in garden)

inhumer   to bury (coffin, treasure), sink, imbed, immerse (in study)

se mêler   to pry into, meddle (in s.o.'s affairs)

mettre en terre   to bury, inter, inhume, place in the ground

miner   to mine (ore, coal)

paperasser*   to rummage among old papers, dig through, sift through (old files)

pelleter   to shovel up (earth, rocks), shovel (at construction site)

percer un tunnel dans   to tunnel through

piaffer   to paw the ground (animal)

piocher   to dig, excavate, dig with pick or pickaxe, take from (deck of cards)

piocher dans le tas*   to dig in, dig into a pile

prospecter   to prospect (oil, ore, minerals)

raviner   to channel (water), furrow (path, ditch), dig a ravine, dig a gully

saccager   to ransack (village)

sarcler   to weed and hoe

sonder   to delve, fathom, sound (water depth)

soulever avec un levier   to pry, pry open (with a lever)

taper dans*   to dig into* (supplies, box, savings account)

terrer   to earth up, dig up (tree, boulder)

se terrer   to dig oneself in, hole up (fugitive, social recluse)

trifouiller*   to rummage, fiddle with, rummage about

tripoter*   to root about, grope, fiddle with

trouver   to find, come across, hit upon (idea), detect, arrive at (conclusion)

De nuit, par le clair de lune pâle, le fossoyeur °fossoie des tombes dans le cimetière. By night, in the pale moonlight, the gravedigger digs graves in the cemetery.

Plusieurs citoyens ont °déterré de vieilles lois afin d'empêcher le passage des nouvelles lois municipales. Several citizens have brought to light old statutes in order to prevent the passage of the new municipal laws.

D'importantes rafales ont °arraché des arbres et des feux de signalisation. Substantial gusts of wind uprooted trees and traffic lights.

Selon ses °fouilles au désert, l'archéologue pense avoir découvert la tombe du pharaon. Based on his desert excavations, the archeologist remains confident he's discovered the pharaoh's tomb.

fourrer   to stick, shove, line with fur

borner   to mark out/stake out with milestones or boundary markers

buriner   to drill (tooth)

caser*   to shove (object), fit (parts)

cheviller   to peg, dowel, assemble using pegs

clouer   to nail, nail down, pin down

clouter   to nail, stud (crosswalk, tires)

cogner   to drive in, hammer in (stud, stake)

combler   to fill in (gap, hole)

creuser   to sink, drive (shaft, well), delve, plough (field), look into (idea)

crever   to stave in (barrel), puncture, pierce (membrane), poke out (eye)

dévisser   to unscrew (bolt, screw)

échopper   to gouge, dig a hole, scoop out (with tool)

encastrer dans   to embed into (slot, opening), fit in (furniture), fit flush, box in

enchâsser   to insert (word), enshrine (holy relic)

enfoncer   to bury, sink (stake, fence post), thrust (hands in pockets)

enfouir   to plant (telephone pole, stake), bury (treasure), plough

faire entrer qn en le poussant   to shove s.o. in

farcir   to cram, stuff (pockets, purse, pillow, tomato)

ficher   to drive in (stake), fasten in, put in file (dossier)

foncer   to sink (well), drive in (post, stake), bore (well)

forcer   to shove open (door), force (mechanism, lock)

former un piquet   to picket (workers on strike, soldiers on guard duty)

fraiser   to countersink (screw), ream, mill, widen hole

se frayer   to shove one's way through (crowd)

garnir de fourrure   to line with fur, fur clothing

gaver   to fill up, cram, gorge, force-feed (animal)

gouger   to gouge, scoop out (with tool), dig out

jalonner   to mark or stake out land

pelleter   to shovel, shovel up (garden, construction site)

percer   to pierce, bore, drill, stab

perforer   to bore, drill, put hole(s) in, pierce

piquer   to puncture, prick, spur, poke with (needle)

piqueter   to mark with stakes or pegs

planter   to stick in, plant (seeds), set, drive in (stake), hammer in (nail)

plonger   to dip, immerse (in good book, in work), dive (submarine)

pousser   to push, shove (crowd), thrust (sword)

pousser violemment   to thrust, jab, stab

presser   to push, press (button), squeeze (sponge, fruit)

sombrer   to sink into (debt, depression, mud), slump (into chair), lapse (into coma)

taper dans*   to dig into* (savings, crate)

tisonner   to poke (coals), knock in (*lit.*
  tisonnier *(m):* a fire iron, poker)

trouer   to bore, make a hole in, pierce, rip a hole (trousers)

visser   to screw in (bolt, light bulb)

Ah, Monsieur et Madame Girard, les fouineurs*! Ils °fourrent leur nez* partout. Nosy Mr. and Mrs. Girard! They stick their noses* into everything.

En sautant du pic en parachute, il s'est °encastré entre les falaises. Jumping with a parachute from the mountain peak, he became wedged between the cliffs.

Malheureusement, ce sont les contribuables qui devront °combler le déficit abyssal des impôts. Unfortunately, it is the taxpayers who will have to make up the deep tax deficit.

En raison des défaillances techniques, la navette spatiale reste °clouée au sol jusqu'à ce qu'elle soit réparée. Because of technical problems, the space shuttle remains confined to earth until it can be repaired.

gonfler to inflate, pump up, blow up (tires)

aérer   to aerate, ventilate (room), air out (bedding)

agrandir   to enlarge, make larger, expand, widen, magnify (image), blow up (photo)

amplifier   to expand, enlarge, amplify (sound, idea)

se ballonner   to balloon up, swell (bee sting), bloat (dead fish)

bomber   to cause to bulge/swell (chest)

bouffir   to puff (cheeks), swell up, puff up, swell (bruise, insect bite)

boursoufler   to bloat, puff up, swell, blister

délayer   to pad out (speech), add extraneous material (school report)

dilater   to expand, distend, expand, dilate (pupils, blood vessel)

enfler   to swell (limb), distend, inflate (budget), bloat (stomach), fill out (physique)

étendre   to distend, spread out (wings, drop cloth), expand (circle of friends, search)

être à plat   to be flat (tire)

être bouffi d'orgueil   to be swollen with pride, have an inflated ego

faire bouffer   to fluff up (pillow), puff up (sleeves)

faire épanouir   to expand, make booming (business), cause to bloom (flower)

faire saillie   to bulge, jut out (mountain crag, jaw, stomach)

fumer   to steam, fumigate, give off smoke, smoke (cigarette, chimney)

fumiger   to fumigate (house for termites)

gazéifier   to aerate, convert into gas, become gaseous (liquid)

gazer   to gas (with nerve gas, mustard gas, toxic fumes)

grossir   to swell (crowd, numbers, river)

insuffler   to blow (air) into

pomper   to pump (air, liquid, gas), pump up, pump out, evacuate liquid

rechaper   to retread (tire) (*lit.* **chape** (*f*): tire tread)

regonfler   to pump up (tire), swell again

saler*   to inflate (bill, charges)

souffler   to blow (breath, wind, glass, candle), inflate, pant, breathe, puff, huff

tapoter*   to plump up (pillow), fluff up

ventiler   to ventilate (room), aerate, evacuate (air/gas/smoke)

J'ai un pneu de bicyclette crevé. Il me faut le réparer et le ° faire gonfler de nouveau. My bicycle tire has a flat. I have to fix it and blow it up again.

À cause des pluies torrentielles, le cours d'eau continue à °grossir et menace de déborder le barrage. Because of the torrential rains, the waterway continues to swell and threatens to overflow the dam.

La veille de la manifestation, des appels à une grève illimitée °se sont amplifiés. The day before the demonstration, calls for an indefinite strike grew stronger.

Si ton discours est trop court tu peux le °délayer avec des blagues. If your talk is too short you can pad it with some jokes.

hacher   to chop, mince, hack

MEMORY AID

The "**hache~**" fragment sounds like the English word *hash*, meaning *a dish of chopped meat and potatoes* (n) and *to chop to pieces or mince* (v). In fact, the English word is derived from the Old French word **hache**, meaning an *axe* used to chop up or hack. The modern-day French word for ground beef is **haché**. Picture an exuberant chef chopping and hacking away at a slab of corned beef, mincing it into a hash. See also **entamer** (to cut into), page 274.

The most logical verb family for **hacher** would include all the words relating to the act of chopping, hacking, cutting, axing, mincing, etc. However, as French cuisine is world-renowned, there are a vast number of terms and expressions that owe their origin to the French culinary arts, so this category also includes verbs and verb phrases related to the kitchen and cooking.

accommoder   to cook, prepare a dish

adoucir   to sweeten, make soft, make milder (to taste)

arroser   to baste (with gravy, with sauce)

assaisonner   to season (food), give relish to, wine and dine (s.o.), dress (salad)

baratter   to churn (butter), stir (sauce)

battre   to beat, whip (cream, batter), scramble (eggs), mix (ingredients)

battre des blancs en neige   to whip egg whites into stiff peaks

beurrer   to butter, coat with butter

bluter   to sift (flour)

braiser   to braise (cook in fat, then simmer)

branler   to shake (ingredients)

brasiller   to grill, broil

brasser   to brew (beer), mash, stew, mix

brouiller   to scramble (eggs, ingredients)

brûler   to parch, dry, roast (corn, peas)

brunir   to brown (meat)

charcuter   to hack, butcher, carve up

chauffer   to heat, warm (food, beverage)

clarifier   to clarify, make clear (butter)

couler   to pour, strain (liquid)

couper   to cut (meat, vegetable), carve (roast), cut (dilute wine), slice

couper en cubes   to cube, cut into cubes (meat, potato)

couper en dès   to dice (vegetables)

couper en rondelles   to slice (lemon, salami)

couper en tranches   to slice, cut into slices, cut into slivers (almonds)

cribler   to sift (through colander), pierce, grade (eggs, fruit)

cuire à la vapeur   to steam (fish, vegetables), cook in a steamer

cuire au feu   to bake

dauber   to stew (*lit.* **daube** (*f*): casserole)

décongeler   to defrost, thaw

dorer   to glaze (pastry), brown

ébrécher   to hack, cut into (meat)

échauffer   to heat, warm, ferment (grain for beer)

écumer   to skim (broth, fat), froth (liquid)

embrocher   to skewer (shish kebob), put on a spit (pig)

enfourner   to put in the oven

épicer   to spice, add spices to

étendre   to dilute (wine), thin (sauce, gravy), water down (alcohol)

être aux fourneaux*   to do the cooking

étuver   to stew, braise, parboil, steam

faire bouillir   to boil

faire cuire to cook
faire cuire à la broche to spit-roast
faire cuire à la poêle to pan-fry
faire cuire à l'eau to boil
faire cuire au gril to grill
faire donner un bouillon to bring to a boil
faire frire to fry, pan-fry, deep-fry
faire la popote* to cook
faire la tambouille* to cook the grub*
faire pâte to batter, paste
faire revenir to brown, cook lightly (meat)
faire roussir to brown (stew meat), sear (steak)
faire une purée to mash, purée
filtrer to strain (liquid)
flamber to flambé (serve flaming in ignited liquor)
fondre to melt (butter), blend, combine (ingredients), dissolve (salt, sugar)
fouetter to whip, whisk (cream, eggs), beat
frémir to simmer (gravy, soup)
fricasser to fricassee (cut in pieces, stew and cook in gravy)
fumer to smoke (fish, meat), steam, cure with smoke (meat)
glacer to ice (cake), freeze, put icing on (donut), glaze (ham, donut)
griller to toast, grill, broil, roast
hacher menu to mince, chop finely
infuser to brew (tea)
larder to insert bacon or fatty meat into lean meat before cooking
lier to thicken (sauce)
mariner to pickle, souse, drench in brine, marinate
mélanger to blend, mix (ingredients)
mêler to blend, mix (ingredients, liquids)
mettre en ragoût to stew
mijoter to stew, simmer, cook slowly
mitonner to simmer, let bread slices simmer in broth
moudre to grind (pepper, coffee), mill
mouiller to baste (a roast), water down (wine)

mouliner to put through the vegetable mill
paner to cover with breadcrumbs
passer to strain (liquid), sift (flour)
pâtisser to make pastry, knead dough
parsemer de to sprinkle with (salt, pepper, spices)
pocher to poach (eggs, fish), cook in simmering liquid (eggs Benedict)
poivrer to pepper, add pepper to, coat in pepper
préchauffer to preheat
purifier to purify
râper to grate (cheese, carrot), grind (pepper)
réchauffer to reheat, warm up
recuire to cook again
réfrigérer to chill, cool, refrigerate
refroidir to chill, cool (dessert gelatin, soup, juice)
relever to flavor with spices
répandre to sprinkle (herbs, salt), give off (odor), spill (soup, wine)
rissoler to brown (meat), roast
rogner to cut, pare, trim (meat), prune, clip
rôtir to roast, toast, broil, parch
rôtir à la broche to barbeque, broach
saler to salt, add salt to
sasser to sift (flour)
saupoudrer to dust, dredge (with flour), sprinkle with salt and pepper
sauter to toss in a pan, sauté
sculpter to carve (ice sculpture)
servir à la louche to ladle out (soup)
sucrer to sugar, put sugar on, sweeten
tailler to cut, carve (meat, fowl)
tamiser to sift, filter, sieve (flour, grain)
tartiner to spread (jam, butter) (*lit.* **tartine** (*f*): bread and butter)
torréfier to roast (coffee)
touiller* to stir (coffee), mix (salad)
trancher to cut, slice (bread, meat)
truffer to garnish with truffles
verser avec une cuillère to spoon s.t. out, pour using a spoon, decant

Tiens! Monsieur le tailleur! Je voudrais ce costume bien coupé et bien façonné, mais on l'a °haché comme des saucisses! Hey! Tailor! I'd like this suit well-cut and tailored, but they've hacked it up like sausages!

°Écumez la graisse de la soupe avant de la servir aux convives. Skim off the fat from the soup before serving it to the guests.

Comme amuse-bouche nous aurons du saumon °fumé sur du pain brun. For appetizers we will have smoked salmon on dark bread.

Le chef °accommoda son mets culinaire le plus célèbre—tartelettes de gibier rôti et gelée de groseilles au porto. The chef prepared his most famous specialty dish—little tarts of roast game and a jelly of gooseberries in port wine.

MEMORY AID

The "**man~**" fragment appears similar to the French word **main**, meaning *hand*. The derivation is from the Latin word **manus** (*hand*). Among ancient artisans, laborers, and craftsmen the hands wielded the greatest creative power. From the Latin **manus**, English has derived words such as *manage, manipulate, maneuver, manhandle*. The "hand" fragment is found in a number of words associated with forming, shaping, or crafting, such as *handmade, handiwork, handle,* and *handicraft*. Picture a multilimbed goddess who wields great creative power with the use of her many hands handling handcrafted handiwork.

Other verbs in this family include: to make, fashion, form, mold, cast, knead, grasp, hold, utilize, manage, structure, forge, devise, transform, convert, alter, manufacture, modify, feel, etc.

bâtir   to build, have built, construct, erect

camper   to shape, construct (s.o.'s image), depict (caricature of s.o.)

confectionner   to make, manufacture, finish (clothing, appliance), prepare (food)

construire   to construct, build, manufacture, create, structure

créer   to create, produce, invent, bring about, give rise to, bring into existence

empaumer   to grasp, catch, hold, take possession of (tool, object), palm (ball)

employer   to use, make use of, employ, utilize (tool, energy, time, money, words)

engendrer   to produce (sensation, mood, electricity, math result), engender

fabriquer   to make, manufacture, fabricate, construct, craft, work (wood, metal)

façonner   to fashion, shape (land, raw material, character, cloth)

faire   to make, do, create (product, building), produce, perform, execute, induce

faire naître   to create, originate, develop, give rise to (product, idea)

faire usage de   to use (tool, force, good sense), make use of (talent, intelligence)

forger   to forge (alliance, counterfeit), form (by hammering), hammer out (metal)

former   to shape, form (clay, design, metal)

foutre*   to do, make, give (a damn)

gérer   to manage (situation, data, business)

gouverner   to manage, control (business, resources, political power)

inventer   to invent (device), manufacture, create, cook up (idea), devise, contrive

malmener   to manhandle (s.o.), mishandle (information, tool, situation), mistreat

manipuler   to handle, manipulate, control (device, power, s.o.), lift, work (clay), hold

manufacturer   to manufacture, process, make, create, turn out (product), build

manutentionner   to handle, pack (merchandise, goods, cargo, freight)

masser   to massage, give a massage to, rub, rub down

ménager   to handle carefully (person, emotions, appliance, device, equipment)

modeler   to model, shape (body, character), mold (clay, personality)

modifier   to modify, change, alter, affect, change, amend, tamper (with device)

moduler   to adjust (price, length), modulate (sound, voice), modify

mouler   to cast (mold), mold (in clay)

se nouer   to form (friendship, alliance, lump in the throat), be formed

œuvrer   to fashion, create a work (of art, of music)

palper   to feel, palpate (physician)

pétrir   to form, mold, knead (dough, clay), manually work (raw material)

prendre   to handle, deal with (person, problem), take hold of, grab, clutch, hold

prendre tournure   to take shape (creation, idea, work of art)

préparer   to manufacture (product), fit, make ready (patient for surgery, speech)

produire   to create, produce (handicraft, artwork, product)

réaliser   to make (furniture), fulfill (obligation), carry out (task), attain (dream)

réinventer   to reinvent, recreate, recraft

réviser   to change, revise, overhaul, rewrite, review

sertir   to set (gemstones in a ring)

se servir de   to use, make use of (talent, tool, object)

structurer   to structure, form, give shape to, develop a structure for (business, phrase)

synthétiser   to synthesize (chemical, new element), add elements to form a whole

tenir   to hold, grasp, wield, grasp, clasp, have, keep, clutch, grab hold of

toucher   to touch, handle, try (precious metals)

toucher à   to handle, meddle with (rules, tradition, law), tamper with (package)

traiter   to handle (data), treat (sewage, minerals, ore), deal with

transformer   to change, modify, transform, convert, alter

travailler   to work, shape (wood, dough, clay, metal)

user de   to use

usiner   to machine, fashion (by machine)

utiliser   to use (tool, influence), utilize, have use of (hands), exercise (authority)

Le sculpteur célèbre sait bien °manier l'argile. The famous sculptor certainly knows how to handle clay.

Pouah!* Tu ne °te sers jamais de savon ni de shampooing? Phew!* Don't you ever use soap or shampoo?

La prise de pression artérielle doit être °réalisée par une infirmière diplômée. Blood-pressure readings should be performed by a licensed nurse.

Le cadre a été licencié pour n'avoir pas réussi à °gérer correctement la situation. The executive was fired for not having correctly handled the situation.

MEMORY AID

Plier is spelled just like the English word *plier(s), a tool with a pivoted jaw for bending, shaping, folding, or cutting.* From **plier** is derived the English verb *to ply—to bend or twist.* In ballet there is a step known as **plié** in which the ballerina *bends at the knees.* Picture a set of pliers (the tool) being used to bend or ply a wire into a shape.

Other verbs in this family include: to wring, warp, distort, press, squeeze, crimp, curl, coil, turn in, make a tuck in, tilt, roll up, model, shape, form, crumple, turn, buckle, flex, disfigure, etc.

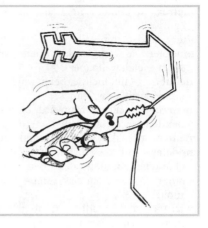

s'affaisser   to sag, cave in, sink (road, soil, body, floor), subside (noise, pain)

assouplir   to make flexible, make supple, relax, soften, limber (muscles)

bossuer   to dent, make a dent in (can, fender), batter

boucler   to buckle (metal), curl (hair)

cabosser   to dent (car), bump, indent

comprimer   to compress (pill, gas), condense, constrict, press together (plywood)

se contorsionner   to contort oneself, twist oneself

contourner   to distort, twist, turn, go around, bend around (road), bypass (town)

couder   to bend, make an elbow turn in s.t.

courber   to bend, curve, warp, make crooked, curl, bend back

crêper   to frizz, wrinkle (paper), crinkle (paper), crimp (fabric)

se crisper   to shrivel (leaf, skin), contract, contort (face), clutch (tool)

débosseler   to take the dents out of (fender, armor)

défigurer   to distort, deform (shape, face), distort (truth), blight (environment)

déformer   to deform, distort, contort (body, face), warp (wood), wring (rag)

déjeter   to warp (wood, plastic), deviate (path)

dénaturer   to distort, disfigure, alter (purity, nature of), deform, adulterate (food)

déplier   to unbend, unfold, open out, lay out (sofa bed, newspaper)

déployer   to unfold, unroll, unfurl, spread out (map, fabric, tarpaulin)

enrouler   to roll up (map, rug), coil (spring), wind up (cable), reel in (fishing line)

érafler   to scratch (e.g., car door), graze

faire dévier   to deflect, cause to deviate (compass needle), sidetrack (s.o., plans)

faire ployer   to bend, sag, cause to bend (knees, back, branch, girder)

faire rejaillir   to reflect (honor on s.o. else), rebound (shame), splash back (water)

faire un trou dans   to make a dent in (budget, meal)

fausser   to bend, distort (color), make crooked, twist, skew (data, test results)

fléchir   to bend, flex (wire, girder), sway

former   to form (shape, design, character)

friper   to crumple (paper), rumple (sheet)

friser   to curl, frizz (hair)

froisser   to crumple (paper), rumple (sheet), crease (cloth)

froncer   to wrinkle, contract, pucker (lips, stitched fabric)

gaufrer to crimp, flute, make pleats in (goffer)

gîter to list (ship), tilt

gondoler to warp, buckle, bulge (wood, sheet metal, wallpaper)

incliner to tilt, incline, bend, angle, curve, slant, bow, lean

incurver to curve s.t. inward, curve, bend (wire, metal, wood)

mailler to make chain mail, make mesh

modeler to shape (metal, clay, character, body), model, mold

mouler to mold (in clay), shape (in mold)

orienter to turn, adjust (knob, mechanism, antenna, lamp, mirror)

pencher to lean, list, tilt, bend, incline, cant, slant

plisser to screw up (face), wrinkle (brow), pleat (skirt), pucker up (lips)

ployer to fold, bend (floorboard, tree branch)

racornir to shrivel up (leather, skin, plant)

se ramasser to curl up, crouch, crouch down, hunker down

recoquiller to shrivel up, turn up (dog-eared book page)

recourber to bend back, bend round, bend again

se recroqueviller to shrivel up, curl up

refléter to reflect, bend back (light, sound)

réfracter to refract, distort (light, sound), bend (light beam)

remplier to tuck, make a tuck in (fabric, sheet, blanket)

replier to coil, fold up (map), bend again, fold down (page corner), tuck in (legs)

retrousser to turn up, roll up, tuck up (pants leg)

serrer to press, squeeze (grip, vise), clamp (jaw), clench (fist), squeeze together

sertir to crimp (tubing, wire)

strier to make a ridge or groove in (wax, metal), striate, groove

tordre to wring, twist (pipe, wire), bend (rail)

torsader to twist (cord, cable, hair), torque (physics)

tortiller to twist, twiddle, roll (twine), squirm (child, worm)

tourner to turn, wind, turn round, bend, rotate, revolve

tournoyer to turn round and round, to wind (spring), twirl (cane), swirl (dress)

travailler to warp (wood, metal)

voiler to warp (floorboard), buckle (metal, wheel)

Ce comique était si marrant que j'étais °plié de rire durant le spectacle entier. The comedian was so hilarious that I was doubled over in laughter throughout the entire show.

L'enquête criminelle s'est °orientée vers le chantage et l'extorsion de fonds menés par la mafia. The criminal investigation was directed toward the blackmail and extortion of funds by the Mafia.

Flûte,* cette chaîne! Ça sature! Ben,* °orientes la touche de sélection des stations. Darn, this stereo! We're getting a distorted signal! Well, adjust the tuning knob.

Surtout, les fausses informations °déforment la réalité et entretiennent un flou entre science et sorcellerie. Above all, the false data distorts reality and creates a fuzzy boundary between science and witchcraft.

MEMORY AID

This verb is very simple to memorize as one of its English meanings is contained within the French infinitive, i.e., **"tap-oter."** Picture a writer engrossed in a new novel he's writing tapping away furiously at the keyboard. In this category are verbs that one would use in an office containing keyboards, typewriters, secretaries, and stenographers.

Other verbs in this family include: to rap, knock, type, flick, flip, snap, drum, drum out, thump, bump, pop, jot down, snap at, drum into, take shorthand, leave a note, etc.

battre du tambour   to drum, beat a drum

brusquer   to snap at (remark)

chiquenauder   to flick (cigarette ash, cigarette lighter), flip (coin, pages)

cliquer   to click (mouse)

cliqueter   to clack (typewriter keys)

cogner   to thump, bump, tap lightly, knock against

copier   to transcribe, copy, duplicate, make a photocopy, Xerox®

dactylographier   to type, type on a typewriter

dicter   to dictate (a letter)

doigter   to finger (musical instrument, keyboard)

donner un petit coup sec   to rap, knock (door)

donner une chiquenaude à   to flick (light switch, cigarette lighter)

donner une petite tape   to pat, touch lightly, hit lightly

double-cliquer   to double-click (mouse)

écrire à la machine   to typewrite

envoyer un mél   to send e-mail (**messagerie électronique**)

faire claquer   to snap (a whip)

faire du traitement de texte   to do word-processing

faire éclater   to pop s.t. (balloon, bubble wrap)

fermer avec un bruit sec   to snap shut (box lid)

fourrer subitement   to pop (bubble, cork)

frapper doucement   to tap, rap (on door, knuckles on desk)

frapper du poing   to thump, hit with fist, punch

gribouiller   to scribble, doodle, scrawl

griffonner   to scrawl, scribble, jot down (notes)

happer   to snap up (bird: beak, dog: muzzle), snatch (in hand)

laisser un mot   to leave a note, leave s.o. a message

manier   to handle, touch, wield (tool, power), finger (keyboard), manipulate, ply

manipuler   to manipulate (keyboard, tool, fabric, item, s.o.), palm (object, ball, coin)

marteler   to drum out (beat), hammer

noter   to note, jot down, take note of, log (in notebook), write down (notes)

paperasser*   to scribble, write hurriedly/carelessly

photocopier   to photocopy, Xerox®

pianoter   to tap, drum one's fingers

pincer   to pluck (guitar strings)

pitonner*   to tap away (keyboard), type, dial (phone), zap* (between TV channels)

prendre note de   to jot down

prendre une lettre en sténo   to transcribe a letter in shorthand

recevoir un mél   to receive e-mail

recopier to transcribe (dictation, report)

seriner qch à qn to drum s.t. into s.o., repeat over and over again

tambouriner to drum, drum one's fingers

taper to tap (keyboard), typewrite

toquer to tap, rap, knock

toucher to touch, brush against, contact, handle, palm

tracer to scribe, trace, draw (outline, hieroglyphic), plot (graph), line (with ruler)

transcrire to transcribe (dictation), record, notate (musical score)

transmettre par télécopie to fax, send facsimile

vérifier le courrier to check one's e-mail

zapper* to channel-surf (TV), click back and forth between TV channels

Le spécialiste de logiciel et internaute °tapotait sur son clavier toute la journée. The computer software programmer and internet surfer tapped away at his keyboard all day long.

Certains parents se demandent si °taper légèrement ou donner une fessée restent dans les limites d'acceptables châtiments. Some parents wonder if a light paddling or spanking are within the acceptable limits of punishment.

L'écrivain prolixe °écrivait à la machine tous ses romans ainsi qu'un recueil de ses autres ouvrages. The prolific writer wrote all his novels on the typewriter, as well as a collection of his other works.

Le conférencier parlait trop vite! J'arrivais à peine à °griffonner quelques mots clefs. The lecturer was speaking too fast! I could barely scribble down a few key words.

6

Verbs in Action

Featured Verbs

contourner to bypass, go around, get around

MEMORY AID

The "**contour~**" fragment is spelled and sounds like the English word *contour*, meaning *a line or surface representing the outline of a figure, body, or mass*. Thus, in using a pen to trace the contour of a shape drawn on paper, one is going around or getting around the shape rather than going through or across it. Picture a driver having a wild ride along a rural road that closely follows the contour of every bend, curve and slope in the terrain. In doing so he is bypassing or going around all the traffic cones placed to mark hazards.

Other verbs in this family include: to wind, snake, swerve, turn, make a U-turn, circumvent, maneuver, dodge, skip, turn round, weave in and out, change course, sidetrack, skirt, etc.

aller à contresens   to go the wrong way, go in the opposite direction

changer de cap   to change course, change direction

circonvenir   to circumvent (obstacle), get around (person, roadblock)

court-circuiter   to bypass (person, department), short-circuit (electrical device)

croiser   to pass or overtake (a car on the road), cruise (boat)

déformer   to distort, deform, warp (wood, metal, judgment), skew (results)

déporter   to swerve, drift, carry off course, deviate

dériver   to divert from proper course, shunt, branch off from (course)

détourner   to divert (river, attention), deflect (bullet, blow), hijack (plane)

dévier   to deviate (from norm), swerve, deflect, sidetrack, go astray, veer

s'emballer   to spiral out of control (inflation), get carried away (with emotion)

s'entrecroiser   to crisscross, interlace (yarn), intersect (lines, roads)

épouser   to follow, hug (curve, road, outline)

escamoter   to get round (difficulty), dodge, skip

esquiver   to dodge, skirt around, avoid, sidestep, elude, evade

éviter   to bypass (destination), dodge, duck, avoid, circumvent, steer clear of

faire demi-tour   to make a U-turn

faire des détours   to dodge, make detours, detour

faire le tour de   to go around, look at from all angles

faire passer   to get through s.t. (difficulty), carry out s.t. (illegal act)

faire un écart   to swerve (car, missile), shy (horse), jump out of the way

faire une volte-face   to make a U-turn (car), make an about-face (opinion)

se faufiler entre   to dodge in and out of (traffic), squeeze between (crowd), sidle

fausser   to bend (wire, pipe), distort (truth, image, judgment), alter (perception)

garer   to sidetrack (train), draw into (rail station), put away (plane: hangar)

longer   to skirt, run alongside, run parallel to (river, road), hug (sidewalk, railing)

louvoyer   to maneuver, dodge, tack (boat)

mettre le cap sur qch   to set out for (destination)

obliquer   to slant, swerve (from path), tilt (boat)

outrepasser to transgress, go beyond (limit), overstep (bounds), override (veto)

passer au large to circumnavigate (globe, island), sail completely around

passer le cap to get over the hurdle of s.t. (difficulty, threshold)

passer par to get through (school, difficulty), go through (countryside)

retourner to turn round, reverse, turn again, turn (idea in head, knife in hand)

revirer to change sides, tack (boat), change (mind), reverse (trend, opinion)

ruser to evade by deceit or guile

semer qn to sidetrack s.o., shake off (pursuer), ditch (s.o.), leave s.o. behind

serpenter to snake, wind (river, mountain path)

shunter to shunt, bypass, move from one track to another, divert route, reroute

slalomer to weave in and out (traffic, obstacles)

tourner to turn, turn round, change direction, deviate (course), veer

tourner autour de to go around, turn around

tourner en rond to drive around in circles

se tourner to move around, turn toward, turn to look back

tournoyer to wind, eddy (water, smoke), fly/buzz around (bee), spin (boomerang)

se tromper de chemin to take the wrong road

varier to change (course, direction), vary (approach, technique)

virer to turn, take a new route, swerve, bear toward (boat), bring about (boat)

zigzaguer to zigzag, move in a zigzag pattern/path

L'automobiliste ivre °contourna la ville car il avait peur de la police. The drunk driver skirted around the town as he was afraid of the police.

Fais attention! Le poids lourd va te °croiser! Be careful! The semi is going to cut in front of you!

La perception des données est °faussée par le malentendu et l'égoïsme scientifique. The perception of the data is distorted by misunderstanding and scientific hubris.

Les motards °se sont croisés plusieurs fois sur l'autoroute. The motorcycle police passed each other several times on the highway.

se cramponner to hang on, cling to, hold fast

s'accrocher to hang on, hook on, latch on, catch on, snag (sweater)

adhérer to cling, hold, adhere (belief, opinion, policy), stick (tape), bind (glue)

afficher to post up, put up, display (results), post (announcement), hang (poster)

agrafer to claw, clutch, grip, hook up, fasten (clothes), staple (paper)

agripper to grip, claw, clutch, snatch, grab

s'arc-bouter contre to lean against (wall, fence), buttress (cathedral wall)

s'attacher to cling to, take hold, attach or fasten oneself, become attached to (s.o.)

avoir le tournis* to feel dizzy, stagger

coller à to stick to, cling to, hold to, adhere to, tailgate (vehicle)

culminer to peak at (salary), reach the highest point, culminate (award, mountain)

descendre to go down, drop off of, fall, subside, come down, lower, descend

descendre en rappel to rope down, rappel (down a cliff)

dévisser to fall (mountain climber)

empoigner to grasp, grab (object, person), grip (emotion)

équilibrer to balance, equilibrate, harmonize, counterbalance (weights, forces)

escalader to climb, climb over (wall), scale, scramble up (hill), clamber up

être en porte à faux to be overhanging (roof), be unsteady (s.o.), slant (wall)

être en recul to be falling (taxes, prices), be declining (civilization, epidemic)

être saillant to be jutting out (rock ledge), be protruding (cliff, jaw)

être suspendu to hang, be suspended

être tendu de to be hung with (curtains, silk)

étreindre to grip (with hands), embrace (friend), hug, clench, grasp

faire de la varappe to go rock climbing

faire de l'alpinisme to do mountaineering, go mountain climbing

faire de l'escalade to go mountain climbing

faire le grand écart to do a balancing act, do the splits

faire le planton* to hang about,* hang around* (bar, street corner, dorm)

faire mariner* to hang around,* wait, cool one's heels,* kill time*

faire saillie to jut out (jaw, cliff)

faire ventouse to adhere to, stick to (suction cup, decal)

fixer à to attach to, tie to, tack on to, clasp to, immobilize

flotter to flap in the wind (flag, banner), hang loose, flutter, flap around (skirt)

gagner les hauteurs* to head for the hills*

gravir to climb, climb up, ascend, clamber up (hill, ladder, wall)

graviter to hang around, gravitate to (person, idea), revolve around (planet)

harnacher to harness (mountain climber)

se jucher to perch (bird on branch), teeter (in high heels, on stilts)

lâcher prise to lose one's grip (rope, tool, situation)

lyncher to hang (s.o.), lynch (s.o.)

pendouiller to dangle, hang, hang loose (pendant, earring)

pendre to hang (by the neck), suspend, dangle, droop, sag

se pendre to hang oneself (with a rope)

placarder to hang, affix, put up (poster)

planer to hang (fog, mist, smoke), look down on (from high perch)

poireauter* to hang around* (with friends)

pondérer to balance, equilibrate (weights), give weight to (relative values)

poser to hang (curtains, painting)

précariser to make insecure (situation), make unstable (position)

se raccrocher to cling, hang on to, grab hold of

se rattraper to stop oneself from falling

rééquilibrer to stabilize, restore balance, re-equilibrate, restore harmony

reprendre son équilibre to regain one's balance

se retenir à qch to hold on to s.t., grab on to s.t., grab hold of s.t.

saisir to grab, seize, latch on to, clutch

serrer to grip, lock, clench (fist, teeth), squeeze, tighten (grip, belt), hold firmly

serrer fort to hold tight, clasp/grip/grab tightly

se stabiliser to find one's balance, become stable (mentally, physically)

surplomber to overhang, project over (awning, cliff, roof)

suspendre to hang, suspend, hang up, dangle, hover (helicopter, bird)

se suspendre à to hang from, dangle from (rope, branch)

tendre to hang, suspend (tarpaulin, hammock)

tenir bon to hold out, hang on,* tough it out* (bad situation), brace oneself

tomber to hang, fall (hair, dress)

zoner* to hang around, bum around,* zone out,* hang out* (with the gang)

Ayant glissé, le randonneur effrayé °se cramponnait au rocher. Having slipped, the hiker fearfully clung to the rock.

Quelle surprise pour le pauvre naufragé—au dessus un vautour °se juche sur le palmier. What a surprise awaiting the poor castaway—above him a vulture is perching on the palm tree.

S'il te plaît, °affiche la date 2 août sur les images numériques. Please label the digital images with the date, August 2.

Des rochers escarpés °surplombent la vallée et les petites péniches sur le canal. Steep cliffs overlook the valley and the small canal barges.

déchaîner to unleash, let loose, unchain

MEMORY AID

"**De-**" means *removal* or *undoing*, and the "**~chaîne~**" fragment is like the English word *chain*. Thus, to "**de-chaîne~**" is *to undo or remove the chain from*. Picture an untrained dog breaking loose from his chain to chase after the mailman. See also **déboucher** (to uncork, unblock, unplug), page 148.

Other verbs in this family include: to unyoke, unbridle, unlatch, unloosen, unravel, unclasp, liberate, release, unrig, untie, unfetter, come undone, disengage, set free, unmuzzle, free, etc.

déboîter to disconnect (mechanical coupling/connection), dislocate (joint)

débrancher to unplug (electrical device), pull out (plug), disconnect (phone)

débrayer to disengage (clutch), operate release mechanism

débrider to unbridle (horse, lust, passions)

débrouiller to unravel (mystery, problem)

défaire to undo (lock), unclasp, unlink (chain), unpin (brooch)

dégager to disengage, extricate, release, clear (leaves), unblock (sinus, nose)

dégrafer to undo, unclasp (hook, clasp), remove staple (paper)

dégréer to unrig (ship's mast), unhitch, strip ship's rigging

délacer to unlace, come undone, come untied (shoelaces)

délier to unloosen, untie (robe, knot), release (from promise), free, undo (bonds)

démêler to unravel (hairdo, rope), disentangle (knot, hair), clear up (mystery)

démuseler to let loose, unmuzzle (dog, censored press)

dénouer to untie, unknot, disentangle, unravel, undo

désaccoupler to uncouple, unlink (people, electrical plugs)

désenchaîner to unchain, remove chain from, liberate, free (prisoner)

désengager to unchain, disengage (talks), pull out (deal), opt out, withdraw (offer)

désentraver to unshackle, unfetter, remove hindrance, free, liberate

désincarcérer to free up, release (prisoner)

dessangler to loosen girth or the cinch (horse)

désunir to disunite (couple), disjoin, break up (matched set), separate (rocks), divide

détacher to untie, take off, remove, detach, unlink (trailer, wagon hitch)

dételer to unharness, unyoke, unhitch (horses, mules, oxen)

déverrouiller to unbolt (gate), set free, release (landing gear), unlock (lock)

dévisser to unscrew (woodscrew, bolt)

lâcher to unleash (dog), let go (prey), release (grip), let slip (word), drop (bomb)

laisser sans entraves to leave unshackled

lever le loquet de to unlatch (door, gate)

libérer to liberate, free, set free, discharge, release, let go

mettre en liberté   to set free, liberate

ôter le joug à   to unyoke, remove yoke (ox, slave)

ôter les fers à   to unfetter (horse, mule)

ouvrir   to unfasten, open (door), unlock (gate), unblock (passage), rip open (package)

relâcher   to release (restraints, grip, prisoner, hostage)

relaxer   to release, acquit (criminal), dismiss (legal charges), discharge (prisoner)

se rompre avec   to break up with, break off with s.o. (relationship)

se séparer de   to break off with, break up with, part (couple), part with, disunite

tirer les verrous de   to unbolt (door, window)

 Qui a lâché et °déchaîné les chiens? Ouah! Ouah! Who unleashed and let loose the dogs? Woof! Woof!

Je ne peux pas °débrancher ce cordon d'alimentation du gaufrier-gril. Il est bloqué. I can't disconnect this power cord from the waffle iron. It's stuck.

Le charpentier a eu recours à une clef à molette pour °dévisser le boulon et l'écrou à oreilles. The carpenter had to use a crescent wrench to unscrew the bolt and the wing nut.

Des secouristes sont parvenus à °dégager une fillette qui avait été bloquée depuis dix heures dans un puits désaffecté. Rescue workers succeeded in extricating a little girl who had been stuck for ten hours in an unused well.

défiler   to march, march past

MEMORY AID

"**De-**" can mean *completely* or *carefully*, and the "**~file~**" fragment is spelled the same as the English word *file*, which means **1.** *a line of persons or objects positioned one behind the other* (n), or **2.** *to march or walk in line* (v). Thus, "**de-file~**" can mean *to be completely in line* and *marching carefully in a line.* There is an English word—*defile*—that derives from the French **défiler**, which means *to march in single file or in columns* (v) or *a narrow gorge or valley* (n). Picture a long line or column of troops filing or marching toward a defile (narrow gorge). Imagine them carrying large carpenter's files instead of muskets to make the visual clues more memorable.

Other verbs in this family include: to filter through, infiltrate, follow one another, parade, strut about, advance, stride, line up, trudge, pace up and down, move forward, set out, etc.

---

aller à grands pas   to stride, stride along, take long or hasty steps

arpenter   to pace up and down, measure, survey (land)

avancer   to advance (troops, idea), move forward, head straight for, go forth, push on

balayer   to sweep past, sweep over (waves, broom, invading troops)

coller   to tailgate, follow s.o. closely

défiler devant   to march past (reviewing stand)

faire la haie   to form a line, get in line, line up

faire la queue   to line up, get in line, form a line

faire les cent pas*   to pace up and down

faire une file d'attente   to form a waiting line

faire une haie d'honneur   to form an honor guard (soldiers)

frôler   to brush against, come close to, border on, brush by, brush past

infiltrer   to infiltrate (cancer, spy), filter through, seep through (liquid)

marcher   to march, walk, troop, pace, parade, tramp

marcher à grandes enjambées   to stride along

marcher à la file   to file off (troops)

marcher à la queue leu leu   to walk in a long line one after another

marcher à la suite de qn   to walk right behind s.o.

marcher à pas de loup   to tiptoe (*lit.* to walk with wolf steps)

marcher au pas   to march

marcher d'un long pas   to walk at a brisk pace

marcher en traînant les pieds   to trudge along

mener le train   to set the pace (race)

se pavaner   to parade about, strut proudly

piétiner   to trample on, tread on, trample

prendre la file   to take one's place in line

remarcher   to walk again, work again (machine)

rentrer dans le rang   to come back into line, get back in line

repartir   to set out again, go away again

suivre   to follow one another, walk behind one another, be in order (pages)

talonner   to be on s.o.'s heels, follow on the heels of s.o.

venir après   to follow, come after (in a sequence, e.g., numbers, pages)

Le sombre cortège funèbre °défilait sur le parvis de l'église devant le tombeau du défunt. The solemn funeral procession was filing past the grave of the deceased on the church square.

Heureusement, le cyclone classé au niveau cinq ne °frôla que légèrement le littoral. Luckily, the category five cyclone only lightly brushed the coastline.

Malgré la chaleur, des dizaines de milliers d'adeptes °faisaient la queue pour pouvoir se recueillir devant le bûcher du gourou. Despite the heat, tens of thousands of followers were waiting in line to pay their respects at the guru's funeral pyre.

L'ouragan André °balaya vivement le chapelet d'îlots et se dirigea vers le continent. Hurricane Andrew briskly swept the chain of small islands and headed toward the mainland.

écarter   <small>to move apart, spread apart, set aside</small>

MEMORY AID

"É" ≈ **"ex"** can mean *away from* or *out of*. The **"~cart~"** fragment is spelled and sounds like the English word *cart*, meaning *a light vehicle moved by hand*, such as a grocery cart. Thus, **"ex-cart~"** can mean *to move a cart away from the path or out of the way*. Or the cart can be set aside. Picture an unattended brat in a grocery store running off with his mother's cart with which he wreaks havoc, spreading apart grocery displays, and moving the cart away from the aisles.

Other verbs in this family include: to spread, widen, move back, avert, swerve, deviate, skid, avoid, go astray, divert, clear out, part, separate, mislead, pull over, turn off, move aside, rove, lose one's way, differ, be on the wrong track, lose one's bearings, change directions, etc.

---

aiguiller   to shunt, divert (water flow, attention), switch (direction)

bailler   to open wide, gape (open mouth, chasm), yawn

balayer   to brush aside, sweep aside (obstacle)

déblayer   to clear away, sweep aside (obstacles), clear the way (for negotiation)

déployer   to spread, deploy (troops)

déraper   to skid (car), sideslip, slip (pedestrian), make a faux pas (s.o.)

déroger   to deviate (from norm, from standards), go astray, depart from (guidelines)

dérouter   to divert (plane, boat), change itinerary (cruise ship), reroute

détourner   to avert, divert, turn off (main road), sidetrack, hijack (e.g., plane)

se détourner   to swerve, change path, turn away, lose interest in

dévier   to swerve, deviate, sidetrack, go astray, divert, realign (tracks), blow (wind)

dévoyer   to lead astray (sheep, youth), lead from the straight and narrow path (Satan)

se disperser   to spread out, disperse (crowd), break (storm clouds), scatter (leaves)

dissiper qn   to lead s.o. astray, corrupt s.o.

diverger   to diverge (light rays, roads), differ (opinions)

divertir   to divert (attention, cash flow)

écarquiller   to spread out, open wide (eyes)

s'effacer   to withdraw, move aside, step aside, take a backseat

égarer   to lead astray (morally), mislead (investigators)

s'égarer   to lose one's way, stray, drift away, get lost, go astray

élargir   to widen (road), let out (pants/skirt waistline), broaden (horizons, mind)

s'éloigner du chemin   to wander off the path, stray from the beaten path

s'engager dans   to turn into (street)

errer   to stray, go astray, rove, roam, wander, freewheel

être en perdition   to be on the wrong path (*lit.* to be in hell)

être sur une fausse piste   to be on the wrong track

éviter   to avoid, shun, stay clear of, evade, eschew

extrapoler à partir de   to extrapolate from, infer by extending known information

faire un pas de côté   to step aside, side-step, move aside

faire une embardée   to swerve, skid, yaw (boat, airplane), rock (boat)

faire une sortie de route   to go off the track (train, vehicle)

se fourvoyer   to go astray, err, be mistaken

se frayer un passage dans   to force one's way through (crowd)

garer   to move aside, pull over (car), berth (ship), park (vehicle)

lever le pied   to take off, clear out, leave

mettre sur la touche   to sideline, bench (athlete), take out of the game (athlete)

mettre sur une voie de garage*   to sideline* (s.o., project)

obliquer   to turn off (road), bear to the side, swerve

ouvrir   to expand, open (passage, the way), open up (horizon, perspective)

perdre la piste   to lose the trail, wander off the path

perdre le nord*   to lose one's way (*lit.* to lose the north star or magnetic north)

perdre ses repères   to lose one's bearings, lose focus (business), lose landmark (ship)

se perdre   to get lost, go astray, lose one's way

se rabattre   to turn off, change one's course, cut in (ahead of car or runner)

se ranger   to pull over, step aside, park (car), step back (pedestrian)

reculer   to move back, withdraw, recoil, step back, shrink back

retirer   to withdraw, recede, move out of the way, retire

revirer   to change sides, change (mind, opinion), reverse (trend)

séparer   to separate, part, move apart, cleave, disperse, disunite, disjoin, break apart

shunter   to reroute, bypass, shunt, move from one track to another (train)

sortir des limites de   to go out of bounds (ball), go out of play

virer   to turn, change directions, turn around, swerve, veer

Les villageois se sont °écartés pour laisser passer l'entourage du roi. The villagers drew aside to let the king's entourage pass.

La piste d'une effraction informatique a été rapidement °écartée par les enquêteurs. The possibility of computer hacking was quickly dismissed by the investigators.

En raison de la défaillance du train d'atterrissage, le vol sera °dérouté vers l'aéroport le plus proche. Due to the failure of the landing gear, the flight will be diverted to the nearest airport.

Pour réduire le risque du cancer de la peau, °éviter les expositions inutiles au soleil. To reduce the risk of skin cancer, avoid unnecessary exposure to the sun.

élancer   to rush forward, dart, dash toward, pursue

accélérer   to quicken, hasten, accelerate, dispatch

s'approcher en courant   to approach quickly, come up to (s.o. or s.t.) quickly

bondir   to bound, leap, spring to, bounce, leap up

cabrioler   to caper, hop, skip, frolic, gambol (child, lamb)

se carapater*   to run, run off, scamper off

charger   to charge (cavalry), make a rush, pick up (taxi)

chasser   to chase, hunt, go hunting

chevaucher   to ride on horseback, ride a horse, sit astride (horse, bike)

converger   to converge (lines, roads, laser beams), focus on (attention)

courir après   to chase, run after, pursue, run around with (friends), chase after (s.o.)

courir une course   to run a race (foot race, car race, horse race)

courser*   to chase after, pursue, follow, chase

danser   to dance, skip, caper, frolic, move rhythmically

darder   to hurl, spear, shoot forth, dart

décocher   to let fly (arrow), dart, deliver (kick, blow), fire off (remark), fire (arrow)

s'ébattre   to frolic, gambol (lamb), sport, jump around

éjecter   to eject (pilot: plane, driver: car crash)

s'emporter   to bolt (horses), flare up (temper), fly into a passion

s'engouffrer   to rush, sweep, surge (wind down a street or in a tunnel)

envoyer valdinguer qn*   to send s.o. flying,* toss s.o. out,* boot s.o.*

faire des galipettes*   to do somersaults, do flips

faire monter en flèche   to send up (like an arrow)

filer*   to rush off, fly by, whisk by, scoot,* dart, whiz by,* skedaddle*

folâtrer   to frolic, be playful, gambol (colt)

foncer dans le tas*   to charge in, plough in (work, project), dig in

foncer tête baissée dans*   to rush headlong into (situation, love)

franchir   to leap over, clear, ride over, stride over (ditch), overcome (hurdle)

frétiller   to jump, frisk, wriggle (fish), squirm (with impatience, worm)

galoper   to gallop (horse), run wild (imagination), run (child), rush around

gambader   to frisk, skip, romp, prance, gambol, caper about

se jeter à corps perdu*   to rush headlong (into a trap, into a relationship)

lancer   to launch (missile, attack), fling, hurl (discus), shoot forth (flames)

se lancer à la poursuite de to chase after, run after, chase down (s.o., animal)

mettre en orbit to launch, put into orbit (satellite)

mirer to take aim at, point at, aim at (target, objective)

monter en amazone to ride sidesaddle (*lit.* Amazons: a mythic tribe of female warriors)

polissonner to run about in the streets (children), scamper about, run wild

poursuivre to pursue (legal action), chase (enemy, elusive dream)

précipiter to hurl, hasten, accelerate, throw, quicken (pace, step)

prendre le galop to break into a gallop

prendre son essor to fly up, fly off, take flight (hopes, airplane, bird)

présenter à l'improviste to spring on s.o. (surprise)

presser le pas to quicken one's stride

se presser to hurry, hasten, accelerate pace

projeter to throw (gravel), project (voice, slides on a screen)

propulser to propel (missile, astronaut), hurl (javelin, projectile)

rebondir to rebound, bounce, bounce back (ball, economy), rally (stocks, athlete)

se ruer to rush, dash, throw oneself, rush at, pounce at (sale item), dash to (exit)

se ruisseler (de) to run, to stream (with), drip with (sweat, water, blood)

sabrer* to hurry over, rush through (homework), go hurriedly through (book)

sauter to leap over, jump, spring, skip over, bound, hop

sauter à cloche-pied to hop, jump

sautiller to hop, skip, jump, leap, prance, bob

sillonner to streak, crisscross (flight paths, ship routes, canals, lightning bolts)

soubresauter to start, jump, plunge, jolt, jerk (motion)

surgir to spring up (plant, building), surge, pop up, crop up, loom up (mountain)

talonner to be on the heels of s.o., hotly pursue

trotter to trot along, scurry about

trottiner to jog along, toddle along (baby)

La cavalerie °s'élança à la poursuite de l'ennemi. The cavalry dashed in pursuit of the enemy.

Une centaine de gendarmes se sont °lancés à la poursuite du criminel de guerre, échappé depuis quarante-huit heures. About a hundred policemen rushed in pursuit of the war criminal, missing for forty-eight hours.

Le prix du pétrole brut a °rebondi après la chute la veille. The price of crude oil rebounded after falling the day before.

Sur la route qui serpente à travers les montagnes, elle °franchit à bicyclette le col de Saverne. On the road snaking through the mountains, she crossed the Saverne Pass by bike.

Le chat parti, les souris °dansent. When the cat's away, the mice will play.

éloigner to move away from, send away, dismiss

MEMORY AID

"É" ≈ "ex" meaning *away from*. Subtracting "g" from the "~loign~" fragment leaves **loin**, French for *far, distant, remote, at a distance*. Thus "**exloin~**" can mean *far away from, at a distance*. Picture a disgruntled host sending an unwelcome houseguest packing or dismissing him far away from his home. See also **reculer** (to recoil, move back), page 210.

Other verbs in this family include: to banish, ban, expel, exile, clear out, send packing, kick out, relocate, disinherit, evacuate, cast out, ostracize, blacklist, secede, relocate, etc.

aller loin to go a long way, go far away

avoir quartier libre to be on leave from barracks (soldier)

bannir to banish (diplomat), expel, reject (person, offer)

bazarder* to get rid of, throw out (person, object)

bouger to move (person, object, animal)

se casser* to clear, clear out, get lost, go away, leave, scram, vacate

changer de place to move to a different locale

changer de secteur to move elsewhere

commuer en to commute, exchange/change legal sentence to a lesser one

congédier to dismiss (employee), discharge, disband (organization)

se débarrasser de to get rid of (person, nuisance, object, burden)

décamper* to clear out,* buzz off,* get lost,* get out*

déhaler to haul off, tow away, tow off (ship)

délaisser to abandon, forsake, give up, neglect, relinquish (legal rights)

délocaliser to relocate (residence, office)

déménager to move house, move furniture out, change houses/apartments

déplacer to remove, transfer (employee), displace (tenant)

déporter to deport (concentration camp), send away

déraciner to uproot (tree, person), eradicate (error, prejudice)

déshériter to disinherit, disown, exclude from rights of inheritance

dessaisir to let go, dispossess, depart with, dismiss (court case)

destituer to dismiss, discharge (from duty), depose (king/queen), impeach (president)

se détourner to turn away, turn aside, lose interest (in idea, s.o.), divert (attention)

détrôner to oust (champion, ruling party), supplant (style, party)

distancer to outdistance, outstrip, outclass (competition), outrun

se distancer de to distance oneself from (s.o. or s.t.)

écarter to dispel, turn aside, avert (gaze), reject (offer, advances), dismiss (idea, s.o.)

éconduire to dismiss (visitor), turn away (salesman), reject (suitor)

s'enfuir d'un endroit to flee from a place

enlever to remove from (child: mother), kidnap

s'enterrer dans un endroit to hide from the world, withdraw from society

envoyer to send away, send forth (troops), send out (alert, messenger)

envoyer bouler qn* to send s.o. packing,* send s.o. away, kick s.o. out*

envoyer en exil to send into exile

envoyer paître qn* to send s.o. packing (*lit.* to send s.o. out to pasture)

être loin de qn to be far from s.o., be at a distance from s.o.

évacuer to evacuate, clear out, clear premises, empty (room, building), flee

exclure to exclude, expel, ban (athlete), banish, prevent entry, marginalize (s.o.)

exiler to exile, send into exile, banish, send away

s'exiler to go into exile, be a self-exile

s'expatrier to leave one's country, renounce one's citizenship, live abroad

expulser to banish, send away, expel, ban

faire la navette entre to commute (to/from work)

faire sécession to secede, formally withdraw (from union, from alliance)

faire son balluchon* to pack one's bags, pack up, leave (*lit.* **balluchon** *(m)*: bundle)

faire son deuil de* to kiss good-bye to,* say good-bye to (dead, old object, old habit)

faire un déménagement to move house, move to a new locale

faire un pèlerinage to go on a pilgrimage

faire un sort à* to get rid of (object), polish off* (beer, plate of food)

ficher le camp* to clear out,* bug off,* go away, leave

fuir to flee, fly, run away, elude (police), avoid (temptation, s.o.), recede

interdire to ban, banish

jeter qch aux orties* to do away with, discard (*lit.* to throw s.t. into the nettles)

laisser en rade* to leave s.o. in the lurch,* leave s.o. out in the cold*

lancer une ruade* to kick out,* send away (s.o.) (*lit.* **ruade** *(f)*: buck of a horse)

liquider to get rid of, sell off, liquidate (stock, inventory)

lourder* to kick out,* send away, dismiss (s.o.)

mettre au rancart* to toss out, chuck, scrap, throw on the scrap heap

mettre en quarantaine to blacklist (political opponent), quarantine (animal)

migrer to migrate (bird, animal)

ostraciser to ostracize, exclude, shun, ban from membership/fellowship (club)

se parer de to ward off (evil), guard against

partir to move away, depart, leave, go away, start off, be off

poser un lapin* to stand up* (a date), not show up for a date

prendre le large* to clear off, put to sea (ship), clear out,* get out,* be off*

quitter to withdraw from (relationship, responsibility, locale), drop out

ramer en arrière* to withdraw (*lit.* to paddle backward)

rapatrier to send back home, repatriate (exile, corpse from overseas)

reculer to move back, shrink back, recoil (in fear or disgust), draw back, back away

refouler to turn back (illegal immigrant), repress (tears, anger, memories)

refuser l'entrée à to turn away, refuse s.o. entry (bouncer, usher, border guard)

reléguer to cast out, relegate, banish, exile, demote (s.o. to a lower rank/status)

rembarrer qn*   to brush s.o. aside,* put s.o. in his place,* send s.o. packing*

se retirer   to withdraw, step down, step back, retire, pull back, clear off

scolariser   to send away to school (pupil), provide with school (community)

séparer   to separate, estrange, break up (friends, couple)

se séparer de   to separate from, sever from, part from, part with

sortir   to throw out, take out (trash)

supprimer   to remove (obstacle, wall), ax (job), withdraw (credits, assets)

tenir qn à distance   to keep s.o. at arm's length

Cette autoroute-ci vous °éloigne de la ville vers la campagne. This highway takes you out of the city to the countryside.

J'espère avoir °quitté cette masure* avant que le prochain locataire n'arrive. I'm hoping to have left this dump* before the next tenant arrives.

Le satellite météorologique °enverra à la Terre en temps réel des images de l'ouragan. The weather satellite will send back to Earth real-time images of the hurricane.

Je t'offre vingt-quatre heures pour °quitter cet arrondissement volontairement sous peine d'être °expulsé de force. I'll give you twenty-four hours to leave this district voluntarily or risk being forcibly evicted.

MEMORY AID

Recall that "**é**" can represent either "*s*" or "*ex*" in English. In this instance *both* peculiarities of punctuation will be utilized. First, "**é**" ≈ "*ex*" meaning *away from*. Next, replacing "**é**" with "*s*" and removing the "**~par~**" makes the "**s-par-piller**" look like *spiller*. Think of a farmer scattering seeds as a *spiller* of the seeds. The seeds are dispersed away from (**ex**) the farmer. Picture an exuberant kid in a candy store overly anxious to get at the gumballs, which end up spilling (*ex-pill* or *s-pill*), scattering, or being dispersed all over the floor, away from the counter. See also **étendre** (to extend, spread out), page 199.

Other verbs in this family include: to sprinkle, strew, sow, disseminate, put in disorder, seed, dissipate, spread abroad, diffuse, litter, swarm, be teeming with, permute, propagate, etc.

aller de guingois*   to go haywire,* go awry, go askew, go wild*

se déposer   to settle (dust, sediment)

déranger   to disarrange, put in disorder, mess up (papers, bedroom)

désintégrer   to disintegrate (atom), split up, crumble, break into pieces (rock, cookie)

disperser   to disperse (fog), scatter (ashes, leaves), break up (collection, crowd)

se disperser   to disband, break up (band, group)

disséminer   to scatter, disseminate (seeds, ideas), disperse

dissiper   to dissipate (fog, clouds), dispel (rumor, fear), scatter, clear up (weather)

écarter   to spread (fingers, legs), throw wide apart, separate, draw open (curtains)

éjaculer   to ejaculate (sudden exclamation, semen)

enfanter (des êtres)   to propagate (beings), create, give rise to

ensemencer   to sow (seeds, field), seed (rain clouds)

essaimer   to scatter, spread (population, business), swarm (bees)

étaler   to spread out (objects, butter, paste), rub on (ointment), roll out (dessert cart)

étendre   to spread out (limb, newspaper), extend (reach, influence), dilute, thin out

être clairsemé   to be thinly sown (seeds), be scattered (rocks, vegetation)

fourmiller (de)   to be teeming (with), swarm (bees, ants, locusts)

fuser   to burst forth, come from all sides (questions), erupt (vapor, lava)

inséminer   to inseminate, fertilize

joncher   to scatter, strew (papers), litter, be strewn over (flowers, corpses), blanket

licencier   to disband (organization), dismiss (employee), disperse

mettre en désordre   to put in disorder or disarray

papillonner*   to switch back and forth (partners, activities), flit about*

parsemer (de)   to strew (rose petals), sprinkle (with) (spices), scatter (quotes: book)

permuter   to change around, permute, change (seats, jobs), permute (math)

propager   to diffuse, spread about (ideas, news, propaganda), circulate (rumors)

se propager   to propagate (faith, ideas), give birth to (religion, theory)

répandre   to scatter, spill, spread (fear, rumor), pour out (liquid), break (news)

saupoudrer   to sprinkle (flour, salt)

semer   to sow (seed), scatter, sprinkle (sugar, salt, water)

Tous ses vêtements étaient °éparpillés partout. C'était un vrai méli-mélo.* All his clothes were scattered everywhere. It was a real jumbled mess.

Aïe! Ton rapport scolaire est °parsemé d'erreurs typographiques. Oh dear! Your school report is riddled with typographical errors.

De fortes rafales de vent ont °répandu le feu de broussailles sur plus de dix mille hectares. Strong gusts of wind spread the brush fire over more than ten thousand hectares (approximately twenty-five thousand acres).

Ses idées portant sur la vie après la mort et le repentir pour le péché °se propagèrent à travers le continent, donnant naissance à un nouveau culte. His ideas regarding the afterlife and repentance for sin spread across the continent, giving rise to a new religion.

Qui °sème le vent, récolte la tempête. Sow the breeze, reap the whirlwind.

to extend, spread out, stretch out **étendre**

MEMORY AID

"**É**" ≈ "*ex*" meaning *away from*. Contained within the verb is the fragment "~**tend**~." One meaning of the English verb *tend* is *to extend* or *move in a certain direction*. Thus, "**ex-tend~**" can mean to *move away from in a certain direction*. The English verb *to extend* means *to stretch out* or *spread to fullest length*. Picture an inconsiderate sunbather reclining to soak up the sun's rays after spreading out and extending his blanket and belongings, crowding other nearby beachgoers. See also **éparpiller** (to spread, disperse), page 197.

Other verbs in this family include: to overrun, expand, invade, take up space, sprawl, abound, widen, prolong, broadcast, deploy, dilute, emit, be influential over, spread to, multiply, etc.

agrandir to enlarge, widen, make greater, augment (size), make spacious (garden)

atteindre to reach, attain (status, goal, end point, finish line)

avoir le don d'ubiquité to be everywhere, be ubiquitous, omnipresent

circuler to move around, circulate (air, money), spread (rumor), pass around (food)

colporter to spread about, spread around (rumor), hawk (merchandise)

se communiquer to spread to (disease, fire), spread around, be transmitted (flu)

déployer to spread out, deploy (troops, riot police)

dérouiller les jambes* to stretch one's legs

se développer to spread (custom), expand, extend, propagate, grow (influence)

diffuser to spread, diffuse (scent), broadcast (TV), air (TV/radio program), telecast

diluer to dilute (wine, medicine), thin out (paint), pad out (speech)

ébruiter to spread (news, rumor, gossip)

écarquiller to open wide (eyes)

élargir to widen, enlarge (scope), stretch (shoes), broaden (knowledge, mind)

émettre to transmit (radio signal), emit (radiation)

enrichir to extend (list), enrich (financially, language, collection)

envahir to spread to, invade (insects, army, plague), overrun, flood (new product)

essaimer to expand (business), spread (population, influence), swarm (bees)

étaler to spread out, display (items), spread (buffet), lay out (dish), show off, flaunt

s'étaler to spread out, sprawl, portend (omen), foretell, be a harbinger (bad news)

s'étendre to stretch (parade), lie down, reach, sprawl, repose, increase (domain)

étirer to stretch out (road, convoy), elongate, stretch (legs)

faire campagne to canvass an area (politician), go campaigning (in a precinct)

faire des étirements to do stretching exercises

faire irruption dans to invade (plague, enemy), burst in (room), barge in (uninvited)

faire tache d'huile* to spread (oil spill) (*lit.* to spread like an oil stain)

faire un duplex entre to hook up TV and radio (for simulcast transmission)

fluidifier to thin out (blood)

grouiller to swarm (clients, tourists, flies), stir, teem (germs), mill around (crowd)

imprimer to transmit (impulse), run off copies (newspaper, magazine)

moquetter to carpet (room) (*lit.* **moquette** (*f*): carpet, wall-to-wall carpet)

multiplier to multiply (math), make manifold, increase (power, effect)

se prélasser to sprawl, bask in the sun

prendre de l'envergure to expand (project, business), increase scope/scale/span of

pulluler to multiply, swarm (flies, rats), abound, congregate (tourists)

radiodiffuser to broadcast (radio program), emit radio signals

radiographier to x-ray, take a radiograph

rayonner to extend over, be influential over/in, beam (with health), glow, radiate

rélargir to widen, let out (clothes)

répandre to spread (news, fashion, terror)

répartir (sur) to spread (over) (time period)

semer à la volée to broadcast (news, rumor, announcement)

tapisser to carpet (room), lay out carpet

tartiner to spread (jam, butter), spread over (article extending over several pages)

télégraphier to telegraph (message by wire)

téléphoner à to telephone, call on the phone

téléviser televise, transmit a TV program

tendre to stretch out, spread, hold out (hand, hat, collection plate)

tenir to take up space, hold a space (seat), hold out (time), contain (volume)

se vautrer to sprawl (on grass), wallow (in mud, in self-pity), slouch (in armchair)

La perspective du sommet °s'étend sur plus de vingt kilomètres. The view from the summit extends for over twenty kilometers.

Quelques 2.000 soldats polonais seront °déployés demain, en remplacement de troupes françaises. Some 2,000 Polish soldiers will be deployed tomorrow to replace French troops.

Le mouvement gréviste menace de °s'étendre à d'autres villes. The strikers' movement is threatening to spread to other towns.

À la suite du naufrage, le pétrolier avait °répandu quelques 80 millions de litres de pétrole brut au long du littoral. As a result of the sinking, the oil tanker had spread some 80 million liters of heavy crude oil along the coast.

MEMORY AID

The "**glisse~**" fragment looks quite similar to the English word *glisten*, meaning *to shine* or *sparkle*. Picture someone shoveling a sidewalk coated with a glistening cover of ice.

Other verbs in this family include: to gloss over, frost, ice up, fall, trip, tumble, tilt, coast, skate, swirl, freeze, lose one's balance, stumble, sled, ski, stagger, sway, reel, spin, whirl, etc.

avoir un vertige   to have a dizzy spell, be lightheaded, have vertigo, feel dizzy

se balancer   to swing, sway, teeter, sway back and forth

buter   to stumble, bump into, trip over (word, obstacle)

caboter   to coast, coast along, sail along the coast of (ship)

chanceler   to stagger, sway (drunkard, dizzy person)

chopper   to stumble, trip, trip over, bumble*

commettre un impair   to blunder, commit a blunder

se congeler   to freeze (food)

se couler   to slip, glide, flow (river), run (cake icing, cheese, faucet)

coulisser   to slide (door, drawer), glide (on track)

dégringoler   to tumble (acrobat), take a tumble (reputation), collapse (stock price)

se déplacer une vertèbre   to slip a disc (back), herniate a disc (spine)

déraper   to skid, slip (on ice), sideslip (skier)

être étourdi   to be dizzy, be giddy, be light-headed, be scatterbrained

être gelé   to be iced, be frozen

être prêt à tomber dans   to teeter on the edge of (cliff, financial ruin)

faire de la luge   to sled, luge

faire des glissades sur la glace   to slip on the ice

faire du ski   to snow ski

faire la trace   to ski on fresh snow

faire tomber   to trip (s.o.), knock over (vase)

faire un dérapage   to skid (airplane, car), wipe out (surfer), drift (car)

faire un faux pas sur   to slip on (ice, marbles)

faire un tête-à-queue   to spin around, whirl around (*lit.* to do a head-to-tail spin)

geler   to freeze (liquid)

se givrer   to ice up (engine, windshield), frost over (lake), frost (cake with icing)

glacer   to ice, frost (windowpane), freeze, glaze (donut), chill (beer mug, person)

glisser sur   to gloss over (details), glide across (piano keys), skate over (subject)

incliner   to tilt, incline (slope, person), recline, lie back

lâcher   to slip, become loose (grip), release (brakes), let loose (swear word), loosen

louper*   to bungle,* make a mess of* (situation)

mourir de froid   to freeze to death

patiner   to skate, spin, ice-skate, roller-skate

perdre pied   to lose one's footing, slip, lose balance

perdre son équilibre   to lose one's balance

planer   to glide (bird, plane, hang glider)

se promener en traîneau   to go sledding, sleighing

se renverser   to fall down, to be spilt (bottle)

riper   to slip, skid, slide

tanguer   to reel, spin, pitch (boat: storm), stumble, stagger

tituber   to stagger (drunkard, s.o. dizzy)

tomber   to fall, fall down, tumble, overturn (car), capsize (boat)

tomber par terre   to fall down, fall to the ground, fall to earth, topple over (tower)

toupiller*   to spin, whirl round and round

tourbillonner   to swirl (smoke, snow), twist (tornado) (*lit.* **tourbillon** *(m)*: whirlpool)

tournoyer   to turn round and round, swirl (smoke, water), swirl around (leaves)

trébucher   to trip, stumble, trip up (*lit.* trebuchet: medieval catapult with trip rope)

vaciller   to teeter, sway, be unsteady, falter, waver, wobble, quiver, lurch

Après de fortes chutes de neige, des congères se sont formées sur les trottoirs. Gare à toi! C'est °glissant! After a heavy snowfall, snowdrifts covered the sidewalks. Watch out! It's slippery!

Permettez-moi de °glisser un mot en faveur de mon collègue. Allow me to put in a good word for my co-worker.

Le ruisseau °glisse parmi les herbes ondulantes. The brook glides among the swaying grasses.

L'avocat hautain °trébucha sur la pierre d'achoppement de son orgueil. The haughty lawyer tripped over the stumbling block of his pride.

MEMORY AID

"**Par-**" means *beyond*, and **courir** means *to run*, so "**par-courir**" can mean *to run beyond*. Picture a marathon athlete running beyond city limits and provincial borders to travel up and down the French countryside covering a great distance.

Other verbs in this family include: to commute between, cross, crisscross, span, snake through, jog along, step across, transfer, cut across, go over, pass in transit, cruise, bridge, etc.

aller son petit bonhomme de chemin* to jog along,* trot along*

battre le pavé* to walk up and down the street (*lit.* **pavé** (*m*): pavement, cobblestone)

bourlinguer* to travel around a lot, voyage, sail (ship)

changer de trottoir to cross the street (*lit.* to change sidewalks)

combler le fossé to bridge the gap (between generations, in salaries)

se communiquer to spread (fire, disease, news)

couper to cut across (route), intersect (lines, roads)

couper à travers champs to cut across country

courir le monde to travel the world, travel around the world, globe-trot

décoller to take off (airplane), lift off (rocket)

se déplacer to travel, move along, get around, travel rapidly

desservir to ply/sail between ports (boats), serve an area (e.g., bus/train routes)

émettre to transmit, emit (sound, light), issue (money, loan), broadcast (TV, radio)

enjamber to span (bridge: river), step across (ditch), stride across, step over (rock)

s'envoler to fly off, take off, take flight

s'étendre de ~ à to reach from ~ to, to stretch from one point to another

être mis en travers to lay across, be placed across (road, tracks), be skewed (image)

faire beaucoup de chemin to cover a lot of ground (runner, vehicle, search party)

faire de la tournée to go around to (stores, cafés, clubs)

faire de l'auto-stop to hitchhike, be a hitchhiker

faire du caravaning to go on a trip in an RV (recreational vehicle)

faire du tourisme to go touring, go sightseeing, be a tourist

faire du tout-terrain to go cross-country racing (car)

faire la correspondance to make a connection, transfer (subway)

faire la navette entre to commute between, shuttle between, travel between

faire la traversée to cross, go across (country, lake, continent)

faire le trajet de ~ à to do the trip from ~ to (destinations A and B)

faire un transfert to transfer (to hospital), make transfer (bus), carry over (sum)

faire une tournée to go on a tour, take a tour

franchir to get over, go through, ford (stream), jump over (ditch), pass over

fréquenter   to go to, frequent (bar, disco), see regularly, run with (same crowd)

jeter un pont sur   to bridge (gap, river)

longer   to run along, skirt along, run parallel to (road, fence), hug (sidewalk, railing)

mesurer   to span (distance), measure (height, width, depth, shoe size)

outrepasser   to go beyond (limitation), transgress (boundary), overstep (authority)

passer   to cross, go over, pass

passer par   to go through (customs, chain of command), get through (difficulty)

répandre   to spread abroad (influence), spread (rumor, terror)

repasser   to cross again, pass again, go past again (same spot), revisit (city, site)

serpenter à travers   to snake through

sillonner   to crisscross, streak through (countryside), travel across (country)

sillonner les routes   to travel the country

survoler   to fly over (in plane), skim over (question), skim through (book)

transférer   to transfer (office, phone call), convey (property), wire (s.o. money)

transiter par   to pass in transit through (city, country)

transmettre   to transmit (TV signal), convey, channel, beam (signal), send, pass on

transporter   to transport, move (merchandise, furniture), freight, ferry, ship (cargo)

traverser   to traverse, span, cross

voler en rase-mottes*   to fly with frequent stopovers (*lit.* to fly to open clumps of ground)

voyager   to travel, take a trip, journey

voyager outre-mer   to travel overseas

voyager par voie de terre   to travel overland

Les trois compagnons de voyage °parcouraient le pays en auto-stop. The three traveling companions traversed the countryside by hitchhiking.
Alors qu'il °se déplaçait de Paris à Londres, les autorités ont découvert son nom sur la liste de surveillance. While he was traveling from Paris to London, the authorities found his name on the surveillance list.

S'il vous plaît, °parcourez cette lettre quand vous le pourrez. Please peruse this letter when you have the time.

Il a °parcouru les numéros du doigt dans l'annuaire téléphonique. He ran his finger down the numbers listed in the phone directory.

Le TGV °sillonnait le paysage à la vitesse grand V*. The high speed train streaked through the countryside at top speed.

MEMORY AID

The **"precipit~"** fragment is found in the English word *precipitation*, meaning **1.** *the physical state of raining (or snowing)*, and **2.** *a headlong fall or rush.* Thus, the reflexive verb of **se précipiter** can be thought of as *to rush oneself.* Picture a sudden downpour causing people to hurry to get out of the drenching rain (precipitation). See also **élancer** (to rush forward, dart, dash toward), page 192.

Other verbs in this family include: to hasten, speed, run, sprint, shoot past, haul ass,* expedite, dispatch, race, rip along,* get a move on,* go double-quick,* rush about, jog, etc.

accélérer   to expedite, quicken, dispatch, accelerate, hasten, hurry up, speed up

accélérer le train   to speed up, hurry up

accourir   to hasten, run up to, flock (to movie star, to sale)

s'affairer   to bustle about, busy oneself (household chores, errands)

affluer   to rush (blood, fluid), flock (crowd, animals) pour in (requests, letters)

aller à la va-vite*   to be in a rush, be in a hurry

aller à toute vitesse   to speed, go quickly

aller au galop   to gallop (horse)

aller dare-dare*   to go double-quick,* hasten, hurry, go at a fast pace

aller grand train*   to go at a brisk pace, hurry, rush

avoir le feu au derrière*   to be in a hurry (*lit.* to have one's butt on fire*)

bâcler   to rush (job), dash off (project, report)

bousculer   to hustle, jostle (crowd, ideas in head)

brûler un feu rouge   to run through/burn through a red light

courir   to run, hasten, race, scurry

courir à fond de train*   to run at top speed

courir à toute allure   to rush about at full speed, run at top speed

courir à toute vitesse   to sprint, race, run at full speed

courir çà et là   to rush about, run here and there

courir vite   to race, run fast, run quickly, sprint

se dépêcher   to hurry, rush, make haste, step on it,* step on the gas,* hurry up*

descendre à toutes jambes   to sprint, race

entraîner brusquement   to rush, sweep along briskly

être pressé   to be in a rush, be in a hurry

expédier   to hurry, do quickly, dispatch (letter), expedite (charges), rush (job)

faire de la course à pied   to go running

faire du jogging   to jog, go jogging

faire en quatrième vitesse*   to do at top speed*

faire la course   to race (competitively)

faire vinaigre*   to hurry up* (*lit.* to hasten wine production too quickly resulting in vinegar*)

filer*   to bolt, run, flash, fly by (time), whiz by*

folâtrer   to frolic, to play, gambol (colt)

foncer*   to bolt for it,* speed along, bolt ahead, bolt

franchir le mur de son   to break the sound barrier (jet)

galoper   to scamper, gallop (horse), run wild (imagination), rush around

gambader   to skip, frolic, frisk, scamper, spring, gambol, leap

griller un feu rouge* to run a red light, speed through a stoplight

griller un stop* to fail to stop (at stop sign)

hâter le pas to speed it up, hasten one's step

se hâter to hasten, make haste, rush, rush into

imposer le rythme to set the pace (foot race, car race)

se jeter to rush oneself, fling oneself, hasten, rush, jump (at chance), pounce

se jeter à corps perdu to rush headlong (into relationship, into project)

lutter de vitesse to race, race against (competition)

se magner* to get a move on,* hurry up,* rush

se magner le derche* to haul ass,* rush

monter to rush up, go up (stairs), move up, rise up

partir à la hâte to hasten, leave in haste

passer à tire d'aile* to pass by in full flight*

passer en flèche* to shoot past,* zoom past,* zip past* (*lit.* **flèche** (*f*): arrow, dart)

passer en trombe* to pass by like a whirlwind*

piquer* to sprint, go into a dive (plane), swoop down (bird)

piquer un sprint* to sprint, run fast

pousser une pointe de vitesse to put on a burst of speed

prendre ses jambes à son corps* to take to one's heels in flight

presser le mouvement to hurry up, rush

presser le pas to quicken one's pace

se presser to rush, hurry

profiler to streamline (process), make aerodynamic (airplane)

rendre aérodynamique to streamline, make aerodynamic *les membres de la medecine*

se ruer to rush, throw oneself, dash toward (sale item, exit)

se secouer* to get a move on,* hurry, make an effort

sprinter to sprint, run at top speed

survoler to fly over, skim through (book), skim over (question), pounce on (s.o.)

tenir le rythme to keep up the pace, keep up with (front runner, hectic pace)

tirer* to rush off, hurry off, leave in a hurry

se tirer vite fait* to be off like a shot,* bolt, take off in a hurry*

tracer* to go fast, rip along,* speed along, belt along*

trottiner to scamper, trot (horse), scoot along (child), scurry about (mouse)

La foule des admirateurs °se précipite vers la limousine de la vedette. The crowd of fans rushes toward the star's limousine.

Une marée d'inconditionnels °se pressa dans la salle pour voir la vedette du feuilleton télévisé. A flood of ardent fans rushed into the room to see the TV soap opera star.

Tous les jours les fidèles °affluent à Lourdes, la cité sainte, pour prier et louer Dieu. Every day the faithful flock to the holy town of Lourdes to pray to and praise God.

Le roi °s'est jeté dans la guerre au mépris de l'avis de ses alliés. The king hastened to war, disdaining his allies' opinions.

MEMORY AID

The **"ramp~"** fragment is spelled like the English word *ramp*, meaning *an inclined passage or platform connecting different levels*. Picture the paired animals of the earth being called to enter Noah's ark before the flood. The limbless snakes have to creep, crawl, and slither up the ramp to reach the ark.

Other verbs in this family include: to wind, stir, snake, limp, halt, hobble, prowl, stagger, wriggle, writhe, prostrate oneself, crouch, lurk, lie flat, fidget, lie down, loiter, linger, etc.

s'abaisser   to lower/humble oneself, be servile, be submissive

aller à cahin-caha*   to hobble along,* toddle along*

aller clopin-clopant*   to hobble along,* toddle along*

s'aplatir   to grovel, lie flat, crouch, go flat (object, cake, carbonated soda)

s'attarder   to loiter, linger, take one's time

avancer au pas   to creep, crawl on all fours

clocher   to limp, hobble, go awry (engine), go amiss (problem, mechanism)

clopiner   to limp, halt, hobble (on crutches)

se coucher   to lie down, go to bed, go to sleep

se coucher sur le ventre   to lie face down, lie prone

s'en aller la queue basse*   to slink, slink away, crawl away

entrer furtivement   to creep in (cat, spy)

être allongé décubitus dorsal   to be lying supine (on back), be supine

être allongé décubitus ventral   to be lying prone (on stomach), be prone

être prostré   to be lying prone (on stomach), be prostrate

gésir   to lie, lie down, lie low, be recumbent

se glisser   to creep, slither

se grouiller   to stir, move, crawl, move slowly

s'humilier   to humble oneself, grovel (before king/queen), lower oneself (status)

marcher à quatre pattes   to crawl (*lit.* to walk on four paws)

se mettre à plat ventre   to lie on one's stomach

se prosterner   to grovel, lurk, prostrate oneself

se remuer   to stir, fidget, move about

rôder   to prowl, prowl about

serpenter   to snake, wind (trail, river)

sidérer*   to stagger* (news headline)

se tordre   to writhe, convulse (with laughter), double over (laughing, in pain)

se tortiller   to wriggle, writhe

se traîner   to crawl along, drag along, lurk, loiter, straggle, traipse

se vautrer   to grovel, wallow (in mud, in self-pity)

Les deux serpents °rampaient aussi vite que possible pour monter à bord de l'arche avant l'averse. The two snakes were crawling as fast as possible to climb into the ark before the downpour began.

Après le déluge, les cadavres du bétail noyé °gisaient à même le sol. After the flood, the corpses of the drowned livestock lay on the bare ground.

Sous l'obscurité nocturne, le renard °se glissa dans le poulailler pour choisir la plus grande poule. Under the cover of night, the fox crept into the henhouse to choose the fattest hen.

randonner   to go hiking, go walking

MEMORY AID

Randonner sounds and looks a bit like the English word *randomly*, meaning *haphazardly, having no specific pattern or objective*. Picture an intrepid hiker with a full day ahead of him and without any specific goal or destination walking, hiking, and wandering the countryside randomly.

Other verbs in this family include: to ramble, jaunt, trek, roam, have wanderlust, venture, stroll, saunter, tramp along, tread, go astray, drift, meander, amble along, be restless, wander, etc.

aller à pas de géant*   to go by leaps and bounds,* take big steps

aller à pied   to go for a walk, tramp, hike

aller faire un tour   to jaunt, take a tour, make a short trip or excursion

aller son chemin   to amble along, walk leisurely

ambler   to amble, with a leisurely gait

s'aventurer   to venture, undertake (risk), take a challenge

avoir la bougeotte*   to be restless, be on the move, be fidgety*

avoir la manie des voyages   to have wanderlust

se balader*   to go for a walk, stroll, gallivant*

battre le pavé*   to walk the streets (*lit.* to beat the pavement)

bourlinguer*   to travel around a lot, sail (ship)

cheminer   to walk, tramp, walk along, progress, advance (troops), wend through

courir à petites foulées   to jog along (*lit.* **foulée** (*f*): stride)

courir le monde   to travel the world, travel around the world

déambuler   to stroll, wander, saunter, walk around, stroll about

divaguer   to ramble, wander, stray (from path, from the topic)

enchaîner   to move on to (next scene in play/movie, next topic)

errer   to wander, roam, rove, stray

faire de la marche à pied   to tramp, hike, go walking

faire du cheval   to go horseback riding

faire du footing   to go jogging

faire du trekking   to go trekking

faire les cent pas*   to pace up and down

faire un périple   to take a long trip/trek

faire une randonnée à bicyclette   to bike ride

faire une randonnée équestre   to horseback ride

faire une randonnée pédestre   to hike, go hiking, go on a hike

faire une virée*   to go for a walk/ride/drive

flâner   to saunter, stroll, roam around, roam aimlessly

fouler   to trample, tread (a path), tramp

se fourvoyer   to go astray, lose one's way, err

se frayer un passage dans   to cut a path through (forest, thick brush, crowd)

se hasarder   to venture, risk, hazard (guess), expose oneself to risk

marauder*   to cruise (for taxi fares)

marcher d'un pas lourd   to tramp along, trudge

marcher d'un pas nonchalant   to saunter along, stroll, walk at a leisurely pace

mener une vie vagabonde   to lead the life of a vagabond/tramp/hobo

mettre le pied   to tread, walk, step, set foot (in s.o.'s house)

se mettre au vert* to take a trip to the countryside (*lit.* to go to the green)

partir en vadrouille* to go on a jaunt, ramble, stroll, roam, wander aimlessly

se paumer* to get lost, lose one's way, lose the trail

se poser to tread (on sensitive subject, on s.o.'s rights), arise (question)

se prélasser to strut, stalk along, jaunt

prendre un raccourci to take a shortcut, take a shorter route

se promener to go for a walk, go for a drive

rayonner to walk in all directions from a central locale

rôder to wander about, wander aimlessly, loiter

serpenter to meander (hiker, trail), snake through (river), snake along (trail)

tâter le terrain to find out the lay of the land, get a feel for the terrain

tâtonner to grope around, feel one's way around, fumble around

traîner dans les rues to roam, rove, wander

se traîner to walk, trudge, trudge along, traipse

trébucher to stumble along, bumble along

trottiner to amble, toddle along* (child), scurry along (mouse), scoot about*

vadrouiller* to rove around, wander around

vagabonder to wander (hiker, mind), roam (imagination)

voguer to wander, drift, sail (boat)

Pendant mes vacances à la campagne, je faisais des °randonnées le long des sentiers balisés. During my vacation in the country, I hiked along marked trails.

Le futur papa °avait la bougeotte.* Il °faisait les cent pas* dans le couloir du bloc d'accouchement. The father-to-be was restless. He paced up and down in the delivery suite hallway.

Un sanglier, échappé de son enclos, °erra durant vingt-quatre heures dans la bourgade avant d'être rattrapé par les gendarmes. The wild boar that had escaped from his pen wandered through the small township for twenty-four hours before being recaptured by the police.

Les aveugles spirituels °tâtonnaient comme des aveugles cherchant la porte. Peuvent-ils trouver la vérité? The spiritually blind groped around like blind men searching for the door. Can they find the truth?

reculer to move back, back away, shrink away

abandonner to abandon (hope), give up, renounce, surrender, desert, abort (data)

avoir des ratés* to backfire* (car) (*lit.* **raté** *(m):* flop, dud, failure)

baisser les bras to give in, admit defeat, surrender, lower one's arms (weapon)

baisser son froc* to take it lying down, give in to punishment

battre en retraite to beat a retreat, retreat (army)

se carapater* to scram,* leave quickly, run away, run off

céder à to yield, give in, give up, yield to (higher power, authority)

cesser le feu to cease fire, observe a ceasefire/truce

chanceler to falter (economy), stagger

contre-pédaler to backpedal, back off from (opinion, prior remark)

culer to go backwards (boat), fall back (*lit.* **cul*** *(m):* butt, bottom)

dater à to date back to (in time)

déclarer forfait to withdraw (from sports event), give up, default, forfeit (game)

se défoncer to give way (bridge), break up (road), freak out, go berserk (on drugs)

se dégonfler* to chicken out*

déguerpir* to move off, be gone, clear out,* clear off,* bolt

délaisser to neglect, desert, leave behind, abandon (s.o., s.t., home)

désemparer to quit, go away, interrupt

déserter to desert, abandon (friends, country, post), give up (cause, effort)

se désister to withdraw (candidature), desist, step down (from job), waive (claim)

s'en aller furtivement to slink away, sneak away, creep away

être en recul to be losing ground (in polls), be declining (civilization, inflation)

faiblir to weaken, die down (voice, sound, energy)

faire machine arrière to backpedal, go astern, go backward, reverse (engine)

faire un pas en arrière to step back (in time), take a step backward

faire une rechute to relapse (bad habit, criminal, illness), fall again (stock prices)

hésiter to falter, waver, vacillate, waffle (decision), hesitate, balk at (offer)

intervertir to reverse the order of (numbers, words), reverse (roles)

inverser to reverse (direction), invert (object, image)

partir discrètement to slip away, leave quietly, leave unnoticed

se plier à to give in to, submit to (authority)

se ployer to yield, fold, give way (to pressure)

quitter to quit, give up, leave (situation, locale)

ramer en arrière* to withdraw, pull back (*lit.* to paddle/row backward)

se ranger to stand back (pedestrian), step back, pull over (car), step aside

rappliquer* to come back, return, turn up* (lost dog, lost item)

se rebattre sur qch to fall back on s.t. (familiar habit)

rebondir to rebound, bounce, bounce back (ball, from illness)

rebrousser chemin to turn back (direction, trajectory), retrace one's steps

rechigner to balk, hesitate, be reluctant

rechuter to have a relapse (illness), backslide (criminal, sinner), fall again (prices)

récidiver to relapse (medical condition, career criminal)

recoquiller to turn back, turn up, bend back (book pages)

refléter to reflect, bounce back (light, sound)

refluer to swing back, ebb (tide), flood back (memories), rush back (blood, crowd)

réfracter to refract (laser beam, light), bend (light beam)

regagner ses pénates* to go back home (*lit.* Penates: Roman gods of the home)

regimber to draw back, resist, balk (animal), jib, kick back (horse), shy away

régresser to recede (pain, flood), regress (knowledge), fall off (sales), deteriorate

se rejeter to fall back on, jump back

se rejeter en arrière to jump backward, recoil

remonter à to date back to (in time) (i.e., ruins dating back to ancient Greece)

se rencogner to retreat, crouch in the corner

rengainer to withdraw, put away, put back (gun: holster), resheath (sword, knife)

renoncer à to give up (smoking, bad habit), waive (rights, claim)

se renverser to fall back, capsize (boat), lean back (in chair), stagger back

se replier to withdraw (troops), draw back, fall back, retreat

se retirer to retire, withdraw, subside, pull back, retreat, lose interest (in s.o.)

retomber to fall again (stock market), relapse (illness)

retourner sur ses pas to retrace one's steps

se retourner to be turned around (situation)

rétracter to retract (statement), recant (testimony), disavow

se retrancher to fall back upon, retreat, entrench (troops), hide behind (law)

rétrograder to go back, fall back (position, ranking)

rétropédaler* to backpedal,* back off from* (opinion, prior remark)

revenir à la mode to come back into fashion

revisiter to revisit (town, museum, subject)

revivre to relive, revive (old style/fashion), reincarnate

ricocher to rebound, ricochet (bullet), bounce off (of), carom (basketball)

rôder to skulk away, lurk, withdraw (into shadows)

soustraire to withdraw, take away, subtract

tanguer to reel, pitch (boat, plane), spin around (room: dizzy person)

tituber to stagger, reel, bumble,* walk unsteadily, stumble

tomber à la renverse to fall backward

vaciller to waver, vacillate, be unsteady, wobble back and forth, teeter, falter

Le lâche °reculait devant son ennemi dès le début de la bataille. The coward retreated in the face of the enemy from the onset of the battle.
Dès lors elle °délaissa sa carrière musicale pour poursuivre un nouveau rêve. From that point on she abandoned her musical career to pursue a new dream.

Les faibles averses du mois dernier n'ont pas été suffisantes pour °inverser la tendance d'un débit d'eau déficitaire. Last month's weak showers were not sufficient to reverse the trend of a deficit in the water capacity.

Le gouvernement refuse de °céder aux exigences stipulées par les ravisseurs. The government refuses to give in to the kidnappers' demands.

La mousson dévastatrice, de catégorie cinq, continue à perdre puissance et est actuellement °rétrogradée à la catégorie quatre. The devastating category-five monsoon continues to lose strength and is currently downgraded to category four.

to lift up, raise, heave, take up **soulever**

accroître to raise (taxes), increase (power, interest), enlarge (size)

arborer to hoist (flag), feature (sale item), display (banner)

assujettir to steady, fix, fasten, keep under (control)

atteindre son summum to reach its peak/zenith (art, civilization)

augmenter to raise (prices), increase (tax), rise, augment, mount (casualties)

charpenter to construct, frame (a house)

construire to build, erect, construct, raise (tower, building)

contrebalancer to counterbalance, equalize balance/weights, offset (weight)

contrebuter to buttress (cathedral wall) shore up, prop up, support (scaffolding)

cultiver to raise (crops), grow (plants), cause to grow, cultivate (farm, good taste)

déferler to unfurl (flag), rise up (waves)

desceller to pull up (rock, masonry)

doper to boost (economy)

dresser to erect, set up, raise, lift, put up (ladder, barrier)

se dresser sur la pointe des pieds to tiptoe, stand on tiptoe

échafauder to raise scaffolding, to construct (thesis), put together (response, project)

édifier to erect, build, construct, edify (person, morally)

élever to raise, bring up, rear, elevate (wall, statue, level, voice, tax, price)

épauler to raise (to the shoulder) (rifle, load), assist, give a hand to (s.o.)

ériger to erect, raise up (monument, statue, building, scaffolding)

s'établir to set up, establish (business, norms, government, rules)

étayer to prop, buttress, shore up (wall, argument, theory)

exalter to elevate (spirit), elate, fire (imagination), overjoy (good news)

faire bâtir to build, have built (house, town)

faire lever to raise, make rise (dough)

faire naître to raise (suspicions), give rise to (idea, fears, difficulty)

guinder to hoist, strain, lift (oneself up, load), force

hausser to raise (prices, salary), shrug (shoulders), increase (taxes)

se hérisser to stand up, stand on end (hair), bristle, fluff (fur)

hisser to lift, hoist (flag), haul up (sails), heave

lever to raise, lift, heave, pull up, lift up, raise up, leaven (dough)

se lever to rise, get up, stand up, stand, lift oneself up

maintenir to uphold (law), maintain (peace, equipment), hold up (wall)

mettre en berne   to fly a flag at half-staff (land) or half-mast (nautical)

monter   to rise, take up, bring up (baggage), mount (gem on ring), pitch (tent)

placer   to put up, place, install, put into place, set in place (furniture)

planter   to erect, plant (trees along street), set (stage for a story)

porter   to carry (cargo), bear (responsibility), support (weight)

progresser   to rise, be on the increase (crime, wind, inflation, unemployment)

rebâtir   to rebuild (house, economy, business)

reconstruire   to rebuild, reconstruct, put together again

redonner du tonus à   to give a boost to (economy, spirit)

redresser   to set upright (statue), right (boat), straighten (plane), put back on track

réédifier   to rebuild, reconstruct, erect again

rehausser   to raise (ceiling, age limit), heighten, make higher (tax), revamp, build up

réinstaller   to put back up, put up again, refurbish, reinstall (stereo), refit (room)

relever   to pick up (chair, economy), lift anew, raise again (statue), right (boat)

remonter   to raise again, pick up, push up, climb up, restore upright (statue)

se remonter*   to get oneself together, get one's act together*

renflouer   to refloat, raise, salvage (boat)

renouer   to renovate, restore, refurbish, renew

reposer sur   to be built on (foundation), rest on (assumption), depend on (result)

rétablir   to restore, reestablish (peace, ceasefire, balance, authority)

réunir   to raise (funds), bring together, put together, gather (for support)

revaloriser   to raise (salaries), increase the value of

revigorer   to cheer, revive, raise (spirits), reinvigorate

soutenir   to hold up, support, sustain, prop up (scaffold, wall, invalid)

se structurer   to develop a structure, develop a platform (politics), take shape (idea)

supporter   to sustain, support (wall, invalid), uphold (law), tolerate (pain), endure

surélever   to make higher, raise height of (roof, high jump bar, wall)

surenchérir   to bid higher (at auction), outbid, outdo, raise one's bid, surpass (limit)

surmonter   to top (with a dome)

surnager   to float (debris/oil on ocean), linger (odor, suspicion)

suspendre   to suspend, hang (lamp, decoration), dangle, sling up (hammock)

tisser   to build up (trust), forge (relationship), spin (spiderweb), weave (fabric)

Sa conduite bizarre et son arrivée tardive le soir °ont soulevé des soupçons chez les policiers. His strange behavior and his late-night arrival aroused the suspicion of the police.

Le clown de cirque arborait une grande coiffure pourpre °surmontée d'un chapeau haut-de-forme. The circus clown sported a large purple hairdo topped with a top hat.

Notre premier ministre montre son ambition en proposant de °revaloriser la contribution hollandaise au budget de l'Union européenne. Our prime minister demonstrates his ambition in proposing an increase in the Dutch contribution to the European Union's budget.

Des manifestants ont °érigé des barricades de fortune pour empêcher l'entrée des autorités. Demonstrators erected makeshift barricades to prevent the authorities' entry.

MEMORY AID

Soustraire means *to subtract*, *take away*, or *withdraw*. It is reflexive, therefore it means *to subtract oneself* or *take oneself away*. Thus, escaping or fleeing is withdrawing or subtracting oneself from a place or situation. Picture a numeral subtracting itself from a mathematical equation in order to flee or escape from being erased.

Other verbs in this family include: to steal away, liberate oneself, break away, extricate oneself, retract, skip out, make off, slip away, get out, vanish, part company, dodge, ditch, etc.

s'absenter   to go away, get away, stay away (from work, school)

s'en aller   to get away, slip away

s'en aller furtivement   to sneak away, slink out, skulk away,* sneak out stealthily

s'arracher   to tear oneself away, get away, break away, drag oneself (from book)

se casser*   to clear out,* scram,* get lost,* leave, depart

se débarrasser   to disencumber, extricate oneself from, get clear, get free from

déblayer   to clear away, clear (terrain), sweep away (debris, leaves, rubbish)

débrayer   to disengage (clutch)

se défiler*   to wriggle out (tight spot, jeans), slip away, duck out,* cop out*

se dégager   to get away from, disengage oneself, get free (person, from obligation)

déguerpir*   to move off, be gone, bolt, take off,* clear out*

déloger   to flee (rabbit), move out (tenant)

se dépêtrer   to extricate oneself from (mud, trap), free oneself, get free

se déprendre   to get loose, detach oneself (from situation, from bondage)

se dérober   to steal away, shy away, shrink away

désemparer   to quit, go away, interrupt (action)

désolidariser   to separate from, dissociate from (person, organization)

disparaître   to disappear, vanish, die, die out (dinosaurs), cease to exist

se dissocier   to dissociate oneself from (group), break up (molecules [chemistry])

échapper à   to escape from, slip away, elude, dodge, get away

s'échapper (de)   to escape, get away, get loose (dog), break away, vanish

s'éclipser   to slip away (s.o.), leave quickly, vanish, slip out (for a moment)

écoper   to bail out (boat), cop out

éluder   to elude, evade, dodge

s'enfuir   to flee from, escape, run away

s'esquiver   to slip away, avoid (question), dodge (responsibility), evade

évacuer   to evacuate, clear (premises), clear out, flee, empty (room, building)

s'évader   to evade, get away, escape, escape from (prison, reality)

s'évanouir dans la nature*   to vanish into thin air*

s'évaporer   to evaporate, vanish, disappear into thin air

éviter   to avoid, dodge, bypass, shirk from (responsibility)

s'exiler   to go into exile, leave one's country, get away from (city, family)

s'extraire   to get out of (car), get free from (relationship), pull oneself away

faire l'école buissonnière* to play truant/hooky,* skip school

faire une équipée* to escape, go on an escapade, jaunt, venture

faire une fugue to run away, run off, take flight, escape

faire une tentative d'évasion to make an escape attempt (prisoner)

se faire la malle* to clear out,* pack one's trunk*

se faire rare* to make oneself scarce*

ficher le camp* to skip out,* clear out,* get out,* leave, depart, scram*

filer* to slip by, make off, vanish (money), skedaddle,* scram,* take off,* run away

fuir to flee from, elude (police), slip away, escape, avoid, fly, take flight

se glisser furtivement to steal away, slip away unnoticed, sneak away

se libérer to liberate oneself, free oneself, break free (shackles, relationship)

mettre les voiles* to clear off,* clear out* (*lit.* to set sail)

omettre to omit, leave out, miss, neglect, fail to include (name on a list)

partir à l'anglaise* to slip away unnoticed

partir discrètement to slip away, sneak away

partir en douce* to slip away, get away unnoticed

passer au travers to escape, avoid (flu)

se paumer* to get lost, lose one's way

planter qn* to give s.o. the slip,* leave s.o. behind, walk out on (spouse)

plaquer qn* to ditch s.o.* (fiancé, spouse), kiss off s.o.,* jilt s.o.*

prendre la tangente* to slip away unnoticed, be on the lam,* sneak away

se quitter to separate, part company, break up (couple, friends)

se raréfier to become scarce (product, commodity)

réchapper to escape (accident, danger, trap)

se réfugier to take refuge (fugitive)

se retirer to retract, withdraw from, hide, keep out of sight, retire (job)

se sauver to escape, make off, abscond, run off, run away, be off, depart

secouer le joug to revolt, break free of the yoke (of oppression)

semer qn* to ditch,* get away from s.o., shake off (pursuer)

sortir to go out, leave, exit, depart, walk out, walk off, walk away, part, get out

s'en sortir to come through (trials), pull through, escape (unharmed), survive

se tailler* to beat it, scram, get out (of place)

se tirer* to extricate oneself, get out (tight spot), clear out,* shove off*

se tirer d'affaire* to get out of a jam,* get out of a tight spot*

trouver une porte de sortie to find a way out, find an exit

vider les lieux* to leave the premises

se volatiliser* to vanish into thin air*

Les jeunes amants °se sont soustraits aux regards de leurs parents pour un rendez-vous amoureux. The young lovers slipped away from their parents' gaze for a romantic rendezvous.

Même si elle parvient à prendre les bastions rebelles, l'armée ne s'attend pas à ce que le mouvement terroriste °disparaisse bientôt. Even if it succeeds in taking the rebel strongholds, the army doesn't expect the terrorist movement to end anytime soon.

L'incertitude avait °fui; j'étais parvenu à ma décision. Uncertainty had fled; I had made my decision.

Les terroristes voulaient que l'armée onusienne °se retire du pays afin qu'ils puissent y imposer leur idéologie malveillante. The terrorists wanted the U.N. army to withdraw from the country so that they could impose their malevolent ideology there.

7

Pile, Pack, Stuff, 'n' Stock

Featured Verbs

s'abonner à   to subscribe to, take out a subscription

MEMORY AID

S'abonner sounds a bit like *Ebony*—the magazine targeted primarily to an African-American readership. Magazines are either bought off the newsstand or *subscribed to*. **S'abonner** also means *to buy season tickets* (for sports activities, theater), *to buy passes or tickets* (for public transportation), or *to subscribe to cable TV or an internet provider*. Picture someone with a subscription, receiving her *Ebony* magazine in the mail.

Other verbs in this family include: to enlist, recruit, sign on, sign up, enroll, hire, ascribe, join in, take part in, register, participate, partner with, renew, associate, belong to, hire, etc.

appartenir   to belong to (item), appertain, pertain, relate to, be a member of (club)

s'associer à   to join, associate with, partner with (organization, business)

cotiser   to subscribe, get up a subscription, contribute toward a subscription

devenir membre de   to join, be a member of (club, organization)

élire   to elect, choose, appoint (president, leader)

embaucher   to sign up, hire, engage, enlist, take on (as employee)

embrigader   to recruit, indoctrinate, instruct in new doctrine (political party)

endoctriner   to indoctrinate (party recruit), brainwash (cult)

engager   to enlist, pledge, engage, induce (involvement, participation)

s'engager   to commit oneself, join in (sports event), enlist (armed forces)

s'engager dans   to enter into (business)

enrégimenter   to enlist (troops, political party)

enrôler   to enlist, enroll (class member), recruit (troops)

enrôler de force   to shanghai (sailor), kidnap for compulsory service (military), impress (force military service upon s.o.)

(se faire) immatriculer   to register (for college, new car), enroll (class), sign up (for class)

faire partie de   to be part of, belong to (club, association, family), be one of (elect)

s'inscrire   to sign on, sign up, enroll, register, become enrolled, log in, sign in (roll)

intégrer   to join (club, business)

se joindre à   to join in (activity), join (club)

louer   to hire, lease, rent, rent out, let out (apartment), book

parrainer   to sponsor for membership, propose, support (*lit.* **parrain** (*m*): sponsor, godfather)

participer (à)   to join, participate in (organization, club, activity, society)

prendre part à   to join in, take part in (activity, club, organization)

racoler   to enlist, solicit (client), drum up (business), accost (passersby: beggar)

se réabonner   to renew subscription (magazine, newspaper), re-subscribe

recruter   to enlist, recruit, enroll (recruits, class members)

référer   to refer (a matter to s.o.), ascribe, refer to (dictionary), consult (authority)

se réinscrire   to reregister, reenroll

se rengager   to reenlist (military)

renouveler   to renew (contact, confidence), reelect (politician)

réunir   to unite (forces), merge (businesses), associate, assemble, join in (activity)

signer   to subscribe, sign (petition, contract), sign in (register), sign for (delivery)

signer le registre   to sign in, register (hotel, court register, for class)

solliciter   to solicit (client, business, votes), apply for (job)

souscrire à   to subscribe to (magazine, theory), take out (insurance policy)

s'unir   to join, unite, band together (club, association), become one

verser (à)   to subscribe (to) (idea, theory), pay (deposit, down payment)

Monique s'est °abonnée au câble comme ont fait ses voisins. Monica subscribed to cable TV like her neighbors did.

Le milliardaire °loua cent chambres à l'hôtel huppé pour accueillir ses invités. The billionaire booked a hundred rooms at the ritzy hotel to accommodate his guests.

Elle est contente de °faire partie d'une organisation qui est la force motrice pour des efforts caritatifs mondiaux. She's happy to belong to an organization that is the driving force behind worldwide humanitarian efforts.

Les œufs que l'on offre aux enfants à Pâques sont °associés à la fertilité, un vestige des rites païens. The eggs given to children at Easter are associated with fertility, a vestige of pagan rituals.

charger to load, charge, burden

accabler de to encumber, burden with (load, troubles), overburden (taxes)

accréditer to authorize, sanction, give official authorization, approve of, credential

adjurer to call upon, to adjure, command under oath or penalty, swear (s.o. to duty)

affréter to charter, freight (ship)

agréer to accredit, qualify, sanction (authorized dealer, professional, expert)

assigner to assign (responsibility), appoint, ascribe (value to), allot (task)

assurer l'intérim de qn to deputize s.o.

autoriser to authorize, empower, give permission (to do s.t.), allow

avaliser to endorse (product, proposal, action), sanction

se coltiner* to lug around* (package, load), get stuck* (with work)

commander to command, order, give an order, boss, charge (with duty/task)

commettre to empower, appoint, entrust (responsibility)

commissionner to empower, order, commission, grant authority, authorize

confier à qn to entrust s.o. with (responsibility, secret, valuables)

contraindre to compel, coerce, force, obligate (s.o. to a task)

convoquer to summon (witness, accused), convene (Congress)

se débarrasser de to unload (problem, load), rid oneself of (nuisance, pest)

déléguer à to assign, delegate to (task, responsibility), discharge duties to (s.o.)

députer to deputize, send, authorize, appoint as deputy (sheriff)

désigner qn pour faire qch to designate s.o. to do s.t., appoint s.o. for a task

diriger to control/run (business), steer (plane), send (convoy), direct (research)

donner l'ordre de to give the order to, command, order to (do s.t.)

donner mandat à to mandate, give authoritative command or instruction

être bondé to be packed, be crowded, be packed full (of people) (bus, train)

être censé to mean to, intend to, be supposed to (do)

faire une ordonnance to write a prescription (medicine)

grever to encumber, burden (debts)

habiliter to authorize (s.o.), give s.o. the authority (legally)

imposer les mains to lay on hands (to ordain to religious ministry or calling)

incomber à to burden with, encumber, devolve upon, pass on duty or authority

lancer un appel to call upon (for service), call for (volunteers, assistance)

mandater   to appoint, elect, give authority, depute (authority), assign

mettre à même de   to empower, invest with legal power, enable, permit, authorize

muter   to transfer (military assignment)

nécessiter   to require (medical care, official action), demand, necessitate

nommer   to appoint, nominate (candidate), call (to office), name, designate

obérer   to burden with debt

obliger (à, de)   to require, force (s.o. to do s.t.), compel (to duty)

oindre   to anoint (leader, king), apply oil or ointment

ordonner à   to order to, give order to, command to

préposer   to set over, appoint, put in charge of

prescrire   to stipulate (parameters, date), prescribe (details), set (method)

pressentir   to approach s.o. about, sound out s.o. (job assignment)

privilégier   to license, privilege, grant (rights, title, promotion), favor (s.o., idea)

promouvoir   to promote (job), encourage (sales), boost (morale, goodwill)

recharger   to reload (gun, camera), recharge (battery), refill (ink pen)

refourguer à*   to unload onto s.o.* (problem)

régler   to order, regulate, adjudicate (hear and judge a case [law]), settle (issue)

reléguer   to relegate (to different status/rank), consign, assign

remplacer qn   to deputize s.o., make s.o. a deputy (sheriff), substitute (teacher)

rendre obligatoire   to mandate, make obligatory (duty, task, service)

requérir   to require (legal sentence, specific need), call for (immediate attention)

responsabiliser qn   to give s.o. a sense of responsibility, put s.o. in charge of

surcharger   to overload (circuit, burden), overburden (work), overcrowd (school)

télécharger   to download (computer)

titulariser   to appoint permanently, give tenure to (professor), pick (athlete)

transmettre son autorité   to give s.o. the authority (to act as proxy in one's stead)

Le patron avait °chargé le nouvel employé d'une tâche accablante. C'était un fardeau formidable. The boss had assigned the new employee an overwhelming task. It was a heavy burden.

Selon un témoin qui avait °requis l'anonymat, il est parti discrètement avec sa maîtresse. According to a witness requesting anonymity, he slipped away quietly with his mistress.

La police °privilégie la piste d'un drame survenu à la suite d'une rupture amoureuse. The police favor an explanation involving an incident provoked by a romantic breakup.

Le juge °ordonna à la mairie de rendre public le dossier portant sur le narcotrafic. The judge ordered City Hall to make public the file dealing with drug trafficking.

emballer to pack, wrap up, package

arranger to rig up, fix up (hairdo), tidy up, straighten (tie), spruce up (room)

arrimer to lash down (ship's cargo), bind

s'assembler to assemble, congregate, gather, collect, come together

bâcher to cover with a canvas sheet or tarpaulin

cadenasser to padlock, lock up with a padlock

clisser to cover with wicker, wicker

comporter to comprise, consist of, incorporate (features, parts), entail

comprimer to compress (air, gas), press together (haystack, straw), pack, compact

conditionner to package (product for sale/display/advertising)

contenir to contain, hold (contents), carry (e.g., contents of a box)

se contenir to keep within bounds, contain oneself (emotions), keep in (suffering)

corder to wrap with cord or string

couvrir to cover, wrap up, coat (paint, varnish), blanket, clothe, protect

empaqueter to pack, package, bundle (up a package)

encaisser to encase, pack (merchandise)

enchaîner to chain up, bind in chains, chain, shackle, link (word), string (beads)

enfermer dans une boîte to box, put in a box, package

enlacer to entwine (ribbon), lace, lace up (shoelaces)

enrouler to roll up (map, rug), wrap, wind up (cable), reel in (fishing line)

entortiller to entwine, wrap, bind

entraver to shackle, hinder, hamper, put in chains (slave)

envelopper to cover, wrap, envelop, encase, bind, wrap up, swaddle (newborn)

faire avec des moyens de fortune to jury-rig, do makeshift repair (boat, motor)

faire ses bagages to pack one's bags

faire un nœud to tie a knot, knot up

faire un paquet-cadeau to gift wrap

fermer à clef to lock, lock up (safe, room, door)

fermer à verrou to bolt (door, window, gate)

ficeler to tie up (string)

fournir une barrière étanche to provide a watertight seal

fourrer* to stick,* shove,* stuff* (into pocket, bag, cupboard)

garrotter to tie up (arms), tie down, restrain by binding arms, pinion

gerber to bind up sheaves of wheat

se grouper to pack, bring together, gather, group (items), consolidate

lier to link (bus routes, communication network), tie together

ligoter to bind, tie up, bind together, tie down, bind (hand and foot)

mettre des sutures to suture or stitch up (wound)

mettre en paquet to bundle, package, wrap up a package/packet, bundle up a packet

mettre le sceau à to seal (container, jar), put a seal on (door, royal decree)

mettre les menottes à qn to handcuff s.o., put s.o. in handcuffs

mettre tout son bazar dans une malle* to put all one's belongings in a trunk

nouer to knot, tie, tie a knot, knot up, fasten

parquer to pack in (people, sardines), herd (animals into cattle car)

peloter to wind up or make into a ball (yarn, string)

plâtrer to set in plaster, put in a cast (broken leg), plaster (stucco wall)

plier bagage to pack bags, pack suitcases

plomber to seal, fill with lead, fill a tooth cavity (**plumbum:** lead [Latin])

recorder to tie up again, restring, decorate with string

recoudre to sew up, sew again

rembobiner to rewind (cassette tape), spool (thread)

relever to wind up (with crank or on spool), roll up (cuffs, sleeves, car window)

remballer to pack up again, repack, repackage

remonter to wind up (watch spring)

remplir to fill, fill up (gas tank, container, questionnaire, application form)

renfermer to contain, comprise, conceal, enclose (contents), hold (container)

rouler to roll up (map, carpet), wind up (cord, string)

sceller to seal (jar, tomb), seal up (package, letter)

scotcher to stick with tape, stick with Scotch® tape, stick to* (TV set)

tasser to pack down, pack, cram (sardines, subway passengers, backpack)

vitrifier to seal through heat fusion (glass, porcelain)

La poupée était °emballée dans un paquet-cadeau pour son anniversaire. The doll was in a gift-wrapped package for her birthday.

Putain!* Avez-vous fini de me °peloter*? Damn it!* Keep your groping hands off me!

La langue °liée de peur, je ne pouvais pas parler. My tongue was paralyzed with fear, such that I couldn't speak.

Jacques estime que la plupart des rapports °contiennent des erreurs majeures et distortions de faits. James figures that most of the reports contain major errors and factual distortions.

empailler to stuff, pack with straw

MEMORY AID

"Em-" means *put into* or *within*, and **paille** in English is *straw*. Thus, **"em-paille~"** can mean *straw put into or within*. Picture a scarecrow stuffed or packed with straw. See also **empâter** (to thicken), page 158.

Other verbs in this family include: to cram, pad, upholster, fill, trim, weave, plait, braid, cushion, soften, line, abound in, fill to the brim, patch things up, be packed with, jam, etc.

---

adoucir to soften (skin), smooth (sheets), make soft, mellow

amollir to soften, soften up, make soft

bachoter* to cram* (for an exam)

bourrer to cram (with food, suitcase), stuff (cushion), jam, fill (pipe)

bûcher* to cram* (for exam)

capitonner to pad, stuff (sofa, mattress, quilt)

doubler to line (clothing), fold in half (blanket, sheet)

endiguer to dam up (lake, river), construct a dike

étouffer to muffle (sound), stifle (emotion), smother (flame)

être plein à craquer* to be crammed full*

farcir to stuff (pocket, pillow, turkey), cram (purse, suitcase), fill (head with ideas)

feutrer to pad, pack, become interwoven, cover/decorate with mats

fourmiller (de) to swarm, to be full of, teem with (bees, ants, people)

fourrer to stuff, line with fur (jacket), pack (a pipe joint [industrial]), fill (cake)

garnir de to fill with (box, case, store department), stock with (refrigerator)

garnir de coussins to cushion (chair, sofa), pad (stool)

insonoriser to soundproof (room), deafen (noise), muffle (sound)

lester to fill (pocket), ballast, fill with ballast (ship)

matelasser to stuff, pad, cushion (furniture), quilt (vest)

natter to mat, plait, braid, weave (hair, rope)

ouater to pad, wad, line (clothing), quilt (vest) (*lit.* **ouate** (*f*): cotton wadding)

parquer to pack in (people: subway car), pen in (cattle, sheep)

ramollir to soften (fabric)

recoller to patch things up, stick back together, reseal (envelope, package)

regorger de to abound in, be packed with, burst at the seams with, teem with

remblayer to embank, fill up (with earth)

rembourrer to stuff, pad, upholster (sofa, pillow, mattress)

rempailler to restuff with straw

remplir to replenish, refill (canteen), fill up, fill in (application, the blank)

remplir à ras bord to fill to the brim (coffee cup)

saturer to saturate (chemical reaction, cloth: water), surfeit, fill up

tapisser to upholster, wallpaper

tresser to weave, braid (ribbon, hair, rope), plait (straw, wire)

L'épouvantail est °empaillé de paille et de chiffons. The scarecrow is stuffed with straw and rags.

Un grand nombre de tentures multicolores °tapissent les murs de son château. A large number of multicolored tapestries hang from the walls of his castle.

À cause de la sécheresse, les particuliers sont interdits de °remplir leurs piscines privées et d'arroser leurs jardins d'agrément. Because of the drought, private citizens are forbidden from filling up their swimming pools and from watering their gardens.

Conformément à la tradition catholique, le jour de la Résurrection, les fidèles mangent du pâté °farci d'œufs durs. Following Catholic tradition, on the Day of Resurrection, the faithful eat pâté stuffed with hard-boiled eggs.

J'ai boulotté* toute la journée. Je °sature*! I slaved away* all day long. I've had enough!*

entasser   to heap, pile up, accumulate, hoard

MONSIEUR
NERFS D'ACIER

MEMORY AID

"**En-**" can mean *put on* or *go on*, and the "**~tasse~**" fragment means *cup* (**la tasse**). Thus, "**en-tasse**" can mean *to put on cups* or *cups going on*. Picture a vaudeville juggler with a tricky balancing act that requires him to stack, pile up, or heap teacups as high as he can. He puts cup on top of cup. Picture cups going on top of cups. See also **ramasser** (to gather, pick up, collect), page 236.

Other verbs in this family include: to collect, gather, assemble, stack up, amass, load with, replenish, add up, total, join to, heap up, put in a pile, compile, draw up, superimpose, etc.

accourir   to flock, gather (crowd, fans, devotees, pigeons, pilgrims)

accumuler   to accumulate, pile up, amass, compile (data, list), accrue (interest)

s'accumuler   to pile up (objects, work, problems, dust)

additionner qch à   to add s.t. to (more water, ingredients, more spices)

ajointer   to join on to, to fit (carpentry, plumbing)

ajouter   to add (salt, spice), join, add together, sum, add up (cost), make an addition

amasser   to hoard, gather, amass, compile, pile, mass, pile up (leaves, clothes, books)

ameulonner   to stack (hay, crops)

amonceler   to accumulate, heap up, mass, amass, pile up

bâter   to load with a packsaddle (horse)

bourrer   to stuff, cram (suitcase, ideas into head)

bousculer   to jostle (subway commuters), crowd (ideas)

capitaliser   to amass (fortune), build up (cash value), add (money/interest)

se caramboler   to pile up (cars in a crash)

centraliser   to centralize (office, business, authority), make central, concentrate

se coaliser   to combine (chemicals, ingredients), unite (nations), coalesce

collectionner   to collect, make a collection of

combiner   to combine (ingredients, chemicals, ideas)

combler   to heap up, fill up (hole, crack), make up for (lost time), fill (void)

compléter   to fill up, add to (collection, registration form)

comprendre   to include, comprise, incorporate (parts of a whole), encompass

conglomérer   to conglomerate (business, enterprise, rock sediment)

dresser   to put up (barricade), set up (tent), lay out (display items), draw up (list)

échafauder   to amass, pile up, stock up, put together (project, formal reply), lay out

empiler   to stack up, pile up, stack, heap up, pile, place in a pile

encourir   to incur (debt, s.o.'s wrath), bring upon oneself (wrath of God)

enfourcher   to get on, mount (motorcycle, horse), straddle (fence)

faire le plein   to fill up (gas tank)

gerber   to stack, pile up/bind up wheat sheaves

joindre à   to add to, join to, fasten to, attach to, link to, unite with

mettre en tas   to put in a pile (dirty clothes, leaves, trash), heap (dirt)

mouliner   to process (compiled data)

percevoir to collect (taxes)

posséder to have, own, possess (wealth, land, common sense)

rajouter to add to, add more of (spice), contribute to (sum), tag on (extra cost)

rassembler to assemble, gather together, collect, put together, clump, hoard, muster

rédiger to compile (encyclopedia), draw up (contract)

remettre to add more, add, put on more (salt, spice)

rempiler to pile up again, pile up (objects), join up again (reenlistment)

remplir to refill, replenish, fill in (questionnaire, form), fulfill (obligation, contract)

superposer to stack, pile up, superimpose (images), overlay (films), stack (bricks)

surajouter to add, add to, tag on (extra cost)

thésauriser to hoard, treasure up (money)

totaliser to add up, total, sum, total up, add

s'unir to unite, join, band together, become one

Les douze étudiants se sont °entassés dans la toute petite Peugeot. The twelve students piled into the tiny Peugeot.

Tout au long de la journée les supporteurs de l'équipe °se rassemblaient au cercle de jeu. All day long the team's fans gathered at the clubhouse.

Le candidat tentait de °dresser le bilan administratif "gauchiste" de son concurrent. The candidate was trying to lay out the left-leaning administrative track record of his opponent.

Pour °ajouter à la confusion, aucune explication officielle n'est prévue actuellement. To add to the confusion, no official explanation is currently expected.

Pierre qui roule n'°amasse pas mousse. A rolling stone gathers no moss.

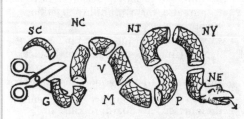

SC NC NJ NY
V
NE
G M P

UNITE OR DIE

MEMORY AID

"**Entre-**" means *between*, and the "**~couper**" fragment means *to cut*. Thus, "**entre-couper**" can mean *to cut between*. Think of it as referring to *cutting something between length markers to yield sections of equal or standardized lengths*. The cuts are interspersed evenly. Picture Benjamin Franklin's famous political cartoon of 1754 ("Unite or Die!"), drawn to admonish the American colonies to unite. Picture a pair of scissors cutting up segments of the snake and gaps interspersed between its sections.

Other verbs in this family include: to divide up, partition, cut up, interweave, make even, standardize, section off, split up, subdivide, quarter, skip, segment, saw up, proportion, etc.

apparier to pair, assort by pairs (socks, gloves, Noah's animals)

baliser to mark out with beacons, buoys, or signposts

bifurquer to divide or separate into parts (tree limb), bifurcate (angle [math])

cliver to cleave, split (into parts, into groups)

cloisonner to partition (room), compartmentalize (sectors)

collationner to collate, arrange in order (papers)

compartimenter to compartmentalize, divide into compartments or categories

couper la file to cut in line, cut ahead of others waiting in line

couper par intervalles to cut by intervals (rope, pipe, cookie dough)

débiter to cut up (wood, stone), distribute (merchandise)

découper to cut up (with knife or scissors), cut out, carve (meat)

dédoubler to divide in two, divide in half

détailler to cut into pieces, break down (analysis of data)

disloquer to dislocate, take to pieces, dismantle, carve up (empire, organization)

diviser to separate, partition, divide (math), split, divide up

doser to grade (exercise level), strike a balance between, proportion, dose (medicine)

écarteler to quarter, divide in quarters

échelonner to place at regular intervals (payments), space, arrange by gradation

échelonner sur to space out over, spread over (regular time intervals)

s'entrelacer to interweave, entwine (ribbon, rope, vines)

entremêler to interweave (different ideas/methods), intersperse (comments)

espacer to separate, leave a space between, space out (objects, numbers, payments)

étaler en éventail to fan out (poker cards, color swatches)

être en pointillé to be marked by stops and starts, be marked with dots and dashes

faire des coupes dans to make cuts in, cut into

faire scission to split into, fission (atoms)

ficher to index, put in file (dossier)

graduer to make gradually more difficult, step up gradually (exercise level, slope)

insérer entre to insert between, squeeze between, tuck between, stick between

s'intercaler entre to come in between (person, object), squeeze between (two people)

s'interposer to intervene, come between (feuding parties, objects)

interrompre to interrupt (TV transmission), break off (negotiations)

jouer à saute-mouton to leapfrog (*lit.* to jump over sheep)

laisser un blanc to leave a gap/blank (on application form, on written exam)

morceler to partition, divide up (inheritance), parcel out (handouts, payments)

se multiplier to multiply (wrinkles, sidewalk cracks, defects, errors, woes)

ordonner to bracket, classify (items, categories), put in order (by age, height, etc.)

parsemer to intersperse, scatter

procéder par paliers to proceed in stages (rocket booster firing, Tour de France race)

quadriller to mark out in squares, form squares

rabâcher to repeat over and over again, keep repeating (history, fabric pattern, word)

régulariser to put in order (papers), regularize (schedule), regulate (heart rate, flow)

répétailler* to keep on repeating, repeat over and over (phrase, TV commercial, song)

répéter to repeat (word, pattern, history), rehearse (show, music)

router to sort (mail)

rubaner to cut into ribbons

saucissonner* to interrupt frequently (TV commercials)

sauter to skip (class, grade)

sautiller to hop, skip, prance, leap

scinder to split up (business), divide, split into parts, break down (math equation)

sectionner to divide into sections, cut off, section, divide up, separate

sectoriser to divide into sectors (pie graph, economic market)

segmenter to segment, divide into segments/parts

séparer to separate, section off, divide, dissipate, cleave, split, segregate, dissever

se séparer en (2, 3, 4 ...) to divide by (2, 3, 4 ...)

subdiviser to subdivide, divide into smaller parts (land, number)

tronçonner to cut into sections (board, movie, pipe), saw up (lumber)

uniformiser to standardize (moral code, exam), make even (design pattern)

Malheureusement, le discours de l'orateur était °entrecoupé de hoquets. Unfortunately, the speaker's talk was interrupted by hiccups.

La grande foule scandait des slogans qui se °répétaient dans tous les coins du village. The large crowd chanted slogans that echoed throughout every corner of the town.

Un arpenteur va °baliser chaque mètre carré des terres que vous venez d'acheter. The surveyor will mark out each square meter of the land you've just purchased.

Le syndicat médical réclame que les soins de garde et d'astreinte soient °échelonnés tous les trois mois. The medical union demands that the daily duties and on-call duties be regularly spaced over time, quarterly.

Charité bien °ordonnée commence par soi-même. Charity begins at home.

entreposer to store, stock, warehouse

MEMORY AID

"Entre-" means *between*, and the **"~pose~"** fragment is the same as the English word *pose*, which means *to place something* (e.g., a model) *into a specific position*. Thus, **"entre-poser"** can mean *to pose something between objects*. Picture someone posing or placing boxes on storage shelves between other boxes, stocking them in a warehouse.

Other verbs in this family include: to fit in, shelve, display, show, exhibit, equip, furnish, supply, place, put in order, retain, stow away, contain, reload, refurnish, fit out, refit, etc.

---

accumuler to accumulate, amass, store, collect, store up, compile, pile up

aménager to equip, outfit, fit out (store)

appareiller to fit out (ship)

s'approvisionner to stock up, get in supplies, stock with provisions

armer to arm (gun, soldier), equip, furnish arms (military), fit out (ship)

arrimer to stow, store (cargo)

assortir to stock (merchandise), supply, store (goods, supplies)

avoir qch en réserve to have s.t. in stock (merchandise)

conserver to keep, store (items), retain, stock, pickle (cucumber), conserve (fruit)

contenir to contain, hold (contents), carry (e.g., box contents), hold in

disposer to arrange (objects); ~ de to have use of, have at one's disposal

doter to equip, grant, fit out, endow (dowry, scholarship)

douer to grant (funding), endow (with power, scholarship)

embarquer to load (cargo)

s'embarquer clandestinement to stow away (ship)

emboîter to fit in, fit, encase, stack, fit together (pieces)

emmagasiner to store, accumulate, warehouse

engranger to store (files, data), file away, enter (in record) (*lit.* **grange** (*f*): barn)

équiper to equip (with tools, appliances, features), fit out, outfit, set up

étager to dispose in tiers (garden terrace, store display, wedding cake)

étalager to display for sale (store items, window display)

étaler to display, show for sale (merchandise), exhibit (sale items)

être bien armé to be well-equipped (store, race car), be well-armed (soldier)

exhiber to exhibit, show (collection, art work)

faire des réserves to get in stock (merchandise)

faire du rangement to put away, tidy up, put in order (store items), put in storage

faire provision de to stock up with, supply with, provision

faire ses provisions to go grocery shopping

fournir to furnish (supplies, proof of purchase, piece of identity)

gadgétiser to equip with gadgets

garnir to equip, fill, fit out, stock (merchandise, equipment, refrigerator)

intercaler to insert (day into calendar), interpose, squeeze in (letter: word)

mettre au rancart to put on the shelf

mettre en rayon to shelve (idea, project, sale item)

mettre en sécurité to put in a safe place

mettre sous séquestre   to sequester (witness, jury), confine, hold (in escrow, hostage)

meubler de   to furnish with, fill with (room: furniture)

montrer   to display, show (item for sale)

munir   to equip (with a good map, soldier), supply, arm, provide (weapon, supplies)

outiller   to equip (with tools)

placer   to put, place, position (s.o., object), set in place, install, arrange, stick in place

pourvoir   to provide (money), supply, equip, fill (position), issue (provisions)

ranger   to put in order, rank, arrange, store away, tuck away, pack up, pack away

rassortir   to stock (a shop), restock (store shelves), resupply

ravitailler   to provision, supply (military, nautical), fuel (car), provide (fresh supply)

réapprovisionner   to restock, resupply

réarmer   to refit (boat), reload (gun, cannon), rearm (soldier)

réassortir   to stock (a shop)

reclasser   to place (object, s.o. unemployed into a new job), redeploy (employee)

régulariser   to put in order, sort out (papers), regulate, stabilize (economy)

remeubler   to refurnish (home, apartment)

remiser   to put away (vehicle), put into storage (snowplow) (*lit.* **remise** (*f*): shed)

renfermer   to contain (box, package), hold (contents)

rengainer   to resheath (sword), put back in holster (gun)

repeupler   to repeople, restock, repopulate (country, island)

réserver   to keep, reserve, have in store, hold in reserve, allot, book (reservations)

stocker   to stock, store, stockpile (weapons, arsenal)

suppléer   to supply, provide (substitute, stand-in), fill in (for s.o.), make up (loss)

°Entreposer dans des aires d'°entreposage sèches dont la température se situe entre 5°C et 37°C. Store in a dry storage area where the temperature remains between 5°C and 37°C.

Vos clichés seront °conservés dans un dossier sénologique. Your films will be stored in a mammography file.

Cette usine est désaffectée et ne °renferme que quelques vieilles cuisinières à gaz. That factory is abandoned, containing only a few old gas ranges.

La cargaison est solidement °arrimée dans la soute de l'aéronef. The cargo is securely stowed in the aircraft's cargo hold.

°Embarquez-le dans le coffre. Load it in the car trunk.

épargner   to save, spare, economize

s'abstenir   to abstain (from overspending), refrain, restrain (urges), curb (desire)

bénéficier   to gain, profit, have (advantage), get (refund), benefit from (investment)

boursicoter   to invest on the stock exchange

budgétiser   to budget for (fiscal year, trip, expenses), calculate, create a budget

calculer   to budget carefully, calculate (cost)

capitaliser   to put at compound interest, add to capital, add to interest, save (money)

centupler   to multiply by one hundred, increase a hundredfold

se constituer un petit pécule*   to build up a nest egg*

daigner   to vouchsafe, deign (grant or bestow favor or privilege, e.g., king)

décupler   to increase tenfold, multiply by ten

dépenser avec précaution   to spare, spend sparingly, spend wisely/prudently

déposer   to deposit (money in bank)

doubler   to double, multiply by two

économiser   to economize, save (electricity, money, time), save up (strength)

engranger   to amass (fortune), reap (benefits)

enrichir   to make rich, enrich (bank account, soil, s.o.'s life)

escompter   to discount (bank note, bill of exchange)

être cupide   to be covetous, be greedy, be grasping

être économe   to be thrifty, be frugal, economize

être lucratif   to be a moneymaker, be lucrative, be a cash cow (investment)

être mesquin   to be stingy, be miserly, be petty, be cheap, be a skinflint

être pingre*   to be stingy, be niggardly, be tight (with money), be a tightwad

être radin*   to be tight, be stingy, be miserly, be a skinflint*

faire des économies   to save, economize

se faire pas mal de thunes*   to make loads of money* (*lit.* **thune*** (*f*): cash)

faire travailler son argent   to put one's money to work (earn interest)

faire un bénéfice   to make a profit, profit from (investment)

faire valoir   to make the most of (situation, investment), invest money

garder   to keep (the change), retain (possession, rights, custody), maintain (figure)

joindre les deux bouts   to make ends meet (financially), survive (on a tight budget)

ménager   to be sparing, save (money, strength, efforts, electricity, resources)

ménager ses forces   to save one's strength

mettre de côté   to save (nest egg, for a rainy day), stash away (money)

monnayer to make money out of, coin into money, mint money

se monter en to supply oneself with

se priver de to deprive oneself of, abstain from

quadrupler to quadruple, multiply by four

quintupler to quintuple, multiply by five

se racquitter to recoup, retrieve one's losses

réaliser to convert into money, cash (bonds, savings certificates)

réaliser une plus-value to make a profit

récompenser to reward, repay (loan), compensate (for loss)

recycler to recycle (aluminum, paper, glass)

redoubler to increase, redouble

rehausser to enrich (coffers), raise the value of (stock), build up (economy, nest egg)

remployer to reinvest (dividends)

remplumer* to retrieve one's losses

rémunérer to reward, remunerate, repay (s.o.)

rendre to pay, reward, repay

rentabiliser to make profitable, make cost-effective

rentrer dans son argent to recover one's money

rentrer dans son fonds to recover one's costs

rentrer dans ses frais to recover one's expenses

replacer to reinvest (funds, dividends)

réserver to reserve, keep, allot (money, expenses), hold in reserve (money)

se restreindre to curtail one's expenses, show fiscal restraint

retenir to retain (heat, scent), keep (profits), hold (attention)

retraiter to recycle (waste), treat (wastewater)

se retrancher to curtail one's expenses, cut back on expenses

rétribuer to remunerate, reward, pay back

s'y retrouver to make a profit

réutiliser to reuse (tool, recycled product)

rouler sur l'or to be rolling in dough, be made of money

sauvegarder to safeguard (investment), maintain (peace, order), save, salvage

sauver to save (money), economize

soudoyer to keep one's pay

tirer profit de to benefit from, profit from (investment, good advice)

toucher de l'argent to get some money, get ahold of some cash

toucher un rappel to get some money back, get a refund

tripler to triple, treble, multiply by three

user d'économie to economize, be frugal

valoir la peine to be worthwhile, be worth s.o.'s while

valoir qch (à qn) to earn s.o. something (interest, income, praise, award)

valoriser to enhance the value of

verser de l'argent to deposit money (bank account)

verser un dépôt to put down a deposit, deposit money (bank account)

°**Épargnez-moi tous les détails sordides de l'affaire. Un point c'est tout!*** Spare me all the sordid details of the affair. Period!*

Il faut monter la colline à pied pour °épargner les chevaux. We have to climb the hill on foot to spare the horses.

Le ministre va °déposer une gerbe de fleurs à la mémoire des victimes de l'attentat. The minister will lay a flower wreath in memory of the victims of the attack.

Les candidats ne °s'épargnèrent aucun coup dans leur joute verbale. The candidates withheld no blows in their verbal jousting.

Nous devons °rendre hommage à ceux qui ont libéré notre pays. We should pay tribute to those who freed our country.

livrer   to deliver, give up, hand over

MEMORY AID

Livrer closely resembles the "*~liver*" fragment in the English word *deliver*. Picture a pizza delivery boy hand-delivering an order, which he hands over to the customer for a cash payment.

Other verbs in this family include: to carry, bring, take out, bring back, exchange, give back to, unload, obtain, transfer, lug around,* convey, export, unpack, bring home, cart about,* etc.

affréter   to freight (ship), charter (boat, plane)

amener   to bring (people), bring about (truce), convey (water supply), haul in (fish)

s'amener   to come along, bring oneself (to party)

apporter   to bring, carry (things), furnish, fetch, get, supply (news, hope, message)

apporter à la main   to hand-carry (envelope, package, pizza)

brinquebaler*   to cart about,* cart around*

camionner   to deliver by truck, haul by truck

céder   to transfer, submit, cede (estate, property), sign over (rights)

charrier   to cart along (person, object), carry along (river), transport (cargo)

charroyer*   to convey, transport

se coltiner*   to lug around* (suitcase, package)

communiquer   to transfer, transmit (data), convey (message), impart (news)

conduire qn quelque part   to take s.o. somewhere

cracher*   to cough up* (money, evidence)

débâter   to unsaddle, unpack (horse)

dégager   to deliver, show (profit, advantage), give off (odor), bring out (idea)

démarcher   to sell door-to-door, canvass (area)

distribuer à   to deliver to, distribute, deliver (mail, pizza), deal (cards)

emmener   to lead away, convey, bring, take/carry (passengers)

emporter   to carry away, take out (food), carry off (wounded), take away, remove

enlever à qn   to take away from s.o. (possession), snatch, remove (tumor), carry off

être à la hauteur*   to deliver the goods,* be up to it*

expédier par voie aérienne   to send by air, send by airmail

exporter   to export, ship abroad, send overseas

extrader   to extradite, surrender an alleged criminal to another authority for trial

faire porte-à-porte   to sell door-to-door, go knocking on doors

faire un virement   to make a transfer (bank account)

se faire livrer   to have delivered (pizza, mail order purchase)

fourguer (à)*   to unload (onto)* (personal problems, emotional baggage)

importer   to import, ship in (overseas product), bring in (foreign cargo)

se livrer à   to give oneself up, surrender (to authorities)

passer à   to hand over to, pass around (hat, communicable disease), pass over to, give to

porter   to carry (voice, sound), convey (message, object)

procurer   to bring (worry, joy), obtain, get, provide (food), furnish (transportation)

raccompagner (à)   to take back (to), return, accompany back

ramener   to bring back, restore, take home (people)

rapporter   to bring back (things), bring home, retrieve

redescendre   to carry down, take down again (luggage, picture)

refourguer à*   to unload on* (problem)

remettre à   to deliver to (letters)

remonter   to take back, bring back up (baggage)

rendre   to deliver, carry, give back (refund), return (s.t.), surrender (license), yield

renvoyer   to send again, send back (letter), return (package)

répandre   to return, take back, exchange (merchandise)

reporter   to take back, carry back, transfer (authority to s.o.), carry forward (sum)

retirer à qn   to take away from s.o. (driver's license, object, car keys)

retourner   to return (letter), give back to (lost object)

revenir à   to give back to, return to s.o.

transbahuter*   to lug, carry away, carry around, schlep*

transborder   to transfer, transship

transiter   to convey in transit (merchandise, delivery)

transmettre   to transfer, hand over, pass on, impart (knowledge), carry (TV signal)

transporter   to transport (cargo), convey, transfer, carry, ship (freight), ferry, freight

trimballer*   to lug around,* carry around (luggage, extra weight)

véhiculer   to convey, transport, carry from one place to another

virer   to transfer (money into bank account), send back

voiturer   to cart (wheelbarrow, handcart), convey, carry away

Oui, on °livre nos pizzas à domicile! Yes, we home-deliver our pizzas!
La tombe du pharaon °livrait des informations précieuses à l'égard de la mode de vie de son époque. The pharaoh's tomb yielded priceless information regarding the lifestyle of his era.
Les provisions de vivres et de médecines ont fait le trajet à bord d'un avion °affrété par la Croix-Rouge. The food and medicine supplies made the trip aboard a plane chartered by the Red Cross.
Le reporteur s'excusa de la mauvaise qualité des informations °transmises par son car de reportage. The field reporter apologized for the poor quality of the information transmitted by his mobile unit.
°Rendre donc à César ce qui est à César. Matthieu 22:21 Render therefore unto Caesar the things that are Caesar's. Matthew 22:21

ramasser   to gather, pick up, collect, assemble

accumuler   to accumulate, accrue (interest), compile, stock up, gather, pile up

acquérir   to acquire (experience, wealth), gain (fame, reputation), buy (property)

s'agglutiner   to gather (crowd), stick together (blood platelets)

amalgamer   to merge, blend (ingredients), combine, amalgamate (metals)

amonceler   to accumulate, gather, pile up, mass, amass

appeler sous les armes   to call up (regiment), enlist

assembler   to assemble, gather, put together, collate (pages), garner (memories)

assimiler   to assimilate (nutrients, knowledge)

attraper   to catch, take in, ensnare, capture, deserve (attention, praise, admiration)

avoir   to have, possess, own, get, have in hand

butiner   to gather (pollen, nectar, information) (*lit.* **butin** *(m)*: booty, loot, spoils)

capter   to catch, harness (energy), acquire (wealth), pick up (TV/radio signal)

collecter   to pick up, collect (donations), gather (information), fund-raise

collectionner   to collect, make a collection (stamps, coins)

conglomérer   to conglomerate (rock sediment, societies), collect, form a mass

convoquer   to call together, convene (assembly, Congress)

cueillir   to gather (fruit), pick (flowers), nab, pluck, catch, collect, grab, snatch

dépouiller   to reap (rewards, votes, spoils of war, booty)

égrapper   to pick (grapes, fruit)

égrener   to pick off (grapes), unstring (beads)

engranger   to gather in (grain), harvest, amass, reap (benefit), store (data), rake in

enregistrer   to take in (information), record (data), tape record, store (on CD, in file)

faire la quête   to take up a collection, pass around the hat

faire rentrer   to collect (taxes)

fondre   to merge, blend, combine (assets, forces, ideas)

froncer   to gather (sewing), pucker (fabric)

gagner   to gain (wealth, fame, recognition, weight)

glaner   to glean (crops, information), harvest, gather (crops), pick up

grappiller   to glean (crops, data), lift* (idea), pick up (votes)

grouper   to group, pool, bulk, consolidate, group together, amass, bracket

harnacher   to harness (horse, wind power, mountain-climbing gear)

jouir de   to possess (charm, good looks), enjoy (good health), have use of

maîtriser   to control (fire), master (subjects, language skills)

masser   to gather (crowd), amass, mass together, mass (troops)

mettre en contact   to bring together (friends), put in contact (electric wires)

moissonner   to harvest, gather (grain)

mouliner   to reel in (fish), process (information)

pêcher   to get ahold of, drag out, fish, fish for* (compliments), catch, trawl (fish)

percevoir   to collect (taxes), receive (payment, salary)

peupler   to stock with people or animals, populate

posséder   to possess (wealth, land, power, self-confidence)

prendre   to take, pick up, pick up oneself (after fall), grab hold, seize, clutch, grasp

procurer   to procure (client: prostitute), obtain, bring about (solution), acquire

quérir   to fetch, go fetch (used as infinitive, prefaced by **aller ~**, **envoyer ~**, **venir ~**)

rabibocher*   to bring together again, reconcile (spouses), make up (lovers, friends)

rafler   to round up, carry off (award), run off with (title), snap up (bargain)

rallier   to rally, rejoin, rally around (flag, leader), muster (troops), bring together

rameuter   to gather together, round up (support), mobilize (troops)

se rapprocher   to get closer (deadline), come together, approach (judge's bench)

rassembler   to gather, assemble, round up, bring together, summon up, clump

ravoir   to recover (back payment, losses), get back (used as an infinitive)

recevoir   to receive (payment, visitor), take, have, get (response), welcome (guest)

rechercher   to collect (s.t.), court (danger), look for (s.o or s.t.)

recoller   to stick back (together), reseal (envelope)

récolter   to harvest, gather (fruit)

réconcilier   to reconcile (differences), patch things up (relationship)

se recouper   to tally, add up (votes, numbers)

recouvrer   to recover (losses), retrieve, collect (taxes), recuperate (tax refund)

recueillir   to gather (harvest, votes, money, data)

récupérer   to recuperate, retrieve, recover (status, lost wages), recoup (expenses)

regrouper   to group together, merge, bring together (people, pieces, companies)

relever   to collect (notebooks), take down (address, notes), pick up, pin up

réquisitionner   to requisition (supplies), commandeer (property, enemy ship)

resserrer   to close in, draw in (fishing net, circle of friends), grow stronger (ties)

retirer   to collect (bags), withdraw (money from bank)

retrancher (de)   to take away (from), deduct, subtract from (math)

réunir   to bring together, collect, raise funds, assemble, join, match, congregate

se réunir   to assemble, unite (countries), reunite (classmates), meet (parliament)

sélectionner   to cull, select, pick (from list, from group), choose

serrer des rangs   to close up ranks (troops)

sonner l'appel   to sound the order to fall in (troops)

stocker   to stockpile (weapons, foodstuffs), accumulate, store, amass

vendanger   to harvest, gather (grapes)

Tous les étés, au bord de la mer, les deux fillettes °ramassent des petites coquilles pour faire des colliers. Every summer, at the seaside, the two little girls collect small seashells to make necklaces.

L'ouragan Luis °gagne en puissance alors qu'il se dirige vers la Jamaïque. Hurricane Luis increases in strength while it heads toward Jamaica.

Dans un premier temps, les apôtres avaient été °convoqués au temple pour des discussions religieuses avec le prophète. Earlier, the apostles had been summoned to the temple for religious discussions with the prophet.

La police a pu °récupérer toutes les traces du vol que le cambrioleur a laissé échapper. The police were able to retrieve all traces of the theft that the burglar overlooked.

to divide, distribute, share among **répartir**

Note: Do not confuse this verb with **repartir**, which lacks the
"**é**" **accent aigu** and means *to start up again* or *to get going again*.

MEMORY AID

"**Re-**" means *repeatedly* or *again*, and the "**~part~**"
fragment is spelled like the English word *part*,
meaning a *division, portion,* or *segment of a whole.*
(Other words derived from "part" include *particle,
partition, partly, partial, partake, participate.*) Thus,
"**ré-part**" can mean to divide into portions
repeatedly. Picture a whole watermelon being
repeatedly divided into portions to distribute or
share among guests at a picnic. See also
subvenir (to supply, provide for), page 243.

Other verbs in this family include: to sort out,
fork out,* portion out, share, subdivide, apportion,
equalize, hand around, parcel out, share in,
bestow, dispense, proportion, give, etc.

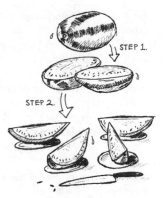

---

accorder   to grant (permission), bestow
(favor, honor, award)

agencer   to dispose, arrange, lay out, set,
put together (sentence, pieces)

assigner   to apportion, assign (property
in payment of a debt)

attribuer   to allot, allocate (inheritance),
award (grant), ascribe (honor), assign
(title)

avoir part à   to share in (reward,
victory), have a share in

concéder   to grant (privilege, right),
concede (goal/point to sports
opponent)

conférer   to confer (honor, award),
impart (wealth), bestow (gift)

daigner   to deign (grant or bestow favor
or privilege, e.g., king/queen)

débiter   to supply (electricity), retail,
yield, produce (factory), discharge
(pump)

débourser   to disburse, outlay (cash),
spend, dispense (favor), deal out, allocate

départir   to distribute, divide, bestow

dispenser   to dispense (cash, candy,
kindness), bestow, give (aid, directions)

distribuer   to distribute, divide, hand
out, parcel, deal out (cards), deliver
(mail)

diviser   to divide, portion out, split up,
partition

donner   to bestow, give, grant, give out,
give away, hand out, impart, donate,
confer

doter   to endow, grant, supply, fund,
provide

douer   to endow (grant), bestow upon
(title, authority), grant (scholarship,
wish)

égaliser   to equalize (portions, shares,
food servings)

équilibrer   to equalize (distribution),
equilibrate, balance (payments, check-
book)

exaucer   to grant (wish), fulfill (desire),
answer (prayer, request)

faire le tri de   to sort out, sort through
(laundry, mail)

faire passer de main en main   to hand
around, pass around (food, collection
plate)

fournir   to supply, furnish (provisions,
example, advice)

fractionner   to divide up, divide into
fractions

fragmenter   to reduce to fragments,
divide up

impartir   to assign (task, mission), allot,
impart, outsource (contract work)

lotir to divide into lots/plots (farm, housing subdivisions), portion out

mettre en tombola to raffle off (prize, tickets)

morceler to divide up, parcel out, divide into shares

niveler to equalize, level (playing field, terrain), level out (social conditions, pay)

obtenir une subvention to obtain a grant or subsidy

octroyer (à) to grant (to), give, bestow (land, title, financial grant)

offrir to give, offer (refreshments, assistance, advice)

parceller to portion, parcel out (land, food rations)

partager to divide up, share, endow, parcel, share in, partake, divvy up,* share with

participer à to participate in, share in, be party to (activity, scheme, expenses, cost)

prendre part à to share, share in (reward), play a part in (success, stage show)

prêter to lend (money, a hand), give, impart (advice, knowledge)

proportionner to proportion (allotments, parcels, prize winnings, food servings)

ramifier to divide, ramify (nervous system, internet links), divide into parts

raquer* to fork out* (money), pay out

rationner to ration, distribute as rations, impose rationing

redonner to give back, give again, return, restore (confidence, self-esteem)

refiler (à)* to give (to), pass (to) (book, measles, flu)

répartir avec parcimonie to dole out (food rations), hand out (welfare checks)

servir to serve (food, drinks), wait on (tables, guests)

subdiviser to subdivide, divide into smaller parts (land, pie, watermelon)

transmettre to hand down, hand over, convey, bestow, impart, pass on (legacy)

troquer (contre) to exchange (for) (goods, services), trade, barter, swap

ventiler to divide into, break into different groups (people), break down (sum)

Jeanne a partagé son gâteau en dix tranches et l'a °réparti parmi ses invités. Jean cut her cake into ten pieces and distributed it among her guests.

Cet objet d'époque est surévalué. Personne n'est disposé à °débourser les 10.000 euros demandés par le propriétaire. This antique is overpriced. No one is willing to spend the 10,000 euros asked for by the owner.

Les électeurs sont unis quant aux réformes mais restent °partagés sur la gestion gouvernementale. The voters are united in their support of the reforms but remain divided over the issue of government leadership.

Les troubles éclatant lundi soir sont °attribués à des voyous* qui assistaient à un match de football. The trouble which broke out Monday night is attributed to hooligans attending a soccer game.

Proverbe français: Qui °donne aux pauvres, °prête à Dieu. He who gives to the poor, imparts to God.

MEMORY AID

The "**sou~**" fragment sounds like **sous**, meaning *under*, *beneath*, or *below*, and **tenir** means *to hold*, *retain*, or *keep*. Thus "**sous-tenir**" can mean *to hold something from below or underneath*. Picture a puppeteer upholding or supporting his Punch and Judy puppets by inserting his hands under their frocks and bearing them up from below. See also **soulever** (to lift up, raise, heave, take up), page 213.

   Other verbs in this family include: to prop up, shore up, rely on, put up with, withstand, tolerate, suffer, allow, strengthen, bear with, comfort, give crutches to, sponsor, console, etc.

(ne pas se laisser) abattre   to bear up (hardship), not let things get one down

adosser   to lean s.t. against s.t. (ladder: wall), perch on (village: mountainside)

appuyer   to support (idea, candidate), uphold, back (political party), prop

avaliser   to back, support (action, idea, proposal, project, cause)

buter   to support, prop up, rest against

cautionner   to give one's support to, back s.o. (candidate), endorse (s.o., contract)

commanditer   to fund, sponsor (project), commission (artwork)

consoler   to console, comfort, support emotionally, sympathize, give solace

consolider   to support, strengthen, prop up, consolidate (strength, support for)

contrebuter   to prop up (wall, girder), support (scaffolding)

donner qn des béquilles   to give s.o. crutches

doper   to boost, give a boost to (economy)

échalasser   to prop up (vines) (*lit.* **échalas** (*m*): beanpole, stake)

endurer   to bear, put up with (pain, suffering, privation)

entretenir   to support, keep up, keep in good order, maintain (yard, health, finances)

étançonner   to shore up, prop up (with beam or timber)

étayer   to support (theory), shore up (wall)

être toujours au poste   to be still manning the fort, to remain at one's post

faire la courte échelle*   to give s.o. a leg up,* give s.o. a boost into the saddle*

hausser   to hoist, raise (taxes, standard of living)

hisser   to hoist (flag), raise (standard)

lever   to lift, raise up, heave, stick up (arms in air), lift up (shoulders)

maintenir   to support, keep in place, maintain (law and order), hold steady (ship)

mettre un échafaudage   to put up scaffolding

mitiger   to alleviate (suffering), mitigate, moderate (force, intensity)

patronner   to support, sponsor, patronize (arts, sports)

pérenniser   to perpetuate, make perpetual, make permanent (treaty), make durable

porter   to bear (fruit), support, carry (emotional burden, child, name of)

rassurer   to reassure, strengthen, put something to rest, restore confidence

réconforter   to comfort (with soothing words, with presence)

redynamiser   to give a boost to (economy)

remédier (à)   to cure (disease, cancer), remedy, relieve (pain), provide relief

se remettre   to make well again, recover (from illness)

se reposer sur   to rely on (s.o.), depend on, be built on (home), rest on (theory)

résister à   to withstand, hold out, resist, fend off (attack), stand up to (threat)

sauvegarder   to uphold (law, order), maintain (peace)

servir d'appui   to serve to support or bear up (financially, politically)

servir de tuteur   to serve as a stake/support (vines, plants)

souscrire à   to sympathize with (s.o., cause), agree with, support (cause)

subir   to bear, suffer, submit to (torture, torment, criticism, suffering)

subventionner   to subsidize, grant funds for

suppléer   to substitute for (teacher), make up for (loss), stand in for (s.o.)

supporter   to bear (burden, sorrow), uphold, support (person, wall)

supporter patiemment   to bear with (patiently)

tenir   to hold up (sign, hand), hold (object), sustain (musical note), stay up (hairdo)

tenir fermement   to keep ahold of, hold firmly, hold in a tight grip

L'échelle faible pouvait à peine °soutenir le gros peintre en bâtiments. The flimsy ladder could barely support the fat house painter.

Le président a °avalisé le déploiement de près de cent véhicules blindés dans le cadre de l'opération "Jour de Tonnerre". The president endorsed the deployment of nearly one hundred armored vehicles as part of "Operation Thunder."

L'adoption de ces nouvelles lois permettra de renforcer et de °maintenir des liens entre les divers groupes sociaux. Adoption of these new laws will permit the strengthening and support of the bonds among diverse social groups.

Il avait fallu trois jours aux sauveteurs pour secourir le rescapé du séisme, qui °s'est aujourd'hui remis de ses blessures. It had taken three days for the rescue workers to free the earthquake survivor, who today has fully recovered from his injuries.

MEMORY AID

"**Sub-**" means *under* or *beneath*, as in *submarine* (*under the water*), and **venir** means *to arrive, reach,* or *come.* Thus, "**sub-venir**" can mean *to arrive under or beneath something.* Picture a stealthy submarine ("sub") arriving from beneath the ocean at a dock to supply or provide much-needed food and munitions for a distant outpost. See also **répartir** (to divide, distribute, share among), page 239.

Other verbs in this family include: to unpack, unload, take care of, attend to, furnish, arm, depose, contribute, aid, provision with, unburden, appropriate, trade, refuel, serve, etc.

aider   to help, aid, assist, succor, be of help, facilitate

approprier   to appropriate (funds), set apart for specific use, suit, fit, adapt (to need)

approvisionner en   to provision with, supply with, stock with (supplies, goods)

assister à   to attend to, tend to, give aid to (homeless, poor)

assurer l'avenir de   to provide for (family, orphans)

commercer   to trade, engage in commerce (countries, merchants)

commercialiser   to market (product), offer for sale

contribuer   to contribute (humanitarian aid, effort), pay

débarder   to unload (lumber), clear woods of (fallen trees)

débarquer   to unload, unship, disembark, land (ship)

décaisser   to pay out (money, reward), unpack (box)

décharger   to unload (vehicle, baggage), empty, unburden (mule)

dédouaner   to clear goods from a customs house, pass goods through customs

délester   to unballast, remove ballast (ship)

dépaqueter   to unpack, unpackage

désembarquer   to unload, unship, disembark (ship)

désenvelopper   to unwrap, open up

développer   to open, unwrap, unfold, develop (plan, product, photo), spread (idea)

distribuer   to distribute, provide, depose, deliver, hand out, share, dole out, parcel out

donner   to give, bestow, grant (loan), provide (dowry), endow (college), fund

doter   to endow, fit out, fit up, equip, fund (scholarship), grant (money)

douer   to grant (financial support), endow (scholarship, college)

entretenir   to maintain (health), support (family, financially)

être surdoué   to be gifted (with talent, good looks, great voice)

faire attention à   to attend to, give attention to (s.o.'s needs)

faire le nécessaire pour   to provide for, provide necessities

faire une enchère   to bid, make a bid (at auction)

fournir   to provide, furnish, supply (supplies, materiel)

se garnir   to furnish or provide oneself with

larguer   to drop off (cargo, supplies)

mettre en vente   to put out for sale, put on sale

munir   to provide, arm, supply (provisions, weapons, equipment)

nantir   to provide s.o. with, give as a pledge, give as collateral/deposit

s'occuper de   to take care of (family, sick, needy, personal affairs)

octroyer (à)   to grant, bestow (allocate, give to)

payer   to pay, contribute, give money to, pay up, remunerate

pourvoir   to provide, supply, endow, provide for, issue (supplies), cater to (needs)

préparer   to make ready, make fit, ready, prepare (dinner), make (plans)

rapporter   to bring in, yield (stock dividends, crops)

raquer*   to fork out,* pay, pay out, cough up* (cash)

ravitailler   to reprovision, refuel, give fresh supplies, provide (fresh ammunition)

refourguer*   to unload* (problem on s.o.), dump* (on s.o.), pass on (bad check)

réglementer   to regulate (price, trade, temperature)

réguler   to regulate (water flow, taxes, traffic)

rembourser   to reimburse, repay (loan), refund

se remonter de   to take on a fresh supply of (provisions)

rendre   to give out (oil well), produce, return (refund), yield (profit)

servir   to serve, wait on (clients, tables)

servir à   to attend to (needs, task)

sortir   to bring out (item for sale), release (new movie, CD), publish (new book)

subvenir aux besoins de   to support (financially)

supporter   to support (financially, physically, emotionally)

télécharger   to download (computer)

Le patron a augmenté son salaire. Maintenant, avec ce qu'il gagne, il peut °subvenir aux besoins de sa famille. The boss gave him a raise. Now, with his current earnings, he can support his family.

Mais t'es nase*—paresseux! Tu sais même pas °décharger une charrette à fumier! You're useless—you lazy bum*! You can't even unload a manure cart!

Veuillez me °rembourser pour ce fer à vapeur défectueux. Be so kind as to reimburse me for this defective steam iron.

La peur déclenche une réaction dans certaines zones cérébrales et °rend le corps prêt à l'action. Fear sets off a reaction in certain cerebral areas and readies the body for action.

8

Be on the Lookout for . . .

Featured Verbs

dérober   to steal, conceal

MEMORY AID

"**De-**" means *removal from* or *undoing*, and the "**~robe~**" fragment is spelled like the English word *robe*. Thus, "**de-robe**" can mean *to remove the robe from*. Picture a thief who has crept into the king's bedchamber to steal the royal ermine robe, removing it from the coat rack. The king will awake to find he has been disrobed.

This category contains words covering a host of illegal, deceptive, and underhanded activities. Other verbs in this family include: to burgle, plunder, ransack, pillage, cheat, swindle, hijack, embezzle, filch,* con,* dupe, fleece,* infringe upon, hoodwink,* feign, rob, snatch, break in, etc.

affabuler   to make up stories, confabulate, replace fact with fantasy (psychiatry)

arnaquer*   to swindle, defraud, scam,* chisel,* cheat

attaquer une banque à main armée   to hold up a bank, pull a bank heist*

attraper   to trick, take in, bamboozle*

barboter*   to steal, rip off,* pinch*

berner   to fool, hoax

blouser*   to con,* swindle, defraud, dupe

braconner   to poach, steal game, take fish or game illegally

braquer*   to hold up (s.o., bank), pull one's gun on, level a gun at, aim a gun (at)

cambrioler   to burgle, break into (house, store), burglarize

caponner*   to cheat, rat on* (s.o.)

carotter*   to cheat, steal, swipe*

chaparder*   to pilfer, steal, commit thievery

chiper*   to pilfer, filch,* rip off*

commettre des malversations   to embezzle (funds, property)

commettre une agression   to mug or attack s.o.

commettre une fourberie   to cheat, deceive, swindle

confisquer   to confiscate (illegal drugs), seize, impound (property)

couillonner*   to con,* dupe, swindle

déplomber   to break into, hack* (computer)

dépouiller   to despoil, deprive of, plunder, raid

détourner   to hijack, embezzle, misappropriate (funds)

détrousser*   to rob, steal from (s.o.)

dévaliser   to rifle, rob, strip, burgle, burglarize, raid (refrigerator)

dévêtir   to divest, deprive of (title, power, possessions, clothing)

dilapider   to embezzle, misappropriate (funds)

dindonner*   to dupe, take in s.o.,* make s.o. the fall guy* (*lit.* **dindon (m):** turkey)

duper   to dupe, take in, gull

écumer les mers   to scour the seas, ply the seas (pirate), prey on ships

embarquer*   to steal, filch,* cart off,* rip off*

embobiner*   to hoodwink,* dupe, bamboozle,* fool (s.o.)

s'emparer de   to seize (power, land, hostage), grab (object), take possession of

empocher   to pocket, snap up, bag,* grab (object, cash)

enlever   to steal, take from (money, object), kidnap

entrer par effraction   to break in (house, bank)

entuber*   to con,* dupe, take in* (s.o.), fool (s.o.)

escamoter   to filch,* make away with, make disappear (money, cards)

escroquer   to swindle, cheat, fleece* (s.o.)

extorquer   to extort, commit extortion

faire casse*   to pull off a robbery/heist*

faire de l'évasion fiscale   to evade taxes

faire des frasques*   to get into mischief (*lit.* frasque (*f*): escapade)

faire des vols à la tire   to pickpocket, pick s.o.'s pocket

faire du chantage   to blackmail

faire mine de   to pretend to (do s.t.)

faire un délit d'initié   to commit insider-dealing or insider-trading

faire un hold-up   to pull a heist*/hold up

se faire avoir*   to be taken for a ride,* be cheated, be had*

se faire gruger*   to be duped, be swindled

se faire posséder*   to be taken in,* be duped, be swindled, be cheated

falsifier   to forge (check), falsify (credentials, document)

faucher*   to steal, rip off,* swipe*

feindre   to feign, pretend, fool s.o.

feinter   to fake,* fake one's way past

filouter*   to steal, swindle, filch,* rob, chisel*

finasser*   to use trickery, finesse (cards)

flouer*   to swindle, trick (s.o.), con* (s.o.)

fouiller   to ransack, rummage, frisk*

frauder   to defraud, commit fraud, cheat, cheat on* (s.o.)

gruger   to dupe, swindle, rob

happer   to snatch up, grab, snap up*

kidnapper   to kidnap

leurrer   to delude, gull, fool (s.o.), trick (s.o.)

marauder   to pilfer, scrounge, filch*

matraquer le client*   to fleece* clients, overcharge (s.o.)

mentir   to lie, be deceptive, tell lies, fib,* cheat

se mettre dans l'illégalité   to break the law

mystifier   to deceive, fool

obscurcir   to darken, obscure (details, truth), dim, make dark (room)

occulter   to conceal, hide, obscure (facts)

pénétrer   to break into (thief), burgle, trespass, enter illegally

piller   to pillage, plunder, ransack, loot (village)

pincer*   to steal, rip off*

piper*   to trick, cheat, decoy

piquer*   to steal, filch,* rip off,* swipe,* pickpocket

pirater   to make a pirated ("bootleg") copy of (song, movie), commit piracy

plagier   to plagiarize, steal s.o.'s writing or ideas

plumer*   to fleece* (rob s.o.), swindle

priver de   to pillage, loot

raboter*   to filch,* pilfer

racketter qn*   to extort money from s.o.

rafler*   to run off with, swipe, steal, rip off,* bag* (jewel)

rançonner   to fleece s.o.,* extort money (from s.o.)

ravir à qn   to rob s.o. of (money, honor)

receler   to conceal, harbor (criminal), receive stolen goods

récidiver   to commit a second offense, be a habitual offender (legal)

récupérer   to hijack (s.o., political platform), take (votes, seat in Congress)

refaire*   to dupe, take s.o. in*

resquiller*   to sneak in (without paying), cut in (line), wrangle, finagle*

rouler*   to con,* dupe, swindle

ruser   to use cunning, use trickery, trick, be crafty

saccager   to sack, plunder, ransack (village), pillage, loot (spoils of war)

simuler   to feign, sham, fake, simulate (real diamond)

sortir au nez et à la barbe de*   to take right (out) from under s.o.'s nose*

soudoyer   to bribe, offer a bribe

subtiliser   to steal, steal from, sneak (into)

tordre qn* to fleece s.o.,* clean s.o. out* (money)

toucher à to tamper with (sealed letter, lock), meddle with

traficoter* to tamper with (engine, mechanism), fiddle with* (account numbers)

trafiquer to tamper with (account ledger), traffic (drugs)

transgresser to infringe, defy, break the law

travailler au noir to work illegally

tricher to trick, cheat, rig (elections)

tromper to cheat, take in, fool, deceive

tromper la vigilance de qn to slip past s.o., sneak by s.o.

truander* to swindle, cheat, con*

truquer* to fix (election, horse race), stack (deck of cards), load (dice)

usurper to usurp (power), seize (possessions)

voler to steal, rob, swipe,* rip off,* pilfer, rustle (cattle)

voler avec effraction to break into (house), burglarize

Le cambrioleur et sa complice ont °dérobé le grand diamant au musée. The burglar and his accomplice stole the large diamond from the museum.

Ma femme m'a °trompé. C'est quelque chose que je ne peux pas pardonner. My wife cheated on me. That's something that I can't forgive.

Le bateau de pirates °écume les mers battant le pavillon d'Espagne. The pirate ship plies the seas under the Spanish ensign.

Elle s'est °fait possédée* par le faux-monnayeur dont les contrefaçons sont indifférenciables des vrais billets. She was swindled by the counterfeiter whose fake bills are indistinguishable from the real ones.

MEMORY AID

"De-" means *removal* or *undoing*, and **voile** means in English *veil—a cloth worn over the face for secrecy, protection, or as an expression of modesty*. Thus, **"de-voile"** can mean *to remove or undo a veil*. Picture a wealthy patron of the arts who has commissioned a bust to be made of him. He removes the veil to reveal or disclose the sculptor's creation.

Other verbs in this family include: to make known, signal, show, highlight, detect, introduce, enlighten, exhibit, uncover, lay bare, expose, unmask, display, present, model, etc.

afficher   to make a show of, display (results), hang (poster), put up (sign, placard)

alerter l'opinion   to alert the public, warn the public, raise an alarm

annoncer   to announce, give notice of, advertise, forecast, herald (news)

apprendre à   to teach, inform, impart

claironner   to shout from the rooftops (news), make known (*lit.* **clairon** *(m)*: bugle)

clamer   to proclaim, announce, give word

débâcher   to uncover, expose (truth) (*lit.* **bâche** *(f)*: canvas, tarpaulin)

déballer   to display (merchandise)

se déboutonner   to expose one's bosom, unbutton oneself

décacheter   to open, unseal, reveal, remove seal (package)

déceler   to discover, detect (error), disclose, reveal, betray (secret), indicate

décolleter   to have one's shoulders bared (low-cut or scoop-neck garment)

découvrir   to unveil, uncover (buried treasure, archeological ruin), discover

défaire   to unpack (baggage), unravel (knot, shoelace)

déferler   to unfurl (flag, ensign)

défourrer   to unwrap, take out of its cover

défrayer la chronique   to be in the news, be widely talked about

défroquer   to defrock, unfrock (priest)

se dégarnir   to strip oneself (of clothing), lose one's hair

démasquer   to expose (liar, traitor), unmask (truth), reveal (hypocrisy)

dénuder   to denude, strip bare (body, tree), disrobe, undress

dépister   to screen (lab test), detect, track down (criminal), unearth (evidence, clue)

déployer   to show, unfurl (flag), unroll (map, fabric), display

dépouiller   to unclothe, strip (clothing), count (votes), go through (document)

détecter   to detect, discover (clue), find out (fact)

diagnostiquer   to diagnose (medical condition, engine malfunction)

discerner   to discern, detect, distinguish

divulguer   to divulge (information), disclose (whereabouts), reveal (secret)

donner sur   to overlook (balcony), open onto (window)

échauder qn   to teach s.o. a lesson, burn s.o.* (bad experience)

éclairer   to throw light on (subject), clarify, enlighten (mind), illuminate (room)

édifier   to enlighten, edify (with knowledge)

éduquer   to educate, train, civilize

élever   to educate (child)

émerger   to emerge (from shadows), appear, stand out (in crowd), come up (sun)

enregistrer to show (profit), tape-record, record (music)

enseigner to teach, instruct, lecture, point out (facts), show

épancher son cœur to pour out one's heart

être exposé to go on display (merchandise)

être mannequin chez qn to be a model for s.o. (fashion designer)

éventer to let out (secret), discover, ventilate (mine), expose to air (grain), find out

exhiber to display, exhibit (art, body part, collection)

exposer to show (product), uncover, lay bare, exhibit (weakness, vulnerability)

faire de la publicité pour to advertise (product), promote

faire flèche de tout bois* to leave no stone unturned* (*lit.* to make arrows out of all wood)

se faire jour to become clear, become apparent, be revealed (truth, answer)

faire part de to announce (news), make known, inform

faire preuve de to show (evidence), prove (intention), exhibit, demonstrate (respect)

faire savoir to make known (intentions), signify, let it be known, announce

faire une démonstration de to demonstrate (technique, product)

faire une photo(graphie) de to take a photograph of, take a picture of

faire voir to show s.t., show off, demonstrate

se familiariser to get to know, familiarize oneself with (**avec**)

figurer to appear (on a list, in phone book), represent, be mentioned, depict, show

frimer* to show off (wealth), be boastful

gesticuler to gesticulate, show or demonstrate s.t. by motions or hand gestures

illuminer to light up (room), enlighten (mind), throw light on (problem), illuminate

impressionner to expose (film, photo)

inaugurer to unveil, open, inaugurate (era, exposition, construction project)

instruire to teach, instruct, educate, give instruction, enlighten (student)

jeter un éclairage nouveau (sur) to cast a new light on (issue, evidence)

lever la voile sur to unveil (statue), expose (truth, plot)

manifester to show, demonstrate, make manifest, evince

mettre à la "une" to put on the front page (newspaper) (**la "une"**: page 1)

mettre à nu to strip, lay bare (facts)

se mettre à poil* to strip stark naked, be in the buff* (*lit.* **poil** (*m*): hair)

mettre (qch) en lumière to bring s.t. to light, illuminate (mind), enlighten (public)

mettre en manchette to headline, put in the headlines (newspaper)

mettre en valeur to show off, show to advantage, highlight (talent, eyes, object)

mettre en vedette to put in the spotlight (singer), feature (film actor)

montrer to show (example, directions), exhibit (object, art)

montrer la voie to show the way (to tourist, by example), show the path (to take)

muer to molt, slough (snake), change into s.t.

offrir à to present (gift), offer (refreshments)

s'offrir aux regards to expose oneself to the public's gaze

ouvrir to unwrap, open (package, one's eyes, one's heart), turn on (TV, faucet)

passer to show (film), play (CD, record)

passer un scan to have a scan (CT, MRI)

percevoir to perceive, detect, sense, realize

photocopier to photocopy, Xerox®

présenter   to introduce (friend), show, present, outline (idea), anchor (TV news)

projeter   to project (slides, image on screen, voice), show

promulguer   to make known (law, decree), declare publicly, announce officially

prouver   to demonstrate, prove, show, substantiate, give proof, show evidence

radiographier   to X-ray, take a radiograph

relooker*   to give a new look to, revamp the image of (product logo, corporation)

remontrer   to reveal again, show again

repérer   to pick out, find (location, landmark), mark (site for biopsy [medicine])

révéler   to reveal, disclose, bring to light, impart, confide, unearth, break (news)

révéler sous son vrai jour   to show in its true light (evidence, truth, person)

rompre le sceau   to break the seal (package, royal document)

signaler   to indicate, signal, report, point out

signaliser   to mark with signs (road)

signifier   to make known, give notice, intend, mean, signify, indicate

sortir   to come out (new product, book), be released (film), bring out (new item)

surexposer   to overexpose (film, skin to sunlight, actor to media)

symboliser   to symbolize, represent, be symbolic of

transparaître   to show through (intentions), be transparent (emotions, film image)

visualiser   to display, visualize (idea), imagine, picture (an idea in mind)

voir le jour   to see the light, originate (idea), germinate (plan, idea)

Le maire °dévoila la nouvelle statue dans le parc la semaine dernière. The mayor unveiled the new statue in the park last week.

Les actes de vengeance tribaux ont été °signalés par l'ONU dans la zone tampon. Acts of tribal retribution were reported by the U.N. in the buffer zone.

Les noms de plusieurs pontes* °figuraient sur la liste de convives. The names of several VIPs appeared on the guest list.

On peut °enregistrer le cliché numérique, puis le transmettre par ligne internet. One can record the digital image, then send it over the internet.

Le joaillier a °fait part de ses doutes quant à l'authenticité du diamant. The jeweler made known his doubts as to the authenticity of the diamond.

MEMORY AID

"**É**" can be equivalent to "*ex*" in English, which can mean *out of* or *from*. The "*~***boue**~*" fragment means *mud, muck, mire,* or *filth*. Thus, "**ex-boue**" can mean *to take something from or out of the mud or mire.* Picture a determined treasure hunter scavenging priceless artifacts in a mud pit, pulling the relics out of the muck. (In France an **éboueur** is a garbage man.) See also **fossoyer** (to dig a ditch or trench), page 166.

Other verbs in this family include: to rummage around, pick over, sort out, follow the trail of, stalk, encounter, run across, recover, fish out, explore, track, trail, hunt, salvage, discover, etc.

aller chercher   to go for, fetch, scavenge, go look for

arracher   to extract, pull up (plant), grub up, pull (tooth), tear out (page), tear off

barboter   to dawdle about (mud), wade (in mud), splash (in mud)

chasser   to hunt (animal, clue), chase, pursue (lead)

chercher   to search for, seek, look for, search (files), explore, hunt, dig for

chiffonner   to pick through rags or trash, be a rag collector

débarrasser   to extricate (from trap, from tight spot), pull from, free from (situation)

découvrir   to discover, uncover (archeological site), detect, disclose

dégager   to extricate, clear, disengage, unblock, free up, release

dénicher   to discover, hunt, find out, take out of the nest, dig up, fish up, unearth

déposer la poubelle   to empty the dustbin

désembourber   to extract from the mud (shoe, horse, tractor)

enlever la voirie   to collect the garbage

être sur la (bonne) piste   to be on the right track/trail

extraire   to extract, pull out, take out, mine (ore), quarry, dig out, free (stuck object)

faire le tour de   to explore (possibilities)

faire le tri de   to sort/shift through (garbage)

faire les poubelles   to scavenge, rummage through trash bins, scrounge

faire une chasse au trésor   to go on a treasure hunt

farfouiller*   to rummage about, search among items, dig about

filer   to track (clues, lead), tail (suspect), track down, shadow (s.o.)

fouiller partout   to rummage, scour, root, ferret, search

fureter   to rummage around, ferret, investigate

jeter au rebut   to throw in the rubbish bin, toss out, discard, chuck*

mettre au rancart*   to chuck out,* throw out, throw on the scrap heap

piller les poubelles*   to scavenge, foray, pick through the rubbish

préserver   to save, preserve (fruits, mummy)

rechercher   to search for (lost item), pry into, seek again, research, seek (honor)

récupérer   to scavenge, recover, retrieve, salvage (old clothes), reclaim (lost item)

rejeter to discharge (waste, gas, fumes)

rencontrer to run across, encounter, strike (object)

repêcher to recover, fish out s.t. (from rubbish)

repérer to locate, find (map coordinates, landmark)

retrouver to follow the trail, recover, find again (lost trail, same clues)

sauver to salvage (parts from wreck), save (face, one's reputation)

sortir la racaille* to take out the trash

suivre to follow (road signs), tail, trail, track (footprints, clue, lead, scent)

suivre la trace de to follow the trail of, be on the track of (criminal, animal)

suivre le fil de to keep track of, follow the trail of, be on the trail of

tirer de to extract, pull from, pull out, haul out, wrench out (s.t. stuck)

toucher à to meddle with, tamper with (mechanism)

traficoter* to tamper with, fiddle with* (radio dial, hairdo)

traquer to stalk, track (Bigfoot, bear), track down (clue, news lead)

trier to pick over, sort out, handpick (employee, partner)

trier sur le volet to handpick (fruit, employee, team)

trifouiller* to rummage about, rummage through (old clothes)

trouver to find, discover, come across

vider la corbeille to empty the waste-basket

vider les ordures to throw out the garbage

L'archéologue intrépide était °éboueur à Paris avant de se lancer sur les traces de la momie. The fearless archeologist was a trash collector in Paris before setting off on the trail of the mummy.

Marc se °trouve à Londres, où son père, un avocat, souhaite que son fils suive aussi des études de droit. Mark is in London, where his father, an attorney, hopes that his son would also pursue legal studies.

Des enquêteurs n'ont °retrouvé aucune évidence probante d'incurie ou de maltraitance. Investigators found no convincing evidence of carelessness or malpractice.

La police a °rencontré une forte résistance dans les implantations des irréductibles retranchés. The police encountered strong resistance in the settlements of the entrenched hardliners.

entrevoir   to glimpse, catch a glimpse of, make out

MEMORY AID

"**Entre-**" means *between*, and **voir** means *to see, observe, witness, view*. Thus, "**entre-voir**" can mean *to see between something*, like seeing something quickly passing between two points. Picture someone in a narrow alley catching only a fleeting glimpse of a man running down the sidewalk because his or her field of vision is restricted.

Other verbs in this family relate to: brief light flashes, flickers, glimmers, and shimmers that one perceives when catching a glimpse of something. Also included are: to shine, reflect, glint, sparkle, glitter, flicker, wink, blink, beam, reflect light, glance at, etc.

apercevoir   to perceive, catch sight of, notice, catch a glimpse of

s'apercevoir de   to notice, perceive, realize, glimpse, note, take note of

apparaître   to come into view, appear, burst upon (scene), become visible

brasiller   to glitter, shine (sea), glimmer

briller   to glitter, shine, sparkle

chatoyer   to shimmer, glisten (rock, gem), sparkle (diamond)

ciller   to blink (eyes) (*lit.* **cil** *(m):* eyelash)

cligner de l'œil   to wink, blink

cligner des yeux   to blink, wink, bat one's eyes

clignoter   to wink, blink, twinkle, flicker, flash intermittently

constater   to notice, take note of, note (details), record (clues at crime scene)

éclater   to sparkle, shine, shine through (talent)

effleurer   to touch lightly, touch upon (subject), graze, skim, brush

entrapercevoir   to catch a fleeting glimpse of

entreluire   to glimmer, gleam, shimmer

étinceler   to flash, sparkle, glitter, twinkle

faire briller   to shine (brass lamp), polish (silverware)

jeter un coup d'œil   to glance at, glimpse

luire   to glitter, gleam, glisten, shine, flash

luire par moments   to glint, glimpse

lustrer   to shine, glaze, give a gloss to, be lustrous (hair conditioner, polish)

miroiter   to reflect light, glisten, shimmer

mousser   to sparkle (wine)

percevoir   to perceive, observe, take notice of, see, catch (glimpse), sense (s.o.)

pétiller   to sparkle (champagne)

prendre connaissance de   to notice, take note of, note, perceive

prendre une vue rapide   to glimpse, see briefly

rayonner   to sparkle, shine, beam, glow, radiate (light, radioactivity)

réfléchir   to reflect (light, sound)

refléter   to reflect (light, sound)

rejaillir   to flash, reflect, reflect back on (glory)

reluire   to shine, glisten, glitter

renvoyer   to reflect (light), echo

répercuter   to reflect, bounce back (echo, sound, light)

repérer   to spot, locate, pick out (locale, s.t. at a distance), scope out (site)

resplendir   to glitter, shine, sparkle

se réverbérer   to be reflected (light, heat), reverberate (sound)

rutiler   to gleam, sparkle, shimmer (*lit.* **rutile** *(m)*: lustrous reddish-brown gemstone)

sauter   to flicker (TV screen)

scintiller   to glisten, sparkle, twinkle, flicker, glitter

sentir   to be aware of, feel, catch scent of (danger, odor), sense (danger)

témoigner (que)   to witness, attest to, bear witness to

tomber sur   to come across, run into, chance upon, meet by chance, hit upon (idea)

vaciller   to flicker (light), oscillate (laser beam), quiver (flame)

visionner   to view, preview (film)

zieuter*   to glimpse, squint at, eyeball* (s.o. or s.t.), eye* (s.o.)

Les frères ont °entrevu le fantôme passant à travers la lucarne de la maison hantée. The brothers glimpsed the ghost passing through the dormer window of the haunted house.

Un témoin oculaire °constata que le taxi circulait à grande vitesse au moment de la collision. An eyewitness noted that the taxi was traveling at high speed at the moment of collision.

Il s'apprêtait à sauter lorsqu'on l'a °repéré. He was getting ready to jump when someone spotted him.

Quoique des altérations de l'ADN °apparaissent, elles ne posent qu'un faible risque d'induire le cancer. Although changes in the DNA may appear, they pose little threat for inducing a cancer.

guetter to watch for, lie in wait for, waylay

MEMORY AID

Guetter is spelled somewhat like the English word *gutter, a drainage channel alongside the street or at the edge of a roof.* Picture a stealthy spy lying in wait in a street gutter, watching for a rival whom he intends to waylay (to attack from ambush). The verbs of this category deal with a host of activities that one would do secretively, cautiously, or with intent to surprise.

Other verbs in this family include: to hide, spy on, conceal, be cautious, look over, shadow, prowl around, eavesdrop, be on the alert, beware of, be watchful, lurk, loiter, keep an eye on, etc.

apercevoir to catch sight of, perceive, notice, take note of

aposter to place in ambush

attendre to watch out for, wait for, anticipate (s.o. or s.t.)

attraper dans un guet-apens to ambush, trap in an ambush, catch in a trap

s'avancer masqué to hide one's hand, conceal one's true intent

aviser to perceive, espy, realize

avoir conscience de qch to be vigilant, be aware of, have knowledge of

avoir la puce à l'oreille* to be suspicious, eavesdrop (*lit.* to have a flea in one's ear)

bigler* to look from the corner of one's eye, eye up,* have a peek at, peep at

brouter to browse (through books)

se calfeutrer to shut oneself away, get cozy (by fireplace)

se camoufler to camouflage/conceal oneself, disguise oneself

se celer to hide, conceal oneself, hide away, be concealed

chuchoter to whisper, murmur, speak in hushed tones

se clapir to hide in a hole (rabbit), squat, cower

couver to lie hidden, lurk, plot (revenge), smolder (hatred, jealousy)

dévisager to stare at, glare at

se dissimuler to hide oneself, pass unnoticed, conceal oneself, hide

écouter aux portes to eavesdrop (*lit.* to listen at the door)

embusquer to ambush, waylay, lie in wait

épier to spy, be on the lookout, spy on (s.o.), watch for (opportunity), look out for

espionner to spy, eavesdrop, spy on (s.o.), be a secret agent/spy

être à l'affût to lie in wait, wait for (*lit.* to be at the gun carriage [**affût** *(m)*])

être aux aguets to be on the watch, watch, watch for, be on the lookout

être aux écoutes to eavesdrop, listen in (*lit.* **écoutes** *(fpl):* ears of wild boar)

être en état d'alerte to be on alert (military), be in a state of alert

être en vigie to be on watch, be vigilant, be watchful

être sur le qui-vive to be on the alert

être sur ses gardes to be on guard, be watchful

être tout ouïe to be all ears (*lit.* **ouïe** *(f):* hearing)

examiner to examine, scrutinize, inspect, observe closely, have a close look, study

faire de l'espionnage to be a spy, to spy

faire disparaître aux regards to hide from sight, conceal

faire gaffe à* to watch out for, be wary of, pay attention (e.g., **fais gaffe!** watch out!)

faire le guet   to pay attention, look out for, be a lookout, watch, patrol

faire preuve de prudence   to be cautious, be prudent

faire sa ronde   to patrol, be on patrol

faire surveiller   to keep a watch, stake out (area), monitor, proctor (exam)

garder la boutique*   to keep an eye on things, mind the store*

garder l'anonymat   to remain anonymous, retain anonymity

garder l'incognito   to remain incognito, stay undercover

garder l'œil sur   to keep an eye on, watch over

guigner   to peer or peep at, ogle

ignorer   to be unaware of, not know, be in the dark (on a subject)

inspecter   to inspect, examine closely

s'isoler   to isolate oneself, seclude oneself, go into hiding

lorgner   to leer, ogle, have one's eye on (*lit.* **lorgnette** (*f*): opera glasses)

loucher sur*   to have one's eye on, squint at

méconnaître   to be unaware of (facts)

se méfier   to beware (s.o., situation), mistrust, distrust, be on guard, watch out for

menacer   to threaten, menace, hang over (threat), jeopardize

mettre qch à plat   to have a close look at

monter la garde   to be on guard, post the guard (prison, castle)

moucharder*   to spy on, sneak, inform on, squeal on,* tattle on,* rat on,* be an informant

se nicher   to hide oneself, nest (bird)

noter   to note, take note of, observe, note down (observations)

noyauter   to infiltrate (spy, cancer) (*lit.* **noyau** (*m*): core, nucleus, center, seed)

observer   to observe closely, study, watch

occulter   to conceal, hide, obscure from sight

offusquer   to obscure, darken, dim (fog), cloud (judgment)

parler tout bas   to whisper, speak in hushed tones

passer inaperçu   to go unnoticed, be unrecognized, pass unobserved/undetected (spy)

patrouiller   to patrol (military, police)

se planquer*   to hide, hide away, conceal oneself

prendre bonne note de   to take note of, note, observe carefully

prendre le maquis*   to go underground, go into hiding (*lit.* **maquis** (*m*): Corsican scrubland)

prendre qn à l'improviste   to catch s.o. unawares, surprise s.o.

prendre qn en filature*   to shadow s.o., stalk s.o., tail s.o.

pressentir   to sense that, have a feeling that (danger)

promener ses regards sur   to look over, eye up*

reconnaître   to recognize, identify, reconnoiter, make preliminary inspection

se recouvrir   to cover oneself up again, disguise oneself

regarder   to look at, look into, glance at, regard, look upon, gaze upon, view, watch

regarder de côté   to look at askance, glance at with suspicion or distrust

regarder qn d'un œil noir*   to look askance at s.o., mistrust, suspect

reluquer*   to ogle (girls at the beach), have one's eye on, leer at

se réserver   to wait, hold oneself back, keep for oneself (best piece of pie)

rester coi   to remain silent, be quiet, remain speechless

rester dans l'ombre   to remain in obscurity, hide in the background/shadows

se rincer l'œil*   to get an eyeful,* see more than expected, see quite a bit

rôder   to lurk, loiter, prowl around, hang around, hover over (s.o.)

sauver   to conceal (undercover, e.g., escapee, runaway, refugee)

scruter   to scrutinize (data, dossier, job applicant)

souffler aux oreilles de qn*   to whisper in s.o.'s ear*

soupçonner   to suspect, surmise, have an inkling, have a suspicion

suivre de près   to follow or watch closely (news), follow close behind (car)

surprendre   to surprise (thief), overhear, intercept, creep up on (s.o.), catch unawares

surveiller   to keep watch over, stake out (enemy lair), guard, watch, monitor

surveiller de près   to keep a close eye on, watch closely

suspecter   to suspect (s.o.), have a suspicion

susurrer   to whisper, murmur

se taire   to be silent, keep quiet, keep silence, hush up, remain silent

se tapir   to lurk, hide away

se tenir en embuscade   to lurk, lie in wait, ambush

se tenir sur ses gardes   to be on one's guard, be alert

toiser   to look up and down, look over (*lit.* **toise** (*f*): measure, fathom [nautical])

tomber dans un guet-apens   to get caught in an ambush or trap

veiller   to be watchful, be vigilant, stay up late (to watch over)

veiller sur   to watch over (flock, sleeping baby, enemy camp)

visionner   to view, see, preview (film)

voir   to see, look, watch, have a look at, perceive

voir venir   to wait and see

Il °guettait l'arrivée de l'espion, bien caché dans l'arbuste touffu. He watched for the spy while well hidden in the bushy shrub.

On °note un aspect séquellaire au niveau du sein gauche mais aucune anomalie probante suspecte d'une métastase. There is noted a postoperative appearance of the left breast but no conclusive evidence of a metastasis.

Elle a °veillé toute la nuit en attendant le défilé du lendemain matin. She stayed up all night long waiting for the parade the next morning.

Le juge °scruta bien toutes les preuves et les témoignages avant de rendre son verdict. The judge carefully scrutinized all the evidence and testimonies before rendering a verdict.

Le tribunal les accuse d'avoir agi de façon concertée pour °occulter les indices et les vestiges ayant trait à l'affaire. The court accuses them of having acted in concert to conceal clues and traces of evidence related to the case.

MEMORY AID

"**Pre-**" means *earlier*, *prior*, or *before* (in time).
Voir means *to see*. Thus, "**pre-voir**" means *to
see earlier* or *see something before it happens*.
With such an ability one can foretell or forecast
the future. A similar word is *preview—to view in
advance or ahead of time*. Picture a gypsy
fortune teller who professes to foretell the
future with her crystal ball that allows her to
see events before they happen.

Other verbs in this family include: to look
ahead, anticipate, warn, prognosticate, imagine,
daydream, prepare for, give alert, conjecture,
plan, envision, forewarn, predict, bet on, etc.

alarmer   to alarm, alert, raise the alarm,
cause alarm

alerter   to alert, warn, notify of danger,
raise alarm

annoncer   to foretell, forecast, give
notice, announce, presage, herald
(news)

anticiper   to anticipate, foresee, think
ahead, second guess, preempt
(decision)

s'attendre à   to expect, anticipate, plan
ahead

augurer   to portend, conjecture,
surmise, augur, predict, foreshadow,
foresee, bode

avertir qn de   to warn s.o. of s.t.,
admonish, caution, forewarn, give
warning

aviser   to notify beforehand

concevoir   to conceive of, imagine,
devise, project, see

conseiller   to counsel, advise, warn, give
counsel to, inform

considérer   to consider, deliberate,
esteem, play with (idea)

convaincre   to convince, persuade,
convert (nonbeliever to faith), prove
(point)

croire   to believe in, have faith in, think,
be of the opinion, trust, believe

déciller   to open s.o.'s eyes, make s.o.
aware of

déconseiller   to advise against, warn
against, counsel s.o. against

décréter l'état d'urgence   to declare a
state of emergency

devancer   to anticipate (question, wish),
preempt (s.o.)

deviner   to guess, predict, divine, infer,
hazard a guess, imagine, reckon

donner l'alerte   to give the alert, raise
the alarm, alert

donner un coup de semonce   to fire a
warning shot (across a ship's bow)

envisager   to envision, conceive of,
contemplate, picture in one's mind

s'étaler   to portend (omen), be a
harbinger (of bad news), foretell,
presage

faire les jeux   to place bets (casino)

se figurer   to imagine, believe, fancy

flairer   to sense, perceive (danger), smell
out, sniff out (clues)

s'imaginer   to suppose, conceive of,
imagine, picture (in mind), visualize

jouer (de l'argent)   to gamble, stake, bet
on, bet money on

se méfier (de)   to be careful (of), be on
guard (against)

mettre en garde contre   to warn against,
alert (s.o.), warn (s.o.)

mettre qn en garde   to warn s.o., alert
s.o.

miser (sur)   to bet on (idea, horse race),
bank on (outcome)

notifier   to notify, inform, give information, apprise

parier aux courses   to bet on the races (horse)

parier sur   to bet on, stake, place a bet on (cards, horse), wager (money), gamble

persuader   to persuade, convince, win approval

précautionner   to warn, caution s.o., alert in advance

prédire   to predict, foretell, make a prediction, foresee

prémunir   to forewarn, caution, prepare for (future), guard against (loss, illness)

se préparer   to prepare for (trip, future), be brewing (storm, plot)

présager   to portend, presage, forebode, foreshadow

pressentir   to sense (danger), have a feeling that, feel out in advance (job applicant)

présumer   to presume, suppose, assume, take for granted

prévenir   to warn, forestall, anticipate, caution, prevent (disease spread)

pronostiquer   to prognosticate (stock market), predict (weather, future), foretell

projeter   to project (future needs), plan in advance, anticipate (needs)

promettre   to forebode, portend, give warning of

prophétiser   to prophesy (biblical prophet), foretell, foresee, forewarn

remémorer   to bring s.t. to s.o.'s mind, recall, remind

se rendre compte de   to realize, become aware of

rêvasser   to daydream, muse

rêver   to dream, muse, dream of, dream up, daydream

songer   to think about, intend, propose, muse on

soupçonner qn de   to suspect s.o. of.

supposer   to suppose, speculate, hypothesize, imagine, reckon

tenir compte de   to take into account, take heed of, make allowance for, consider

tenter sa chance   to try one's luck, take a chance, chance it (sports bet, slot machine)

tirer au sort   to cast lots, draw lots (to determine order)

tirer les cartes   to read one's fortune (cards)

La météo °prévoit des passages nuageux plus fréquents pour le week-end. The weather report predicts more frequent cloudy periods this weekend.

Bien qu'il fût °averti de l'incendie il n'eut pas le temps de se servir de l'extincteur. Although he was alerted to the fire, he didn't have time to use the fire extinguisher.

Si ces problèmes administratifs ne sont pas résolus d'ici lundi, une nouvelle solution sera °envisagée. If these administrative issues aren't resolved by next Monday a new solution will be contemplated.

Les détecteurs permettent aux scientifiques d'observer la subduction des plaques tectoniques et de °donner l'alerte en cas d'ondes sismiques. The detectors permit the scientists to observe the subduction of the tectonic plates and to set off an alert in the event of seismic waves.

MEMORY AID

The French prefix **"sur-"** can mean *on* or *upon*.
Venir means *to come, arrive, reach, occur*, or
happen. Thus, **"sur-venir"** can be thought of as
something coming upon or arriving on. Picture
an astonishing happening—a wondrous
occurrence taking place—a fleet of alien
spacecraft arriving on the horizon, coming upon
the city, and landing on numerous downtown
rooftops.

Other verbs in this family include: to turn up,
take place, arrive, appear, dawn, crop up, show
up, express itself, loom up, run across, result in,
hit upon, be a result of, be caused by, etc.

aborder to arrive at, land (ship), reach
(goal), attain (objective), address
(issue)

advenir to happen, occur, come to pass
(event), befall (misfortune)

alunir to land on the moon

s'amener to turn up, arrive, show up,
appear

amerrir to land on the water (seaplane),
touch down on the sea

arriver to happen, occur, turn up, reach
(destination), come about (reform)

atterrir to land (airplane), touch down
(space shuttle), land on (space station)

s'avérer (que) to prove to be, happen
(that), turn out (that)

avoir lieu to occur, happen, take place,
play out (sequence of events)

avoir pour origine to be caused by,
originate in, have for cause (problem,
disease)

avoir recours à to resort to (force, harsh
measures), turn to (s.o. for help)

comparaître devant to appear before
(tribunal, judge)

se concrétiser to materialize (hope,
project, threat), come true (dream)

se dérouler to take place (event), unfold
(fairy tale), set (story background)

échoir to happen, befall (misfortune),
fall due (deadline)

émaner de to come from, emanate from
(odor, sound), issue from (light)

entrer en passant to drop in, drop by
(visitor), pay a visit to

entrer en vigueur to come into
play/place (factor), be in effect (rules),
be effective

être pris au dépourvu to be taken
unawares, be taken by surprise

se faire to happen, take place, occur,
acquire (reputation), make (friend,
rule)

figurer to appear (on a list), represent
(item), symbolize, depict

improviser to improvise, ad lib,* do on
the spot

intervenir to arise (new perspective,
new data), occur, happen (event)

jaillir to occur (idea), spring up
(thought, inspiration)

se manifester to express itself (emotion,
phenomenon), be apparent, be revealed

s'observer to occur (phenomenon,
illness), take place (chemical reaction)

paraître to appear, come into sight,
come out (new book), appear to be,
seem to be

se passer to happen, take place (event),
come along

se passer par hasard to happen by
chance

se pointer* to turn up, arrive, show up

présenter à l'improviste to spring on
s.o.* (surprise party), surprise (s.o.
with s.t.)

se présenter to appear, present oneself, crop up (problem, occasion)

se produire to happen, occur, take place, come along, come about

provenir (de) to issue, originate, proceed, spring (from), be a result of

radiner* to show up, arrive

se ramener* to turn up, happen, occur

rappliquer* to arrive, turn up, come back

réapparaître to reappear, come back, turn up again (old friend)

se réceptionner to land (from a fall or jump)

relever to turn up (evidence, contradictions, clue)

remonter to reappear, come back, go back to (in time), date back (in time)

reparaître to reappear, turn up again, show up again, recur, happen again

se reposer to crop up again (problem), settle again (dust, bird)

se représenter to present itself again, crop up again (problem), occur, show

se reproduire to happen again, reappear, recur (problem, curse, cancer)

ressurgir to resurface (problem, issue), return (strength), reappear

résulter to result in, come of, ensue, be a result of, cause

se retrouver to find oneself (in same spot), end up (in prison), meet again (s.o.)

revenir à soi to come back to (person) (boomerang, self-addressed envelope, curse)

sortir de to come of, result in (as a consequence of an action)

sortir par hasard to come up (number), arise, happen by chance, happen by accident

surgir to appear suddenly, loom up (mountain), arise, pop up,* spring up

surgir du néant to spring out of nowhere (animal, car), be a bolt out of the blue

surprendre to surprise, catch unawares

tomber dans le voisinage to be in the vicinity, be in the neighborhood

tomber sur to run into (friend), run across, come across (bargain), chance upon

toucher terre to land, touch down (plane)

trouver to hit upon (solution), come across (good seat), find (restaurant)

venir to come (person, to mind), happen, arrive, occur

venir à l'esprit to come to mind, cross one's mind

se voir to take place, happen (event), occur, show up, show (emotion, strain)

To express something happening *unexpectedly*, *by chance*, or *without intention*, one can combine a verb from column A meaning *to happen* with an adverb or adverbial phrase from column B. These can be mixed in a variety of combinations:

A: *To Happen*	B: *Adverb*	
arriver [...]	à l'improviste	unexpectedly, unawares
advenir [...]	inopinément	unexpectedly, unforeseen
se passer [...]	d'une manière inattendue	unexpectedly, unforeseen
se faire [...]	d'une manière imprévue	unforeseen
se dérouler [...]	imprudemment	unguardedly
venir [...]	à son insu	unawares
avoir lieu [...]	subitement	suddenly
se produire [...]	soudainement	suddenly, all of a sudden
se ramener [...]	tout à coup	suddenly
se voir [...]	de but en blanc	without warning
etc.	par hasard	by chance, fortuitously
	sans invitation	uninvited, without invitation
	sans intention	unintended
	involontairement	unintentionally, unwillingly
	par mégarde	accidentally, by mistake
	sans avertissement	without warning
	au pied levé	at a moment's notice
	au fur et à mesure	as one goes along, on the fly
	contre toute attente	without any warning
	dans un moment d'inattention	in an off-guard moment

Ça pourra aller!* Appelez-moi s'il °survient quelque chose de bizarre. That's close enough!* Call me if something strange happens.
L'opération pratiquée °s'est déroulée sans difficulté particulière. The operation was performed without any complication.
La collision entre la comète et le projectile devrait °se produire vers 18 h 30. The collision between the comet and the projectile should take place around 6:30 P.M.

Le maire précise que les nouvelles lois °entreront en vigueur le 8 juin. The mayor specifies that the new statutes will come into effect on June 8.

De la discussion °jaillit la lumière. From debate comes enlightenment.

Fais ce que dois, °advienne que pourra. Do your duty, come what may.

9

Oops! Ouch!

Featured Verbs

barbouiller (de) to smear (with), cover (with), daub

MEMORY AID

The first two syllables of **"bar-boui**-ller," when spoken, sound a bit like the first two syllables of the English word *barbeque* (**bar-be**-que), or **Bar-B**-Q. Picture an outdoor barbeque chef vigorously smearing, coating, and daubing the steaks on the grill with barbeque sauce.

The following verbs deal with the act of brushing on or covering something with a coat or finish. Other verbs in this family include: to coat, smudge, splash, gloss over, glaze, brush, varnish, veneer, apply, whitewash, wax, weatherproof, resurface, paint, polish, lubricate, oil, etc.

appliquer to apply (makeup, paint, ointment), stick, spread on (varnish)

arroser to baste (with gravy), sprinkle (with liquid)

asperger to apply hastily, spray (cologne), splash (water)

badigeonner to whitewash (picket fence, wall), disguise defects, paint

barioler to streak with several colors (*lit.* **bariolé:** gaudy, multicolored)

brosser to brush, brush on (paint, sauce)

caraméliser to coat with caramel, caramelize (candied apple)

colorer to varnish, dye, color

éclabousser (de) to splash (with), spatter (with paint), dash (with liquid)

émailler to enamel, coat with enamel

enduire to smear, coat (with paint, glue, grease), plaster (wall)

être tapissé de to be covered with (wallpaper), be lined with, be carpeted with

farder to paint (makeup), varnish, gloss over

farter to wax (skis)

flanquer* to slap a coat on* (paint)

gainer to cover, sheathe (sword), place a protective cover or sheath on (biopsy probe)

gloser to gloss (a text, i.e., to furnish critique), gloss over (remarks)

goudronner to tar, cover with tar (road), apply tar to (roof)

graisser to grease, oil, lubricate

se grimer to put on makeup (theatre)

huiler to oil, lubricate (machine parts)

imperméabiliser to weatherproof (raincoat, fabric)

incruster to superimpose, overlay (TV captions or headings)

laminer to laminate, cover with (wood, sheet metal)

laquer to lacquer, paint with lacquer coat, apply lacquer

lubrifier to lubricate, grease (engine)

lustrer to gloss, glaze, give luster to, make lustrous

se maquiller to make up or paint oneself, put on makeup

mettre à la va-vite* to apply, slap on* (paint)

meurtrir to make black and blue, bruise (flesh, fruit)

noircir to smudge, blacken (smoke), dirty (ink, coal)

patiner to give a patina or sheen to (wood, metal)

peindre to paint (portrait, house), apply paint, color

peinturer to paint (Canadian French), daub, apply hastily (paint), slap on (paint)

plaquer to plate (jewelry in gold), veneer (wood)

plastifier to coat with plastic (sofa cushion, driver's license)

provigner to layer (vines)

recrépir to apply a fresh coat of plaster, repaint

refaire surface to resurface (road)

repaver to repave (road)

retoucher to touch up (paint, photo)

revêtir to cover, put on (coating, top coat of paint), endow with

satiner to glaze, put a glossy coat on, give a satin finish to (wood, hair)

savonner to lather, soap, soap up

tacher to stain, spot, taint, blur

teindre to dye, stain, color (fabric)

vernir to varnish (wood, pottery, leather), glaze, apply varnish to, apply nail polish

vitrer to glaze, make shiny, furnish with glass window

zébrer to stripe, streak with lines, paint/draw stripes on

Mince alors! Le mécanicien a les mains toutes °barbouillées de graisse.
My word! The mechanic's hands are all covered with grease.

Les Indiens utilisent le venin paralysant du serpent dont ils °enduisent leurs flèches et leurs lances. The Indians use poisonous snake venom which they smear on their arrows and spears.

Nous °appliquerons la loi "tolérance zéro" face à la gravité des violences. We will apply the full force of the "zero tolerance" law considering the severity of the violence.

Le phare jetait un grand flot de lumière sur les vagues qui °éclaboussaient les rochers. The lighthouse cast a wide flood of light on the waves that splashed against the rocks.

démonter to take apart, disassemble, dismantle

MEMORY AID

"**De-**" means *undoing*, *reversal*, or *removal*, and **monter** can mean *to assemble, erect, raise*, or *fix up*, as in putting up a tower, building, or apparatus. Thus, "**de-monter**" refers to the *undoing or removal of that which has already been assembled or erected*. Picture a giant construction worker disassembling or dismantling piece-by-piece an edifice that has already been erected, such as the Eiffel Tower, or a child taking apart a house of blocks. See also **emplafonner** (to smash into), page 110, and **terrasser** (to bring down, strike down), page 132.

Other verbs in this family include: to collapse, cave in, fall, crumble, break up, dismember, ruin, scuttle, sabotage, destabilize, take to pieces, tumble, damage, demolish, destroy, shatter, wreck, etc.

abaisser to let fall down, push down, pull down (price), bring down (tax rate)

s'abaisser to fall down, tumble, drop (price, tax), lower oneself

abattre to fell (tree), cut down, pull down, demolish (building)

s'abattre (sur) to tumble down, crash, beat down (rain), swoop down (bird, enemy)

abîmer to wreck, ruin (book), damage (building)

s'affaisser to cave in (floor, road), collapse (building, person), subside

anéantir to annihilate, utterly destroy (building, civilization), crush (bad news)

bousiller* to break, damage, wreck, ruin, bungle,* botch*

briser en pièces to shatter, crash, break into pieces (glass, windowpane, vase)

causer des ravages to damage, wreak havoc, ravage (village), desolate (land)

causer la ruine de to ruin, cause the collapse of (business, civilization)

chuter to plummet (s.o., price), fall, fail, slump (economy), tumble, drop (value)

claquer* to conk out,* break down (car), tucker out* (baby, old person)

crouler to collapse (under weight of), fall in, give way (wall), crumble (dam)

débâtir to take down basting/tacking (i.e., holding stitches used in sewing)

dédramatiser to play down importance of (situation), make less alarming

défoncer to smash, plow down, batter down (wall, door), demolish, knock down

dégonfler to cause to collapse, deflate (raft, tire), reduce (swelling, staff, numbers)

se dégonfler* to cave in, chicken out,* go down (local swelling)

dégringoler to tumble down, tear down, crash, topple over, collapse (currency, wall)

se délabrer to fall into decay, go to ruin, fall to pieces, collapse, tumble, fall (s.o.)

démanteler to dismantle, break up, demolish, break into pieces

démantibuler* to break up, break (into pieces), dislocate (joint)

démembrer to dismember (limbs), break up (business), carve up (empire)

démolir to demolish, wreck, pull down (house, neighborhood)

désagréger to break up, crumble (rock), disintegrate, split (partnership)

désamianter to remove asbestos (from pipe, ceiling, old ship) (*lit.* **amiante (m)**: asbestos)

descendre en roulant to tumble, fall down, collapse

déstabiliser to destabilize (currency, economy), unhinge, perturb, trouble

diminuer to fall, abate (interest, activity), decrease (value, staffing), run low (gas)

s'ébouler to collapse, fall in, cave in (coal mine, wall)

échouer to run aground (boat, beached whale), miscarry, fail (plot)

s'écrouler to collapse (building), cave in (ceiling), be overcome (with emotion)

s'effondrer to collapse (in tears), break down, collapse (dreams)

effriter to crumble, cause to crumble, weather (rock cliff), erode (beach)

émietter to crumble (bread, cheese), break up (empire), eat away at (strength)

faire des dégâts to ruin, damage, harm, cause harm to (storm, flood, fire)

faire tomber to knock down (building), wreck (wall), bring down (government)

faner to wither away, droop, debilitate, wilt (person, flower)

flétrir to wither away, fade, shrivel up, parch (skin, earth)

foirer* to fall through (plans), flunk,* screw up,* botch*

fracasser to shatter, break in pieces (object, jaw, limb), smash down (door)

péricliter to be in a state of collapse (business)

plastiquer to blow up (with **plastique** explosives)

raser to raze, demolish (to the ground), level (city with bomb)

recaler to fail (exam), stall again (engine)

réduire en morceaux to smash to pieces, smash to bits

ruiner to wreck (building), ruin (relationship), damage, bankrupt, destroy, undo

saborder to scuttle (ship), ruin one's chances

saboter to sabotage, botch,* ruin, bungle,* bumble*

saper to undermine (efforts, support beam), sap (energy)

tomber to fall (wall, speed record), fall down (tower), droop, sink, topple

tomber en désuétude to fall into disuse, fall into disrepair (factory, appliance)

tomber en panne to break down (car engine)

tomber en poussière to crumble into dust (statue, civilization)

tomber en ruine to fall in ruins (building, temple, society)

tomber évanoui to faint, fall unconscious, lose consciousness, pass out

tomber par terre to fall down, collapse, fall to the ground, fall to earth, fall over

tomber raide to drop to the ground, fall straight down, fall precipitously

Lors d'un nettoyage de son fusil, l'armurier a °démonté le mécanisme de déclenchement qui était coincé. While cleaning his shotgun, the gunsmith dismantled the trigger mechanism which was jammed.
Ouah!* Un grand éclair a °fracassé la verrière au-dessus. Wow!* A big lightning bolt shattered the glass roof overhead.

Dû à une voiture piégée le grand mur °s'est effondré. A car bomb caused the collapse of the big wall.

À la suite du grand incendie le plafond de l'usine °s'est écroulé. As a result of the large fire the factory ceiling caved in.

écouler   to leak out, flow out, pass

abreuver   to water (animals, ground), give water to

affluer   to flow into, flow (blood, fluid), flood in (light, water), pour

arroser   to sprinkle, water (lawn), wet, irrigate, soak, hose (lawn)

arroser à la lance   to hose down (burning house: fireman)

arroser au jet   to hose or water (garden)

asperger d'eau   to sprinkle with water, spray with water

assécher   to drain (pond), dry out (laundry)

avoir une voie d'eau   to have a leak (boat)

bouillonner   to bubble, foam (sea), boil, roil

brouillasser   to drizzle (rain)

bruiner   to drizzle, splatter (liquid), rain lightly

circuler   to circulate (traffic, air current), flow (blood, traffic)

clapoter   to splash (waves), swash, undulate (waves)

couler   to flow (stream), trickle, leak (blood, paint)

déborder   to overflow (river), spill over (dam), boil over (soup)

découler   to trickle, flow, spring, follow (derived idea)

dégazer   to empty tanks, decarbonate (water), bleed (pipes), clear out (fuel tanks)

dégouliner   to trickle, drip (paint, gravy)

dégoutter   to drip, trickle, fall in drops (rain, sweat, blood, water)

dessécher   to drain, dry up, parch (tongue, earth), shrivel up (skin, leather)

déverser   to pour out liquid, tip (pitcher, vase), profuse, decant

distiller   to trickle, distill, drop, exude (sweat, sadness)

drainer   to drain (liquid, farmland, swamp, bank account)

éclabousser   to splash, splatter, dash (liquid)

épancher   to pour out (love, sentiment), discharge, extravasate (blood [medical])

s'évaporer   to evaporate

s'éventer   to leak out (freshness), lose aroma (perfume), go flat (champagne)

faire eau   to spring a leak (boat)

faire la vidange   to change the oil, drain the oil (car)

faire pleuvoir   to rain down (blows, criticism, projectiles), shower down (praise)

filtrer   to seep through, filter through

fluidifier le sang   to thin the blood, dissolve blood clots

fuser   to spurt, burst forth, liquefy, erupt (lava)

gicler   to squirt, spout, spurt, whoosh*

goutter   to drip (faucet, blood, raindrops), dribble

humecter   to moisten (washcloth), dampen (eyes, grass)

s'infiltrer   to seep in, filter through, soak

insinuer   to seep into (odor, liquid), invade (cancer)

irriguer   to irrigate (farm), water (lawn)

jaillir   to gush, spring (fountain)

jeter   to discharge, flow (river), empty, dispose of

liquéfier   to liquefy, make liquid (chemical), to melt

mouiller   to moisten, wet (towel, s.o. by accident), baste (roast), water down (wine)

noyer   to drench, soak, drown (sorrows in a glass of wine)

passer   to go by, pass (comet), pass by (stream), percolate (coffee), run (brook)

patauger   to splash (in puddle)

pleurer   to drip (faucet), weep tears, run (eyes)

pleuvoir   to rain, rain down, pour

pleuvoir des hallebardes*   to rain cats and dogs* (*lit.* to rain halberds: medieval weapon with an ax-like blade and steel spike on a long pole)

pleuvoter   to drizzle

prendre de l'eau   to leak, take on water (boat)

projeter   to spurt, send out (sparks), cast (reflection)

purger   to drain (radiator), bleed (brake fluid), purge (political party)

réhydrater   to moisturize (skin), rehydrate, remoisten (chapped lips)

rejaillir   to gush, spring, splash, spurt, cascade

rendre humide   to dampen, moisten

répandre   to spill (liquid, oil), pour out, slosh

reverser   to pour out some more, pour again (wine)

saillir   to gush, spurt (liquid, blood)

sécréter   to secrete (bodily fluid, venom, bile)

seringuer   to squirt, inject (with a syringe)

sortir en bouillonnant   to gush out

sourdre   to spring, gush (well), well up

suinter   to ooze, sweat, weep, leak, run out, seep

tomber goutte à goutte   to drip (faucet, blood)

transvaser   to decant (wine), pour off liquid (leaving sediment behind)

tremper   to soak, wet, drench, steep, dunk (doughnut in coffee)

vaporiser   to vaporize, mist, spray (cologne)

verser   to pour, discharge, empty, spill (liquid, grain, blood), shed (tears)

vidanger   to drain (cesspool, reservoir, swimming pool), empty

vider   to empty (container, room), drain (tank, pool)

Bien des années s'étaient °écoulées. La veuve avait pris le deuil et s'était retirée dans un couvent. Many years had passed. The widow had gone into mourning and had joined a convent.

Notre pays est sacré! Beaucoup de sang a été °versé sur cette terre sainte. Our country is sacred! Much blood has been shed over this holy land.

À la suite d'une alerte rouge la salle de conférence a été entièrement °vidée sans incident. Following a red alert the lecture hall was completely emptied without incident.

Dès l'origine, des informations contradictoires ont °circulé sur l'état de la santé du roi. From the outset, contradictory information has circulated regarding the state of the king's health.

engourdir to numb, deaden, dull

MEMORY AID

"**En-**" can mean *put into* or *go into*. Contained within **engourdir** is the word *gourd*, which in English refers to *the fruit of several varieties of vines having bulbous-shaped, hard rinds*. Thus, "**en-gourd**" can mean to put something *into a gourd*. Picture a patient in an operating suite with a large gourd-shaped belly undergoing anesthesia in preparation for surgery. An anesthetic needle will be put into his gourd-like abdomen to numb it so as to deaden or dull any sensation.

Other verbs in this family include: to soothe, calm, anesthetize, ease, curb, cushion, paralyze, kill the nerve, etherize, hypnotize, allay, mitigate, alleviate, assuage, moderate, comfort, etc.

adoucir   to allay, mitigate, soften (skin), mellow (s.o.), ease (pain, suffering)

affaiblir   to lessen, weaken (sound, strength), dim (light), impair, drag down

alléger   to alleviate (pain, suffering), assuage, ease (tension)

amortir   to deaden, allay, moderate, weaken, soften (blow), cushion (impact)

anesthésier   to anesthetize, block (pain impulse), do a nerve block

apaiser   to allay, pacify, mitigate, calm, soothe (pain, suffering, spirits)

s'apaiser   to abate, subside (uproar, fuss, hunger, thirst, passion, fever)

assourdir   to deaden, muffle (sound), stun

atténuer   to take the sting out of (remark, criticism), dull (sensation)

calmer   to calm (nerves), soothe, quiet (fear), ease (pain), salve, relieve (pain)

dévitaliser   to kill the nerve (tooth), do a root canal (procedure)

diminuer   to abate, diminish, lessen (pain, sensation), decline (activity), fade (light)

émousser   to dull (sensation, intellect), deaden, take the edge off (pain), blunt (edge)

endormir   to put to sleep, allay (worry), deaden (pain)

éthériser   to etherize, administer ether (anesthesiologist)

être anesthésié   to be anesthetized, undergo anesthesia

faire une piqûre de novocaïne   to give a shot of novocaine

glacer   to paralyze (with fear), chill (one's blood), send a chill (up one's spine)

hébéter   to dull, besot, make stupid, daze, induce a stupor

hypnotiser   to hypnotize, mesmerize

insensibiliser   to anesthetize, render insensitive, desensitize (nerve, skin)

mater   to deaden, make flat or dull (gloss finish, sound, pain)

mitiger   to mitigate, alleviate, make milder, moderate (quality, condition)

modérer   to moderate (pain), mitigate, tone down (mood), calm down

pacifier   to pacify, calm, bring peace to (relationship, country)

paralyser   to paralyze (muscle, limb), render immobile, disable (motor, economy)

rabattre   to smooth down, abate (ambition, pretensions), lose (one's illusions of)

réconforter to comfort, relieve (suffering, pain, distress)

rendormir to put back to sleep, put to sleep again (baby)

rendre moins aigu to make less sharp (knife, pain), lessen intensity (pain, symptom)

soulager to alleviate, allay (pain), soothe, comfort, quell (thirst), relieve

ternir to dull (shiny finish), deaden, tarnish, lose shine

tétaniser to paralyze (toxin, fear) (*lit.* **tétanos** *(m)*: lockjaw from tetanus toxin)

tranquilliser to tranquilize (surgery patient, animal), calm (nerves)

transir to benumb, paralyze (with fear), numb senses, stun

Le froid °engourdit la peau; une piqûre l'anesthésie. Cold will numb the skin; a shot will anesthetize it.

Une torsion de cheville? Vous °calmerez la douleur avec une vessie remplie de glaçons. An ankle sprain? You'll ease the pain with an ice bag filled with ice cubes.

La décision prise devrait contribuer à °alléger le doute et l'incertitude. The decision that was made should help to alleviate the doubt and uncertainty.

Ce rabais devrait °amortir la facture énergétique pour tous les foyers. This discount should soften the impact of the energy bill for all the households.

entamer   to cut into, wear down, make an incision

MEMORY AID

"**En-**" can mean *into*, *put into*, *within*, and the "*~tame~*" fragment is derived from the Greek root word *temnein—to cut* or *slice*. As a prefix or suffix it appears as *temno* or *tomo*; English words using this root include *tome* (one book *cut* from a work of several volumes) and *tomography* (a fancy X-ray machine that takes parallel image "*slices*" through the body). Thus, "**en-tame**" can mean *to cut into* or *put slices into* something. Picture the unfortunate victims of the French Revolution, paraded up to the guillotine to await the heavy cold blade that will cut or slice into their necks. See also **transpercer** (to pierce through, run through), page 134, and **fourrer** (to stick, shove), page 168.

Other verbs in this family include: to incise, cleave, split, cut open, notch, gouge, sever, slash, amputate, carve, disjoin, disunite, cut back, scalp, circumcise, butcher, dissect, slice, trim, etc.

---

affaiblir   to weaken (economy, authority, person)

amaigrir   to make thinner, thin (waistline, hair)

amincir   to slim down, thin down, beat out (gold: hammer), make thinner

amputer   to amputate (limb, word)

atténuer   to weaken, attenuate, diminish, decrease (effect)

balafrer   to gash, slash, scar

battre en brèche   to breach (enemy lines), make a gap/hole in (castle wall)

bissecter   to bisect, cut in half (angle, tissue sample)

briser en éclats   to splinter, break into pieces

chaponner   to caponize, castrate/neuter a rooster or fowl

charcuter*   to butcher, hack,* mangle, carve up (roast, text)

châtrer   to neuter, castrate (bull), geld (horse, pig), cut back (shrub), fix (dog)

circoncire   to circumcise

cisailler   to pare, clip, cut, shear (sheet metal, scalp), prune (branch), hack

cliver   to split (group, into parts), crack, cleave

couper   to cut, clip, pare, make an incision, behead, slit (throat), shave, incise, hack

couper en rondelles   to slice, slice up (sausage, lemon)

crevasser   to split, crack (wall, soil, rock, glacier), chap (lips, skin)

débiter   to cut up (wood), chop, distribute

déboiser   to clear of trees (terrain)

déchiqueter   to shred, tear to pieces, tear to shreds (paper), pull to pieces (meat, s.o.)

déchirer   to tear, rip, split asunder, split apart, tear up, rend (silence, fabric)

décortiquer   to dissect (tumor, word), husk (rice), peel (shrimp), decorticate (tree)

découper   to cut out, cut, carve (meat, fowl), cut up (fabric), cut to shape (wood)

défricher   to clear or cut away (forest)

déliter   to cleave (rock, i.e., planes between rock/mineral strata)

démailler   to get a run in (nylon stocking)

dépecer   to cut up, tear limb from limb, carve

déplomber   to hack into* (computer)

dépouiller   to strip, divest, denude, skin (animal)

désosser   to bone, debone (meat)

détruire   to undermine (support, s.o.'s efforts)

disjoindre   to disjoin, disunite, disconnect (hoses), take apart, break apart (rock)

disséquer   to dissect (frog, surgical tissue), cut apart (organ, problem)

dissoudre   to break up, dissolve (sugar, solute, worries), disband, break up (marriage)

ébouter   to cut the end off of (pole, branch)

ébrécher   to hack, chip (tooth, plate), nick, notch, indent

échancrer   to make a crescent-shaped cut, cut low (dress neckline)

écharper   to slash (limb, s.o.), cut, hack up, cut to pieces (troops, meat)

échopper   to gouge (wood with tool), gouge out (eyes)

éclater en   to break into (tears, sobs, pieces)

éculer   to wear thin (heel, story), be hackneyed (expression), be well worn (joke)

émincer   to slice thinly, chop (meat, vegetables)

entailler   to cut, notch, gash, nick

épiler   to pluck (eyebrows), epilate (i.e., to remove hair from)

éplucher   to pick, peel, clean (shrimp, fruit, vegetables)

épointer   to break the point off of (spear, pencil)

équarrir   to cut up (carcass), square off (corners of stone, brick or wood)

érafler   to scratch, make a scratch (skin), key (i.e., to vandalize car paint)

être amputé de moitié   to be cut in half

étriper   to cut open, gut, disembowel

éventrer   to disembowel, gore, tear open, rip open

évider   to gouge, gouge out (eyes), hollow out (log), core (apple), scoop out

éviscérer   to eviscerate, cut out the internal organs, gut

exciser   to excise, remove by cutting, remove surgically (wart, cancer, mole)

faire des coupes dans   to make cuts in, cut into

faire scission   to split away, split off (molecules)

fendre   to cleave, split, cut open, crack, ax, chop down, splinter (wood), cleave

filer   to get a run in (nylons, pantyhose)

graver   to cut, engrave, etch (glass, metal), carve, cut (music record)

hacher   to chop, mince, hack, chop up (meat)

inciser   to incise (wound), cut into, lance (boil/pustule)

macérer   to macerate (i.e., to separate solid into parts by soaking in water)

manucurer   to manicure (nails, lawn)

mettre en charpie*   to pull to bits (lit. charpie (f): lint)

opérer   to operate (surgery), operate on, perform surgery

peler   to peel (sunburned skin, fruit), peel away (layers, old paint)

picorer   to peck at, peck about (bird, picky eater)

plumer   to pluck (fowl), fleece (sheep)

pourfendre   to cleave asunder

rabattre   to cut back (trees)

raser   to shave off (beard), scrape (car on curb)

se raser   to shave oneself, shave, shave off

recadrer   to crop (photo), reframe (picture, question)

recéper   to cut back, clear (woods)

recouper   to cut again, cut some more (bread, sausage)

refendre   to quarter (timber), cleave, split

retrancher   to cut off from (fellowship, membership)

rogner   to cut (corners, meat), crop, pare, clip (wing, hedge), prune, trim (nails)

saboter   to sabotage, damage willfully (lit. sabot (m): wooden shoe used to jam machines by saboteur)

sabrer   to cut to pieces, tear to pieces, cut with a saber

saper   to undermine, chip away at (morale, resistance)

scalper   to scalp, remove s.o.'s scalp

scier   to saw, cut with a saw, saw off, hew (timber)

sculpter   to carve, sculpt, sculpture

sectionner   to sever (artery, nerve), section (pathology specimen), cut (cable)

séparer   to sever, cleave, divide, split (into parts), disjoin

sillonner   to furrow, grove, plough (field)

subir une opération chirurgicale   to undergo surgery, have an operation

taillader   to slash, gash

tailler   to cut, cut up, carve (wood), hew, prune, trim, engrave, sharpen (pencil)

tailler sur mesure   to tailor (suit, dress)

tondre qn*   to cut s.o.'s hair, give s.o. a haircut

trancher   to slice, cut, cut off (limb, tree branch, fish head)

tronçonner   to saw, saw up (lumber, tree)

La critique interminable du patron °entamait le moral de ses employés.
The boss's incessant criticism undermined his employees' morale.
Vite! Emmenez-moi chez le dentiste. J'ai °ébréché l'émail de mon incisive.
Quick! Take me to the dentist. I chipped the enamel off my incisor.
Si vous perdiez votre témoignage vous seriez °retranché de l'église. If you
were to lose your testimony you would be cut off from church fellowship.
Le bûcheron °tronçonne des bûches avec une tronçonneuse à gaz. The woodcutter
saws the logs with a gas-powered chainsaw.

MEMORY AID

"**É**" or "*ex*" in English means *out of* or *without*, and the "*~***puis***~*" fragment is derived from the French noun **puissance**, meaning *power* or *force*. So, "**ex-puis**-er" can mean *without force* or *out of power*. Picture an exhausted, battered boxer slumping in his corner, completely out of energy. He does not have the strength to continue the fight. See also **traîner** (to drag, lag behind, trail, droop), page 45.

Other verbs in this family include: to tire, subside, fail, wither, wilt, weaken, deteriorate, pass out, worsen, enfeeble, wear away, use up, exhaust, expire, diminish, waste away, faint, etc.

affaiblir   to weaken, enfeeble, fade (sound), dim (light), deteriorate (condition)

s'aggraver   to worsen, get worse, aggravate (situation, health, economy)

alanguir   to enfeeble, make weak, make languid

s'aliter   to confine to bed, take to one's bed, be bedridden (ill)

aller en eau de boudin*   to fizzle out* (*lit.* to go into the water of blood sausages)

amincir   to make thinner, thin down (soup), beat thinner (gold leaf)

amoindrir   to lessen, decrease, diminish, make weaker, weaken (authority)

arriver à terme   to come to an end, expire (contract), come to term (loan)

atténuer   to weaken, attenuate, make thinner/feeble, decrease (effort)

attraper la turista*   to get diarrhea, get the "runs"*

avoir le coup de pompe*   to feel tired, feel drained (*lit.* to have a knocked-out pump)

avoir une syncope   to pass out, black out, have a syncopal episode

claquer*   to tire out, wear out, conk out* (engine), fatigue

se consumer   to waste away (with illness, e.g., tuberculosis), wear out

crever*   to be exhausted, be worn out, puncture, die

débander   to lose one's erection, relax (archery bow), slacken (spring)

décharger   to empty (gun), unload (gun), discharge (gun, battery)

décroître   to decline (interest), dim (light), fade (memory, color), slacken (effort)

défaillir   to weaken (strength, energy), faint

(se) dégarnir   to grow thin, thin out, lose leaves (tree), go bald

délayer   to thin out (paint, color), drag out (speech), add water to (powder)

se démoder   to go out of style (clothes), be out of fashion, be outdated/outmoded

dépenser   to use up (energy, resources), consume (gas), spend (money), burn (money)

dépérir   to wither away (ill), waste away, decline (health), wilt (plant), sicken

se désempeser   to become limp (flag, plant, penis)

se dessécher   to wither (plant, leaf), waste away, parch (soil), dry up (skin)

diluer   to weaken (power), dilute (wine, monetary assets), thin out (paint)

dissiper   to dissipate (energy, effort), waste away, disappear

drainer   to drain (liquid, swampland)

édulcorer   to water down (text), tone down (harsh rhetoric)

s'égrener   to drop one by one, fall from the stalk (seed), be strung out (parade)

élimer to wear out, become worn down, become threadbare (fabric)

émietter to erode (power, authority), waste away, dissipate (energy)

empirer to worsen, deteriorate (condition, health), get worse, decline (economy)

énerver to debilitate, weaken, unnerve

époumoner to exhaust, make winded (exercise, hike) (*lit.* poumon *(m)*: lung)

éreinter to exhaust, tire out, do in, wash out (energy), wipe out

s'éteindre to be exhausted, die out, be extinguished (flame, hope, light), peter out

s'étioler to waste away, wilt (plant, s.o.), decline (memory), grow sickly, weaken

être à l'article de la mort* to be at death's door,* have one foot in the grave*

être à plat* to be run down, be tired, be beat,* be exhausted

être alité (par) to be laid low (by) (illness, injury)

être cuit* to be done for,* be done in,* be exhausted

être exténué to be worn out, be enfeebled, be drained, be wasted

être flagada* to be washed out,* be beat,* be exhausted, be dead beat*

être groggy* to be washed out,* be fatigued, be drunk

être las to be tired, be weary, be exhausted, be jaded

être lessivé* to be all washed up,* be done in,* be tired out

être patraque* to be peaked,* out of sorts, be sickly, be pale

être recru to be fatigued, be tired, be worn out

être vétuste to be worn out, dilapidated, be antiquated, be out of date (style, clothes)

s'évanouir to faint, vanish, black out, lose consciousness, die out (sound), pass out

s'éventer to go flat (soda), go stale (perfume, wine)

expirer to expire, die, come to an end, die away, go out (fire), die out (sound)

faiblir to get weaker, grow fainter (daylight), dim, weaken (voice, muscle)

faillir à to fail in, fail to do, fail at, miscarry, waver, falter

faner to wilt (flower, s.o.), wither, languish, debilitate (illness)

fatiguer to fatigue, tire, wear out, wear down, make weary

finir to use up, finish, end, conclude, finish off (opponent), polish off (plate)

se flétrir to wither, wilt (flower), fade (beauty), shrivel up (face, skin)

fondre* to slim down, lose weight, diet, lose pounds

fragiliser to weaken, undermine, make fragile

handicaper to handicap, hinder, impede

languir to languish, sag, flag (sales, stock prices, enthusiasm)

lasser to tire, weary, fatigue, wear out

lessiver* to wash out* (energy), tire out

limer to file down (wood, metal), smooth down (rough edge), file (fingernails)

macérer to cause to become lean (starvation), emaciate, macerate

maigrir to reduce, grow thin, grow skinny, lose weight, make look thin (photo)

se maigrir to lose weight, grow skinny, slim down

manquer de punch* to lack dynamism, lack energy

mincir to grow thinner/slimmer, attenuate, slim down (figure)

miner to wear away, sap (energy), waste away (s.o.), erode (foundation)

minorer (de) to reduce (by) (amount or percent, i.e., taxes, rates)

monter en graine to go to seed (garden, cornfield), weaken

pâlir to grow pale, grow dim, turn pale (face, light, moon)

se pâmer to swoon, faint, be overcome (with emotion/laughter)

pendre mollement to flag, slacken, decline in vigor (*lit.* to hang feebly)

perdre du poids   to lose weight
pomper*   to tire out, exhaust
ne pas pouvoir tenir le coup*   to lack stamina, lack energy
prendre du bouchon*   to grow old
prendre la bouteille*   to grow old
se ramollir   to enervate, go soft (butter, clay), go to seed (s.o.), weaken
raréfier   to make thin (ozone layer), make less dense (gas), make scarce (product)
se rendre   to be worn out, give up, surrender, give in
se rétrécir   to grow narrower (road, valley), shrink (wool), grow smaller (group)
stagner   to stagnate (pond, relationship)
tarir   to dry up (source, lake)

se tasser   to subside, shrink, slow down (mental process, agility)
tempérer   to ease (pain), temper (harsh climate, cold weather)
terminer   to finish, end, terminate, conclude, bring to an end, complete, sign off, ace
tomber dans les pommes*   to pass out, faint, lose consciousness
tomber dans les vapes*   to pass out, lose consciousness, faint
s'user   to wear oneself out, tire oneself out
utiliser tout   to use up (resources, all of shampoo)
vanner*   to tire out, poop out
vieillir   to age, grow old, become obsolete

Le mari °s'épuisait à expliquer à sa femme toutes ses disparitions nocturnes. The husband grew tired of having to explain all his night-time disappearances to his wife.

Ses paroles rassurantes °dissipèrent toute crainte. Her reassuring words made all fear disappear.

Les dirigeants se sont pliés à une inspection de la fabrique afin de °dissiper les soupçons qu'ils mènent un entrepôt pour des armes nucléaires. The directors consented to an inspection of the factory in order to lay to rest the suspicions that they are running a storage facility for nuclear weapons.

Des variations de température ont °fragilisé les poutres du bâtiment et sont indubitablement à l'origine de son effondrement. Variations in temperature weakened the building's girders and undoubtedly caused its collapse.

gaspiller to waste, squander

MEMORY AID

Gaspiller looks very much like *gas-spiller* in English. Picture a service-station attendant who becomes distracted while pumping gasoline. He inadvertently spills the fuel all over the car and the ground. Thus, the *gas-spiller* wastes and squanders precious fuel.

Other verbs in this family include: to misuse, lay waste, abuse, go to waste, ruin, be neglected, rot, get moldy, spoil, mar, go stale, be useless, go rotten, dissipate, misallocate, misplace, etc.

abuser de to abuse, misuse, exploit (natural resources), overuse

bâcler* to botch,* mess up,* screw up* (at work, project)

claquer* to blow,* waste (money), spend (money)

dépenser sans compter to spend extravagantly/lavishly, spend freely, overspend

dépenser sottement to spend (money) foolishly, blow hard-earned cash, burn (money)

dévaster to devastate, lay waste, ruin (culture, crops)

devoir de l'argent à qn to be in debt, be indebted to s.o., owe s.o. money

dévorer to squander, destroy, waste (time, resources)

dilapider to squander (one's inheritance), dissipate (energy), waste (money)

dissiper to squander, dissipate, waste (energy, time, money)

échouer to fail, miscarry (exam, attempt, plans)

égarer to mislay, misplace (keys, object)

émietter to squander (fortune), fritter away* (time, money)

s'endetter to get into debt, run into debt

être dans le rouge* to be in the red,* be in debt

être dépensier to be a spendthrift, be one who squanders money, be prodigal

être en friche* to go to waste (talent), be neglected (country), lie fallow (farmland)

être endetté to be in debt, be indebted (to)

être nul* to be useless, be worthless (in math), be of no use

être prodigue to be extravagant, be spendthrift, be wasteful

être redevable à qn to be in s.o.'s debt, owe s.o. (money, favor)

faire faillite to go bankrupt, become insolvent, declare bankruptcy

faire le rabat-joie* to spoil the fun, be a killjoy,* be a spoilsport*

flamber* to gamble/wager large sums of money

gâcher to waste (money, youth, opportunity), ruin (one's life, chances)

gâter to waste, spoil (child), mar, ruin (view, fun), harm (mind, judgment)

laisser passer to waste (chance), let go by (opportunity), lose the chance

mal affecter to misappropriate (funds), embezzle

mal analyser to misdiagnose (medical condition)

mal attribuer to misallocate (funds)

mal calculer to miscalculate

mal compter to miscount, make an addition error

mal employer to misuse (time, energy, resources)

mal répartir to misapportion (shares, votes)

manger* to squander, run through (money, resources)

manger de l'argent* to spend money foolishly, squander money

manquer to spoil, miss, miscarry (plot), be shy of (goal), lose (contact), neglect

mésuser to misuse, abuse

moisir to go moldy, rot (in prison, apple)

perdre du temps à faire qch to waste time doing s.t.

perdre son argent to waste one's money

pourrir to spoil, rot, go bad, go rotten, decay, molder, decompose

se priver to go without, do without (food, water), deny oneself (medical attention)

prodiguer to waste, squander, lavish (money), be a spendthrift

se putréfier to go rotten, spoil, become putrid, decay

rancir to go rancid, go stale, spoil (milk)

se rassir to go stale, spoil (food)

rater to miss (opportunity), fail (exam, train), spoil, mess up,* backfire,* go wrong

rétamer* to fail (exam), be fatigued

se saigner* to drain one's purse or wallet (of cash)

Être fainéant; quelle perte de temps et quel °gaspillage de talent! To be an idler; what a waste of time and talent!

Alors que j'essayais d'escalader le mur mes jambes me °manquèrent tout à fait. While I was trying to climb the wall my legs completely failed me.

Qu'il °pourrisse au bagne pour ses crimes commis contre l'humanité! May he rot in jail for the crimes he's committed against humanity!

Le patronat de cette entreprise a mal géré la crise financière, donc il a °fait faillite. This firm's management handled the financial crisis badly, so it went bankrupt.

souiller to soil, dirty, muddy, sully

MEMORY AID

Taking the **"souil~"** fragment and removing the **"u"** leaves *soil*, which as a verb means *to make dirty*, *begrime*, or *smudge*. **Souiller** is also spelled similarly to **soulier**, meaning *shoe*. So the verb brings to mind both *soil* and *shoe*, hence a *soiled shoe*. Picture a soccer game played in a downpour, turning the field into a quagmire of mud. The players' shoes are all muddied, soiled, and dirtied.

Other verbs in this family include: to tarnish, stink, splash, bespatter, stain, taint, make greasy, smudge, make a mess of, spoil, spray, corrupt, pervert, contaminate, get soaked, pollute, etc.

adultérer to adulterate (wine, medicine), corrupt (morals)

asperger to splash, spray, spray with (water, perfume)

assombrir to darken, cloud, throw a gloom over (sky, mood, party)

avancer en pataugeant dans la boue to slosh through the mud

barboter to dawdle about in the mud or water

barbouiller to soil, dirty, smear

cendrer to cover with ashes, smear on ashes

cochonner* to mess up* (clothes, page) (*lit.* **cochon** *(m)*: pig, hog)

colorer to stain, color, dye

contaminer to contaminate, soil, infect, transmit (infection, disease)

corrompre to corrupt, infect, taint, spoil (meat)

crotter* to dirty, bespatter, soil (*lit.* **crotte** *(f)*: mud, rubbish, booger)

déparer to spoil (nature), detract from (beauty, quality)

détremper to soak, waterlog

dévergonder to debauch, corrupt (morals, innocence)

écheveler to dishevel, disarrange (hair, clothing)

éclabousser to splash with liquid or mud, soil, stain

s'embourber to get stuck in the mud/mire, get bogged down

empourprer to color purple or red (with paint or stain)

encrasser to foul (motor), make dirty, foul up, dirty, clog (machine, drain)

enduire to smear, coat with (paint, glue, grease, plaster, enamel)

enlaidir to make look ugly (person), become ugly, deface (painting)

entacher to taint, sully, mar (paint finish)

s'entartrer to be covered in scale (faucet, kettle), be covered with tartar (teeth)

enténébrer to plunge or wrap in darkness (night, fog), become gloomy

être dans la panade* to be in a real mess*

être trempé jusqu'aux os to be soaked to the bone, be drenching wet

se faire saucé* to get soaked (in rainstorm)

gâter to ruin, spoil (child, fun), damage (environment, mind)

graisser to make greasy, to grease (frying pan), lubricate (car chassis)

huiler to oil (motor), make oily, lubricate

infecter to infect, contaminate, taint, stink

mâchurer to daub, smudge, apply paint with hasty strokes

maculer de to stain with, blur, smudge, blemish (*lit.* **macula**: spot, blemish [Latin])

marqueter to spot, speckle, checker, mark with checkered pattern (fabric, tablecloth)

mettre la pagaille* to mess things up,* muddle up,* put in shambles*

moucheter to spot, speckle, stipple (i.e., to design with dots and short strokes)

mouiller to wet (by accident), moisten, soak, dampen

noircir to smudge, blacken (smoke), dirty (ink, coal), darken (sky, black dye)

patauger to splash (in puddle), flounder (in predicament)

pervertir to pervert, corrupt (morals), taint (food)

puer to stink, smell of, reek of (odor)

puer le bouc* to stink* (*lit.* to stink like a goat)

puer le fauve* to stink* (*lit.* to stink like a wild beast)

rembrunir to darken (tan, skin), grow darker (sky)

rendre défraîchi to make shop-soiled, make faded, tarnish

rendre terne to make dingy (room), make dirty (color), make drab/dowdy

rougir to redden, blush, color red (with paint or stain)

salir to soil, dirty, taint, sully, besmirch, grime, blot, foul, mess*

saloper* to make a mess of,* botch,* mess up,* muck up,* bungle*

se tacher to stain one's clothes, become stained (napkin, shirt)

tacheter to stipple, dapple (with splotches of color/paint)

teinter to stain, tint, tinge (fabric)

ternir to tarnish, sully, blemish

tomber dans le vulgaire to lapse into vulgarity, become crude/coarse/gross

se tremper to get steeped/soaked in (water, mud)

vicier to taint, pollute, contaminate, foul (water, air), corrupt

À cause de sa coquetterie au bureau et de ses robes moulantes, Marie a °souillé sa réputation. Because of her office flirtations and her tight-fitting dresses, Mary sullied her reputation.

En tant que dirigeant, ses opinions politiques étaient souvent °teintées d'idéologie gauchiste. As a leader, his political opinions were often colored by left-wing ideology.

Les gants du chercheur ont °contaminé le cobaye avec le virus de la grippe aviaire. The researcher's gloves infected the guinea pig with the avian flu virus.

La poussière du charbon °noircit le pavé du petit village. The coal dust blackened the little town's cobblestone street.

soupeser to feel the weight of, weigh in one's hand

MEMORY AID

The fragment "**sou~**" is similar to **sous** meaning *under* or *below*. **Peser** means *to weigh, to lie heavy, to be heavy*. Thus, "**sou-peser**" can mean *to be heavy* or *weigh down on something below*. Picture the god Atlas, of Greek mythology, who is condemned to bear the weight of the earth and heavens upon his shoulders. He squats under or below the earth, heavily weighed down by his tremendous burden. See also **charger** (to load, charge, burden), page 220, and **sombrer** (to sink into, sink, founder), page 43.

Other verbs in this family include: to make cumbersome, burden, encumber, crush, hamper, pressure, push down, put a strain on, squeeze, strain, overdo it, overload, bring down, etc.

---

accabler to crush, overwhelm (responsibility, heat), overburden (workload)

affaisser to weigh down, press down, cause to sink, sag, overwhelm

aller au fond to sink to the bottom

alourdir to weigh down, make cumbersome

s'alourdir to grow heavier, be more burdensome (death toll, taxes)

appesantir to weigh down, make heavier, burden, encumber

appuyer to exert pressure, burden, press on (button, gas pedal, trigger)

calculer to weigh, reckon, calculate, weigh up (chances, consequences)

se coltiner* to get stuck with* (task), lug around* (object), have to put up with

combler de to overwhelm, weigh down, fill with (dirt), burden with

couler to sink (boat, company), strain, drop (politician: polls)

crouler to give way (wall, support), collapse (under weight of, house)

crouler sous le poids de to collapse under the pressure of

déclasser to downgrade, lower s.o. in status, reduce in rank/standing

écraser to crush, overwhelm, run over (car), mash (potato), flatten (egg carton)

embarrasser to hinder, hamper, obstruct, clutter up

s'embarrasser to burden oneself (concern, work), trouble oneself (with)

empêcher to hinder (plans), prevent, oppose (progress)

empiéter to impinge, infringe, encroach (territory, neighbor's property)

encombrer to encumber (passageway, progress, with burdens), hinder

enfoncer to sink, push down (thumbtack) drive down (stake), smash down (gate)

entraver to hinder, hamper, hold up (traffic), prevent (progress), handicap, hobble

essuyer to sustain, undergo, endure (insult, failure, loss)

être abattu to sink (heart, soul), be downcast, be despondent

être sous la contrainte to be under pressure, be under constraint (deadline)

être sous pression to be under pressure, be pressured

faire baisser to push down, lower (TV volume, thermostat, prices, window shade)

faire obstacle à to hinder, stand in the way of (s.o., progress), be a stumbling block to

faire tomber au fond to sink s.t. (old ship)

se faire du mouron* to worry oneself sick,* agonize over (problem), worry over

forcer to overdo it (medicine, exercise), strain (voice, muscle)

fouler to oppress, trample down (enemy, crops), press/crush (grapes for wine)

grever to burden, encumber (with debt), put a strain on, burden with

grossir to put on weight, get heavier/larger, round out, get fatter (cattle, fruit), grow

jauger to measure, size up (opponent, competition)

mesurer to weigh up, assess, measure, size up (problem, situation)

mettre à rude épreuve to strain, put to severe test (loyalty, car engine)

mettre en balance to weigh (object, options), weigh against (odds, evidence)

mouiller l'ancre to drop anchor, make port (ship) (*lit.* to wet the anchor)

opprimer to oppress, crush (weight, emotional burden, guilt)

pâtir de to suffer because of, suffer on account of

peser to weigh, press down (burden, guilt)

peser à qn to press s.o., weigh on s.o. (guilt, burden), matter to s.o.

peser le pour et le contre to weigh the pros and the cons, consider the options

peser lourdement sur to put a strain on (financial, marital), carry weight (issue)

peser sur to lie heavy, weigh on, bear upon (guilt, burden, worry)

plafonner to reach a ceiling, put an upper limit to (job promotions, taxes)

ployer sous un poids to strain under a weight, bend under weight, yield to a burden

pousser qn to press s.o./push s.o., shove s.o., push s.o. (to achieve a goal, physically)

prendre du poids to put on weight, gain weight, get heavier, get fat

presser to press (a record), squeeze (fruit, sponge), compress, squash

pressurer to press (fruit), pressure s.o., pressurize (space suit, diving suit)

rabattre to pull down (dress, covers), slam shut (door), knock down (wind)

repasser to press, iron (clothes)

repeser to reweigh (evidence, fruit), weigh against, weigh some more

résorber to reduce (tax), bring down (deficit), resorb (hematoma), diminish (deficit)

stresser to put under pressure, stress out (person), stress (syllable)

subir des pressions to come under pressure, be pressured

surcharger to overload, weigh down, overfill (bin, tank), overburden (work)

tomber au fond to sink to the bottom

Il °soupèse toute la responsabilité qu'il porte sur ses épaules. He feels the weight of all the responsibility he carries on his shoulders.

Le tunnel était trop exigu pour le poids lourd qui était contraint d'°empiéter sur la voie opposée, forçant les autres véhicules à le contourner. The tunnel was too cramped for the semi, which had to encroach upon the oncoming lane, forcing the other vehicles to drive around it.

La hausse du prix du pétrole est à la suite de la marée noire, ce qui fait °peser un risque plus grave, selon les Verts. The rise in the price of gasoline is a result of the oil spill at sea, posing a greater risk, according to the ecologists.

Le bilan des morts et des blessés continue à °s'alourdir dans la zone sinistrée, cinq jours après le raz de marée. The toll of dead and injured continues to become heavier in the disaster zone, five days after the tidal wave.

Glossary
Conjunctions, Adverbs, Adjectives, and Compound Prepositions

French-English

à bon escient   knowingly, wittingly
à cause de   because of
à ce qu'on dit   apparently
à cet égard   in this respect
à chaque instant   constantly
à compter de   (as, reckoning) from
à condition que   provided that
à contrecœur   reluctantly
à contretemps   at the wrong time
à côté   beside(s)
à coup sûr   definitely, without a doubt, surely
à courte échéance   before long
à en juger par   judging by
à fond   thoroughly
à gogo   galore
à jamais   forever
à juste titre   rightly so
à la bonne franquette   informally, simply
à la différence   in contrast
à la fois   at the same time
à la limite   if need be
à la régulière   fair and square
à la rigueur   if necessary, in a pinch
à l'égard de   concerning
à l'encontre de   contrary to
à l'époque   of/at that time
à l'époque actuelle   nowadays
à l'exception de   except for
à l'instar de   like (in imitation of)
à l'insu de   unbeknownst, unknown to
à l'inverse   conversely
à longue échéance   in the long run
à l'origine   initially, originally
à maintes reprises   over and over again
à mesure que   as
à moins que   unless
à part   aside from, other than
à partir de   from, as from (time, date), beginning in
à partir de maintenant   from now on
à peine   scarcely, barely
à peu près   nearly, roughly, around
à plusieurs reprises   several times, repeatedly

à présent   at present
à propos   by the way
à propos de   about, in connection with, concerning
à proprement parler   literally
à qui le droit   to whom it may concern
à raison de   at the rate of
à supposer que   supposing
à tort   wrongly
à tout instant   any minute now
à tout prendre   all in all, on the whole
à tout prix   at all costs
à vrai dire   actually, to tell the truth
à vue   visually
à vue d'œil   visibly
accessoirement   in addition (to)
actuellement   currently, presently
advienne que pourra   come what may
afin de   in order to (with infinitive)
afin que   in order to (with subjunctive)
ailleurs   elsewhere
ainsi   thus
ainsi que   as well as
aléatoire   uncertain, hazardous
alentour   about, around
alors que   while, whereas
alors que même   even though
antérieurement   previously, formerly
apparemment   apparently
approfondi   thorough, in-depth
approximativement   approximately
après coup   afterwards
assez   rather
assurément   assuredly, surely, certainly
attendu que   inasmuch as
au bas mot   at least
au cas où   if need be
au contraire   on the contrary
au demeurant   after all, incidentally
au fait   by the way, incidentally
au firmament de   at the height of
au fond   basically
au hasard   at random
au moins   at least
au moyen de   by means of

au pied levé   unawares
au plus fort de   at the height of
au point nommé   at the right moment
au premier abord   at first sight
au regard de   compared to
aucunement   not at all, not in the least
auparavant   formerly
aussi   also
aussi bien   even, anyhow, in any case
aussitôt que   as soon as
autant   as many, as much
autant que je sache   as far as I know
autrement   otherwise
autrement dit   in other words
aux yeux de   according to, in the eyes of
avant tout   above all
avec équité   fairly
avec reconnaissance   thankfully
bêtement (tout ~)   simply (quite ~)
bien entendu   of course
bien évidemment   of course
bien que   although
bientôt   soon, shortly
bienveillant   kindly
brièvement   shortly, soon
çà et là   here and there
ça se peut   that may be, perhaps
carrément   really, honestly
censé   supposed, reputed
cependant   however
certainement   certainly
certes   certainly, indeed
ces derniers temps   lately
c'est selon   that depends on
comme   as, like, such as, since, because
complètement   completely, entirely,
   thoroughly
compte tenu de   considering, given
concernant   regarding, concerning
constamment   constantly
contre toute attente   contrary to all expectations
couramment   1. fluently 2. commonly
coûte que coûte   at all costs
crûment   roughly, crudely
d'ailleurs   besides
d'alors   of that time
dans la mesure où   inasmuch as, insofar as
dans le fond   basically
dans l'ensemble   on the whole
dans les (numéro)   approximately (number)
dans l'intervalle   meanwhile
d'après   according to
d'autant plus   so much the more
d'autant que   seeing that
d'autre part   on the other hand

davantage   more, anymore
de bon gré   willingly
de ce fait   for this reason
de ce pas   directly, at once
de crainte que   for fear that
de façon que   so that
de façon surprenante   surprisingly
de fait   in fact, indeed
de fortune   makeshift
de loin   by far
de même   likewise
de nouveau   again
de peur que   lest, for fear that
de plus   besides
de plus en plus   more and more
de près   nearly
de prime abord   at first glance
de rigueur   compulsory
de sorte que   so that
de surcroît   moreover
de temps en temps   from time to time
de tous les instants   constant
de tout au tout   completely
de toute façon   anyhow
de toute manière   anyhow
de vive voix   in person, personally
depuis peu   lately
depuis que   since
dernièrement   lately
des fois*   sometimes
des fois que*   just in case
dès l'origine   from the outset
dès lors   from then on
dès lorsque   as soon as
dès que   as soon as, since
désormais   henceforth
d'habitude   usually
disertement   fluently
donc   therefore
d'ordinaire   usually, ordinarily
dorénavant   from now on, henceforth
d'ores et déjà   already
du coup   as a result of
du premier coup   straight away
du reste   besides
dûment   duly
d'un instant à l'autre   any minute now
effectivement   precisely, quite right
également   likewise, also
en cas de   if need be, in case of
en ce moment   of that time
en connaissance de cause   knowingly
en dépit de   despite
en effet   as a matter of fact
en fait   as a matter of fact, in fact
en fonction de   according to

en grande partie   largely
en guise de   by way of
en outre   moreover, besides, in addition to
en particulier   in particular
en quelque sorte   in some ways
en raison de   because of
en réaction à   in response to
en regard de   1. facing 2. taking into account
en règle générale   as a general rule
en revanche   on the other hand
en soi   in itself
en sus   in addition (to)
en tant que   as
en temps voulu   in due time
en termes concis   concisely
en tous cas   in any case, whatever happens
en tout point   in every respect
en vigueur   in force
encore   still, again
entièrement   entirely, completely
entre autres   among others
entretemps   meanwhile
environ   around, about, nearly
essentiellement   essentially
et ainsi de suite   and so on
étant donné que   given that
éventuel   possible
éventuellement   possibly
évidemment   obviously
excepté   except for
exprès   on purpose, expressly
expressément   explicitly
face à   given
facultatif   optional
faute de   for lack of
forcément   necessarily, inevitably
formellement   strictly, precisely, definitely
franchement   frankly, to be honest
gérable   manageable
globalement   overall, all in all
grâce à quoi   whereby
grossièrement   roughly
guère   hardly
habituellement   usually
honnêtement   honestly
hors   except for
hors de propos   irrelevant
hors du commun   extraordinary
il y a grandes chances (que)   chances are
   (that)
immanquablement   inevitably
immédiatement   immediately
incessamment   immediately
incidemment   by the way, incidentally
indémodable   classic
inespéré   unexpected

inopiné   unexpected, unforeseen, sudden
inopinément   unexpectedly, suddenly
insolite   unusual
instamment   urgently, expressly
intempestif   untimely
inutile de dire que   needless to say
jadis   formerly
jamais   never
journalier   daily
journellement   all the time
jusqu'à   until
jusqu'à ce que   until
jusqu'à présent   as yet
jusqu'alors   up until then
jusqu'ici   until now
justement   as a matter of fact, exactly
là-dessus   thereupon
le cas échéant   if need be, if the need arises
littéralement   literally
lors de   at the time of
lorsque   when, at the time
l'un dans l'autre   all in all
maintes fois   often
mais   but, why
malgré   despite, in spite of
même   like, even, same
modestement   humbly
momentanément   for the time being
moyennant   by means of, by way of
moyennant que   on condition that
mûrement   more closely, at leisure
naguère   lately
naturellement   naturally
néanmoins   nevertheless, nonetheless
nécessairement   necessarily
n'empêche que   nevertheless, nonetheless
n'en déplaise à   with all respect to
nettement   distinctly, clearly
nommément   notably
non que   not that
nonobstant   in spite of, nevertheless
notamment   specially, particularly
nuitamment   nightly
nullement   not at all, by no means
obligatoirement   necessarily
où que   wherever
outre mesure   excessively
ouvertement   openly
par ailleurs   otherwise, moreover
par-ci par-là   here and there, now and then
par conséquent   therefore
par contre   on the other hand
par égard pour   out of consideration for
par hasard   by accident, accidentally
par la suite   afterwards
par le fait   in point of fact

par le temps qui court   nowadays, these days
par mégarde   inadvertently
par moments   now and then
par périodes   from time to time
par rapport à   in comparison with, compared to
par suite de   as a result of
par surprise   by surprise
parallèlement   at the same time, also
parce que   because, since
pareil   similar, like, such
pareillement   likewise
particulièrement   specifically
pas du tout   not at all, not in the least
passablement   fairly, quite a lot
pendant ce temps   meanwhile
pendant que   while, whilst
peu commun   unusual
peu souvent   seldom
platement   humbly
plutôt   rather
ponctuellement   irregularly, from time to time
postérieurement   subsequently
pour la petite histoire   incidentally
pour le moment   for the moment
pour l'instant   for the time being
pour peu que   if only, if ever
pour que   so that
pour sûr   definitely
pour tout dire   actually
pour un temps   for a time
pourtant   however
pourvu que   provided that
préalablement   beforehand
préalablement à   prior to
précité   aforementioned, aforesaid
presque   nearly, almost, hardly
presque jamais   hardly ever
présumé   supposed, reputed
prétendu   supposed, presumed
primitivement   originally
principalement   mostly, mainly, principally
probant   convincing
probatoire   preliminary
prochainement   soon
proprement   literally, correctly
puisque   since, because
quand même   anyhow
quant à   as for
quasiment   almost, nearly
que   but, that, than, as, yet
que de fois   how many times
quelque peu   rather
quelquefois   sometimes
question ~   as far as ~ is concerned

question de   because of
qui que   whoever, whomever
quoi que ce soit   whatever
quoi qu'il en soit   be that as it may
quoique   although
raison de plus   all the more reason
récemment   lately
réellement   really
relativement à   in relation to
requis   required
rien que   simply, nothing but
rudement*   very, awfully, really*
sans aucun doute   without a doubt, no doubt, undoubtedly
sans cérémonie   informally
sans doute   without a doubt, no doubt
sans égard pour   without considering
sans façon   informally
sans quoi   otherwise
sans se faire prier   willingly
sciemment   knowingly
séance tenante   then and there
selon   according to
selon toute probabilité   in all probability
semblable   such, like, similar
sensiblement   noticeably, appreciably
seulement   only, but, solely, merely
si bien que   so that
simplement   simply, merely
sinon   otherwise
sinon que   except that
soi-disant   so-called
soit dit en passant   by the way
soit l'un soit l'autre   either one or the other
soit que   whether
soit [...] soit   either . . . or
sous peu   shortly
sous tous les rapports   in every aspect
souvent   often
spécialement   especially
spécifiquement   uniquely
strictement   absolutely (usually negative)
subit   sudden, unexpected
sur ces entrefaites   at that moment, meanwhile
sur-le-champ   immediately
sur le compte de   about
sur le fait   in the act
sur le moment   at the time
surtout   particularly, above all, especially, mostly, mainly, principally
susmentionné   aforementioned, aforesaid
tandis que   while, whereas
tant bien que mal   so-so
tant s'en faut   far from it
tantôt   presently, soon, by and by

tel   like, such, similar
tel quel   such as it is
tellement   so many, so much
texto*   word for word
touchant   concerning, with regard to
toujours   still, always, ever, forever
tout à coup   suddenly
tout à fait   quite, thoroughly, entirely
tout compte fait   all things considered
tout d'abord   in the first place
tout de bon   seriously, truly

tout de même   all the same
tout d'un coup   suddenly (stronger emphasis)
tout entier   entirely, completely
toutefois   however
ultérieurement   later, later on
uniquement   only
véritablement   truly
vraiment   truly
vraisemblable   likely
vraisemblablement   most likely, probably

English-French

about   à propos de, sur le compte de, alentour
above all   avant tout, surtout
absolutely (**usually negative**)   strictement
accidentally   par hasard
according to   d'après, selon, aux yeux de, en fonction de
actually   à vrai dire, pour tout dire
aforementioned   précité, susmentionné
after all   au demeurant
afterward   après coup, par la suite
again   encore, de nouveau, encore une fois
all in all   à tout prendre, l'un dans l'autre, globalement
all the more reason   raison de plus
all the same   tout de même
all the time   journellement, toujours
all things considered   tout compte fait
almost   quasiment, presque
already   déjà, d'ores et déjà
also   aussi, également, parallèlement
although   bien que, quoique
always   toujours
among others   entre autres
and so on   et ainsi de suite
any minute now   à tout instant, d'un instant à l'autre
anyhow   de toute façon, de toute manière, quand même, aussi bien
anymore   davantage
apparently   à ce qu'on dit, apparemment
appreciably   sensiblement
approximately (**number**)   approximativement, dans les (numéro)
around   alentour, environ, à peu près
as   à mesure que, comme, tel que, en tant que
as a general rule   en règle générale
as a matter of fact   en effet, en fait, justement
as a result of   du coup, par suite
as far as ~ is concerned   question ~

as far as I know   autant que je sache
as for   quant à
as from   à compter de, à partir de
as many   autant
as much   autant
as soon as   aussitôt que, dès lorsque, dès que
as well as   ainsi que
as yet   jusqu'à présent
aside from   à part
assuredly   assurément
at all costs   à tout prix, coûte que coûte
at first sight/glance   au premier abord, de prime abord
at least   au moins, au bas mot
at leisure   mûrement
at once   de ce pas
at present   à présent
at random   au hasard
at that moment   sur ces entrefaites
at the height of   au firmament de, au plus fort de
at the rate of   à raison de
at the right moment   au point nommé
at the same time   à la fois, parallèlement
at the time (of)   lorsque, lors de, sur le moment
at the wrong time   à contretemps
awfully*   rudement*
basically   au fond, dans le fond
barely   à peine
be that as it may   quoi qu'il en soit
because   parce que, comme
because of   à cause de, en raison de, question de
before long   à courte échéance
beforehand   préalablement
beginning in   à partir de
besides   d'ailleurs, du reste, à côté de, de plus, en outre
but   seulement, mais, que, sauf que
by accident   par hasard
by and by   tantôt

by far   de loin
by means of   au moyen de, moyennant
by no means   nullement
by surprise   par surprise
by the way   incidemment, soit dit en passant, au fait, à propos
by way of   en guise de, moyennant
certainly   certainement, certes, assurément
chances are (that)   il y a grandes chances (que)
classic   indémodable
clearly   nettement
come what may   advienne que pourra
commonly   couramment
compared to   par rapport à, au regard de
completely   de tout au tout, complètement
compulsory   de rigueur
concerning   à propos de, concernant, à l'égard de
concisely   en termes concis
considering   compte tenu de
constant   de tous les instants
constantly   à chaque instant, constamment
contrary to   à l'encontre de
contrary to all expectations   contre toute attente
conversely   à l'inverse
convincing   probant
correctly   proprement (definitions)
currently   actuellement, couramment
daily   journalier
definitely   à coup sûr, pour sûr, formellement
despite   en dépit de, malgré
directly   de ce pas
distinctly   nettement
duly   dûment
either one or the other   soit l'un soit l'autre
either . . . or   soit ... soit
elsewhere   ailleurs
entirely   complètement, tout entier, entièrement
especially   spécialement, surtout
essentially   essentiellement
even   même, aussi bien
even though   alors que même
ever   toujours, jamais
exactly   justement
except for   à l'exception de, excepté, hors
except that   sinon que
excessively   outre mesure
explicitly   expressément
expressly   exprès, instamment
extraordinary   hors du commun
facing   en regard de
fair and square   à la régulière
fairly   avec équité, passablement

far from it   tant s'en faut
fluently   couramment, disertement
for a time   pour un temps
for fear that   de crainte que, de peur que
for lack of   faute de
for the moment   pour le moment
for the time being   pour l'instant, momentanément
for this reason   de ce fait
forever   toujours, à jamais
formerly   antérieurement, auparavant, jadis
frankly   franchement
from   à partir de (time)
from now on   à partir de maintenant, dorénavant
from the outset   dès l'origine
from then on   dès lors
from time to time   de temps en temps, par périodes, ponctuellement
galore   à gogo
given   face à, compte tenu de
given that   étant donné que
hardly   guère, presque
hardly ever   presque jamais
hazardous   aléatoire
henceforth   désormais, dorénavant
here and there   çà et là, par-ci par-là
honestly   carrément, honnêtement
how many times   que de fois
however   cependant, pourtant, toutefois
humbly   platement, humblement, modestement
if ever   pour peu que
if necessary   à la rigueur
if need be   à la limite, au cas où, en cas de, le cas échéant
if only   pour peu que
if the need arises   le cas échéant
immediately   sur-le-champ, immédiatement, incessamment
in a pinch*   à la rigueur
in addition (to)   accessoirement, en outre, en sus
in all probability   selon toute probabilité
in any case   en tous cas, aussi bien
in case of   en cas de
in comparison with   par rapport à
in connection with   à propos de
in contrast to   à la différence
in-depth   approfondi
in due time   en temps voulu
in every respect   en tout point, sous tous les rapports
in fact   de fait, en fait
in force   en vigueur
in itself   en soi

in order to   afin de (w/ infinitive), afin que (w/ subjunctive)

in other words   autrement dit

in particular   en particulier

in person   de vive voix

in point of fact   par le fait

in relation to   relativement à

in response to   en réaction à

in some ways   en quelque sorte

in spite of   malgré, en dépit de, nonobstant

in the act   sur le fait

in the eyes of   aux yeux de

in the first place   tout d'abord

in the long run   à longue échéance

in this respect   à cet égard

inadvertently   par mégarde

inasmuch as   dans la mesure où, attendu que

incidentally   au demeurant, incidemment, pour la petite histoire

indeed   certes, de fait

inevitably   forcément, immanquablement

informally   à la bonne franquette, sans cérémonie, sans façon

initially   à l'origine

insofar as   dans la mesure où

irregularly   ponctuellement

irrelevant   hors de propos

judging by   à en juger par

just in case   des fois que

kindly   bienveillant

knowingly   à bon escient, en connaissance de cause, sciemment

largely   en grande partie

lately   ces derniers temps, récemment, dernièrement, depuis peu, naguère

later   ultérieurement

lest   de peur que

like   comme, tel, même, pareil, semblable, en tant que, à l'instar de

likely   vraisemblable, vraisemblablement

likewise   de même, également, pareillement

literally   littéralement, proprement, à proprement parler

mainly   surtout, principalement

makeshift   de fortune

manageable   gérable

meanwhile   dans l'intervalle, entretemps, pendant ce temps, sur des entrefaites

merely   seulement, simplement, rien que

more   davantage

more and more   de plus en plus

more closely   mûrement

moreover   de surcroît, en outre, par ailleurs

most likely   vraisemblablement

mostly   pour la plupart, le plus souvent, principalement

naturally   naturellement

nearly   quasiment, de près, à peu près, presque, environ

necessarily   forcément, nécessairement, obligatoirement

needless to say   inutile de dire que

never   jamais

nevertheless   néanmoins, n'empêche que, nonobstant

nightly   nuitamment

no doubt   sans doute

nonetheless   néanmoins, n'empêche que

not at all   aucunement, pas du tout, nullement

not in the least   aucunement, pas du tout

not that   non que

notably   nommément

nothing but   rien que

noticeably   sensiblement

now and then   par-ci par-là, par moments

nowadays   à l'époque actuelle, par le temps qui court

obviously   évidemment

of course   bien entendu, bien évidemment

of that time   à l'époque, d'alors, en ce moment

often   souvent, maintes fois

on condition that   moyennant que

on purpose   exprès

on the contrary   au contraire

on the other hand   d'autre part, en revanche, par contre

on the whole   à tout prendre, dans l'ensemble

only   uniquement, seulement

openly   ouvertement

optional   facultatif

originally   à l'origine, primitivement

other than   à part

otherwise   autrement, par ailleurs, sans quoi, sinon

out of consideration for   par égard pour

over and over again   à maintes reprises

overall   globalement

particularly   notamment, surtout

perhaps   ça se peut

personally   de vive voix

possible   éventuel, possible

possibly   éventuellement

precisely   effectivement, justement, formellement

preliminary   probatoire

presently   actuellement, tantôt

previously   antérieurement

principally   principalement, surtout

prior to   préalablement à

probably   vraisemblablement, probablement

provided that   à condition que, pourvu que
quite   tout à fait, assez, entièrement
quite a lot   passablement
quite right   effectivement
rather   assez, plutôt, quelque peu
really   réellement, carrément, rudement*
regarding   concernant
reluctantly   à contrecœur
repeatedly   à plusieurs reprises
reputed   censé, présumé, prétendu
required   requis, de rigueur, obligatoire
rightly so   à juste titre
roughly   crûment, rudement, grossièrement,
   à peu près
same   même
scarcely   à peine
seeing that   d'autant que
seldom   peu souvent
seriously   tout de bon
several times   à plusieurs reprises
shortly   sous peu, bientôt, brièvement
similar   semblable, pareil, tel
simply (quite simply)   simplement, seulement, (tout ~) bêtement, rien que
since   dès que, puisque, depuis que, comme
so-called   soi-disant
so many   tellement
so much   tellement
so much the more   d'autant plus
so-so   tant bien que mal
so that   de façon que, de sorte que, pour que,
   si bien que
sometimes   des fois,* quelquefois
soon   bientôt, prochainement, tantôt
specially   notamment, surtout
specifically   particulièrement
still   toujours, encore
straight away   du premier coup
strictly   formellement
subsequently   postérieurement
such   tel, pareil, semblable
such as   comme
such as it is   tel quel
sudden   subit, soudain, inopiné
suddenly   tout à coup, tout d'un coup
   (*stronger emphasis*), inopinément
supposed   censé, présumé, prétendu
supposing   à supposer que
surely   assurément, sûrement, à coup sûr
surprisingly   de façon surprenante
taking into account   en regard de

thankfully   avec reconnaissance
that depends   c'est selon, ça dépend
that may be   ça se peut
there and then   séance tenante
therefore   donc, par conséquent
thereupon   là-dessus
these days   par le temps qui court
thorough   approfondi
thoroughly   complètement, entièrement, tout
   à fait, à fond
thus   ainsi
to be honest   franchement
to tell the truth   à vrai dire
to whom it may concern   à qui le droit
truly   tout de bon, vraiment, véritablement
unawares   au pied levé
unbeknownst to   à l'insu de
uncertain   aléatoire
undoubtedly   sans aucun doute, sans doute, à
   coup sûr
unexpected   inespéré, inopiné, subit
uniquely   spécifiquement
unknown to   à l'insu de
unless   à moins que
until   jusqu'à ce que, jusqu'à
until now   jusqu'ici
untimely   intempestif
unusual   insolite, peu commun
up until then   jusqu'alors
urgently   instamment
usually   habituellement, d'habitude, d'ordinaire
very   rudement,* vrai, même, véritable
visibly   à vue d'œil
visually   à vue
whatever   quoi que ce soit
whatever happens   en tous cas
when   lorsque, quand
whereas   alors que, tandis que
wherever   où que
whether   soit que
while   alors que, pendant que, tandis que
whoever/whomever   qui que
with all respect to   n'en déplaise à
with regard to   touchant
without a doubt   à coup sûr, sans doute
without considering   sans égard pour
willingly   de bon gré, sans se faire prier
wittingly   à bon escient
word for word   texto*
wrongly   à tort

Index of French Verbs